Transforming learning across the c

Transforming learning across the c

II TRANSFORMING LEARNING ACROSS THE CURRICULUM

Transforming Learning Across the Curriculum

(from upper primary to sixth form)

Julia Strong and Pie Corbett

IV TRANSFORMING LEARNING ACROSS THE CURRICULUM

Talk for Writing
15 Branch Street
Huddersfield
West Yorkshire
HD1 4JL

Contact Nick Batty at orders@talk4writing.com
07514034010
www.talk4writing.com

First published, 2020

Copyright   ©Pie Corbett and Julia Strong

All rights reserved. The handouts within this book may be reprinted to support in-school training only, but they remain the intellectual property of Pie Corbett and Julia Strong and are subject to copyright. It is forbidden to use the handouts for commercial gain, place them on the internet or share them with other schools or institutions. Except for the handouts and the use of brief extracts for review purposes, no part of this publication may be reproduced or transmitted in any form or by any means, electronic or mechanical, including photocopy, recording, or any information and retrieval system, without permission in writing from the publisher (Talk for Writing) or a license from the Copyright Licensing Agency Ltd, Barnard's Inn, 86 Fetter Lane, London EC4A 1EN (www.cla.co.uk).

ISBN: 978-1-9998942-4-5

British Library Cataloguing in Publication Data
A catalogue record of this book is available from the British Library

- Typeset by creativeguru.co.uk
- Conference film clips by quickstepfilms.com
- DVDs produced by imgfactory.co.uk
- Cover design by www.knownaim.co.uk
- Photographs: Julia Strong & Talk for Writing Training Schools

This book can only be ordered from www.talkforwritingshop.com

Dedication

Transforming Learning Across the Curriculum is dedicated to all the teachers and Talk for Writing schools and trainers who have helped develop Talk for Writing across the years. In particular, we would like to thank all the teachers and schools who have contributed to this book. A special mention goes to The John of Gaunt School, whose enthusiasm for the approach has enabled this book to contain many chapters written by subject specialists across the secondary curriculum. To see the process in action and for information about training, visit www.talkforwriting.com/training

Julia Strong and Pie Corbett

About the authors

Pie Corbett is an inspirational trainer, poet, author and editor of over 250 books. A former teacher, headteacher, lecturer and English inspector, Pie is famous in the education world for the transformational Talk for Writing approach. He has been working with Julia Strong on developing this approach since 2005. Julia is a former English teacher, deputy headteacher and Deputy Director of the National Literacy Trust. She is an outstanding trainer for secondary schools, and is also the author of a number of bestselling books including the *English Frameworking* series, *Literacy Across the Curriculum* and *Talk for Writing Across the Secondary Curriculum*.

Pie and Julia have co-authored the following books:

- *Talk for Writing in the Early Years* (Open University Press, 2016)
- *Talk for Writing Across the Curriculum* (Open University Press, 2011 & 2017)
- *Jumpstart! Grammar* (David Fulton, 2014 & 2016)
- *Creating Storytellers and Writers* (Talk for Writing, 2017, 2018 & 2020)

Endorsements for this book

"Who'd have thought Talk for Writing could make such a difference to maths, PE and science? Packed with riches, the powerful TfW approach is applied in this book to the entire curriculum by the experts Pie and Julia, with outstanding results. You will find everything you need to be transformative in developing students' language acquisition and confidence in writing, no matter what the subject. Detailed rationale, links with cognitive science, endless practical examples across the upper primary and secondary curriculum and exemplary chapters written by teachers: get started!"
— *Shirley Clarke, Formative Assessment Expert, UK*

"In *Transforming Learning Across the Curriculum*, Pie Corbett and Julia Strong offer a compelling and eminently practical approach to mobilising effective writing in the classroom. This book is packed full of useable strategies, whether it is for English or maths, or in primary or secondary school classrooms. A wealth of interesting school case studies bring alive the thorough, step-by-step 'Talk for Writing' approach for the teacher-reader. Highly recommended!"
— *Alex Quigley, National Content Manager, Education Endowment Foundation (EEF)*

Foreword by Pie Corbett

In the early 1970s, James Britton and Douglas Barnes explored the notion that children learn through exploratory talk, noting that the language of subject areas was a potential barrier to learning. However, we believe that teaching the language of subjects enhances learning and can be acquired by every student. For years, articles have been written, courses and conferences run and yet, what *Language across the Curriculum* means in practice has remained evasive. The recent EEF guidance *Improving Literacy In Secondary Schools* is strong on theory but has not so much to say about what it might practically look like. This book fills that gap.

For thirty years, Julia Strong has been investigating and developing the practical realities of language across the curriculum. Her conclusions about what it is and how it might be practically developed to raise standards across schools are the core of this book. Insights range from Year 5 art to A-level philosophy. I doubt whether there is anyone else, who has devoted so much time to studying what disciplinary language teaching might look like across all school subjects, developing ideas both in primary and secondary schools.

Simply put, learning in any subject is inextricably linked with language. Students with small vocabularies will inevitably fail. To succeed, all students have to acquire the language that they need to investigate, think, learn and express themselves in different disciplines. They have to be able to 'talk the text'. Subject teachers have to teach the language needs of their subject. The language that GCSE business studies requires is different to the vocabulary, sentence and text structures needed for GCSE physical education: students' subject learning is inextricably linked with the acquisition of relevant language. Each knowledge area is bound within its language.

Years of working with schools combined with the fact that Talk for Writing focuses on language acquisition has led us to the point where we can clearly identify key strategies rooted in the Talk for Writing process that can be adapted by all schools to raise standards. The first 7 chapters of this book set out the generic strategies and understandings that are required and can be used in all subjects. The 8th chapter touches on research that supports this work. As soon as we saw the work of Barak Rosenshine, and insights such as 'dual coding' through neuroscience into the 'science of learning', we recognised what was being said as a direct reflection of what we had been practically developing for years. The rest of the book provides case studies in different subjects. The enthusiasm for the Talk for Writing approach from the teachers shines throughout these case studies. They set out how to teach the tune of their subject (disciplinary language) and improve learning. Reading through them, it becomes clear that the patterns of language in the different disciplines reflect the patterns of learning. Every subject has its tune.

If we are to transform the life opportunities of every child, then teaching subjects through this approach is vital. After about half a century, we now know what language across the curriculum looks like and how to use it to raise standards. The aim of this work is about whole school transformation and, therefore, the transformation of students' lives.

Index

Reading suggestion: Hopefully, members of school management teams will find the whole book useful. Subject/class teachers may prefer to read the opening section and then focus on the chapters and pages relating to what they teach, using this index and the following, more detailed index. If you are interested in what Talk for Writing looks like in different subjects, we recommend you read both the primary and secondary chapters, if available, regardless of which sector you actually work in, as we can learn a lot from each other.

Foreword: Pie Corbett

Section 1: A guide to Talk for Writing across the curriculum

Chapter 1:	The simple solution	1
Chapter 2:	The Talk for Writing process	11
Chapter 3:	Getting the model right	37
Chapter 4:	Vocabulary matters	55
Chapter 5:	Linking ideas coherently	73
Chapter 6:	Co-constructing understanding	87
Chapter 7:	Reading matters	111
Chapter 8:	Useful research overviews	129

Section 2: Talk for Writing in subject areas

Chapter 9a:	TfW in English – the power of short-burst writing	135
Chapter 9b:	TfW in English (Y6)	151
Chapter 9c:	TfW in English (Y8)	173
Chapter 9d:	How TfW supports struggling students (secondary)	179
Chapter 10a:	TfW in maths (Y6)	189
Chapter 10b:	TfW in maths (secondary)	195
Chapter 11a:	TfW in science (Y5)	208
Chapter 11b:	TfW in science (Y10)	217
Chapter 12a:	TfW in history (Y5)	231
Chapter 12b:	TfW in history (Y8)	240
Chapter 12c:	How TfW supports religious education (Y5)	250
Chapter 12d:	TfW in geography (Y7 & Y10)	255
Chapter 13:	How TFW complements PE (secondary)	263
Chapter 14:	TfW in modern foreign languages (secondary)	271
Chapter 15:	TfW in computer science (Y7& Y10)	280
Chapter 16a:	TFW in art is revolutionary (primary)	290
Chapter 16b:	TFW in art (KS3 & KS4)	295

Section 3: Getting Talk for Writing going in your school

Chapter 17a:	Becoming a TfW secondary school	303
Chapter 17b:	Getting TfW going in your school	313

Index: subjects, management, teaching tools, video clips & handouts

The video clips plus accompanying teacher's notes and handouts are online.
Go to www.talk4writing.co.uk/tl and follow the instructions 'Code: 1224'.

Curriculum/ Management	Teaching tools	Chapter (Ch), Pages (pp), Videos & Handouts (H) Key references in **bold**
Art		Ch **16a-b** ; pp: 62-65, **290-302**; Videos: 58, 59
Accounting		pp: 20, **89-90**; Videos: 3, **28**
	Actions and mime to support understanding	pp: 20, 22, 44, 45, 46, **62-64**, 70, 81, 154, 176, 178, 200, 209, 211, 221, 227, 233, 268, 274
Business studies		pp: 1,10, 21, 32, 41; Videos: **3**, 9, 19, 60
	Boxing up structure: planning your writing	pp: 10, **16-18, 23-25,** 29, 47, 54, 95, 99, 110, 177, 185, 191-192, **196,** 201-203, 253, 262, 267, 278, 305, 317; Videos: **3, 9, 11,** 15, **19, 28, 36, 39,** 60
Computer science		Ch **15**; pp: 53, 77, **280-289**
	Cold to hot process: basing teaching on formative assessment	pp:**13-14**, 16, **34-35**, 54, 84-85, 90, 104-6, **134**, 152-3, 177, 181, 187-8, 189, 192, 195, 197-8, 216-7, 232, 239, 246-8,257, 262, 272, 277, 281, 284, 289, 311, 320; Videos: **6,**15, **27,** 61
	Co-constructing learning	Ch **6**; pp: 21, 25, **28-9, 87-110,** 80, 146, 189, 224, **242, 244, 277, 324**; Videos: **3**, 13, **28, 29,** 30, **31,** 34, 35; H: **2, 3, 4, 5d, 6a, 7a,b, 8, 9**
	Coherence/linking text /sentence signposts	Ch **5**; pp: 17, 18, 22, **25-9, 31-33, 38-40, 41-2,** 45, 47-8, 50, 62, **73-86,** 97, 102, 100-1, 183, 240, 243, 256-7, 261, **266,** 276; Videos: **12,** 15, **27, 35,** 50, 57; H: **2**
	Confidence	pp: 2, 10, 16, 24, 32, 61, 87, 91, 96, 107, 191, 200, 208, 216, 239, 249, 261, 289, 303, 308, 328; Videos: **3, 9,** 16
Design & technology		pp: 18, 23, 27, 50, 124; Videos: 11, **27,** 59
	Dialogic talk/booktalk (also see talking the text & co-constricting learning)	pp: 7, **10,** 12, 37, 61, 87-88, **96, 102,** 103-6; **106-10, 122,** 124, 149, 172, **190-196,** 205; 257, **269**; Videos: **28, 30, 31, 34,35;** H: **6a-b, 7a-b, 8, 9**
	Differentiation	pp: 32, 34, 133, 175, 214
Drama		pp: 1, 74, 81, 106-9, 154, 237
	Echo reading	pp: 21, 52, 81, 93, 102, 124, 125,
	Embedding learning	pp: 61, 69, **71,** 102, 109, 129, **144,** 174, 193, **205-6,** 247, 308, **310-14, 323-5**
	Explaining to others	pp: 7, 21, 29, **33,** 69, 80, 205, 216, 318; Videos: 3, 6, 30, 28
English		Ch **9a-d**; pp: 6, 11, 14, 26, 30, 47, **54,** 72, 74, 79, 82, **106-110,** 117, **125, 135-188,** 303, 306-8, 317; Videos: 5, **13, 20,** 23, 25, **32-37;** H: **1-5, 7-11**
	Feedback & marking	pp: 9, **32-4,** 86, 97, 98, 102, **122, 167,** 177, **180, 197-8,** 260, 261, 270, 275, 286, 288, 293, 305, **310,**
History		Ch **12 a-b**; pp: 29, 59, 79, **83-4, 90-103, 231-249**; Videos: **12, 26,** 48, **49, 50**
Geography		Ch **12d**; pp: 61, 64, **67-8, 255-262**,
	Hook	pp: **13, 19, 20,** 131, **152,** 198, 209, **220;** Video: **4,**
	Impact	pp: **7-10,** 62, **199, 208, 216, 223, 229, 290, 293, 303-313**; Videos: **1-4,** 27, 61
Maths		Ch **10a-b**; pp: 8, 16, 35, **60,** 66, **133, 189-207;** Videos: **6,** 10, **14, 38, 39,** 40
	Magpieing	pp: **18,** 46, **63-4,** 66, **89,** 83, 91, 105, 139-40, **168,** 176, 179, **177, 221-2, 232**-3, 244, **257,** 264, 273, **299, 321; 319;** Video 32
	Models/model text	Ch **3**; pp:12, **23-4,**16-18, **21-3,** 27, 29- 33, **37-54,** 75-80, 121, 128, 151-161, 189, 193, **196, 200, 223-4, 227, 242-48,** 264, 277, 287, **291-294;** Videos: **12, 14 ,27**
Modern foreign languages		Ch**14**; pp: 70, **271-279**, 322; Video: 57
Music		pp: 41-2,61-62, 86

Philosophy		pp:103-106, 127,
Physical education		Ch 13; pp: 63, 70, 263-70, 304; Videos: 53,54,55,56
	Planning units	Ch 2; pp:13-38; 167, 175, 196, 217-30, 240-9, 261, 271, 280, 290-294, 310;H:1
	Pri/sec transfer	pp: 1, 30, 37, 316; H:10a&b (last section)
	Progression Also see cold to hot	pp: 7, 8, 11, 14, 37, 55, 63, 71, 87, 89-90, 130, 132, 135, 178, 179, 195, 203, 215, 223, 242, 253, 265-6, 259, 270, 280, 290, 294, 319, 323-5;
Project team		Ch 17a-b; pp: 7-10, 117, 303-326; Videos: 1, 2, 3,60,61; H: 1,1a & all handouts
Psychology		pp: 106, 304; Video: 29
	Punctuation	pp: 26-28, 33, 39, 79, 155, 159-60, 178
	Reading: (also see echo reading & booktalk)	Ch 7; pp: 4, 7-8, 42, 46, 52, 55, 87, 104, 132, 134, 140, 144-5, 160, 166, 213, 233, 260, 283, 111-28, Videos: 11, 30 – 32; H:10a&b
Religious education		Ch 12; pp: 250-254, Videos: 7,16,30, 51,52
Science		Ch 11a-b; pp: 4, 19, 20, 22, 24, 27, 31, 44-46, 51-2, 56-8, 63, 66, 70, 88-9, 208-30, 304, 311, Videos: 4,8, 17 – 18, 21-22, 41-47: H: 7b
Management		Ch 1,17a &17b; pp:1-10, 117, 303 – 326; Videos: 1,2,61; H:12
	Shared writing	pp: 29-31, 32, 36, 98-101, 136, 141-3, 145-6, 157, 159, 166-7, 176, 180, 186-7, 235, 240, 276, 293; Videos: 13, 14, 33-35; H:3&4
Sociology		See Chapter 12e online
Special needs		Ch 9d; pp: 133, 179-188, 285, 303
	Spelling	pp: 14-15, 26, 33, 62, 71-2, 252, 286, 296, 297, 333
	Talking the text (talking frames)	pp: 7, 16, 33, 50, 56, 61, 63, 90, 92-102, 190-2, 196, 246-7, 257, 317
	Text mapping	pp: 21-3, 46, 50-52, 89, 106, 154, 184, 200, 213, 217, 222-3, 230, 242-3, 248-9, 252, 260, 263-5, 274, 286, 291, 295-6, 307, 322; Videos: 7-10, 17,18, 29 49, 54
	Toolkits	pp: 26-7, 87, 101, 129, 146, 157, 167, 189, 193, 291; Videos: 34-35; H:2,11 &12
	Topic sentences	pp. 17, 26-7, 41-2, 49, 54, 95, 97, 102,
	Transferring learning	pp: 6-7, 24-7, 77-8, 122, 132, 306, 317,
	Vocabulary	Ch 4; pp: 3, 6, 11, 22, 17, 18, 19, 23, 25, 29, 55-72, 112, 121-2, 124, 128, 132, All subject chapters include vocab focus; Videos: 5, 20-26, 40, 44-47,49; H:5a-d, 6a-b, 7a-c

A guide to educational gobbledygook

Education drowns in a sea of tedious acronyms and weird terminology. I've tried to avoid this and explain it when it has to appear, but a bit has crept in unexplained:

- **A-level:** Advanced level qualifications
- **AQA:** Assessment & Qualification Alliance – an examination awarding body in England, Wales and Northern Ireland
- **BEC:** (Business Environment & Concepts) – see **video clip 54**
- **GCSE:** General Certificate of Secondary Education
- **Key stage 1,2,3,4:** In the curriculum in England and Wales, this term is used to refer to specific groups of years. **KS1** = 5-7-year olds; **KS2** = 7-11-year olds; **KS3** = 11-14-year olds; **KS4** = 14-16-year olds. **KS5** refers to 16-18-year olds but the old phrase for this, **6th form**, is usually still used, a left-over from the days when the secondary years started with 1. They still do in Scotland and Northern Ireland.
- **MAT:** Multi-Academy Trust: a single entity set up to undertake strategic collaboration to try to improve & maintain high educational standards across a number of schools in England.
- **SATs:** Standard assessment task – the phrase originated in America for multiple choice testing. It is the commonly used term in England to refer to the end of KS1 & 2 tests.
- **SENCO:** Special Education Needs Co-ordinator

Chapter 1: The simple solution

If you ask a room full of secondary teachers if they read for pleasure, the majority will say that they do; change the question to, "Do you write for pleasure?" and the chances are that very few will say they do. If questioned, the few who do are not thinking about the sort of writing that secondary schools typically require of students. In primary schools, teachers are liable to be more positive in their own attitudes to writing because the sort of writing they teach tends to be more creative and thus more enjoyable for pupil and teacher alike.

Typical writing tasks facing Year 11s

Science: State and explain the trend in reactivity down group 1 and group 7 of the periodic table.	**History:** 'The Papal Bull was the most important reason for the execution of Mary Queen of Scots.' How far do you agree?
Art: Compare the work of two artists that have impressed you.	**Music:** (listening test): Explain how the composer describes a train journey.
ICT: Explain how increasing the size of the cache would improve the performance of a computer.	**Geography:** In a hot desert, what opportunities & challenges are there for economic development?
D&T: How did your solution fulfil the original brief?	**MFL:** Describe what you did in your summer holidays. (Question & answer in French)
RE: "For Muslims, Adam is a more important Prophet than Ibrahim." Evaluate this statement.	**English Language:** How does the writer use language to explain her first experiences of cycling?
Business: Using your business knowledge & case study evidence, investigate whether venture capital investment was the right way to finance the business.	**Maths:** In a chess club, there are x boys & y girls. If 5 more boys & 8 more girls join, there would be half as many boys as girls. Show that $y = 2x + 2$.
Drama: (Question refers to given extract from *The Crucible*.) Explain how you and the actor playing Abigail might use the performance space and interact with each other to show the audience the **relationship** between the two characters.	

Now look at the complexity and breadth of a few of the writing tasks that typically face Year 11s. The secondary curriculum requires students to write challenging text for a very wide range of purposes and contexts, typically making precise, concise, factual writing demands – creativity is rarely on the menu. It is a challenge that defeats many students and is particularly daunting for disadvantaged students.

The GCSE year will be the most challenging writing year of any student's life – whatever they select to do after that age, any writing demands will be more focused on their choices. This problem is exacerbated by the fact that the primary and secondary curriculums are becoming ever harder and content heavy, thus encouraging teachers to put their focus on covering content at the expense of considering how the pupils will be able to really understand or express that content. In addition, there is the seemingly ever-present problem of pupils tending to go backwards when they transfer from primary to secondary: the writing advances they were making in Years 5 & 6 are often not built on and many complain that they are just doing things they have already done. As Ofsted's telling document *KS3 The Wasted Years* states:

> *Inspectors found that too many secondary schools did not work effectively with partner primary schools to understand pupils' prior learning and ensure that they built on this during Key Stage 3. Worryingly, some secondary leaders simply accepted that pupils would repeat what they had already done in primary school during the early part of Key Stage 3, particularly in year 7.*

2 TRANSFORMING LEARNING ACROSS THE CURRICULUM

If we do not help pupils, whether of primary or secondary age, build on their existing knowledge and, if we do not motivate them to learn and help them become effective communicators of their knowledge, then all they learn is that they are not good at it. As they reluctantly write, they are constantly repeating their errors. Practice only makes perfect if you are practising the right thing. A large number of pupils will be defeated by the challenge that non-fiction writing often presents, which dents their confidence in their ability to succeed which, in turn, undermines motivation. We need to build pupils' skills as writers and communicators across the curriculum in a simple coordinated way. This is where Talk for Writing can help.

We are not expecting students, when faced by typical secondary writing tasks, to think, "Goody, goody, writing tonight!" because it's not the sort of writing that most human beings could respond to with enthusiasm, but Talk for Writing will help them feel confident in their ability to rise to the task. They will know how to plan an answer and the patterns of language and technical vocabulary that such a writing task requires. Moreover, the process will have helped them comprehend and recall the content, so they have something to write. And, when they've finished, they will feel proud of themselves, which will make them feel good in a different way.

I first started thinking about how we could better help students become powerful learners, communicators and writers, way back in 1975. The message that every school should develop a policy for language across the curriculum had come from above that year in the form of the *Bullock Report* which ran to almost 600 pages. Its official title was *A language for life*. In a nutshell, it looked at how the use of English was being taught, covering reading, writing and speech from birth but with a particular focus on "language in education". When you look at the report's many excellent recommendations, you may wonder why, nearly 50 years on, progress in some areas, especially in achieving a meaningful approach to language across the curriculum, has been so painfully slow.

It's worth taking the time to read *chapter 12: Language across the curriculum*. Just look at the quality of thought in the third paragraph of that chapter reprinted below (overlooking the dated use of 'he'; language changes over time):

> The primary school teacher responsible for the whole or most of the schoolwork of his class already has it in his power to establish a language policy across the curriculum. Whether or not he is taking that opportunity **will depend upon the extent to which the various uses of language permeate all the other learning activities, or to which, on the other hand, language learning is regarded as a separate activity. The distinction is a crucial one, and a great deal follows from it. For language to play its full role as a means of learning, the teacher must create in the classroom an environment which encourages a wide range of language uses.** The effectiveness of this context for the purpose can be judged by the answers to a number of questions. For example,

> how often does a child share his personal interests and learning discoveries with others in the class? How far is the teacher able to enter such conversations without robbing the children of verbal initiative? Are the children accustomed to read to one another what they have written, and just as readily listen? Are they accustomed to solving co-operatively in talk the practical problems that arise when they work together? How much opportunity is there for the kind of talk by which children make sense in their own terms of the information offered by teacher or by book? What varieties of writing - story, personal record, comment, report, speculation, etc - are produced in the course of a day? Over a longer span, what varieties occur in the output of a single child? These are straws in the wind. **What they indicate is the degree to which learning and the acquisition of language are interlocked ...**

It is a very perceptive statement reflecting the fact that literacy giants like Douglas Barnes and James Britton were on the committee that produced the report. The next paragraph turns to secondary schools:

> By his training and experience, the primary school teacher is likely to conceive of his task in terms of integrated rather than subject-oriented work. In the secondary school, however, it is traditional practice to move more or less directly into a programme of specialist teaching and a subject timetable. Clearly it is here that the proposals to be made in this chapter principally apply. **A primary school teacher may happen to be unaware of new conceptions of the role of language, but he would not generally regard them as matters outside his concern. However, they are certainly regarded in this way by secondary school teachers of most subjects.** The move from an integrated to a specialist curriculum constitutes in itself a considerably increased demand upon the linguistic powers of the pupil, but the most obvious demand, that for a wider and more specialised vocabulary, is not the principal difficulty. **In general, a curriculum subject, philosophically speaking, is a distinctive mode of analysis. While many teachers recognise that their aim is to initiate a student in a particular mode of analysis, they rarely recognise the linguistic implications of doing so. They do not recognise, in short, that the mental processes they seek to foster are the outcome of a development that originates in speech.**

These paragraphs are worth reading carefully as they contain so many deep truths; I have highlighted the most salient points. How is it then that so many of the important points made here so long ago have not been put into practice effectively?

The key lies, perhaps, in the penultimate sentence of chapter 12: **"We strongly recommend that whatever the means chosen to implement it a policy for language across the curriculum should be adopted by every secondary school."**

4 TRANSFORMING LEARNING ACROSS THE CURRICULUM

This rather suggests that it is the policy that is important rather than the means selected to achieve it. Moreover, each of the chapters had accompanying recommendations at the end of the report: a mere 41 pages of recommendations containing 333 things that were to be done. It's not surprising then that many of the excellent seeds within the report fell on barren ground. Here are the recommendations for chapter 12:

> 137. In the primary school the individual teacher is in a position to devise a language policy across the various aspects of the curriculum, but there remains the need for a general school policy to give expression to the aim and ensure consistency throughout the years of primary schooling.
>
> 138. In the secondary school, all subject teachers need to be aware of:
> (i) the linguistic processes by which their pupils acquire information and understanding, and the implications for the teacher's own use of language;
> (ii) the reading demands of their own subjects, and ways in which the pupils can be helped to meet them.
>
> 139. To bring about this understanding every secondary school should develop a policy for language across the curriculum. The responsibility for this policy should be embodied in the organisational structure of the school.

The report emphasised creating policy, rather than helping teachers adapt their practice to achieve a meaningful policy: so, schools focused on creating documents for people to obey. The documents told you what to do but not how to do it and this often remains the problem today. A policy needs to be developed through effective practice so there is buy-in for the approach, see **page 313–314**. In this way, practice will exemplify the theory and make it meaningful, and both will flourish. As practice develops, the policy can be further refined. What basically happened in many schools is that they started at the wrong end and invented paper policies which were then supposedly imposed on practice but, in the end, made very little difference to what happened in the classroom: hence all those strange unit planning sheets with a column for literacy, as if it were a separate thing. And publishers jumped on the bandwagon producing textbooks with all the content of the subject in the main chapters as usual, alongside weird appendices called *Literacy*. One science book comes to mind, where this appendix consisted of biographical details of a few key scientists followed by some tedious comprehension questions – the language of science clearly having nothing to do with literacy.

At the school I was then working in, endless meetings (which in themselves were a bit of a novelty in those relatively meetingless days) came up with the glorious idea of a monster poster relating to a few regularly misspelt words that was to be displayed on the walls of all classrooms. These gently faded: the teaching beneath carried on as before, as did the spelling. This helped entrench the problem the *Bullock Report* had identified: "While many teachers recognise that their aim is to initiate a student in a particular mode of analysis, they rarely recognise the linguistic implications of doing so." It's not so much that they are unwilling to do it; it's just that they don't know how to do it.

Why, then, weren't we saved twenty-two years later, when again a large number of impressive experts gathered to consider how to improve literacy? Strangely, the resultant National Literacy Strategy only focused on reading and writing and chose to miss out the key element that Bullock had rightly identified, **speech**. So, though the laudable aim of the strategy was to change practice and to provide the training to help teachers do this (and many of its training materials were excellent), it initially missed out the most important aspect of that training, only rectifying the error many years later. In addition, buy-in was not on the agenda. Literacy consultants were told what to tell the teachers to do and there was no avenue to feedback on what worked to co-construct the way forward, even for the consultants, let alone the teachers. As a result, a generation of teachers was created with a tendency to wait to be told what to do. Through these errors, the world's most extensive and expensive teacher training initiative failed to be as successful as it could have been.

There has, perhaps, been one further significant obstacle that has prevented progress and that is the way literacy itself is examined in primary schools in England. In order to separate the sheep from the goats, there has been an ever-increasing emphasis on disjointed skills, doubtless because it is easier to test these: just look at the way English grammar is examined with its focus on the naming of parts rather than on constructing effective sentences; or reading with its exam focus on disembodied assessment domains which encourages teaching towards specific skills rather than holistically. These lists of reading skills arose through testing regimes trying to isolate skills to test but, when you look at them, they all interact and depend upon each other, just as meaningful grammar is the sum of its parts. Another example is the phonics check that tests the ability to bark at print but doesn't test whether the children know what the words mean or can write them down correctly. Learning and the acquisition of language are indeed interlocked.

So, here we are, nearly 50 years on, still trying to achieve an effective practical way of making a focus on language permeate all teaching, as suits the needs of the subject being studied. Some progress has been made as evidenced by EEF's findings on *Improving Literacy in Secondary Schools*, see **pages 132–133**. The whole purpose of this book is to help teachers teach the linguistic tune of whatever subject they are teaching (its *disciplinary literacy*, in the language of the academic world) so that they recognise the literacy underpinning whichever discipline they are teaching and help learners internalise its patterns.

How to do this is particularly challenging in secondary schools where every 50 minutes or so the lesson changes along with the teacher and, therefore, the learning focus. Primary teachers know that teaching literacy is down to them. Secondary teachers, on the other hand, have long resisted appeals that literacy is their baby – an error that has been exacerbated by a tendency for anything related to literacy in secondary schools to be very English-teacher centric rather than adapted to suit the demands of different disciplines. Hence the frequent calls for extended writing weeks that would somehow solve the problem of poor writing. This solution is strange in two ways: first, most departments don't require extended writing so just exactly what are they supposed to do in those weeks – invent spurious writing tasks? Secondly, if you're not very good at writing, the last thing you need is to be required to do lots of it. But, if you have been taught how to structure and express short pieces of writing well, matching audience and purpose to structure in a co-ordinated manner, it is easy to extend that skill to any length of writing required. Again, this is where Talk for Writing can help.

When I became the deputy director of the National Literacy Trust, a very small part of my job was to develop training on literacy across the curriculum. So, I had the motivation to find out more about the best of what research told us about literacy across the curriculum. When the massed resources of the National Literacy Strategy started focusing on across-the-curriculum work in secondary schools, I thought that aspect of my work would become redundant, but the reverse turned out to be true because many of the materials circulated were, yet again, written from an English-teacher perspective.

Slowly, through looking at research and what worked in practice, and listening carefully to what teachers of different subjects told me about the language and related writing demands of their subjects, I built up a whole range of ideas about what would help. One key thing that I discovered by focusing on the different types of writing different subjects require is that every subject has its tune, linked to the type of phrasing and the technical vocabulary that it spins around (the EEF uses the academic term disciplinary literacy – **see page 132**). If you want to know how to write up a science experiment effectively, an English teacher is not the person to ask. I recently discovered that Professor David Crystal had come to the same conclusion. If you haven't read his books, do. All of them are marvellous. But it wasn't until I came across Pie Corbett's Talk for Writing that I found the missing link that could make literacy across the curriculum a practical reality.

Talk for Writing provides a simple underpinning process that supports pupils both in their learning in any subject and in transferring key communication skills across the curriculum. Its pedagogy is based on how human beings learn, moving from imitation to innovation to independent application, as pictured below. If you reflect on anything that you can do well (speak a language, ride a bike, carry out a science investigation, put up shelves, etc) when learning any of these skills, you will have gone through this process. Thus, it makes complete sense to put this process at the heart of how we plan to teach anything. The secret is to spend time at the imitation stage helping students internalise the language and the procedures that they will need to use to succeed at whatever they are learning.

The term Talk for Writing not only describes all the talk that surrounds the teaching of writing but also the wider learning within a unit – for example, the

Talk for Writing across the curriculum
  Planning stage
  ○ Cold-task baseline
  ○ Adjust model text & planning

1. Imitation stage
   ○ Hook audience
   ○ Warm-up vocabulary
   ○ Internalise model (text map)
     - Box-up structure
     - Co-construct key ingredients toolkit

2. Innovation stage
   ○ Shared-write innovation
   ○ Students have a go

3. Independent-application stage
   ○ Complete hot task on own
   ○ Reflect on learning: compare cold/hot tasks
   ○ Decide next steps

text mapping process that helps students internalise the expression of a unit also helps the students remember the content of the unit. The process revolves around providing models of what is required, including the way in which an effective teacher models the language needed and thinks aloud, articulating thought processes as well as readerly, writerly and practical approaches. The students are engaged in talking through ideas before applying their ideas in practice, refining their spoken and written understanding alongside their understanding of what they are doing – their mental road map. By involving them in explaining to others, Talk for Writing enables the students to develop their understanding of whatever is being studied. And, of course, in the process, it improves their reading: the more familiar you become with the tune of a subject (its key technical vocabulary and language patterns), the easier it is to read any related text because the generic language patterns have been internalised. Becoming a skilled reader, underpins effective learning. Talk for Writing helps students become better speakers, listeners, readers, writers and thinkers.

In effect, Talk for Writing is a spiral of progress which not only helps students build their skills and understanding from unit to unit within subject areas but also enables them to transfer these skills across the curriculum so that skills learnt in one area can be applied in another.

If your school is in England, all this will help meet Ofsted's latest inspection programme, which includes these questions: "What cross-curricular links are there (in particular in the development of literacy and numeracy across the curriculum)? How are you developing progression as pupils move through the school?"

If you compare the Talk for Writing process with Rosenshine's very useful *10 Principles of Instruction*, you'll see that not only does it encapsulate these principles but it has a number of additional features that transform it into a powerful learning process that can be applied to any subject, rather than just a list of good things to remember to do. Similarly, the key recommendations of the EEF's very useful document *Improving Literacy in Secondary Schools* are reflected in this book but TfW provides a more holistic approach. This is explained in Chapter 8 as it seemed more logical to explain Talk for Writing first.

The impact of the approach

The Talk for Writing process has shown itself to be very effective in raising the

8 TRANSFORMING LEARNING ACROSS THE CURRICULUM

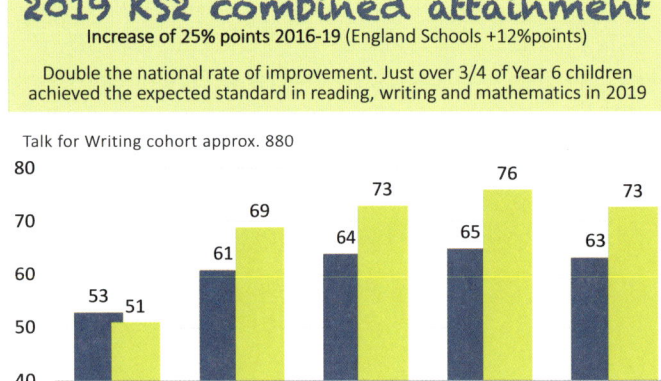

attainment of pupils in primary schools. In 2019, the combined results of the 16 Talk for Writing primary training schools in reading, writing, spelling & grammar and maths show that Year 6 pupils outperformed the national average by an impressive 11% (as this bar graph shows) despite having around 30% pupil premium, compared with a national average of 23%, and having 42% EAL, around double the national average. Thousands of primary schools are adopting the approach not only because it motivates the pupils but, importantly, it also motivates the teachers.

Secondary schools which have applied the approach across the curriculum report excellent progress; lessons and schools have been graded as *Outstanding*. Not only have results improved but students and teachers have been energised by the approach. The potential of Talk for Writing in secondary schools is summed up by these quotations from school leaders:

> *"I've worked quite a bit in some primary schools and I'm aware of what an impact Talk for Writing has had … Knowing what I know of Talk for Writing, this is an ideal vehicle for us to move on in this school and address some of the literacy and the learning outcomes that we want to address. It's best to have a consistent approach … I walk around the school every day and, when I see Talk for Writing in place, they are exciting lessons."* – Paul McAteer, when head of Slough and Eton Business College, **see video clips 1 & 2**.
>
> *"Talk for Writing is a pedagogical model that has transformed teaching and learning in this school."*
> – Karen Roberts, Executive Headteacher, Rainham Girls School
>
> *"Irrespective of whether your school is outstanding or making the exciting journey from special measures, Talk for Writing is a whole-school philosophy to teaching and learning that will catalyse improvement and raise aspirations across the school."*
> – James Munt, Executive Headteacher Havant Secondary Academy, Front Lawn Primary Academy, Portfield Primary and Seal Primary Schools
>
> *"As soon as it became evident that improving the quality and depth of writing across the curriculum was a developmental necessity for Wexham School, we began to research how best to achieve this. Talk for Writing was put forward as a suggestion and the consistent and unified approach across a wide range of subject disciplines at*

> *all key stages made us believe that this was an initiative that could help us in our ambitions for our students. Now in its second year of implementation, Talk for Writing is having a transformational impact on teaching and learning across the school."*
> – Ruth Corrie, Assistant Deputy Headteacher and TfW project leader, Wexham School, Slough

And this is what subject teachers have said:

> *"Because of the success of the Talk for Writing process, my mindset has changed: I plan lessons differently now ... it's literally filled my heart with joy."* – Emma Cooper, science teacher, The John of Gaunt School (**see chapter 11 and video clip 43**).
>
> *"It's been brilliant and makes it a pleasure to teach so I hope what I've written helps to explain the beauty of Talk for Writing*
> – Stu Gray, history teacher, The John of Gaunt School, (**see chapter 12b and video clips 12 & 26**).
>
> *"At last a literary consultant who really understands the phrase 'across the curriculum' rather than trying to make us all English teachers."* – Conference delegate
>
> *"The students feel pride in their own improvement and success ... It's slashed the time we have to spend on marking ... There's a real sense of 'Let's see what we can do now' – and there's much more conversation about teaching and learning now."*
> – Hiri Arunagiri, when Head of Science, Slough and Eton Business College. (see Hiri using text mapping on **video clip 17**).
>
> *"Making notes in a box on the 5 key ideas has totally changed the way we teach. It's revolutionised the way the students can answer the unit 4 questions and it's even transformed accountancy! We feel like we are walking on water."*
> – Marissa Bow, Head of Business Studies, Slough and Eton, (see **video clips 3, 28 & 60**).

It's worth listening to what Marissa has to say because, in many ways, she sums up the simple power of Talk for Writing to transform the quality of learning. She explains with great clarity why the process has proved to be so transformational for the students in all the subjects she teaches – business studies, economics, law and accountancy – as this extract illustrates:

"Talk for Writing has totally changed the way that we do things in the department. We have adapted our teaching style quite significantly...

"It is so simple and it really makes sense and it blows you away that you didn't think of these things yourself. We work with students that very often haven't come across in business and accounting the terminology that they are expected to use and that they get graded on during the examinations. And applying the Talk for Writing principles, especially something as simple as boxing up the text, has really revolutionised not only our lives but theirs as well. Because, all of a sudden, what they do has structure; it has meaning and understanding. They've learnt to engage with the text. It's not simply reading a bunch of words that they then try and memorise knowing that somewhere in the question they are going to recognise a word and know that little bit of knowledge in the back of the head is what they have to give back.

"They now actually understand the information that they are working with; they understand what the terminology means; they know how to apply the terminology to situations, and it has greatly improved the results they are achieving ... They actually understand what is being asked of them and they understand how to apply it. A big piece of information, a whole page of written work, is no longer intimidating. They have the power and the knowledge to look at that info, take their highlighter, bring out the text that's relevant to them and discard the information that's not. And that's a very, very, powerful tool: to be able to sift through the rubble of a lot of information and take the facts that are relevant and go and apply it to the result ...

"We're now putting them in the mark grades of As and Bs where previously we were getting Ds, hoping for Cs. And that has empowered them, and it's given them confidence: and the confidence in one subject goes through into confidence in the next subject. They stand up a little bit more straight. They know their opinion matters and it's easier to talk to them in class. They know they've got an opinion and they know they've got an educated opinion and it makes a big difference. They are talking in language that makes me go, 'Wow, my kids are arguing rules of prudence,' where previously they wouldn't have known what prudence meant."

– Marissa Bow, Head of Business Studies, Slough and Eton

Chapter 2: The Talk for Writing process

The Talk for Writing process for whatever age of learner you are teaching moves from imitation to innovation to independent application because that is the sequence that underpins all effective learning. This chapter guides you through that process using examples from a range of curriculum areas and ends with downloadable **handout 1**, which you may want to annotate so you can begin to think about how you would adapt your units. Some of the aspects of the process will probably be long familiar to you but some will be new.

In the imitation stage, if learners are being introduced not just to new content but also to new language that the content is expressed in (its tune), then students are liable to be unfamiliar with the key vocabulary and the pattern of language as well as the information and activities that make up the unit. The more unfamiliar the students are with the tune of the subject at this stage, the longer this stage will take so that the students can build up the appropiate patterns of language and have co-constructed understanding of the content. Once this understanding is in place, they can build on this knowledge and move through innovation to independent application.

Progress is a continuum: initially the balance of learning within units is liable to be heavily weighted towards the imitation stage because it is essential to get some of the basic patterns in place. As students become more familiar with subjects, more of these basic patterns will be in place, so the focus will switch to the innovation stage and, by the examination stage, the focus will be more biased towards independent application as students focus on adapting their knowledge to a range of potential questions and tasks. The three stages will still be present: it is just that the weighting will have changed.

Moreover, depending on what you are teaching, the way the stages relate to your unit will vary. A primary English language unit would usually follow the classic 3-stage process (see page 150) with the content (which in this case would be expression based) being introduced at the imitation stage and then embedded throughout the unit. Non-fiction units, especially in subjects across the curriculum in secondary schools, may have a more complex structure with additional content being introduced regularly

The Talk for Writing process across the curriculum

Planning stage
Cold-task baseline – adjust model text & planning

1. **Imitation stage**
   - Hook audience
   - Warm-up vocabulary
     - vocabulary, perform, text map, explain to others → content ← key phrases & concepts, dialogic talk to develop comprehension, echo reading
   - Internalise model (text map)
     - Box-up structure
     - Co-construct key ingredients toolkit (Plan it, Link it, Express it, Check it)

2. **Innovation stage**
   - vocabulary, perform, text map, explain to others → content ← key phrases & concepts, dialogic talk to develop comprehension, echo reading
   - Shared-write innovation
   - Students have a go

3. **Independent-application stage**
   - Complete hot task on own
   - Reflect on learning: compare cold/hot tasks
   - Decide next steps

Initially, main focus of unit = co-constructing understanding of content + imitation

KS3 practical subjects' main literacy focus throughout is vocab & explaining to others about what doing – not writing

As class progresses, main focus probably switches to innovation

By exam years, focus on real independence – adapting knowledge to suit different circumstances & exam questions

throughout the unit. As illustrated in the diagram above, each time content is introduced, a wide range of Talk for Writing elements will be relevant to help the students understand the content, retain it and be able to explain it to others. If you look at the science unit on atoms, **chapter 11b**, you will see that the whole process is repeated 3 times within the unit as the students' understanding of the complex issues they are studying grows. This is not Woollies pick 'n' mix where you can just select a little bit on warming up the words and think job done. It is a process that will support all subjects, but which needs to be adapted to suit the needs of different subjects, as the subject chapters of this book illustrate.

Planning your unit

Just as you can't write a good introduction to an essay before you have thought through the content of the essay, reading about planning a unit is probably best done once you understand the Talk for Writing process. So, if you are a new comer to Talk for Writing, you may want to speed through this bit and return to it in more detail later when it will have more meaning.

Every subject is different – in some, writing will be key while in others, especially maths or in practical subjects up until the end of KS3, very little writing may be required – and so planning will reflect these differences. Below are some of the key issues when planning any unit – all of them can be supported by applying the principles of Talk for Writing:

- How are you going to engage the students in what they are about to learn?
- How are you ensuring they understand the key vocabulary and phrases of the unit?
    - Which words and phrases will you focus on?
    - How will you ensure this language becomes embedded?
- What content needs to be included, in what stages, and how are students going to be helped to understand and retain this information?
    - How is regular review being built in?
    - What opportunities are there to explain what they have learnt to others?
    - Which concepts/activities should be focused on and how can dialogic talk be used to support understanding?
- If writing is required, what is the model for that writing?
    - Have you tested the model by seeing if it is structured clearly, or analysed it to see if it has significant (recyclable) generic features that will help build the class's ability to express themselves in your subject and recall what they have learnt?
    - How are students being helped to write this sort of writing so that, by the end of the unit, they can do it independently?
- If practical application is required, what is the model for that practice?
- How are students being helped to explain and evaluate what they have done?
- How will students be helped to embed their learning?

Bookending units with cold and hot tasks

Assessment should underpin all planning. What the students already know about what you are planning to teach them, and how well can they express/perform their knowledge, is key to pitching the unit at the right level and building in the next steps appropriately.

Set a cold task (a brief activity to allow students to show what they already know) at the beginning of the unit (if possible, do this a week before you actually plan to start the unit because you need time to adjust what you are going to teach in the light of what the students show they can already do). Always warm up the topic in some way so the focus is clear, but don't teach anything about how to express it, and then give the students a short amount of time (e.g. 4 minutes) to complete the task plus one minute to check it through as far as they have got and improve it if needed. Building in the importance of checking your work from the very beginning pays off. If some students feel they can't really begin, given the nature of the task, ask them to explain what the barriers are.

In the example below of a cold task, the teacher of 6-year-old children wanted to know how well the class understood how to do information writing. She hooked the children and warmed up the topic by inviting a bat woman (a woman with a bat) to tell the class about bats. At the end of the visit, she asked the children to write down the key information they now knew about bats. The example here is typical of what the children wrote. This told the teacher the child did understand what information means. However, there is no evidence that the child has planned the three bits of information that she has listed in any way, so she needs to be shown a simple way of planning. Equally, there is no sign that the child knows how to join the points together, so she needs to be shown how to link ideas. Clearly, the child does know how to write simple sentences that are fairly accurate and her spelling is good for her age, so she must have checked her work, but the vocabulary used is very limited and there is no attempt to engage the reader: you are very glad that what she wrote is very short!

> **Initial cold task**
> **- Year 1 pupil's information writing**
>
> Bats Han upside down.
> Bats like new homes.
> Bats like to eat inses.

Analysis of cold tasks enables you to focus your teaching of the whole class on what the students really need by altering your teaching plan and model text accordingly so that all the class is appropriately challenged to make progress. It is key to Talk for Writing that all students in a class initially work on the same model so that we don't doom students by deciding in advance that they won't be able to do it. Because different students will show different levels of attainment when completing the task, it enables you to assess what needs doing to support different groupings so that all can succeed: you will see which students need extra help to cope with the planned work, and which students are already showing progress in this area and will need to be challenged appropriately to develop their skills.

Because the text pictured above was typical of what the children in that class wrote about bats, analysing their work has enabled the teacher to know she needed to help her class:

- o **Plan**: so they know how to structure simple information text
- o **Link**: so they know how to make their ideas flow simply, in this example by using rhetorical questions and key conjunctions (joining words) like *and* and *but*
- o **Express**: so they know how to extend sentences from simple to compound and make them more interesting by including relevant detail and vocabulary.

> **Fox facts**
>
> Foxes are not tame pets.
>   What are they like? Foxes are elegant, dog-like creatures with sharp noses, bushy tails and reddish-brown fur.
>   What do they eat? They usually eat small, furry animals, feathery birds and they are very fond of tasty, plump chickens too. But they also eat insects and juicy berries.
>   Did you know that foxes are nocturnal? That means they come out at night. Foxes are famous for being cunning and pouncing on their prey. Their homes are called dens. Their babies are called cubs.
>   And they can swim!

As a result of this understanding, the teacher then produced a simple model text (reproduced here) that the class could imitate so they could internalise the structure and language they need to make progress. The whole idea of a model text is that it is full of generic features that the students need to know in order to be able to write such text themselves.

Making progress is key to effective learning. Once a student feels they can do something, they are immediately motivated. The idea is to repeat a similar task at the end of the unit so that the students can see the progress they have made. The simple idea of putting blue stickers to show the cold task at the beginning of the unit and a red sticker at the end enables students to see the progress they have made and is highly motivating (see **page 34**).

Dot-dot-dot spellings you are unsure of

> **End of unit hot task**
>
> Hedgehog Facs
> Hedgehogs are wild animals not pets.
> What are they like. They have sharp spins on ther bakes but undernif they are soft.
> What do they eat? They eat slipuriy slugs crushey bittls tickley spids and juciy catppl. They like frat too. They gring wort. Badgers are the alle anmls that eat hedgehogs.
> Did you now. Hedgehogs are nkctnl that mens they come out at nit. Hedgehogs hibnat that mens they sleep in the winter. Their nest is called a hibnacl. Ther babys are coled hogllos.
> And …… they can sime!

If you look at the hot task here that the same child wrote independently at the end of the unit, you can see the power of the approach because all the features the teacher had chosen to focus on are now present in the child's writing. One teacher famously commented, "You can tell the writing's getting better – the spelling's getting worse." This is a very important thing. The most difficult thing about the English language is the very wide range of vocabulary and the inconsistency of the spelling. If children start to think that correct spelling is more important than using just the right word, they are condemned to writing *big* for the rest of their lives because they can't spell *enormous*. This matters because fear of misspelling can be very damaging. There is a gloriously simple cure. When writing on the flipchart, demonstrate to the class that if they are unsure of the spelling of a word, they should still use it but just put …… underneath and carry on regardless. Breaking the flow when writing to worry about spelling, makes writing very hard. At the reading-through stage, worry about the spelling. This is a great relief to every teacher/teaching assistant when adding words to the flipchart, let alone the children.

Using prior learning grids to build on prior learning and frame learning

Another useful resource at the beginning of units, which can take both the form of a cold task and to use as a way of framing learning, are prior learning grids. These are based on the KWL grids developed by David Wray et al for the Exeter Project. The initials stood for *what do I KNOW, what do I WANT to LEARN and what have I Learnt*. Education is awash with acronyms, so I try to use as few as possible and just use the *say what it does on the tin* approach, so we all know what we are talking about.

Activating prior learning grids have proved very successful because they are a good way of establishing if the students already know anything about the topic you are about to teach. In other words, they help establish prior knowledge of content, not expression. They work well like this. The teacher fills in the middle column with the key learning points of the unit, in the order in which they will be learnt, expressed as questions. Every student is given a grid at the start of the unit and they fill in the first column – leaving it blank if they cannot recall any prior knowledge. As the unit develops, the *What have I learnt?* column can be filled in after class discussions that have co-constructed the key learning points. These are a great way of helping students know what they are learning and are very helpful for any adult who wants to provide support. They are also useful for revision and retaining what has been learnt. They can be adapted in a wide variety of ways to frame learning as illustrated here. In this example, from Wexham School in Slough. The key things to be learnt in the French unit are listed down the middle. In the left-hand column (tabbed in blue) students initially listed the words and phrases they already knew in French in relation to what they were going to learn and, in

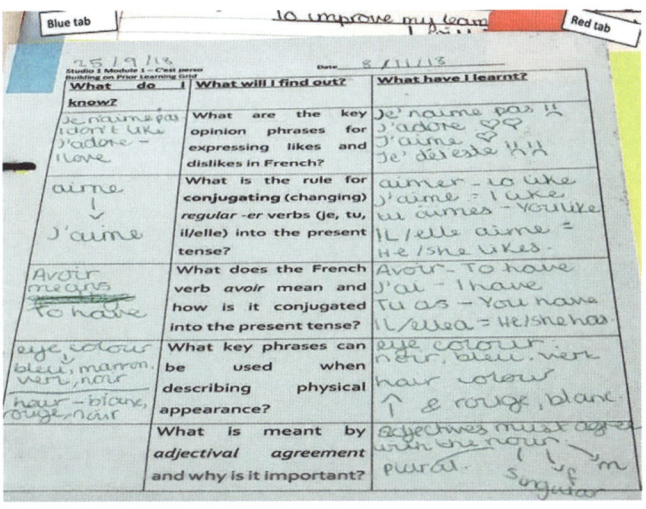

the final column (tabbed in red as the hot task), students have written in French what they had learnt. (**See page 277** for a unit based on this approach.)

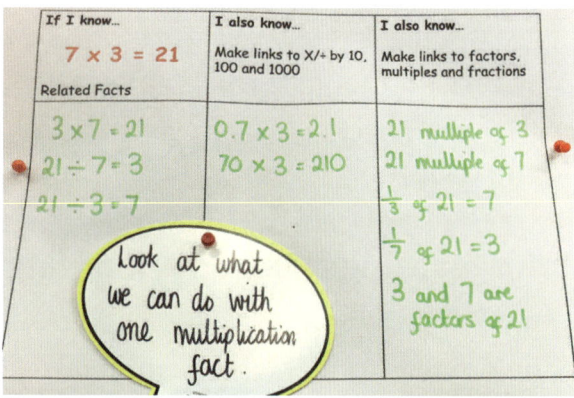

These grids lend themselves to all sorts of useful adaptations – just look at the clarity of this wonderful maths example on display in a Y5 classroom in St Matthew's, Birmingham, alongside references to what the fluency in reasoning focus was. When you look at this, you begin to understand how a school with a going rate of 88% pupil premium regularly scores 90% in the maths SATs. **See chapter 10a (pages 189–194)** to learn more about how this school gets such high maths results.

The centrality of the model

Whatever we are expecting the students to do, there needs to be some sort of a model to show them what to do. A model is absolutely key so it's worth spending time on testing whether the models you are using are good. We all need to know what a good one looks like if we are being expected to present, create, make, perform or write a good one ourselves. If you are expected to wire an electric circuit, you need a model showing you how it is done. In the same way, if students are expected to write something in relation to what they are learning in a unit, there must be a model of what this looks like and that model needs to be internalised so the students will have the right pattern in their heads. In this way, they will have the confidence to put pen to paper. If the words, "I don't know how to start, Sir/Miss," are familiar to you, that means there hasn't been a model or the model hasn't been sufficiently internalised to be of use. Teachers who use the Talk for Writing process effectively tell me that they no longer have students who don't know how to start writing. Those words were horribly familiar to me when I taught. I used to think it was the fault of the students who said they couldn't start since I suffered from the belief that I had explained everything very clearly – now I realise it was my fault. I had done too much talking and not given the students enough opportunity to talk the text themselves.

Model text MOT test

Some sort of model – usually a text – will be key to the success of a unit, so it needs to be thought about carefully. It's worth running it past the model text MOT test. Always check, for a class of this age and attainment, that it:

1. **lends itself to being memorised** (ie **is it short** – no more than 400 words preferably less.) (Most curriculum areas only require a few, and some just one, well-crafted paragraphs. If your subject requires extended writing, break it down into manageable sections and work on one or two at a time.)
2. **models a key type of text** the students will need to write
3. **boxes up** into a clear structure

THE TALK FOR WRITING PROCESS 17

4. includes **topic sentences**, where appropriate
5. contains **generically useful phrases** that are typical of this sort of text
6. includes good **sentence signposts** that link the text together coherently
7. illustrates a good use of appropriate **technical vocabulary**
8. uses the appropriate **tense**/s
9. **makes sense and flow well**.

In the light of this analysis, always ask yourself, 'How could I improve this model?'

If a model doesn't have significant generic features that will help the students internalise the tune (the rhythms and patterns of language underpinning your subject), including technical vocabulary and the phrasing regularly used, then it won't be worth internalising it, so it is important to select and develop models carefully.

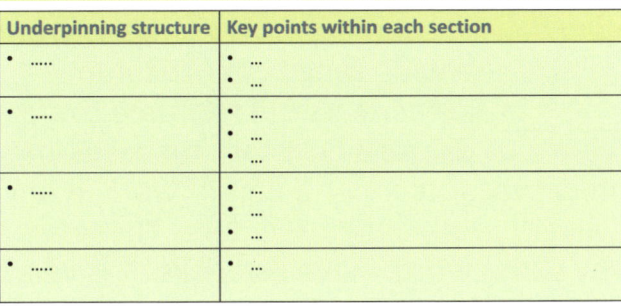

Here is an example of a good model for how to write a product evaluation for design and technology based on one written by the D&T department at Graham School, Scarborough. How can you test that it is good? First of all, establish whether your model has a clear structure that is typical of the sort of text required by exams in your subject. The best way to do this is to box it up at the planning stage to make certain your model is useful. Doing this yourself at this stage means that you will be well prepared to guide the students in how to box up the text when you come to teach it.

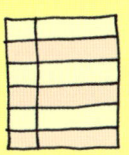

Boxing up is a very simple way of devising a grid to see what the underpinning structure is of any piece of text. Make a grid that reflects the number of paragraphs or sections of a text and put the heading of each part in the left-hand column. If you are just focusing on one paragraph, then divide it up into its key parts: introductory statement; key points; rounding off. The right-hand column of the boxed-up grid can then be used to bullet-point brief notes of the key points

18 TRANSFORMING LEARNING ACROSS THE CURRICULUM

Test 1. Does the structure box up logically?	
Intro product	For my controlled assessment, I designed and made a MBBM for children and men of all ages. My machine provides essential bubble blowing in a mega way, using SMART materials to provide structure and support for the bubbles.
Key design features	It has been designed to ergonomically fit into the user's hand, with a soft-grip palm support for added comfort and user safety. It is lightweight and easy to carry and can easily be folded away for storage. In addition, the appearance of the MBBM is traditional in shape but has a contemporary feel and touch.
Durability	The product can be used both indoors and outside due to hardwearing and robust materials that were chosen as a result of extensive testing of a range of possible materials.
Price	To keep costs low, I would use computer aided design and manufacture, possibly a 3D printer and ABS plastic. The cost for each product will be between £10 - £15 which, through my survey of users, is a price that consumers felt was reasonable.
Tests and modifications	The prototype I made was thoroughly tested by a range of possible users. From their feedback, I made a number of modifications including thickening the handle and including a non-slip surface to the handle.
Conclusion	In conclusion, I believe I have fulfilled the needs of my clients as specified in the design brief.

made in each section or insert images to sum up the content. So let's see if our D&T text passed the boxing up test. As you can see, it has boxed up very well. The product being evaluated has been clearly introduced and the key content of product evaluation has been included referring back to the design brief. This is further illustrated in the imitation section of this chapter (**pages 23–25**).

Now you know your model has passed the structure test, see if it passes the ingredients test. A good simple way of analysing the ingredients is to:

- highlight generically useful phrases in green (the ones the students can magpie and use when writing similar text – hence the Talk for Writing magpie icon)
- highlight sentence signposts in magenta (the linking phrases that hold the text together)
- highlight all technical vocabulary in blue

If all of these are clear, you know you have a good model. When you look at how well this D&T text passes the analysis test (**see page 25**), you realise that you have a very useful model on your hands that, once internalised, will enable students to move swiftly toward being able to write quality product evaluation independently.

Establishing what vocabulary to focus on

Warming up the words: Never-heard-the-word grids for all subject areas			
Key words	Never heard	Heard – not sure of meaning	Know what means – jot down meaning or image
1. prediction			
2. variable			
3. compare			
4. describe***			
19. inspire*			
20. expire*			

Vocabulary should be a key aspect of any unit – research tells us both that it is the key element for comprehension and that it tends not to be well taught. Because of its importance, **chapter 4** is devoted to ways of teaching vocabulary with examples from a wide range of curriculum areas. A useful resource to use as a cold task for assessing students' understanding of the key technical vocabulary of a unit of work in any subject is a never-heard-the-word grid (NHTW grid), illustrated here. These are explained fully in chapter 4, including why some words have asterisks. It is very useful to return to this grid at the end of the unit to establish progress made. **See page 71**.

Once the planning is in place, the teaching of the unit can begin.

1. The imitation stage

Start with a hook

The opening of any unit is obviously key to its success. If students are not interested in what is about to be taught, the chances of them learning anything is greatly reduced. But time is not on our side, given that the curriculum seems to be ever-increasingly stuffed full of content at the expense of the time to engage with it and understand it. So quick ways of grabbing students' interest need to be devised, like the one here, where Tom Killigrew, formerly a science teacher at The John of Gaunt School in Trowbridge, is pictured explaining to his fellow teachers how a simple statement in detective mode like, "Sand is in court accused of being a liquid not a solid," can be used to hook student interest. In **video clip 4** from which this image has been taken, Tom explains why he has found Talk for Writing powerful for teaching science. In his words, "It's just good teaching."

"Sand is in court accused of being a liquid not a solid."
– Tom Killigrew, science teacher, John of Gaunt

Warming up the words

Following on from the NHTW grid to establish which words to focus on most, an essential element of warming up any unit will be to focus on the key vocabulary that will be needed in order to build student confidence in using key words that may be unfamiliar. As explained above, vocabulary is so important that a whole chapter has been devoted to it so just one method is focused on here. Isabel Beck's simple 'basic routine' is a very useful quick way to start to learn some of the identified target words. The teacher says the target word, for example, *contradictory*, and provides a simple definition. (This needs preparing before the unit starts as it is very hard to make up good simple definitions off the top of your head and, if you reach for the dictionary, the chances are you will be confronted by a whole raft of other words that also need explaining.) Then the teacher says "Contradictory means …?" and the class, with the teacher's help, parrots the response: "… statements oppose each other so they cannot all be true." Then the teacher reverses it, beginning with the definition: "If statements oppose each other so they cannot all be true, they are …" and pauses for the class to fill in the word, "contradictory". This goes back and forth quickly. Then the teacher starts to use the word in context coming up with

The Isabel Beck routine:

1. Say word aloud: *contradictory*
2. Give a **simple** definition: *Contradictory means that statements oppose each other so they cannot all be true*
3. Involve students in saying word and definition
4. Use in sentences
5. Help them use it several times in different contexts

several examples and asks the students to come up with their own examples. It's quick, interactive, engaging and effective because everyone gets to say the words. See **video clip 5** of a Year 6 class at St Matthew's in Birmingham for an example of this approach in action.

Introducing the content

The next part of the imitation stage focuses on introducing the content of the unit. Many of the different aspects of the TfW process will be useful here, see image on **page 11**. Different subjects will have very different content that is sourced and presented in a wide range of ways but, whatever the subject, there will be words, phrases and concepts that will need to be focused on to help students internalise the patterns and key underpinning ideas of whatever is being taught. Here are a few examples. Text mapping, explained on **page 22**, can be a very powerful and engaging way of helping students remember content as can all sorts of ways of involving students in their learning through drama or mime, **see page 63**.

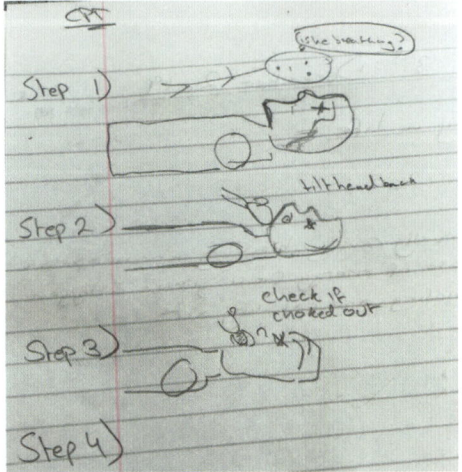

I recently watched a short part of a wonderful science lesson at Wexham School, Slough, where Hannah Thompson happened to be about to teach CPR. It embodied the way Talk for Writing can support the teaching of content. She hooked the class by telling them that not only was this part of the curriculum but a really useful skill that could help them save lives. She had a dummy with which to illustrate the process, and used actions and wit to help the students understand the vocabulary and follow the instructions. The picture shows her illustrating exactly where the trachea is with students choosing to imitate her action, as the photograph shows. When one student referred to this as the windpipe, she reminded them to use the correct terminology saying, "Not the windpipe, the oesophogus, ladies and gentlemen; this is GCSE." While listening, students were asked to text map the key points, as illustrated by one student's work here. Everyone was watching, listening, text mapping: totally involved in learning.

Introducing content through text

If text is being used as a way of introducing content, then oral comprehension will be key to checking the students' understanding of what is being read. The more open the questions, the more time students have to discuss and confer in small groups, the more likely they are to have understood the content. This sort of oral questioning and the wider significance of reading is the focus of chapter 7. Echo reading key extracts will also help the students' understanding of the passage and increase their reading fluency and mileage. In echo reading, the teacher reads a sentence clearly with good intonation and then gets the class to copy exactly how the sentence should be read. Building real understanding of whatever is being focused on will enable students to explain what they are learning. Explaining to others should be at the heart of the learning. If students can't explain what they have read and supposedly learnt, then they haven't learnt it (and they probably haven't understood it). So all sorts of talk and co-constructing understanding activities need to be devised to help students understand what they are learning so they will increasingly be able to explain it clearly and apply what they have learnt independently (see **chapter 6** on co-constructing understanding). If they can explain it, they will remember it. **Video clip 6**, relating to maths, is a good example of how the TfW process supports learning and leads to students being able to explain what they have learnt.

Introducing the model

Throughout any unit, the teacher should act as a model of how to explain whatever is being taught. At whatever stage is appropriate, the teacher will introduce the model of the sort of work they want the students to be able to do by the end of the unit. The centrality of models should be obvious but, surprisingly, many teachers don't provide clear models of *what = good* for whatever they are asking the students to do. If you don't provide a model, the students will probably think *good = long, neat and spelt correctly*. So, it's important to model clearly what is required and show that well-expressed, appropriate content is king.

What makes Talk for Writing so powerful is its emphasis on orally internalising the model before actually seeing the text – I managed to not think of this in the 25 years that I taught and that is why the words, 'I don't know how to begin, Miss', were just too familiar to me: not their fault but mine as explained earlier in this chapter. Oral rehearsal is key to effective learning. If the students do not have the tune of your subject securely in their heads so that they can explain their learning coherently using technical language appropriately, then they won't be able to do the writing that is required of them. In these circumstances, the best way to introduce the model is orally, supported by a text map as explained below. If you are teaching upper KS2 in a primary school where Talk for Writing is established, you may find that you can move straight to retelling the gist of the text activities because your class has already internalised the underpinning tune of the subject. However, if you are teaching Year 7 in a secondary school where most of the intake has not benefitted from the Talk for Writing approach, internalising the model orally will probably be the best way to begin. If you teach a subject like business studies that only begins in Year 10, the text map and oral way in will be equally relevant. As students' linguistic competence increases, more sophisticated ways of internalising model text can be introduced as explained in Chapter 3. But it's worth remembering that oral recall of short models and text mapping is very engaging and can work well with learners of all ages and levels, as sixth formers from The Dyson Perrins Academy in Malvern illustrate on **video clip 7**.

Text mapping

The secret of helping classes internalise model text successfully is to prepare a simple text map of the model that will help everyone remember the key content and linking phrases. Here is a text map for the model text about the fox on **page 14**. A text map should have just a few key images to help you remember the gist of the text – there should not be an image for every word – too many images just cause confusion. Also, if you happen to be artistic, resist the temptation to make your images good. The students will soon be doing their own text mapping and may well be put off if they think the quality of the drawing matters – they are just squiggles to aide memory – and they have to be done quickly. Display the text map on the whiteboard or flipchart so that everyone, including you, can see it clearly.

Make certain you have internalised the text thoroughly yourself and work out a few key actions to help the students recall the text. Again, don't come up with too many actions – just enough to act as an aide memoire. Then perform the text for the class line by line getting the class to listen to the intonation of the words and watch any actions, and then copying the actions and the intonation. If the students come up with better ideas for the actions than you have thought of – go with their ideas.

It often works best if you get the students to stand – a few minutes relief from the torture that is usually school chairs will probably be welcome. If you look at the **video clip 8** of this process in action in science with a Year 9 class, you can see why it is engaging and an excellent way both of helping students remember key content and of expressing it clearly. Moreover, text mapping can be invaluable in giving students the confidence to explain to others. Listen to **video clip 9** as business studies teacher Isabel Hutton explains how she developed the approach and how surprised she was by how effective it was.

Here's some useful advice to help you help a class to internalise text:

- Stress the triggers (language features) which are key to coherence
- Strengthen recollection of key content through actions
- Begin as a performance then back off and increasingly hand over to class. Get the students to do the telling
- Say the lines expressively – if the students are dull, then you were dull
- If someone doesn't want to join in, let them sit and watch.

It won't take long for the students to recall the model and once they are familiar with the process they will begin to internalise models quickly. Once they can recall the basic model:

- get the students to sketch their own text map (people remember things much better from their own images so outlaw clip art and don't use it yourself when text mapping content (except, perhaps, in computer studies)
- move from whole class, to groups, to pairs. Once they can do it in pairs, they have remembered it.

It should be obvious why ensuring that the model is of high quality is key. Since time is being spent on this process, it is very important to select a few key models that underpin expression and key content in your subject as explained on **pages 16–18 above**.

Once the students have internalised the text, they are then shown it in written form and can begin to analyse the key features. A great advantage of internalising the text orally before you see it is that, by the time the students get to see the text, they can all read it fluently because they have internalised the pattern of the language, and have already understood vocabulary and key concepts because these have been well introduced. This helps them become confident users of the key vocabulary related to the topic and it's entertaining and memorable, as **video 10** of maths teacher Mr Roy from Royd's Hall, Huddersfield, illustrates.

Boxing up the text

The first thing to do once the students see the actual text is to get the class to box it up so they understand how it is structured.

The beauty of boxing up, introduced in the planning stage on **page 17**, is that once you have boxed up the structure of the model, you can then use the same boxing up as a planner. This enables the students to plan their own version of a similar text and jot down a series of notes in each section so they know what content to include. The first example here is a boxed-up version of the simple information model text about a fox above (**see page 14**). It is easy to see how you could use this same structure to write information text relating to any other animal. The second example is the boxed-up structure for the D&T product evaluation. Again it is easy to see how this structure could be used to evaluate any product.

Boxed-up plan for information text on an animal

Underlying structure	Key points
• Introduce animal	
• Appearance	
• Diet	
• Habits	
• Conclusion	

Having asked many thousands of primary and secondary teachers over the years whether students plan their work, the overwhelming response is that they normally don't, with the result that they often head off in the wrong direction and waste their time writing something that is of little use, and then end up feeling a failure. The best things in teaching are always simple. This shouldn't exactly be ground-breaking stuff but you will be amazed at the power of boxing up if, every time students are expected to plan something in any subject, they are required to box it up. Very quickly, they will be able to box up structure independently and will automatically use boxing up to plan their work. This, in itself, is miraculous. Somehow they seem to be willing to do boxing up – probably because it is fundamentally simple and they can see how it helps them. It helps them construct a mental model of what they have to do. Just listen to a student from Slough and Eton explaining why boxing up has made a big difference (**video clip 11**).

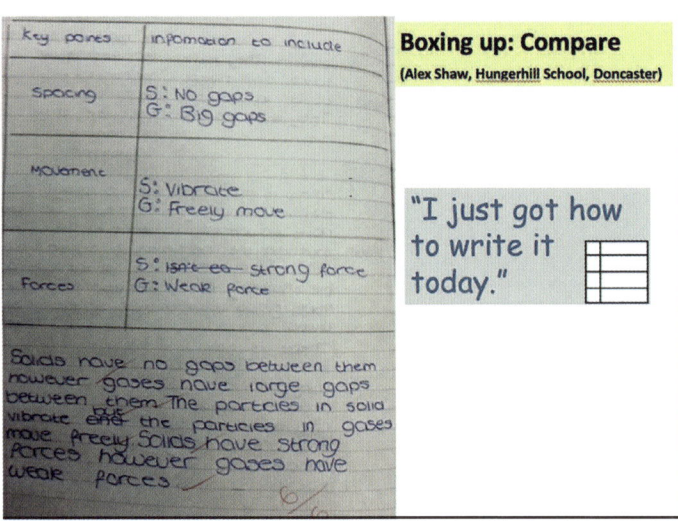

Boxing up gives students confidence. It enables them to understand the structure of what they are trying to write as powerfully illustrated by this example from science teacher Alex Shaw from Hungerhill School, Doncaster. The student has boxed up a simple plan listing the headings he needs:

- Spacing
- Movement
- Forces.

Next to each heading he has bullet pointed the key content required. Underneath he has written a paragraph following this 3-part structure. Bingo! His explanation of the difference between solids and gases has won him full marks. The student's comment is very telling: "I just got how to write it today." Too often in secondary school, if students are required to write, they feel they cannot do it and failure leads to failure. Using this method, success builds on success across the curriculum.

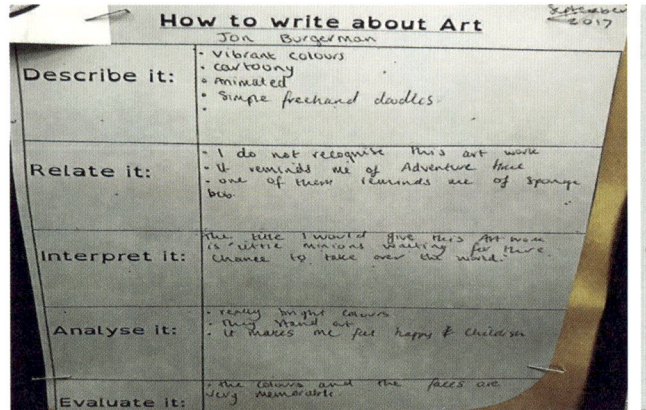

Have a go yourself at boxing up the structure of the answer to a typical question in whatever subject you are teaching. Here are two examples that teachers jotted down in a few minutes. You can see from this how powerful this could be in transferring learning skills across the curriculum.

And, of course, once students are familiar with boxing up and are using it across the curriculum, they will be able to box up any well structured text very quickly independently and identify the underpinning structure, so, over time, very little time will be taken up with this. Students often find boxing up transformational.

Co-constructing the toolkit

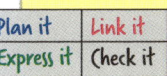

Evaluating my Mega Bubble Blowing Machine (MBBM)
For my controlled assessment, I designed and made a MBBM for children and men of all ages. My machine provides essential bubble blowing in a mega way, using SMART materials to provide structure and support for the bubbles.

It has been designed to ergonomically fit into the user's hand, with a soft-grip palm support for added comfort and user safety. It is lightweight and easy to carry and can easily be folded away for storage. In addition, the appearance of the MBBM is traditional in shape but has a contemporary feel and touch.

The product can be used both indoors and outside due to hardwearing and robust materials that were chosen as a result of extensive testing of a range of possible materials.

To keep costs low, I would use computer aided design and manufacture, possibly a 3D printer and ABS plastic. The cost for each product will be between £10 - £15 which, through my survey of users, is a price that consumers felt was reasonable.

The prototype I made was thoroughly tested by a range of possible users. From their feedback, I made a number of modifications including thickening the handle and including a non-slip surface to the handle.

In conclusion, I believe I have fulfilled the needs of my clients as specified in the design brief.

Once the students have boxed up the model text so they understand the structure, the next thing to do is to get them to analyse key ingredients of the text. The best way to do this is through simple highlighting, asking them to identify specific features, as illustrated here. Consistent different-coloured highlighting is best, as illustrated by this example. Here, and throughout this book, generic text is highlighted in green and the sentence signposts that link the text together and guide the reader are in magenta, whereas technical vocabulary is in blue. The more the students have to pick out the features themselves, the more they will come to understand them. In primary school, consistency within each year is easy because most of the lessons will be taught by the same teacher. In secondary schools, consistency across the curriculum is somewhat of a nightmare. But colour coding the key ingredients of model text is a great way to achieve coherent understanding. When you walk round Wexham School in Slough, you can see that in every subject where text matters, the students are very familiar with the following:

- generic (recyclable) text – highlighted in yellow
- linking text (sentence signposts) – highlighted in pink
- technical vocabulary – highlighted in blue.

It is a very easy way to begin to achieve transfer of understanding across the curriculum.

It's also a good idea to start flip-charting key sentence signposts and display them so that phrases like *In addition*, *From their feedback*, *In conclusion* become familiar to the students and they can use them automatically where appropriate. These signposts are the glue that links each topic together coherently. For detailed work on sentence signposts **see chapter 5**. This will enable each subject area to identify the key writing tools that are required for their subject.

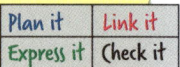

Establishing flexible writing toolkits

A key problem for students is that the demands of writing are many and varied. We need to find a way of helping them transfer their writing skills from one subject to another by being aware of which skills are similar for any particular piece of non-fiction writing required and which ones are different. If you ask yourself if all the different types of non-fiction writing we ask students to do have got any features in common, you will probably come to the conclusion that they all need to be:

- planned in some sort of way to provide a logical structure
- linked well to provide coherence
- expressed well to facilitate understanding
- checked for relevance and accuracy.

This has led to the development of *plan-it, link-it, express-it, check-it toolkit* grids (see **Handout 2** online) which have proved to be a very useful way of helping students co-construct understanding of the types of writing that different subjects require. They enable students to develop a flexible writing toolkit in their heads, so they know how to handle any writing task they are faced with.

Generic writing toolkit

Plan it	Link it
• Analyse the task • Think audience & purpose • Box up structure. (logical/chronological) - Begin with an introduction - End with a conclusion	• Introduce paragraphs with a topic sentence • Use sentence signposts to link the text and make it fit together
Express it	**Check it**
• Express points clearly • Keep reader engaged • Include detail to illustrate key points • Use technical vocabulary appropriately	• Read it to check it flows, makes sense and fulfils purpose • Check punctuation and spelling

This is relatively easy for teachers in upper primary as the Year 5 teacher could introduce the approach and then adapt it as appropriate across the curriculum and the Year 6 teacher inherit it and build it further. The idea in secondary schools (assuming that many of the intake will not be familiar with Talk for Writing) is that the English teachers early on in Year 7, through analysing a variety of non-fiction text with their classes, co-construct a generic writing toolkit like the one here, having identified the key features that the writing has in common. This approach can be supported by posters available from Talk4Writing.com once the understanding has been co-constructed. These generic writing toolkits in A5 format can also be downloaded from Talk for Writing website so that they are accessible to all classrooms that require writing. Classes can then decide whether the writing they are being asked to do has the same key features as the generic writing toolkit or whether it differs in any way. The students working on their own or in pairs could:

- tick all the features that are the same
- amend any features that need altering
- add any additional key features
- annotate the grid with examples from the model text.

The class could then confer and agree on what the toolkit is for this type of writing.

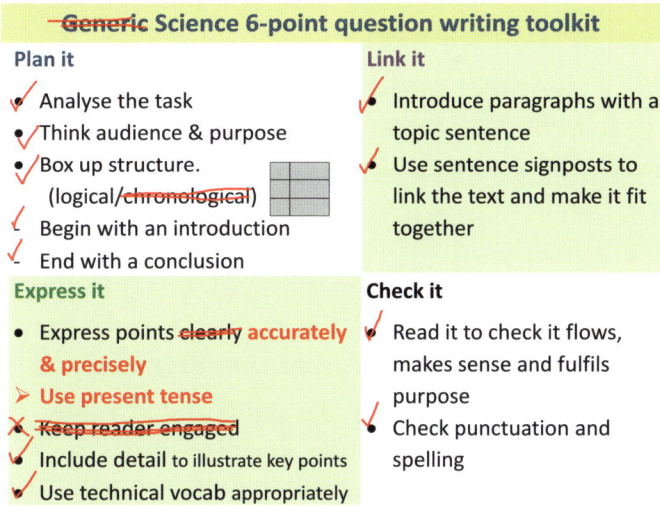

Beginning from a consistent generic model will help students recognise the similarities while emphasising the key differences. The example here for a 6-point science question emphasises the fact that the type of writing required has to be very accurate and precise – keeping the reader engaged is not a requirement (English teachers may not like this but it is a fact!). If the class also annotates the model with examples to illustrate this, it would help them grasp what being accurate and precise means as well as the difference the present tense makes.

Below is an annotated example for the D&T model text on **page 17**. As you can see, very little of the generic writing toolkit has been changed. The students have identified that the order of the points being made is logical not chronological and that keeping the reader engaged is not an issue but covering the key points of the brief is. They have then found examples of the key features from within the model text to strengthen their understanding of the type of text required.

Helping students analyse the different writing demands of different types of non-fiction text consistently will help them internalise these differences so they automatically write the right sort of text. This simple procedure enables students to transfer their understanding about writing easily from subject to

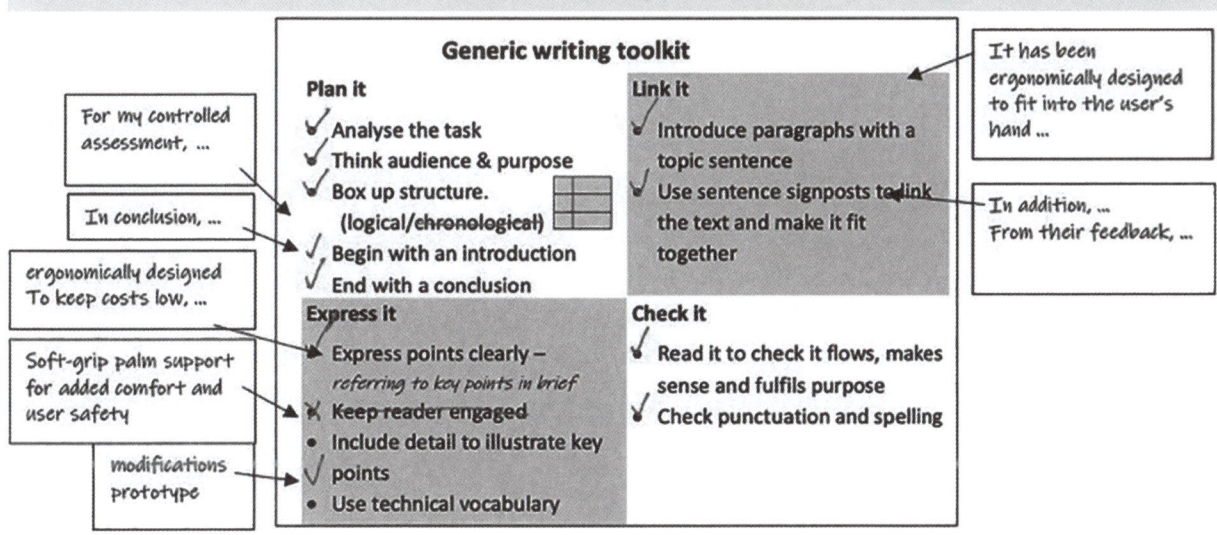

subject and maintains the importance of planning, linking, expressing and checking their work appropriately.

Get the punctuation right

If you look at the examples of the sentence signposts above, you will see that each one has the comma that should follow it attached. In primary schools now, the children and their teachers have become familiar with this (technically, it is the comma that separates off a fronted adverbial from the sentence that it introduces). The pupils will probably all know the term *fronted adverbial*. It is strange to secondary teachers because it is a recent addition to the grammatical world but, to the students, this term is not strange because it is part of the grammar test that they will have done at the end of key stage 2. They should enter secondary school automatically putting these commas in but, if we are not careful, they will lose the skill in secondary school because we don't consistently use the feature. In secondary schools, if the term *fronted adverbial* is too technical, just remind them that putting a comma after sentence signposts at the beginning of sentences matters. So, in all poster displays of sentence signposts used to introduce sentences, remember to include the comma at the end of the signpost.

Why co-constructing learning matters

At all stages, but most importantly at the imitation stage, co-constructing learning is key, so the students understand what they are learning. If we are not careful, learning becomes a form of painting by numbers where the student is provided with so much support that they have not internalised, that they collapse as soon as they are left to their own devices and feel that they have failed. Through co-constructing learning, we can build independence. Just as only writing down definitions doesn't help you internalise the meaning of words, writing frames including lists of sentence signposts don't help students to structure and link their own work independently. If students are given writing frames listing the key language they need to use, they will just copy it and fill in the gaps. They won't internalise the essential phrases.

If you look at the writing the student has written above, on the surface it looks good because it is coherently structured and linked. But the problem is that, as soon as you look at the support that was given to enable the students to do the writing, you can see that all this coherence has just been copied rather than internalised. The chances are that, left to their own devices, the same student will not know how to begin or continue coherently because they do not know how to plan independently and the sentence signposts that link such text together cannot be remembered. Most of the work here has been done by the teacher and the student has only had to copy. The idea is to scaffold the student's learning in such a way that increasingly the teacher has to do less and less work and the students more and more because they know how to do it, as illustrated by **video clip 12** which shows that students quickly become used to identifying key signposts and using them effectively within well-structured work. The power of co-constructing learning is demonstrated in **chapter 6**.

2. Innovation stage

Talk for Writing is founded on co-constructing understanding through good models that are initially internalised orally then analysed for structure and key ingredients, often referred to as writing tools. Boxing up provides a consistent means of analysing the structure of different writing purposes so students can use this independently to structure their own writing to fit whatever purpose is required. Alongside this, internalising the meaning of key vocabulary and the sentence structures needed, plus using the generic writing toolkit to establish how the writing required conforms or differs from standard non-fiction requirements, provides students with a flexible framework in the head which will help them write appropriately for whichever non-fiction writing is required.

Once the basics of this are in place through the imitation stage, it is time to move on to the innovation stage. The idea is to innovate on the model by applying the same underpinning structure and phrasing to different content. The teacher will then introduce the new content, warming up any new vocabulary and key phrases and using text mapping techniques and oral techniques like oral comprehension and explaining to others, to help students understand and remember the content.

Boxed-up plan for information text on an animal

Underlying structure	Key points
• Intro topic	• badger
• Appearance	• b&w striped snout • stumpy • size of small pig
• Diet	...
• Habits	...
• Conclusion	...

Shared writing

At the innovation stage, to stick to the simple fox information text example from **page 14** for a moment, instead of a fox, a different animal could be introduced. The same planning structure could then be used, as illustrated here, to discuss and make notes on what the content would be if the animal were, for example, a badger. This sort of innovation on the boxed-up plan should initially be done in front of the students so they understand the process. Once they are familiar with the

process, they should be able to do it independently, perhaps feeding back on the information they have planned to include and magpieing ideas from other students' examples. Once the new plan is in place, and the teacher has orally rehearsed some possibilities with the class, the teacher can then interactively model for the class through shared writing how to adapt the original model to suit the new content. This is best done on a flip chart (because typing on a keyboard does not illustrate the writing process the students are faced with, assuming they are writing on paper). The writer should be supported by the new boxed-up plan of key points on the washing line or working wall plus any word or phrase banks and toolkits that have been created. In addition, the original model text should be displayed on the white board so the class can see how to use the boxing up and toolkit to support their writing and innovate on the model to suit the new content.

Doing shared writing effectively requires real skill on the teacher's part which, in turn, requires thorough preparation (see **Handouts 3 & 4**). In primary schools where Talk for Writing is well established, classes will have moved beyond the simple substitution phase before the end of KS1 (around the age of 7). Sadly, many children still transfer to secondary schools lacking basic writing skills, so it is always a question of judging where your class is. Some Year 7 classes, when they first start secondary school, may still be at the simple substitution stage, or a group within the class may need support at this level. Where a class still has significant difficulties in writing coherently, then the shared writing should hug closely to the original so that:

> *Foxes are not pets.*
>   *What are they like? Foxes are elegant, dog-like creatures with sharp noses, bushy tails and reddish-brown fur …*

might become:

> *Badgers are definitely not pets.*
>   *They are stumpy, pig-like creatures with distinctive black and white striped faces and greyish fur.*

Hopefully, you may be in the position to demonstrate a more sophisticated way of writing focusing on the sort of features that are central to the writing required for your subject. So the innovation could be

> *Badgers are wild animals that are rarely seen because they are nocturnal, which means they come out at night.*
>   *They are immediately identifiable by their distinctive black and white striped faces that contrast with their stumpy grey bodies …*

Shared writing is an art that, hopefully, primary teachers and English and MFL departments in secondary schools are very good at. For examples of how to do shared writing effectively, see **video clips 13, 33 & 35**.

Creating Storytellers and Writers has a whole section focused on the art of shared writing supported by a range of video clips that will be useful if you require more support in this skill.

In creative writing, there are many ways to express, say, *suspense* effectively. So it makes sense for the teacher to share-write one example with the class and then challenge everyone to write their own version which should be significantly different from the model the class 'wrote together'. But the more factual the writing required, the less scope or need there is for variety in how the text is innovated on. Science will want the facts presented as accurately and as briefly as possible – once you have a good example of this, trying to find alternatives may not be time well spent, but time spent on making text coherent will pay off as explained below.

Modelling writing

Sentence combination – my turn:

- Many scientists support the asteroid theory
- An asteroid collided with Earth around 65 million years ago.
- The dinosaurs were destroyed.
- Dinosaur fossil records did not gradually die out over the years.
- Dinosaur fossil records abruptly disappeared.

Many scientists argue that the dinosaurs were wiped out by an asteroid that collided with Earth approximately 65 million years ago. Key evidence for this theory is the fact that dinosaur fossil records did not die out gradually over the centuries but abruptly disappeared.

Shared writing can be very daunting for teachers who aren't language specialists so modelling writing is a more simple alternative at the innovation stage because you can fully prepare everything in advance focusing on how to link facts coherently. First, bullet point whatever key content is required in your boxed-up plan. For example, if your model text had focused on how to support a theory with evidence, your boxed-up plan for the innovation could include 5 bullet-pointed facts relating to, say, the asteroid theory, as illustrated here.

Then, in *Blue-Peter* style, show how to express such information coherently by using text you have prepared earlier, underlining the sentence signposts that give the text its coherence, as illustrated above.

Sentence combination – your turn:

- Dust from collision of asteroid with Earth obliterated Sun
- Dinosaurs could not cope with such a drop in temperature
- Dinosaurs' main sources of food were wiped out
- Dinosaurs quickly became extinct
- It is estimated 50% of all animal species died out

Next, provide the students with the rest of the bullet points from the boxed-up plan to see if they can coherently link the points, explaining that there are many different ways in which these points can be coherently linked. Asking the students to write their version on mini-whiteboards can be very useful as you can quickly see which versions are good and the students can see a range of alternative good solutions. The facts remain the same; it is the coherence that is being innovated on. Here's just one example:

> *One example answer: there is a wide range of ways of expressing this coherently*
>
> 1. Dust from the collision of the asteroid with the Earth blotted out the sun which caused a sharp drop in temperature. Dinosaurs were ill equipped to cope because this swiftly wiped out their main sources of food. As a result, they quickly became extinct along with an estimated 50% of all other animal species.

Alternately, put an incoherent version on the whiteboard and ask the class in pairs to discuss how it could be improved. Then ask the students to explain how to improve it.

Differentiating by outcome not input

If all students are going to be given a chance to succeed, it is important that all students have access to the curriculum rather than, as stated earlier, the teacher deciding in advance who is going to fail. So, at the imitation stage, all the students will have had access to the content and related model/s that the unit is focusing on. At the innovation stage, when the students start writing their own innovations, the teacher may decide to give different levels of support to groups of students according to their attainment so far. Those students whom the teacher knows will find the writing required too challenging if left entirely on their own, could be gathered together and talked through the process by the teacher while the rest of the class finishes the innovation on their own. Some teachers have found it useful, at this stage, to have groups working together on the problem, so that small groups 'shared write' their own versions which are then displayed to the whole class and, together, the class decides which version works best. Again, the more understanding can be co-constructed, the better.

Providing effective feedback

> *Assess work: establish what needs focusing on*
>
> | The problem: | Possible cure: |
> |---|---|
> | • Misunderstanding | Revisit concept: set up explaining to other activities |
> | • Lack of cohesion | Sentence combination |
> | • Lack of range | Provide more model text with additional features |

Obviously, live marking is always best as the advice is oral and can be acted upon immediately and there is a chance for the student to discuss what they don't understand, but it is rarely possible to get round the whole class in this way.

When the work is taken in and marked, the teacher will be able to recognise which elements are creating the greatest problems. There is no point in marking the work if, when it is handed back, students aren't required to immediately improve their work in some sort of way following brief input from the teacher on what to do. The first two bullet points pictured here are common problems. Clearly, if a significant number of pupils are having problems with aspects of the content, this needs to be revisited and explaining-to-others activities set up. The second one, sentence combination, which research has shown to be the most effective way of helping students improve their expression, means that more work needs to be done on showing students how to combine information coherently – as illustrated above by the text on the demise of the dinosaurs.

So, when the students' work on combining the dinosaur text was marked and handed back, the teacher might want to begin by talking the students through a possible way of combining these sentences, for example:

> *Dinosaurs were not able to cope with such a drop in temperature since it rapidly wiped out their main sources of food. Consequently, they quickly became extinct as did an estimated 50% of all other animal species living at the time …*

They could also include any good alternative examples written by the students so the class can see a number of coherent alternatives.

In the happy situation where some students' work was so good that it did not require improving in any way, those students could be asked to support other groups in explaining the content to others or combining information coherently. For the students providing the support, nothing will help them embed their learning more than explaining to others and, for the students who need more help, a different voice explaining what to do, especially when it is a fellow student, can really help build understanding. As one primary pupil kindly told their teacher, "Everything's so much clearer when Tyrone explains it." Alternately, students who are progressing very well can be provided with more challenging models to extend the range of what they can do.

Marking schemes across the curriculum

Simple, focused marking works best

Spot the error for the pupils to correct themselves
(– green for areas for all to focus on when work is handed back)

- a dot in the margin to guide them towards **basic errors** (spelling/punctuation/capitals) to correct in that line. Three dots = 3 errors in the line, etc.
- a squiggly line to indicate that a sentence is **not coherent** and needs recasting
- a pair of parallel lines to indicate that the **paragraphing** needs adjusting
- A line down the margin to indicate where **content is inaccurate**

When you look at some school's marking schemes with endless lists of symbols signifying errors of one sort or another, you can't help thinking they have been devised by members of senior management who no longer have to put their ideas into practice, since they no longer teach and thus don't actually have to mark work. A simple system like the one pictured here offers a good basis for coherent feedback across the curriculum and, importantly, puts the emphasis on the students correcting the errors themselves. If you add in the requirement that all students have to have checked their work through and written a brief comment on how well they think they have completed the work, before giving it to a teacher to mark, this will greatly cut down the number of careless errors. Then, when marking, the teacher can focus on which aspects of the content or expression need revisiting and decide on activities to remedy any errors as soon as the work is handed back. Obviously, teachers can add to the list as suits their needs when focusing on specific features.

It's also useful to add to this a simple 2-colour marking system that is consistent

across the school with one colour (for example, pink) to signal excellent work and one colour (for example, green) to signal need for improvement. The simplicity and clarity of this is obvious and the students can use the same colour scheme when discussing each other's work. When work is handed back, attention can immediately be focused on anything in green.

Independent application stage

At the end of a unit, there should be some opportunity for the students to show what they now know independently – the hot task. This means that they can apply what they have learnt using different content. For example, this could be a different context or a different question relating to similar content, or a different problem to solve using the same method as has just been learnt.

Independent activites may very well be differentiated so that different groups of students are given different challenges related to the progress they are making. There is no point in making students do activities that you know they can't do – this just increases a sense of failure. This differentiation may just amount to some students being provided with supporting flipcharts to scaffold their work, or being grouped for more innovation, while others are working entirely independently.

Comparing the cold to hot tasks

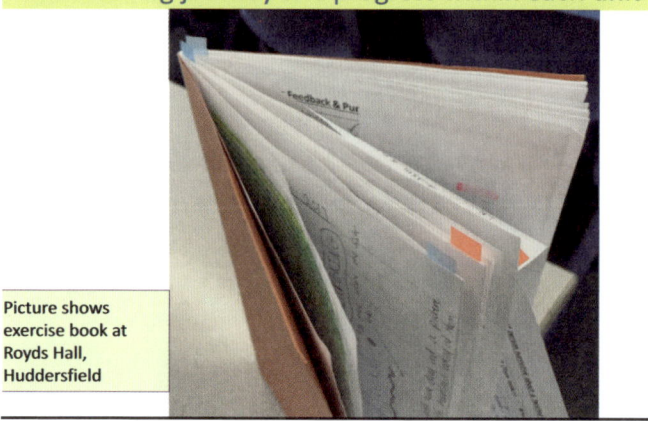

Blue tabs (*cold task*) and **red** tabs (*hot task*) show the learning journey and progress within each unit

Picture shows exercise book at Royds Hall, Huddersfield

At the end of the unit, it is important that the students are given time to reflect on what they have learnt and to compare their cold task to their hot task. Sometimes learning walks can seem like looking at stuff, stuff and more stuff, and you suspect it feels like that to the students as well. The whole point of the cold to hot process is to show what the students have learnt so that you and they can compare what they could do at the beginning of the unit and what they could do by the end of the unit. It should be highly motivational. For this reason, it is a good idea to make the cold task at the start of each unit and the hot task at the end of the unit highly visible. A simple way of doing this is to give the students blue and red tabs as illustrated here – or blue and red highlighter pens can be used to shade the top edge of the paper. It's important to make the learning journey visible and to encourage reflection on progress.

It is a very empowering process. Students from all years at a Talk for Writing after-school event at Royds Hall in Huddersfield were invited to bring their work and show the progress they were making. They were very keen to explain how motivated it made them feel. It was an inspiring event; inspiring most of all because of the confidence and pride that the students now had in their learning.

Teachers from a wide range of subjects have found the approach useful as is illustrated by **video clip 6** from a Year 8 maths lesson in Slough & Eton. One maths teacher commented that watching it made her more aware of students' potential misconceptions when faced with a task: when you are good at a subject it can be hard to imagine how it is perceived by someone unfamiliar with the process and the technical words related to it.

The process really can transform results within any subject and, when applied across a whole school, is even more powerful. Look at **video 61** from Thomas Becket Catholic School in Northampton to see how it was in-school evidence from the cold to hot tasks that helped convince staff that the TfW process would work for them. The project lead at Dyson Perrins in Malvern had enthusiastically told me about Billy, from a traveller background, for whom Talk for Writing had been truly transformational. Listen to Billy on **video clip 16** telling his story about how the approach is helping him achieve his dream of becoming a PE teacher.

A special plea to avoid an obsession with exams

I've been talking to students and teachers for nearly 50 years now about their teaching and learning and one big change is very noticeable in that time. The focus of the teaching has become more and more exam obsessed, doubtless caused by external pressures, but the solution is in our hands. Now, depressingly, the answer to questions like, "Why does this help?" is nearly always framed in exam-passing terms rather than in helping gain understanding, interest or competence. I fear for the children who, in a normal year, have just emerged from their Year 6 in primary, where the SATs are ever-present, to find that the first thing they do in secondary schools is activities explicitly linked to the Year 11 exam criteria. Of course, the exams matter, but developing a love of learning, an interest in things, a desire to think, understand and be creative is also important, alongside having a love of language so you can make the words dance.

It is perfectly possible to thread all the elements needed for success in exams into our teaching in Years 7-9 without making them the sole focus of our teaching and, hopefully, this book will show just how to do this. Then, in the months before exams, we can focus on honing specific exam techniques confident that our students have the skills, nous, knowledge, understanding and motivation to soar over all the strange hurdles that exams can pose. And, in the process, of course, this will help schools in England meet the latest curriculum inspection requirements of Ofsted: "Don't spend a disproportionate amount of time on test or exam preparation at the expense of teaching."

The handout below, which is also available on the website, may be useful in helping you to adapt the approach to fit your needs. Each stage is set out in order with suggestions for how it works in practice. You may want to print this off and make notes as you read on how you could apply the process to a unit you will be teaching soon.

Talk for Writing adapting-a-unit planner

Handout 1.

How am I ...	Practical suggestions	Notes
PLANNING STAGE		
• using baseline assessment?	Devise cold task to assess baseline	
• ensuring using best model text/ process to support progress?	Ensure your model provides the support the students need	
1. IMITATION STAGE:	**Warming up words**	**Warming up words**
• flagging up key words? & building on prior knowledge? • supporting students in understanding these words and using them orally in context?	1. Never-heard-the word-grids 2. Word clumping activities 3. Sorting activities 4. Using image to picture words 5. Mime 6. The Isabel Beck routine	
Warming up phrases	**Warming up phrases**	**Warming up phrases**
• supporting students in using the sentence signposts and typical phrasing of my subject?	• Raiding the reading – magpieing • Clumping sentence signposts • Sorting sentence signposts • Sequencing • Analysing signposts /highlighting	
Introducing new content	**Introducing new content**	**Introducing new content**
	text mapping; oral comprehension; echo reading; acting out/miming; explaining to others;	
internalising text	**Internalising the text/process**	**Internalising the text/process**
• helping the students to internalise the language patterns they will need for this unit? • helping students analyse & understand the key ingredients?	• Talking the exemplar text • *What = good* activities • Using icons to talk the gist of a text • Helping students infer meaning • Boxing up • Sorting activities • Co-constructing toolkits & learning	
2. INNOVATION STAGE:	**Innovating on the model**	**Innovating on the model**
• helping students adapt model to suit different topics/ needs?	• Shared writing innovating on model • Building up range of model text	
3. INDEPENDENT application stage	**Independent application stage**	**Independent application stage**
• helping students show what they can do independently?	• Remedying key problems resulting from innovation work • Independence challenge	
Consolidating learning	**Consolidating learning**	**Consolidating learning**
• helping students embed their learning? • helping students reflect on the progress they are making? • helping them identify next steps?	• Hot task then comparing with cold • Revisit framing learning grids • Revisit never-heard-word grids • Word dominoes • Annotating exemplar text	

© Julia Strong – Talk4Writing.com This resource may be reprinted to support in-school training but should not be forwarded to others or used for commercial gain.

Chapter 3: Getting the model right

The quality of the models we use and the language we model shapes the learning that takes place. This chapter answers frequently asked questions about model text before focusing on more sophisticated ways of internalising model text. Chapter 5 concentrates on modelling key patterns of language.

When writing, we all rely on some sort of model of *what = good*. Once you're a confident writer, this takes the form of a flexible model in your head built up over years of reading, listening, talking, discussing and writing that helps you know how to plan, what to write and exactly how to write it, assuming, of course, that you have reasonable knowledge of the content to be covered.

How many models? turns out to be a truly tricky question though, definitely, *the fewer the better* is a useful rule. But different subjects will need a different number of key models depending on how many different types of writing/problem solving students are expected to do when answering questions in that subject. Each teacher with oversight of a curriculum area in primary schools and each department in secondary schools has to think about this.

How do you build in progression? is an easier question. Subject units in KS1 need to be developed across KS2 so that the sentence signposts become increasingly sophisticated and varied, depending on the subject focused on. Ideally, models taught in primary can be built on once the pupils transfer to secondary schools so that hard-won skills aren't lost or pupils bored by repetition. Over time, the models supporting a particular strand of work should get progressively more difficult. Subjects taught from Year 7 in secondary should, by the end of Year 9, have supported students in internalising all the patterns of language they need to answer questions in the end of KS4 exams, thus allowing more time to be spent focusing on new information, so that they can innovate on the patterns and write independently on any aspect of the course by Year 11. But someone needs to consider progression across subjects and across the school. This is returned to in **chapter 17b**.

Where do I find the models? Whatever age you are teaching, it is important to use your cold task to help you decide on what aspect your class most needs to focus on first when it comes to clearly expressing their understanding of your subject. For secondary teachers, an obvious source of model text is to look at the example answers provided by exam boards and work backwards from there. You will probably find that you need to adapt an exam board model text to meet the needs of your class or write the model yourself. For upper KS2 & KS3, key elements can be threaded into your model, building skills progressively, without endlessly telling students this will be useful when it comes to the exam. The focus should be on encouraging good understanding and communication in your subject.

38 TRANSFORMING LEARNING ACROSS THE CURRICULUM

What we can learn from the cold task & writing our own models

Sometimes the best source of a model text is just to look at the sort of writing the students already do in your subject as the cold task and then write what they should have written. In many ways, the example pictured here is thoroughly depressing. It is deliberately small to make the point that even when you are too far away to read it, you can see that this student had no idea how to structure their writing. When you get close enough to read it, you discover a few more important things, not least that this student actually knows quite a lot about the topic; it's their inability to express their knowledge coherently that is holding them back. This is even more depressing when you realise that this student has already left school and is old enough to be in college and yet has managed to get through the schooling system and not be a more able writer. So, have a look at the opening lines below and ask yourself this: if this was typical of the writing in your subject in a group you had just inherited, what would help most?

> ***The role of early years professionals in early years settings in meeting the needs of children who are unwell.***
>
> *Within my placement we have a child who is asthmatic, throughout the day the practitioners support that child by asking them throughout the day whether they need to take their inhaler, if the child does need to take it then a practitioner who is trained and is within the room at all times will assist the child in taking their inhaler. By persistently asking the child whether they need their inhaler or not is effective as the child may not realise they need it until they are asked if they need it, or they may be too scared or worried to ask for their inhaler. The disadvantages to persistently asking the child whether they need their inhaler or not is that you may be constantly reminding the child about their condition which may lower their self-esteem. Another disadvantage to this is that the child may become dependent on the practitioner asking them if they need their inhaler or not, this may reduce the chances of them asking the practitioners for it when they need it. The setting keep the child's inhaler within a designated area, this is effective as it ensures that the practitioners can find it every time that the child ... (222 words)*

Content is clearly not the key issue – the student's points are relevant; it's the way they are ordered and expressed that is painful. When I ask groups of teachers what should be focused on first, often someone suggests improving the punctuation. But punctuation is not the key issue here. If you just corrected the punctuation, even throwing in a niftily-used semicolon or two, it would still be poor writing. The problem is the ideas are unstructured, unclearly expressed and endlessly repeated so the reader is in danger of losing the plot, and certainly the will to read on. The central problem here is the lack of structure. If the student had boxed up a plan and bulleted a few key points, they could at least have divided up their points and had more of a chance of expressing them coherently.

Students need to get in the habit of reading their work through, preferably aloud. As soon as they do that, they will hear the repetition and, hopefully, also hear where the text needs to be punctuated. Interestingly, the spelling is excellent – perhaps assisted by spell checker.

When students write like this, the sooner they are helped through the *plan it, link it, express it, check it* process, the sooner they are likely to be able to express themselves clearly.

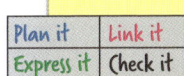

Undoubtedly, this student needs a model so they understand what is required, which probably means you will have to write it yourself because you need to start where the students are and create a model that moves them forward. Here's my attempt at writing the beginning of the model to rectify the errors of the cold task. I've annotated it on the right to explain why I've made the changes I made. Following it are some suggestions of how to use such a model.

To meet the needs of children who are unwell, early years professionals need to understand the children's needs and be trained and ready to support them as necessary, which will include having medicines or support equipment to hand and stored efficiently and safely. But there is still the tricky question of do you keep on raising the child's possible needs or do you leave it to the child to signal a problem?

What is the role of early years professionals in meeting the needs of children who are unwell?

I simplified the awkwardly expressed title (see page above) and turned it into a question for clarity.

On attempting to recast the content, I realised it had not directly addressed the question asked so I inserted this introductory paragraph to raise the complexities that the original text had raised, but only in relation to asthmatic children, and generalised the points. The original just dived straight into a recount of personal experience at a work placement.

> *For example,* there is an asthmatic child in my placement. *Throughout the day,* practitioners support that child by asking them whether they need to take their inhaler: *if* the child does need to, then a practitioner *who* is trained and within the room at all times, assists the child. The setting keeps the child's inhaler within a designated area, *which* is effective *as* it ensures that the practitioners can find it efficiently.
>
> *On the one hand,* persistently asking the child whether they need their inhaler is effective *as* the child may not realise they need it *until* they are asked if they need it, *or* they may be too scared or worried to ask for their inhaler. *However,* by doing this, you may be constantly reminding the child about their condition *which* may lower their self-esteem. *Moreover,* the child may become dependent on the practitioner asking them, *which* may reduce the chances of them asking the practitioners for it *when* they need it. (252 words)

I then recast the original, thinning it down considerably by getting rid of all repetition and introduced it as an example illustrating the introductory point. I moved the text relating to where the inhaler was stored so the 2nd paragraph focused on what the practitioners did.

The third paragraph then discusses the advantages and disadvantages of constantly asking the child about their needs, which brought out the complexity of the issue while omitting unnecessary phrasing. I used sentence signposts (signalled in magenta here) to emphasise the contrasted points and additional arguments that give the text coherence.

The most interesting thing about this is that it wasn't until I forced myself to write a model that I really understood the strengths and weaknesses of the original. (When reading through the draft chapter, I had just left a note to myself to do this, but I hadn't done it so I was tempted to delete my note and press on because no one would ever know: I knew that writing a model would be a bit too much like hard work. It was, but it was worth it.) **The benefits of doing ourselves the type of writing we ask the students to do cannot be overemphasised.**

I could present this as a model text for the students to analyse, but it might be more effective to present it side by side with the original text and ask the students to identify the differences starting with boxing up the structure of both and finding out what that difference is. Once they had done that, we could discuss why I had made the changes I made. I could talk them through any points they hadn't grasped, focusing on the fact that the first thing is to get the plan right. Then, express all the points clearly making certain they are well linked, and then check it – first for sense and coherence and then for accuracy. It nearly always comes down to *plan it, link it, express it, check it*.

Recognising the key role of boxing up

The centrality of boxing up – of helping students understand the underpinning structure of whatever they are reading/planning/writing – has been covered on **pages 17–18 & 23–25** and **video clips 3, 9, 11, 36 & 47.** Here, I just want to emphasise the importance of getting the students to analyse the structure themselves, so they really come to understand the difference that it makes. **Video clip 19** shows Sanjeet, a business studies teacher at Slough and Eton, explains how getting students to analyse the structure of 3 different model answers (a weak answer, a medium answer and a really good answer) made all the difference when it came to the students actually knowing how to write a good answer themselves. As she admits, previously, she thought she had made this clear, but she hadn't. Working out the differences in the structure of the varying quality of the answers themselves, rather than being told them, is what made the difference.

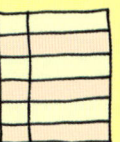

Recognising the role of topic sentences as paragraph signposts

Identifying the key features of model text:
GCSE Music question: What compositional devices have you included which match the compositional strand? (6 marks)

<u>The compositional devices I have used fall under the strand of the Western classical tradition</u>. In section A, complex harmony has been used creating a primary and secondary contrast within <u>chordal</u> use. Antiphonal parts have been added which are passed within the string section, creating links to early Bach Brandenburg Concertos. The overall composition uses a ternary structure cementing links with classical controlled structure.

Model text for music by Barrie McArdie, Queensbury School, Bradford

Most paragraphs in non-fiction text should begin with a topic sentence that clearly introduces the reader to what the paragraph is about. Such topic sentences play a particularly important role in single paragraph answers like the model text here about compositional devices in music. It orientates the reader and should be clearly related to the question: they function like super signposts that introduce whole paragraphs.

If the cold task indicates that writing good topic sentences is a problem for your class, you may want to start with simply boxing up the text together and getting the students to decide on a single word or very short heading for each box/paragraph. Then show how that heading has been turned into the opening sentence of each paragraph to help the reader understand what is about to be explained. Use the boxed-up planner to plan a similar text, and model for the class how to turn one or two similar headings into topic sentences. Then get the students to write their own topic sentences for the remaining headings. This activity forms part of an extended activity on the Fire of London on **page 95.**

42 TRANSFORMING LEARNING ACROSS THE CURRICULUM

Understanding what topic sentences do
- Select a sentence that sounds like a topic sentence and one that doesn't.
- Could any be topic sentences that round off a paragraph?

1. Cats have a limited diet.
2. Often the reasons are to do with laziness.
3. Then they worked in the mines.
4. So English became an international language.
5. There are many reasons why a new supermarket is not needed in this area.
6. In this case, light intensity is known as a limiting factor.
7. The average student score was 75%.
8. Living standards rose in the twentieth century.
9. Their demise marked the end of an era.

If topic sentences need improving, you may also want to set up an activity like this one. Substitute my choice of sentences with a range from your unit so that you have a number of relevant examples of sentences that could be topic sentences and ones that couldn't. If you want to add a challenge, include topic sentences that round off rather than introduce paragraphs. Once the class, in pairs, have had the time to decide on their answers, get a pair to tell you a good example of a topic sentence. If they answer, for example, *There are many reasons why a new supermarket is not needed in this area*, use this as an opportunity to talk the text and co-construct orally with the class how that paragraph might continue: "The first reason is that there are already three supermarkets in …" etc. Chanting this together will help familiarise them with the tune of your subject. In this way, you will help them get the pattern in their heads. The students who are good at this sort of activity will all be good readers because they will have internalised this pattern through reading. If they are not good at it, you need to include more reading of the sort of text you are wanting them to write.

The power of colour coding

Now let's analyse the music model text. The class has been asked to identify 4 features:

- <u>the topic sentence</u>
- sentence signposts
- generic text
- technical language

Identifying the key features of model text

GCSE Music question: What compositional devices have you included which match the compositional strand? (6 marks)

The compositional devices I have used fall under the strand of the Western classical tradition. In section A, complex harmony has been used creating a primary and secondary contrast within chordal use. Antiphonal parts have been added which are passed within the string section, creating links to early Bach Brandenburg Concertos. The overall composition uses a ternary structure cementing links with classical controlled structure.

_{Model text for music by Barrie McArdle, Queensbury School, Bradford}

You can see that the most dominant feature is the correct use of technical terms. The model is only 64 words in length, of which 24 are the technical language of music. It may be short, but it is challenging as expressing the concepts needed to fulfil the demands of the question is not easy. When presenting the model text to the class, it is very important that when they see it, it is in black and white and in plain font (like the version on page 41) so that all the analysis is done by them. Cutting learning corners and presenting them with pre-analysed text won't work in the long term. You will have done all the work and they will understand remarkably little. If they have to co-construct understanding, the analysis is going to be meaningful.

GETTING THE MODEL RIGHT 43

Once the class has highlighted different features in different colours, then it's useful to present the analysed text on screen again but this time matching their colour coding. The colour coding makes a big difference as suddenly the students can see the different functions of different parts of the text: the tune begins to come clear. This colour coding is most powerful if it is consistent across the school as suggested in the image here. The colour coding selected should be tested out on your schools' ICT system as the colours vary significantly from system to system. Also, test your choice on any colour-blind students or staff to see if the colour coding works for them.

You can see from the quote below what a significant difference the colour coding of key features can make, because it turns a somewhat abstract concept into something much more concrete. As a result, the same teacher introduced colour coding of model text to her A-level group and focused on its effectiveness as her action research, which included this statement: *"The year 13 class had produced a similar evaluation a few months previously without the support. 5 out of the 6 students had found this section particularly difficult, and 3 of the 6 had not submitted the work by the deadline, because they found it very difficult. The average mark for the class was 3/9. By the time this project was undertaken, 5 students were continuing with the course. Within 24 hours of completing discussing the colour-coded exemplars, all 5 students had submitted their work and the average mark for the class was 6.8/9, with 2 students gaining 8/9. As a result of this, the students were motivated to return to their previous piece of coursework which had not yet been submitted and were able to significantly improve their overall mark."*

> **Impact of colour-coding model text**
>
> - "The effect of this was instantly amazing and therefore I used a similar method with my year 7 who were writing a report on the uses of ICT in society.
> - "The results with all 3 classes astonished me. I had expected improvements, but not on the scale seen."
>
> – Katherine Mobberley, Assistant Headteacher, Chenderit School, Oxfordshire

This is the power of colour coding. Think how much more powerful it would be if all teachers across the school used the same colour for identifying the key generic features of text. Teachers could use any other colours to identify other subject-specific features they wanted to focus on. The effectiveness of establishing this as a whole-school approach is illustrated on **page 78**.

Why internalising a good model text matters

Perhaps the best way of illustrating the power of model text to help students start to have the confidence to express themselves is this example from a science investigation, which seems to have inspired lots of great units in primary and secondary schools alike. It also illustrates how to adapt the approach to suit different subject needs. Here, the students don't move from imitation to independent application of the writing up of investigations in one unit, but rather over time over three separate units, or longer, because investigations usually don't suit innovating on. It, therefore, makes more sense to wait for the next investigation to innovate on the model. This isn't the full text for an investigation, only the first four paragraphs are included to illustrate the approach.

This example is for a Year 7 class whose first investigation has focused on the effect of exercise on the heart. The teacher wants them to get the pattern of writing-up investigations in their heads so that by the end of the first term they can be doing this independently. Once the students have completed all the interesting work of actually carrying out the investigation, and they are faced with writing up their investigation, the text map for the model text pictured here is introduced. First, the class internalises the text orally, led by the teacher and supported by the text map and related actions. Once the class has internalised the text, which won't take them long, ask them to quickly jot down their own text map, as working out their own symbols will help them remember the text and key information about the investigation more easily.

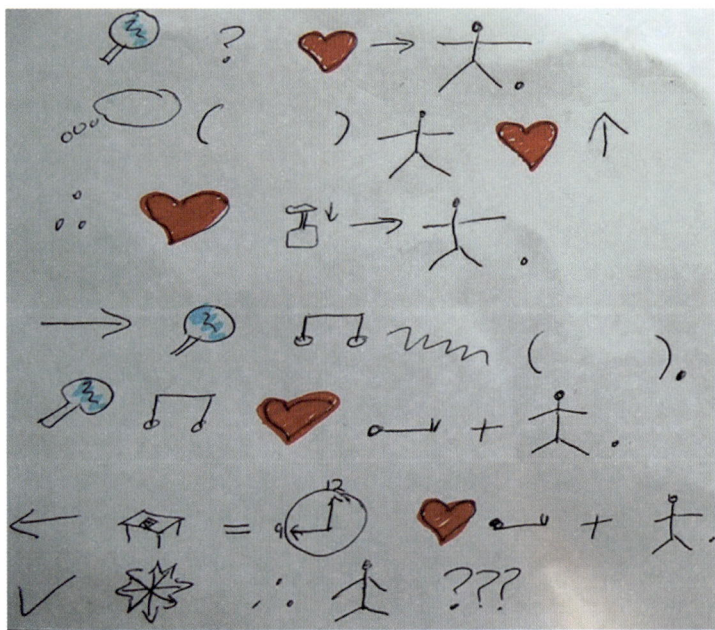

The teacher then shows them the actual text (see left below). Because they have internalised the text, they should all be able to read it and, because of earlier work done on vocabulary and the purpose of the investigation, they should all be able to understand what the model is saying. A few quick questions could be inserted here to check their understanding and see if they can summarise the key points. They can quickly box up the model, as illustrated below, to establish the structure of how you write up investigations.

GETTING THE MODEL RIGHT 45

> I am investigating what happens to my heart when take exercise.
>
> My prediction, what I think will happen, is that exercise will make my heartbeat faster because the heart has to pump blood faster to enable me to do the exercise.
>
> To carry out an investigation, you must compare at least two variables: things which change or vary. For this investigation, I will compare my heart rate when I am resting and when I am taking exercise.
>
> However, it is important to make the test fair. To make this test fair, I must record my heart rate for exactly the same amount of time when I am resting as when I am exercising. It is essential that all the other conditions remain the same because, otherwise, I would not know if it was the exercise or something else that was making the difference.

Boxing up science investigations – establishing the structure

• What is being investigated?	
• Best guess (prediction)	
• The variables	
• Making it fair	

Feedback from this can help the class create an agreed boxed-up structure to display on the washing line/working wall.

> All generic phrases (useful for any investigation): **green**
> Sentence signposts: **pink**
>
> I am investigating what happens to my heart when I take exercise.
>
> My prediction, what I think will happen, is that exercise will make my heartbeat faster because the heart has to pump blood faster to enable me to do the exercise.
>
> To carry out an investigation, you must compare at least two variables: things which change or vary. For this investigation, I will compare my heart rate when I am resting and when I am taking exercise.
>
> However, it is important to make the test fair. To make this test fair, I must record my heart rate for exactly the same amount of time when I am resting as when I am exercising. It is essential that all the other conditions remain the same because, otherwise, I wouldn't know if it was the exercise or something else that was making the difference.

Next, the class analyses the model text, in order to identify generic phrases for investigations and any useful sentence signposts. This can then be fed back and a class version established. As you can see, all the generic science text is in green with the sentence signposts highlighted in magenta; this leaves the text that is specfic to this particular investigation in black.

The students could then see if they could write up the investigation just using the text map and the pattern in their heads. If they can write it down exactly as they internalised it, then that is success.

Innovating on the model

The next time the class does an investigation, once it comes to the moment to write up the investigation, the class could first (with the help of the earlier text map) recall how to write up an investigation. They could then use the boxed-up structure for science investigations that they had created above to co-construct the key points to make for the investigation they had just conducted. Next, by innovating on the plan and the generic text skeleton from the previous investigation (pictured here), they could orally co-construct what the text would be for this second investigation. The class could devise the actions to go with it and quickly

> **Generic text skeleton for a science investigation**
>
> I am investigating what happens to ... when ...
>
> My prediction, what I think will happen, is that ... because ...
>
> To carry out an investigation, you must compare at least two variables: things which change or vary. For this investigation, I will compare ... when ... and when ...
>
> However, it is important to make the test fair. To make this test fair, I must record ... when ... as when ... It is essential that all the other conditions remain the same because, otherwise, I would not know if it was. ... or something else that was making the difference.

46 TRANSFORMING LEARNING ACROSS THE CURRICULUM

jot down their own text map. Having rehearsed the pattern in their head, they should then be in an excellent position to write up the experiment. Hopefully, by the third investigation they would have the pattern of how to write up investigations sufficiently in their heads to be able to quickly box up the key points to make in their own plan, jot down a few key images in their plan, and write up the investigation independently. Of course, we don't want students to be parroting out exactly the same frame each time but, once they have the basic pattern in their heads, they will easily learn how to adjust it to suit different circumstances.

More sophisticated ways of internalising the model

As explained on **page 21**, when students become more confident with the pattern of language within subjects, less time needs to be spent on internalising the patterns of language, and imitating text orally, and more sophisticated ways of internalising patterns of language can be used. Text mapping a short model and getting the students to internalise the text with a few supporting actions remains the best way of internalising the tune of a subject for students who are relatively new to the tune – so it can be appropriate for students of any age. A-level students facing the challenge of much more complex text have found it very useful, see **video clip 29**. Once students are more familiar with the basic tune of a subject, additional model text can be introduced in a variety of more sophisticated ways. Here is a range of alternative ways of helping students internalise the pattern of text and magpie useful phrases. All of these methods also have the advantage of boosting students' reading skills as they all involve different ways of interrogating text.

    a. **Sequencing the text to box it up and then analysing it**
    b. **Selecting the best short model then establishing the key ingredients**
    c. **Text mapping a short model text and talking the gist of it**
    d. **Text mapping a text from hearing it being spoken aloud**
    e. **Colour coding each clump of meaning & reading it aloud**
    f. **Working out what the question was from the model answer**
    g. **Identifying useful generic phrases to magpie from a model**
    h. **Using a really challenging model**

Christians also agree with the First Cause Argument. The Christian philosopher Thomas Aquinas said that if you have nothing and add some more nothing, you will end up with nothing so there must be something else that will cause a change, and that something is God.

Additionally, some people have asked if everything has a cause, what caused God to exist. While many theists say that God exists outside time so that God does not need a cause, many atheists would argue that this is a weak response.

The First Cause is a strong argument in favour of the existence of God but it doesn't prove that God is like the deity described in Christianity and Islam.

Does the First Cause Argument prove that there is a God?

Ghazali's idea is very logical because we see it everyday. Just like a table only exists because it has been made so, therefore, something must have caused the universe to exist.

The First Cause Argument says that because the universe exists, this proves that God exists. This is an idea developed by the Muslim philosopher Al Ghazali who wrote that everything that exists has a beginning and so therefore has a cause. So, as the universe at one point began to exist, therefore, the universe must have had a cause.

As well as Muslims and Christians agreeing with the first argument, it would be fair to say that non-believers can also recognise that every event has a cause and so it is logical for there to be a cause for the universe. However, non-believing critics would argue that just because there is a cause for the universe, it doesn't have to be the idea of God seen in the Bible or the Qu'ran. It could just be a scientific cause like the Big Bang.

a) Sequencing the text to box it up and then analysing it

Here you can see how RE teacher Richard Wolfendon, at Royds Hall, Huddersfield, introduced a model text as a sorting activity. The students' first task was to sort the text into its correct order and then decide what the heading would be for each section, a good way to make boxing up very concrete and active. When you try to box this text into the *correct* order, a lot of people, especially if they are English teachers like me, are surprised by the order in which, according to RE teachers, it should be boxed up. Have a look at the correct order below:

	Does the First Cause Argument prove that there is a God?
Intro answer	The First Cause is a strong argument in favour of the existence of God but it doesn't prove that God is like the deity described in Christianity and Islam.
Explain First Cause argument – Muslim perspective	The First Cause Argument says that because the universe exists, this proves that God exists. This is an idea developed by the Muslim philosopher Al Ghazali who wrote that everything that exists has a beginning and so, therefore, has a cause. So, as the universe at one point began to exist, therefore, the universe must have had a cause.
Expand explanation	Ghazali's idea is very logical because we see it every day. Just like a table only exists because it has been made so, therefore, something must have caused the universe to exist.
Christian perspective	Christians also agree with the First Cause Argument. The Christian philosopher Thomas Aquinas said that if you have nothing and add some more nothing, you will end up with nothing so there must be something else that will cause a change, and that something is God.
Non-believer perspective	As well as Muslims and Christians agreeing with the first argument, it would be fair to say that non-believers can also recognise that every event has a cause and so it is logical for there to be a cause for the universe. However, non-believing critics would argue that just because there is a cause for the universe, it doesn't have to be the idea of God seen in the Bible or the Qu'ran. It could just be a scientific cause like the Big Bang.
Additional point rounding off	Additionally, some people have asked if everything has a cause, what caused God to exist. While many theists say that God exists outside time so that God does not need a cause, many atheists would argue that this is a weak response.

The opening paragraph reads like some sort of conclusion, from the English teacher perspective. But this is exactly the way you should introduce an RE answer according to the rubric of the RE examiners, an important point for RE teachers to emphasise and illustrate through model text. The model certainly passes the first test: *does it box up well*? To establish its usefulness, it has to pass the second test: *does it include good examples of the typical features of this type of text?* This means checking for:

- **balance:** the argument should be fairly presented with a range of differing perspectives treated fairly
- **generically useful phrases** that are typical of this sort of text
- **good sentence signposts** that link the text together coherently
- a good use of appropriate *technical vocabulary*
- the **appropriate tense**, i.e. all general points in the present tense as suits this sort of discursive text, with specific references to the past actions of individuals in the past tense
- errors and ensuring the whole text makes sense and flows well.

	Does the First Cause Argument prove that there is a God?
Introduction: sums up what is to follow.	The First Cause is a strong argument in favour of the existence of God but it doesn't prove that God is like the deity described in Christianity and Islam.
Balance: the text presents the views of Muslims and Christians coherently and fairly, as well as referencing the perspective of non-believers.	The First Cause Argument says that because the universe exists, this proves that God exists. This is an idea developed by the Muslim philosopher Al Ghazali who wrote that everything that exists has a beginning and so, therefore, has a cause. So, as the universe at one point began to exist, therefore, the universe must have had a cause. Ghazali's idea is very logical because we see it everyday. Just like a table only exists because it has been made so, therefore, something must have caused the universe to exist.
Correct use of tense: present tense used consistently to sum up arguments (is, says, proves, doesn't argue); **past tense** is used consistently when referring to specific past actions/statements (x said, x wrote)	Christians also agree with the First Cause Argument. The Christian philosopher Thomas Aquinas said that if you have nothing and add some more nothing, you will end up with nothing so, there must be something else that will cause a change, and that something is God. As well as Muslims and Christians agreeing with the first argument, it would be fair to say that non-believers can also recognise that every event has a cause and so it is logical for there to be a cause for the universe. However, non-believing critics would argue that just because there is a cause for the universe, it doesn't have to be the idea of God seen in the Bible or the Qu'ran. It could just be a scientific cause like the Big Bang. Additionally, some people have asked, if everything has a cause, what caused God to exist? While many theists say that God exists outside time, so that God does not need a cause, many atheists would argue that this is a weak response.

This annotated version shows that this is an excellent model text. The argument is balanced, well-structured and flows coherently. There is a wide range of generically useful phrases that will help the students internalise the tune of this sort of text and technical vocabulary is well used. The changes in tense that this sort of text requires are well handled.

GETTING THE MODEL RIGHT 49

Matching ingredients of First Cause model text against generic writing toolkit

Generic writing toolkit

Plan it - plan balanced response **Link it**
- ✓ Analyse the task
- ✓ Think audience & purpose
- ✓ Box up structure.
  (logical/~~chronological~~)
- ✓ Begin with an introduction
- ✓ End with a conclusion — *summing up what is to follow*

- ✓ Introduce paragraphs with a topic sentence
- ✓ Use sentence signposts to link the text and make it fit together

Express it *Mainly present tense, past for past actions* **Check it**
- ✓ Express points clearly
- ✓ Keep reader engaged
- ✓ Include detail to illustrate key points
- ✓ Use technical vocabulary appropriately

- ✓ Read it to check it flows, makes sense and fulfils purpose
- ✓ Check punctuation and spelling

Plan it	Link it
Express it	Check it

We have a model! This is important. Sometimes the models used fall very short of being good.

Quickly getting students to identify any significant differences between the RE model and the generic writing toolkit will help them remember them, so they know just how to tackle RE questions.

b) Selecting the best short model then establishing the key ingredients

Comparing possible models: what = good?

- Select which of the 4 openings of model text is best if the task were to **write clear instructions for an experiment to show how water affects growth of cress seeds**
- Establish what '**key ingredients**' help make it good and co-construct the toolkit

1. **Instructions for cress experiment** We had to get 4 petri dishes and put some cotton wool and cress seeds into each …	2. **Instructions for cress experiment** a. Put the same small amount of cotton wool into 4 petri dishes. b. Press the same amount of ..
3. **Instructions for cress experiment** Growing cress is a good laugh. First, I wanted to see how to grow the best cress seeds in the class. What we did was to put some cress seeds in a petri dish…	4. **Instructions for cress experiment** Equipment: 4 petri dishes… I will try to set up four sets of the equipment just like our teacher showed us …

This activity is suited to short, single-paragraph model texts like the music model above. The idea is to present the class with 4 different possible versions of the whole paragraph or the opening section, as illustrated here. When selecting your texts, it is most useful if, apart from the good model, you present 3 alternative texts containing the type of errors the students are tending to make. Here, text number 3 is a classic example of the student who wants to write the story of everything regardless of the task. Number 1 is an example of just recounting what happened and number 4 is a strange sort of future recount. The students have to look at the purpose and decide which is best given the task. Clearly, number 2 is the only possible choice given the task.

The students then, in small groups, decide what the key ingredients for success are and start to establish their own toolkit. They can then confer with another group. Get the groups to feed back so the class co-constructs its own toolkit which would include things like:
- Box up the instructions in chronological order
- Begin each instruction in the imperative (bossy verb)

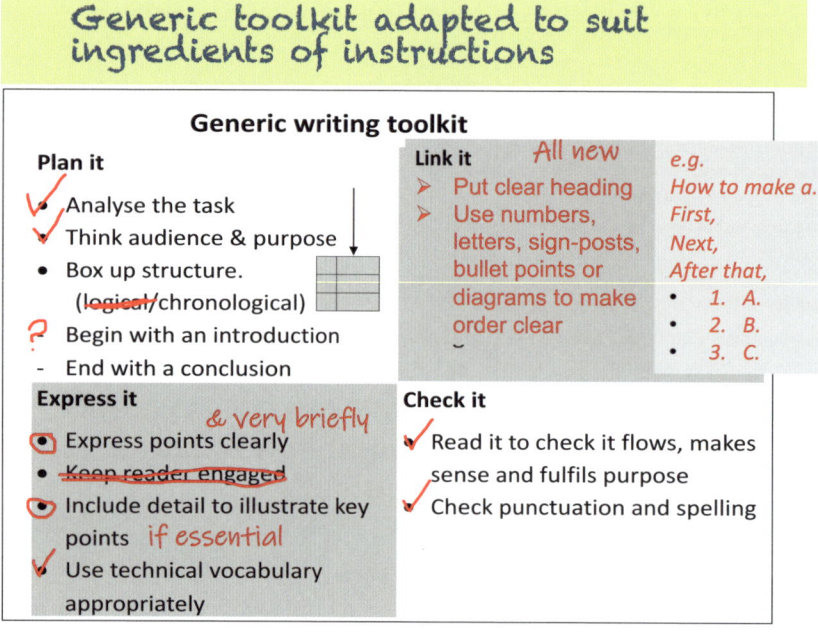

Interestingly, writing instructions is often presented as easy but writing clear instructions is a real skill, as you discover when trying to follow instructions for a walk written by someone who appears to have never actually done the walk. If you look at the generic writing toolkit that has been annotated to meet the requirements of instructions, you will see that it requires more amendment than any other text type. The planning remains very similar but, after that, it could be all annotated diagrams and no other writing at all. If there is writing, it should be pared down to the minimum necessary. The linking is all completely different; only the checking remains the same.

c) Text mapping a short model text and talking the gist of it

This is a great activity that is both entertaining and very effective. Assuming that your class is already familiar with text mapping, just display the model text on screen (or read them the text, as in the following activity). Then give the class a short amount of time to text map the text – insist on silence for this part of the activity as text mapping requires total concentration. The example on the slide from Portslade Community College, Brighton, has been adapted from the work of D&T teacher Jo Tyrell-Baldwin who decided to come up with an entertaining, daft product to help students internalise the pattern of product evaluation – which explains why the student is sporting a toilet roll on his head to ensure tissue is always to hand when you have a cold.

GETTING THE MODEL RIGHT 51

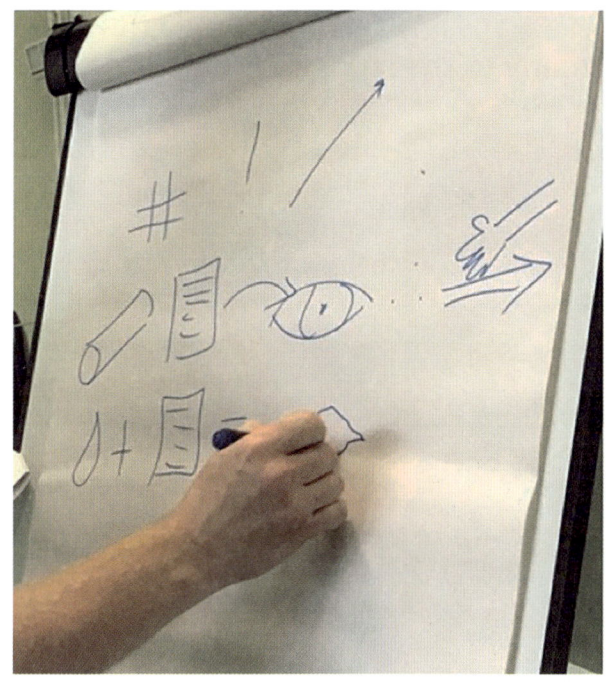

Once they have text mapped the paragraph, ask them to focus on it for a minute to help them internalise the images and the flow of the text. Then, blank out the screen, and ask them to talk the text to their partner – tell them you are not expecting it to be word for word the same as the original but rather their aim is to talk the gist of the text. At the end of the activity, get one or two students to present their versions to the class. (They can add to points if they like but it must be coherent). This activity helps the students internalise both the content of the text and how it is expressed.

Assuming the students who present to the class have done this well, then change the scenario somewhat. Most people, when feeding back on this, do it with great seriousness because they are concentrating on remembering what their images meant, so change the scenario to one that is more relaxing. For example, you are the design inspector for the area, and you are telling a friend all about the completely ridiculous design you've seen today. If they look insecure, model how to start: "You just won't believe the stupid design I saw today!" Hopefully, they will then be able to relate the main details in an entertaining way. Such activities help students gain confidence in their ability to manipulate text. And if you ever require students to present something to a large audience, don't let them have notes – they will just read them and bore everyone solid while making themselves miserable. But if they have text mapped the key points they want to say, they will be able to remember them without having to look at them. With a little practice, to build up confidence, they will be able to make an excellent presentation which, in turn boosts confidence further.

d) Text mapping a text from hearing it being spoken aloud

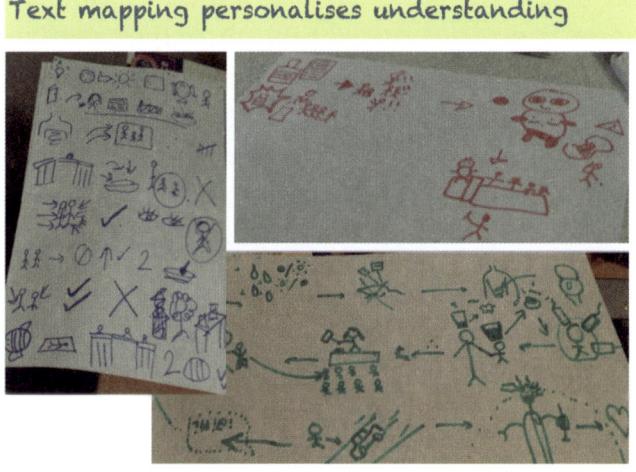

One of the very interesting things that the science department at Slough and Eton found was that the text mapping didn't only help the students express their science more clearly, the process also helped them remember the actual content of the science, because the process of text mapping (dual coding) pinned the learning in their minds. Here you can see three text maps of the same content from 3 different students. These text maps are personal – only they have to understand them. This appealed greatly to the students.

To see the power of this in practice, look at **video clip 17** from Slough and Eton filmed at the end of this class's Year 9. Here the teacher is explaining the science behind vaccines and the class is text mapping what she is saying. It was mid-June and they had just moved to their new teacher, Hiri Arungari, who would be teaching them in Year 10. Because the whole department taught in Talk for Writing style, she knew her class would be familiar with text mapping. I suggest you spend the first minute trying to text map alongside the class and then just watch the class, all of whom are totally concentrating and all of whom are keeping up with the task.

Once the students have the tune of your subject in their heads, this sort of advanced text mapping can provide a more sophisticated way of internalising text. If you tried to text map alongside the class, you will have discovered just how hard you have to concentrate. This makes you really focus on what is being said and helps you picture the relationship between things. It is this that contributes to the power of text mapping.

e) Colour coding each clump of meaning & reading it aloud

One good way of building fluency with the tune of text in your subject is to get the students all reading a model text aloud in pairs. Display a two-colour version of the text where the colour changes every time a new phrase or clause begins, to highlight how words are clumped together to provide meaning (see below). You may need to warm this up through echo reading **(see page 21)**. For students who have difficulty reading, provide one copy of the text per student and encourage them to use a ruler to follow where they have got to.

GETTING THE MODEL RIGHT 53

<u>Describe the characteristics of magnetic & solid-state secondary storage.</u>

Secondary storage is required to store data and programs that would otherwise be lost when power is lost to the computer system. These devices can be split into categories such as magnetic, optical and solid state. The characteristics of magnetic and solid state are as follows: magnetic devices, such as a hard disc drive, have a large storage capacity and are cheaper than solid-state storage. However, due to the fact that they have moving parts, they are less reliable and are also susceptible to heat or magnetic fields.

On the other hand, solid-state devices, such as a solid-state drive, have no moving parts and are, therefore, not sensitive to movement. This makes them ideal when portability is important, for example, taking files from school to home. However, these devices are more expensive per gigabyte than magnetic storage and have a limited number of read/write cycles.

Therefore, it is important to consider the characteristics of these devices before purchasing them to ensure they are suitable for their purpose.

Adapted from work of Sharon Lake, computer science, Hungerhill School, Doncaster

f) Working out what the question was from the model answer

Another excellent way of getting students to focus on the content of a model and reflect on what it means is to provide students with the model text but without any heading (see second image here). The task is to work out what the question was. This helps students recognise the importance of planning their answers, so they answer the question asked, as well as building familiarity with the tune of model answers. And here's the answer: *Explain what specificity is and why it is important. Describe how it could be applied to one sport.*

If this is the model answer, what was the question?

Specificity is matching the training to the demands of the activity.

It is important to consider specificity in order to make sure the training is relevant to the performer and it has a positive effect on their performance. For example, the training should focus on the same muscle groups, energy systems and movements that are used in the activity.

There are several ways a footballer would apply the principle of specificity to their training. First, they would focus on improving the strength in their hamstrings and quadriceps as they use these muscles to run and kick. Secondly, they would use a combination of aerobic and anaerobic training methods. This is because they need an efficient aerobic system that will allow them to run for 90 minutes. They also need a strong anaerobic system to enable them to sprint up the pitch and receive a pass. Finally, they would practise skills such as passing, dribbling and shooting in their training sessions as they would be performing these movements in a game.

Adapted from work of Lucy Wright, PE department, Hungerhill Secondary School, Doncaster

g) Identifying useful generic phrases to magpie from a model

Identify useful phrases to magpie from short models & relate to toolkit

- Good use of sentence signposts to link text
- Precise phrasing that explains the science clearly
- Technical terms well used

- **Text 1:** In conclusion, the acetone evaporated fastest. We can see this because the temperature went down by 8°C. This happened because the particles with the most energy evaporated first.

- **Text 2:** The role of a root hair cell is to absorb water from the ground. It has adapted to do this by having a long thin hair. This helps because it gives it a large surface area.

- **Text 3:** This graph is showing the relationship between heart rate and the length of time of the exercise. The heart rate is shown on the vertical axis and the time is shown on the horizontal axis. These are the variables. As one thing changes, the other changes. As the amount of time increases, the heart rate increases.

Adapted from work of Alex Shaw, Science department, Hungerhill Secondary School, Doncaster

Once students are familiar with the tune of a subject, then additional model texts can be sourced to help students identify and become familiar with the sort of phrasing they will need to express their knowledge effectively. Here the way the model text is expressed is matched to key science toolkit features.

h) Using a really challenging model

Year 9 cold task: Earlier work on *The Curious Incident of the Dog in the Night-time* before the use of model text:

> Christopher is a very intelligent and logical young man. He is also extremely bright. Because of his disability, he finds it hard to communicate or chat. But he is quite clever so he will be able to learn, like he already has.
>
> Christopher's relationship with his father is quite unique. They are very understanding of each other. Father has grown used to Christopher and never gets too angry, unless Christopher steps out of line. However, father has quite a short temper.
>
> Christopher's relationship with his mother is quite different to that of his father's. Christopher doesn't really feel any emotion and he talks about her quite a lot. I don't think he knows what he feels about his mum.
>
> I think Christopher should stay at his dad's but …

Year 9 hot task: Same student's work after use of model text:

> In modern day Britain, the harsh reality of life is often shielded from young people with disabilities. This is mostly the case in this wonderful book. This book acts not only as a pleasurable read but as a sort of campaign. It opens your eyes as to how dismissive and ignorant one can be in everyday situations. A wonderful insight into the human mind, Haddon keeps you flying high right to the end.
>
> Haddon's novel tells of a fifteen-year-old boy named Christopher, who suffers from Asperger's Syndrome. He lives in the bubble of a well-organised life until he finds the dog of one of his neighbours in their front garden. Christopher's bubble is instantly popped, and his life is thrown into many twists and turns. Shocks for the reader come in their dozens and hit the reader straight on. The ups and downs in Christopher's life throughout the course of this book play a main role in the plot.
>
> Haddon's choice to have the story narrated by Christopher may not seem an appropriate choice but it is truly effective and engaging …

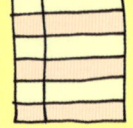

The simple focus of a challenging model text as a source of a really good structure to innovate on, plus great phrases to magpie, can be extremely powerful. This technique enabled English teacher Andy Breckenridge from Blatchington Mill School, Brighton, to move students who had promise but were failing to reach their potential, from mediocre writing to achieving writing that could have come from the *Guardian Book Review* page as illustrated here.

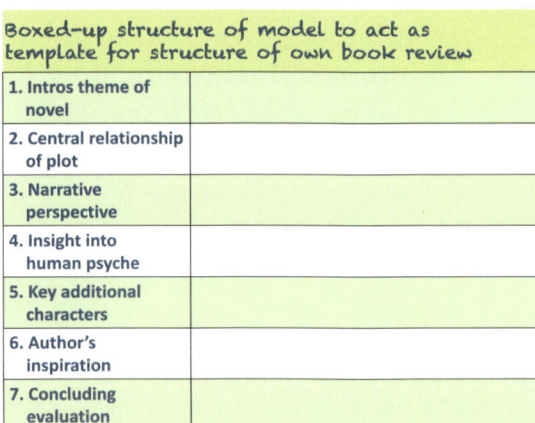

Boxed-up structure of model to act as template for structure of own book review

1. Intros theme of novel	
2. Central relationship of plot	
3. Narrative perspective	
4. Insight into human psyche	
5. Key additional characters	
6. Author's inspiration	
7. Concluding evaluation	

The quality of the transformation is such that the reader shifts from thinking, "I can't really bear to read any more of this," to wanting to read on. The teacher achieved this transformation by challenging a potentially able but somewhat lazy class by presenting them with an ambitious model text in the form of a *Guardian Book Review* which he gave to the class and read aloud to them. The class then boxed up the review so that they could see that it didn't slavishly follow the plot of the novel, as exemplified by the boxing up here: the plot is covered in one section only.

Key sentence signposts/sentence stems
- In the introduction to …
- One of the reasons why …
- In X's hands …
- In addition to …

Useful generic phrasing
- It is this sentiment which resonates as one reads …
- Characters that particularly stand out are …
- To reveal that the story …
- The growing relationships between … are central to the plot
- It gives a unique and compassionate voice to a narrator.
- … human inhumanity to humans…
- … sometimes misleading, sometimes all too true …
- This is a beautifully balanced piece of storytelling …
- … glimpses of what is yet to come …
- We meet all shades of …
- … able to give a remarkable insight …

He then got them to colour code the model, underlining topic sentences and identifying useful generic phrases they could magpie for their own reviews as illustrated here. The class then innovated on the boxed-up plan making it fit their class novel and wrote their own reviews, working together to redraft their work. And the writing was transformed.

The importance of providing a good model cannot be overemphasised. If the students are involved in analysing how it is structured and what features make it *good*, they will then be able to use such structure and such features in their own work and be more able to read such text independently.

Chapter 4: Vocabulary matters

Vocabulary really matters – it is a powerful indicator of future success. Research has shown that vocabulary size at the age of 5 is a good predictor of a child's GCSE results. If students arrive in secondary school with a poor vocabulary, that's even more of a reason to focus on vocabulary. There is a mass of research into vocabulary all of which, in some way, tells you how important it is to individual and educational progress. Words allow you to explain the world and explain yourself to the world. These three important findings are perhaps the most relevant to teachers' practice:

a. **Vocabulary is key to comprehension:** "Enhancing children's vocabulary development is more effective at improving reading comprehension than teaching students comprehension strategies." – *The York Project*, 2010: Clarke, Snowling, Truelove and Hule. They found that the most effective method of boosting comprehension was focusing on oral comprehension rather than writing answers down.

b. **Lack of vocabulary is caused by lack of opportunity not a lack of ability:** The research that clearly shows what causes young children to have a wide or a narrow vocabulary is *The Early Catastrophe – The 30 Million Word Gap by Age 3* – Hart & Risley, 1995. Unsurprisingly, what they found was a parallel between the language the children heard at home and the language they could use: language in – language out.

c. **Vocabulary should be directly taught:** "What is missing for many children who master phonics but don't comprehend well is *vocabulary*, the words they need to know in order to understand what they're reading. Thus, vocabulary is the 'missing link' in reading/language instruction in our school system ... If education is going to have a serious 'compensatory' function, we must do more to promote vocabulary." – *Teaching Vocabulary Early, Direct and Sequential*, Biemiller, 2000.

Curing poor decoding cannot be done across the curriculum, since that requires specialised phonics teaching, but every teacher across the curriculum can increase the vocabulary and world knowledge of the students by focusing on the language and the words to explain the knowledge linked to whatever subject they are teaching. Without the related vocabulary, the knowledge won't develop, so time needs to be spent on growing vocabulary. If we are serious about closing the attainment gap, we must make certain we all teach vocabulary well. That leaves us with two key questions:

1. Which words to teach?
2. How best to teach them?

This chapter focuses on these questions as teaching vocabulary needs to be done as efficiently, effectively and engagingly as possible; given the pressing

56 TRANSFORMING LEARNING ACROSS THE CURRICULUM

demands of the curriculum, time is not on our side and there are an awful lot of words to learn. TfW's focus on talking the text helps since the key elements of the approach also boost vocabulary development.

1. Which words to teach?

English is a very word-rich language with a vast wealth of synonyms (you don't need a thesaurus for any other language except, apparently, Japanese); this offers a challenge as there are just so many words. It's also important to remember that we all have an active and a passive vocabulary, whatever language we speak. Our passive vocabulary is words we are aware of and know but don't always have course to use; these are the ones we tend to forget: *use it or lose it* very much applies to language. Alex Quigley's very interesting book *Closing the Vocabulary Gap* tells us that children need to reach 50,000 words to be able to survive in school and beyond. The other really useful book on vocabulary, *Bringing Words to Life* by Isabel Beck, is an excellent guide not only to which words to focus on but also how to teach vocabulary. She talks about 3 tiers of vocabulary: tier 1 are everyday words used for basic communication that require little, if any, instruction; tier 2 are words not in everyday use but often encountered in written form that will help children through life e.g., *anxious, furious, circumstance;* tier 3 words are subject-specific or technical words linked to topics or subjects and these will need explicit teaching if such language is key to understanding a topic. **See page 240** for an example of how these tiers have been planned for in a history unit.

The main issue is that there are too many words to teach and not enough time to teach them all. We need to foster schools where teachers not only plan and explicitly teach vocabulary but, just as importantly, where they encourage pupils to develop an interest and growing autonomy with words through helping them see the links between words with similar roots and the origins of words. In many ways **video 20** says it all. Tyler, a new pupil, had entered Tom Wriglesworth's Year 6 class in Selby Community Primary. To put Tom in the picture, Tyler told him: "I'm just letting you know that I do maths but I won't do poetry. Call me Mr T." This video shows what a teacher who knows how to make his pupils savour vocabulary can do.

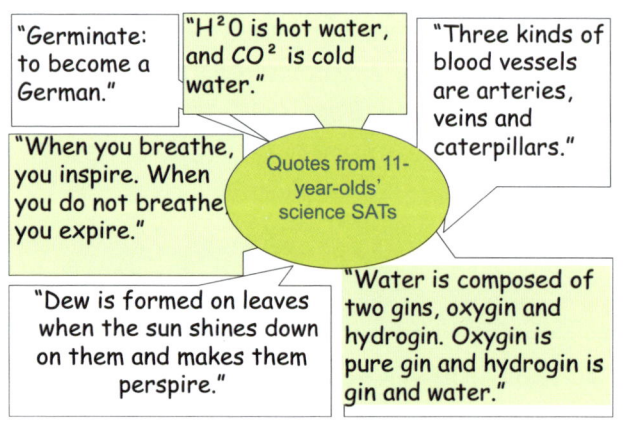

2. How to teach vocabulary

Just look at these Year 6 gems from the days when there were science SATs. We laugh at the children's errors but, in the end, the source of the error is liable to have been not the child but how the child had been taught; doubtless we can all add grand examples from moments when our teaching fell below par.

VOCABULARY MATTERS 57

Just consider the glorious sentence, *"Three kinds of blood vessels are arteries, veins and caterpillars."* You don't need to be Sherlock Holmes to deduce that the teacher was talking about *capillaries*, but the child heard the word as something they knew about, *caterpillars,* and nothing ever happened to enlighten them. If we could look in the science books of the children who made these errors, we would probably find the key words written down with appropriate definitions carefully copied or stuck into the books. But somewhere along the line, the words have failed to impinge on the children's vocabulary, so the world knowledge is somewhat lacking.

Research tells us that vocabulary tends to be *taken as read* and not well taught. If we are not careful, we assume that the students understand words they do not understand as exemplified in the maths chapter, **page 199**. Hopefully, every teacher will already have a number of nifty activities focusing on building vocabulary through helping students use the new words, which can be shared at staff meetings. Chapter 2 introduced Isabel Beck's *basic routine* (**page 19**). Here are a few other practical suggestions that help embed understanding:

1. **Begin by establishing what words the students do and don't know**
2. **Help students understand words by associating an image with a word**
3. **Make the words visible**
4. **Focus on making the students say the words in a range of contexts**
5. **Devise talk frames**
6. **Help students understand words by associating an action with a word**
7. **Devise sorting games that encourage discussion of meaning**
8. **Help students see how one word leads to another**
9. **Review and embed vocabulary**
10. **Understand why you need to teach exam command terms very carefully**

But first **a word of warning**: the 10 activities below are interactive, often involving some sort of sorting in pairs or small groups, so that the students have to talk about the words and co-construct their understanding. That's exactly what's wrong with many off-the-shelf vocabulary activities like the one pictured here. The task is to match each word to its definition by drawing a line to link them. Have a go yourself and you will find that the activity is more of a time-filler than anything else because trying to match the words on the page with their definitions is self-defeating – even more so if you are unfamiliar with many of the words. The process involved is counter intuitive as the more links you make, the more confusing the sheet becomes. Being able to physically sort the words and the definitions with a partner would solve the problem and turn this into an excellent

activity because the process would help to clarify thinking and lead to discussion, which in turn helps to familiarise students with the vocabulary. And to ice the cake, these off-the-shelf activities are often laid out so that the text is very small and squashed into the corner of the page, just like my example above, which I have kindly not attributed to the science textbook from whence it came! But publishers tell me books like these sell very nicely.

1. Use *NHTW grids* to establish the words the students don't know

Never-heard-the-word grids (NHTW grid) – first mentioned in Chapter 2 because they make good cold tasks for vocabulary, help establish what words the students are already familiar with – as well as those that need focusing on. They work particularly well with non-fiction topics. It brings to the front of the students' minds vocabulary they may have heard before but had forgotten about and flags up all the key vocabulary coming their way soon, as well as reminding you of which words must be focused on.

To create the grid:
- Identify the core vocabulary associated with the unit and list the words on a sheet. If your unit requires more than say 25 words, select the ones needed first and create another NHTW grid later in the unit.
- Mark words that have at least two meanings (so the meaning can only be determined by context) with an asterisk, for example *inspire**. *Describe* has won three asterisks to signal extreme danger – as explained later in this chapter.
- Give every student a copy of the sheet and present it as a challenge. If you think they haven't met the terms before, reassure them that they don't have to worry if they get none of the words right at the beginning of the unit, but the aim is for everyone to get full marks when they revisit the sheet at the end of the unit, and they ought to be able to spell them (see **page 71**).
- Say each word clearly and repeat it in a sentence which provides context but doesn't give away its meaning, e.g., '*symptoms: I don't have any symptoms.*' It's important for students to understand that you know a word by the company it keeps.
- Allow enough time after each word for the students to tick the *never heard the word* column, *heard it but not sure of its meaning* column, or to quickly jot down a meaning and/or example or image to sum it up.
- Ask the students to put their score at the end of the activity.
- Let them know that you are not going to go over any of the words in isolation but will introduce each word in context as it's needed for the unit.

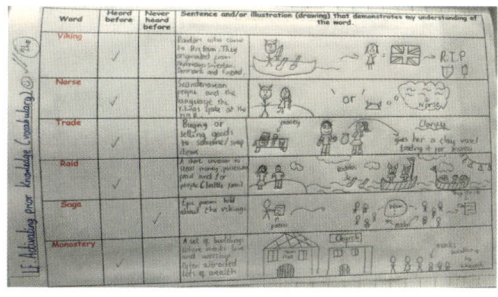

If you try to go over the words immediately, probably most of the class won't listen beyond word two, even if they are quiet. Moreover, 20 or so words are too many to introduce at once. The history example here from Hallsville Primary, Newham, shows that this child was familiar with all the words except for *saga* which they had clearly returned to later and explained and provided an image to help them remember. The next example is an excellent RAG-rating version. You can see at a glance which words the student was initially completely befuddled by, only feeling secure with one word. Looking at the images added later, you can see they now have a good idea of what the words mean.

NHTW grids have proved very popular: not least because they are easy to produce, very logical, entertaining and effective; there are numerous references to them in the subject-based chapters. It is important to remember that these grids initially don't teach the word. Apart from helping the teacher establish which words need concentrating on most, what these grids are also designed to do is flag up for the students the key words they will be concentrating on within the unit and help to remind the teacher that these words need to be nurtured so that they form part of the vocabulary that students can understand, use confidently and spell, if they need to write them down. They're also an excellent resource to return to throughout the unit (reviewing learning at the start of units or adding in images and definitions as the words are encountered in context within the unit and returning to at the end of the unit – see **page 71**). It's also worth asking the students to add words to the list that they encounter in the unit which they didn't know. It's important to nurture a culture where asking what words mean is seen as good. Look at **video clip 26** and hear Stu Gray, Director of Learning in Humanities at John of Gaunt, as he feeds back to staff on how NHTW grids and warming up the words has made a difference. He's honest enough to say that he counts himself amongst the guilty who hadn't previously paid enough attention to helping the students understand the key words of his subject.

2. Help students understand words by associating an image with a word

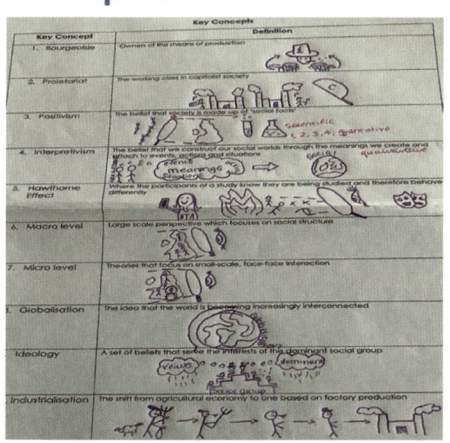

The more accustomed students become to deciding what images will best help them remember the meaning of words, the easier it will be for them to understand and recall words – and it's entertaining. Including the images is important because, later on, the students will be helped by text mapping the key content of your subject and, the more they have visual images to help them do this, the easier it will be for them both to recall the content and the meaning of the words within it.

An additional method to help students have a firm grasp of tricky concepts is to give the students the words and simple definitions and ask them to come up with the images that will help them remember the meaning of the terms. The image above shows an A-level student's images to help recall key sociological concepts like *the bourgeoisie*. Look at the images for *industrialisation* and you will see how useful it is as it supports real understanding. This, combined with discussion using these terms and regular revisiting of the vocabulary, will do the job.

3. Making the words visible

Poor vocabulary was a significant issue at Wexham School, Slough when the school started its TfW project. Now, as you walk from lesson to lesson, you can see how teachers are really helping the students enrich their vocabulary.

One simple technique is to insert key words from the NHTW grid into a pocket chart (see right above) and display them prominently in the room to remind student and teacher alike that these words matter. In another room, students were asked to place words in the pocket chart that they were unsure of to ensure the teacher covered these (see middle image). Listen to the school's deputy headteacher and TfW project lead Ruth Corrie (**video clip 25**) as she explains the difference making a real focus on vocabulary has made. Vocabulary was a focus in every room I walked into and was included in the elements that students highlighted when analysing model text. From the first image above you can see that the maths department has divided some of its key vocabulary into mathematical processes as opposed to other key words associated with maths.

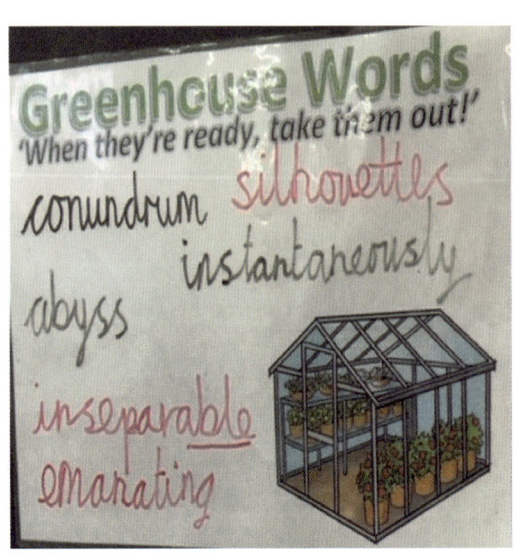

The John of Gaunt School includes vocabulary reviews in its lesson warm-up quizzes to make certain every teacher focuses on vocabulary, see **video clip 44**. This is further strengthened by including the key vocabulary for each unit in the students' curriculum organisers. Tom Wriglesworth, when teaching Year 5 at Selby Community Primary School, came up with the idea pictured on the left of keeping the words focused on in the greenhouse – a whiteboard where words could be added when introduced and removed once sufficiently nurtured.

VOCABULARY MATTERS 61

Don't miss a trick: If you are showing an engaging film clip to a class to boost understanding of whatever unit you are teaching, pre-watch the video to establish all the useful words it could help introduce or embed. I recently watched a geography lesson including the most stunning film of a Tsunami I've ever seen – the commentary was also illuminating and full of interesting words. If these had been flagged up before the students saw the film and the students asked if they could explain their meaning from watching the film and hearing how they were used in context, it would have been a great vocabulary opportunity. See **page 297** for an excellent example of this approach in art.

4. Focus on making students say the words in a range of contexts

How can we efficiently and engagingly make certain our students understand the words, can use them appropriately and recall them when needed? Getting students to write down the definitions of words is a very common method used, certainly in secondary schools – the trouble is that on its own it will make little, if any, difference, apart from keeping the students quietly occupied. You can copy definitions down without thinking at all about what you are writing. The key is talking about the meaning of the word, making the students say it and understand it in context and helping them picture the meaning of the word. You have to speak a word several times in different contexts to start to have confidence in remembering it when others use it let alone using it yourself. This is where Isabel Beck's simple *basic routine* introduced on **page 19** is so useful. It's quick, interactive, engaging and effective because everyone gets to say the words. See **video clip 5** of an example of this approach in action in a Year 6 class at St Matthew's in a very challenging area of Birmingham, which gets outstanding results despite having an 88% pupil premium intake.

Sorting activities to establish key words

	Characteristic 1		Characteristic 5
rhythm	Is the music high or low?	pitch	Is the music fast or slow?
tempo	Characteristic 1 How loud or soft is the music?	mood	Characteristic 6 Are the sounds long, short, constant, varied?
melody	Characteristic 3 Does the tune move in steps, or in leaps?	dynamics	Characteristic 7 How complex is the music?
texture	Characteristic 4 How does the music make you feel – sad, calm happy etc		

A useful alternative to the Isabel Beck routine is to provide the students with the words and simple definitions to sort. This has the advantage of making the students interrogate their understanding of the words by having to agree the matches with a partner. This approach is particularly suited for helping students understand the key terms that a subject spins round. Clearly, the more secure the students are with this vocabulary, the easier it will be for them to build their understanding of the subject, so time spent embedding this vocabulary pays off. Moreover, if you've got the words in this format, then the activity can be given to students in any class you are teaching this subject to who need to strengthen their understanding of the words. The examples here relate to the underpinning terminology of music, but they could easily be adapted to suit any subject. The students, in pairs, are being asked to match the word not to its definition but to the characteristics that sum up its meaning. If you use definitions, devise simple ones, otherwise you'll need definitions of the definitions which rather defeats the point.

62 TRANSFORMING LEARNING ACROSS THE CURRICULUM

Flexible word walls for key words/phrases

Key terms	Opening Ravel's *Bolero*	Opening Dukas' *Sorcerer's Apprentice*
tempo		
pitch		
dynamics		
rhythm		
texture		
melody		
mood		

This can then be followed up by an activity that involves the students in generating vocabulary related to the words they have been working on. The more the students are involved in generating the linking words, the more they will understand and recall them and be able to use them confidently. Each pair of students is given a sheet of paper with the key terms on. The students then listen to extracts from two well-known pieces of music and jot down all the words relating to each in turn. Tell them to put a dotted line under any word they are not confident in spelling – the list they come up with must not be constrained by whether the words are correctly spelt (see **page 14**). The teacher can then flipchart the words generated, clumping the words relating to say *tempo* into categories like *fast* and *slow* to aid students' understanding of all the words. In a different colour, they can then add in the more technical vocabulary the students need to know, for example words like *lento* and *adagio* to the *slow* category. In this way, the students' dormant vocabulary is revived and they begin to learn new words.

Generating key vocabulary – art

Key terms	Portrait by Van Gogh	Portrait by Picasso
use of light		
use of colour		
texture		
level of realism		
texture		
context		
mood		

The teacher can then create a *word bank* for the unit they are teaching and display it, preferably on a washing line, when they want to refer to it and add words as the unit develops. If this *word bank* is not relevant to the next class, it can be removed. In this simple way, the washing line becomes the *work in progress* area for each class and supports their learning. Lists on walls which are always displayed and rarely referred to just become wallpaper and, of course, you haven't got enough walls to display all the words and phrases you need for all the classes/subjects you teach. The example here shows the same approach but this time for art appreciation.

5. Devise talking frames

Talking frames are easy to construct for whatever subject you teach. Just think of the sentence stems needed to express understanding, or discuss issues, and help students internalise these so they can talk their way to understanding.

See **pages 190–191** for an explanation of how Tracey Adams has devised talking frames focusing on the key vocabulary of each of her maths units. She feels these have revolutionised her teaching because of the impact on the children's understanding.

6. Help students recall words by associating an action with a word

The power of actions in helping students both remember words and relish their meaning will be well known to any teachers familiar with the Talk for Writing method of using text maps and actions to help students internalise model text. Actions can be used to great effect to warm up the meaning of key words. It's worth looking at **video 21** of a group of Year 1 children in a science lesson at Yew Tree Community Primary, Birmingham, to remind ourselves about how engaging words can be. The next stage will be to ensure that the students can use these key technical words and any related command terms appropriately as **video clip 22** from the same school illustrates. The term *predict* is useful both to comprehension in reading and to discussion in science. If such understanding can be secured at such an early age using these methods, just think of the potential for expanding vocabulary across primary school and into secondary school. If we are not careful, we are the barrier to progress: we decide in advance that a word is too difficult and do not teach it. Using actions for words, works with students of all ages. If you look at the Year 9 science group at John of Gaunt – **see video clip 8** – you can see that the class is enjoying coming up with actions to help them recall key words.

Using mime to help boost recall: As imitating the text activities show, actions can very much support students in remembering both content and individual words and, of course, it's entertaining and provides a welcome respite from sitting at desks. So, whenever an action can help recall the meaning of a word, it's a good idea to use it. The sorting activity below has been strengthened by adding in mime, not hard to do when the subject is PE.

- Ask the students in small groups to match the key terms about motor skills with their simple definitions and then add an example for each. (Explain why there is no example for motor skills as this is the generic term and all the examples are types of motor skills.)
- Ask the groups to come up with at least 3 examples for one type of motor skill (allocate different types to different groups).

PE vocab sorting & mime activity

Key term	Working definition	Example
motor skills	ability to perform certain movements with control and consistency	
open motor skills	ability to perform movements affected by the environment or by others	making a tackle in football
closed motor skills	movements performed in stable conditions where performer has almost total control	a free throw in basketball
fine motor skills	involves movement of small muscle groups	flick of the wrist as the ball is released
gross motor skills	involves movement of large muscle groups	a sliding tackle

Adapted from material produced by K Ford, PE Department, Old Hall School, Rotherham

If the students were then asked to feed back their suggestions, the chances are the class wouldn't listen, but if you asked each group to mime their examples and the class had to identify the activity, then they would stay involved. The more they are involved in generating the examples, the more they will understand the concept. Mime is an extremely powerful learning technique because, when you mime something, you have to go through the sequence you are miming in your head – in effect, it makes you talk to yourself about whatever it is you are trying to mime. So, for anything that can be sequenced, use mime. It can also help pupils comprehend text, **see page 81**.

7. Devise sorting games that encourage discussion of meaning

Grouping words activates prior learning

1. UK	2. Europe	3. Asia	4. Africa
5. The World	6. Climate	7. Landscape & forms	
the Tropics	River Nile	**volcanoes**	Kenya
Sahara	Egypt	**drought**	hospitals
rivers	**earthquake**	**erosion**	health
Europe	Tokyo	**flooding**	London
nuclear power	India	less developed	Ben Nevis
Scotland	Farming	hot climate	migration
equator	oil	Sao Paulo	Italy
Mississippi	religion	poverty	tourism

Adapted from material developed by Lawrence Collins, Head of Geography, Lincoln Minster School, Lincoln

Vocabulary sorting activities pay real dividends – students see them as a game, so they are engaged. Sorting activities to activate prior knowledge can be used to embed key terminology that has already been introduced and that will be needed for forthcoming units or to see what students remember about something that has been previously taught. The idea is to make a card-sorting activity based around the key topics that will already have been studied and its related key vocabulary. Present the topics on shaded card to distinguish them from the vocabulary, as illustrated in the geography example here. The words immediately under *Landscape and forms* have been shaded here to illustrate the process. The students' task, in pairs, is to take each heading in turn and decide which vocabulary best matches the heading. Several of the words will probably be a good match for a number of different headings. This activates prior learning and warms up dormant vocabulary as well as helping the teacher know how much the students already know. It would be useful to also have the activity on screen so the students can hear the words being read aloud before they start the activity. This will help them recall the words.

The art example below could be a useful sorting activity at the beginning of Year 10 to help students recall the language of art evaluation. Some of the words would fit more than one category which makes it a better activity as this leads to more discussion about the words.

VOCABULARY MATTERS 65

Artist's intention	Mood	Form/composition	Use of tone, colour, texture
exaggerate	distort	recreate	reflect
express	explore	evoke	suggest
happy	sad	haunting	evocative
frightening	awesome	entertaining	nostalgic
balanced	symmetrical	arrangement	composition
design	angular	curved	foreground
vivid	sombre	bright	dull
clashing	pastel	matching	rough

Adapted from material developed by the Art Department at Hampstead School, Camden, London

Sorting activities to help pupils recall prior-learning

Related to circular shapes	Related to multi-sided shapes	Related to triangles	Words related to 2 or 3 dimensions
radius	square	triangular	regular
diameter	rectangle	three-sided	edge
circumference	kite	isosceles	face
concentric	parallelogram	equilateral	surface
spherical	rhombus	scalene	angle
cylindrical	oblong	congruent	centre
curved	pentagon	pyramid	right angle
semicircle	polygon	triangle	line

Here is a similar activity to bring back to students' minds the words they hopefully encountered in primary school for geometry. Again, the card sorting activity is to be completed in pairs. First, they have to clump the words, into the 4 categories given selecting the best fit. Then, since these terms are best understood visually, ask them if they can come up with an image to represent each word. Next, get the pairs to share their conclusions with another pair. The more opportunities the activity provides for them to actually say the words, the better. Moreover, many of the words have roots or prefixes that regularly recur in key vocabulary in maths or science so at the same time these links can be brought out – see activity 8 below.

8. Help students see how one word leads to another

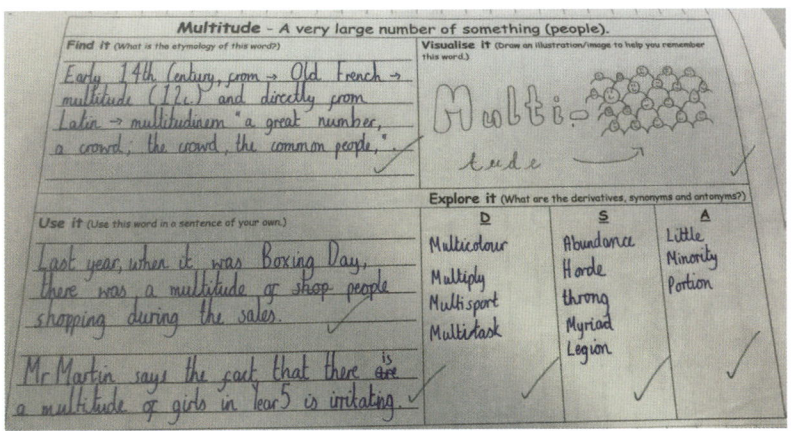

Words very much form the content of English teaching so teachers of English hopefully take the time to build vocabulary by helping students see how one word can lead to another. Look at this page from a Year 5 pupil's book in Daniel Martin's class at St Matthew's, Birmingham. It follows a tried and tested process so the pupils are used to finding out the roots of words, how they are used, coming up with a visual image to help them remember the base word focused on, and then finding words derived from it; then words with the same and opposite meanings. This provides them with a wealth of words to magpie. Many of the children enter this school with very few words in English, way below the national average, but they leave with vocabularies far beyond the national average. Such a methodical focus on building vocabulary is part of the key to their success. In primary schools, it makes sense for class teachers to take such a holistic approach to teaching vocabulary including introducing understanding of roots, prefixes and suffixes in English and then enhancing understanding as relevant across the curriculum, as illustrated above. In secondary schools, teachers of English can further develop learners' understanding of roots and affixes while teachers of all other subjects across the curriculum can look out for extra ways of extending vocabulary, including drawing on the roots and affixes that are particularly relevant to their subjects, as illustrated here.

The image to the left from science shows how useful it is for students to automatically be able to associate a tricky technical term with an image that helps bring clarity. The more students can associate an image with the words, the more liable they are to remember them and the easier it will be for them to text map. If these words have roots or prefixes that regularly feature in your subject, then it is time well spent to bring out these links. Much of the technical vocabulary of maths and science, originates in Latin or Greek. Here knowing that *therm* comes from the Greek word for *heat* immediately leads to related words like *thermostat, thermos flask, hypothermia, thermal, thermometer* etc. That leaves *exo* and *endo*. The link with the Latin word *ex*, meaning *out of*, is immediately useful since it relates to so many words *(exit, extend, exceed, exclude)*. *Endo* is not so obliging. It is the Greek for *within, inner, containing,* and is used in a range of highly technical words like *endothelium* – it's worth linking to these if you know they will be part of the syllabus you're teaching. For activities related to roots and affixes see the online **handouts 5a–c**.

9. Understand why you need to teach exam command terms very carefully

When introducing NHTW grids on **page 18**, I suggested putting an asterisk on words with more than one meaning and recommended putting 3 asterisks on *describe*. Here's why. Key command terms can be very tricky because they can be hard to pin down and, in some cases, can actually mean different things in different subjects. Take the word *describe*. In English, this usually means selecting a range of well-chosen words, often including imagery, to help the reader picture the place, the things, the people or the feelings that are being described. It tends to be very subjective. In science, it means providing a brief factual explanation. It must be objective. It would be harder for two *definitions* of the command term *describe* to be more opposite: context matters.

VOCABULARY MATTERS 67

The text sorting activity in the chapter on co-constructing understanding of science command terms **(see page 88)** is a good activity to do to help students be wary of the term *describe*. Having experienced through that activity how tricky it could be to reconstruct an exam board's explanation of what its command terms mean, with a definition of the term, and the text that exemplifies it, I was very interested when I saw a noticeboard in a geography room. It showed each of the geography command terms (all 15 of them!) their definition – according to AQA – and some example text to illustrate them. So, I decided to turn it into a sorting game, just like the science command term activity on page 88. I did what I always do. Type everything up, print it off and cut it up into its constituent parts to see if I could put it together again. I couldn't, even though I had recently typed everything.

I decided to get rid of the examples and set myself the much easier task of just matching the command term to the definition. I still couldn't do it. So, then I thought, make it easier. I clumped some of the causes of the confusion by shading various words and their definitions to lessen the choices you had to make: as illustrated here.

Sorting games to internalise key information
Match the command term to the definition that is the best fit.

• Calculate	• Discuss
• Complete	• Compare
• Describe	• Evaluate
• Outline	• To what extent
• Explain	• Justify
• Identify	• Suggest
• Give	• Assess
• State	

Geography command terms – the definitions

work out the value of something	finish the task by adding given information	set out main characteristics
identify similarity and difference	set out characteristics	set out reasons or purposes
name or otherwise characterise	provide an answer from memory	express in clear terms
present a possible case	support a case with evidence	make an informed judgement
judge the importance or success of something	judge from available evidence	present key points about ideas or strengths/weaknesses of an idea

I still couldn't get it right first time. So, this was even more interesting. I've tried it out with groups of extremely intelligent teachers. No one so far has got it right – as judged by what the exam board says is correct. At one school, where I had the whole staff playing the game, I was told, by coincidence, there was an AQA geography examiner on the staff. I couldn't help watching with interest as she tried desperately to get it right. She didn't either – not far out but still two command terms and their explanations were misplaced. So, here's the game (see above) and its downloadable from the website **(see Handout 6)** along with the answers.

68 TRANSFORMING LEARNING ACROSS THE CURRICULUM

What's important about this is that it tells us that we must test things out for ourselves (including examples from exam boards) before setting them as tasks for the students, just as we should try to write the model answers to exam questions (see page 40). In this way, we may discover levels of difficulty which will help us devise ways of helping the students. In the geography example, I would play the game with the students letting them know in advance that the chances are they won't be able to match everything up. And then discuss what the problem is and how the shades of difference don't seem to be clear. Then give advice on how to handle this when it comes to actually answering the questions.

10. Review and embed vocabulary

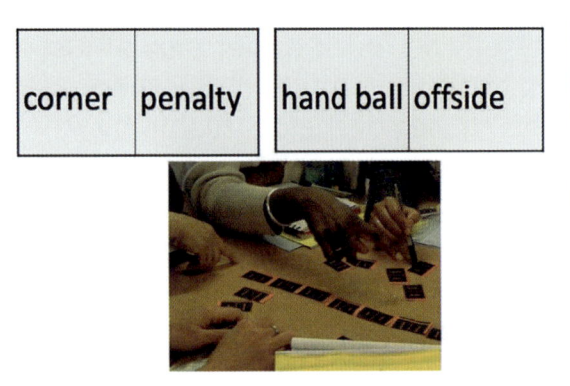

Word dominoes: The more students are encouraged to use the key terms and concepts related to a subject in a variety of contexts (oral, read and written), the more likely they are to understand, retain and develop their understanding. Word dominoes is a useful resource to embed vocabulary at the end of units and build pupil confidence in using the words. They are a sure-fire hit as it is a very engaging activity. Source the words on the dominoes from your NHTW grid lists for the topic and additional key vocabulary focused on within the unit.

- The idea is to create around 10 to 20 dominoes (too many makes it confusing). Each domino contains 2 words or phrases that are key to the unit. The ones pictured here relate to some of the subject-specific language of football.
- Give groups of students a set of dominoes and ask them to lay them all out on the table so that everyone in the group can see them and pick any domino as the starter domino. In the example here, the starter domino is *corner/penalty*. The group then looks at all the other dominoes to try to find a word that links with *penalty* and selects *hand ball*.
- Explain that they can only link the two dominoes together if they can coherently explain the link between the two words. For example, *If a member of the opposition handles the ball in the penalty area, the other team is awarded a penalty.*

The students' explanations of the links have to be articulate – this is the whole purpose of the activity; knowing that there may be an audience to judge the quality of their answers, will help achieve this. To ensure that they stay on task and don't rush through by *chucking any old domino down*, explain that when they have finished, another group will be asked to referee the links that they have made.

VOCABULARY MATTERS 69

The activity is popular because it is challenging, engaging and competitive. Very quickly, whole classes get involved as do large halls of teachers from all subjects as the pictures of teachers in North Wales playing dominoes illustrates. If an inspector called, they are definitely "on task"! It's worth reflecting on why it's important to devise activities that challenge the students – activities that are too easy are tedious and not worth paying attention to.

Dominoes is an ideal activity to set at the end of a unit to help embed vocabulary. Even when you are familiar with the terms, explaining a link coherently is quite challenging. The same activity can also be revisited if a new unit relies on the terminology that has already been taught. You can download what a set of dominoes might look like **(Handout 7)** – adapt it to suit your subject.

When creating your dominoes, it is a good idea to start like this:

- List the words that you plan to include; you may need to include synonyms for some of the words to ensure there are sufficient linked words and this will help strengthen the students' range of vocabulary.
- Make the game open-ended not closed by ensuring that there are at least two possible links for each word. If it's open ended, it's more challenging and engaging; if there is only one reasonable link for several words, it will probably be too hard to complete.
- Produce a rough copy and check that it works (i.e. that it is possible to go out by linking all the words) and that all the words are spelt correctly, before going into production. Also, only use a capital letter if that word always begins with a capital.

- If possible, print them out so that when you reverse each domino, the same words appear in reverse order so that *corner/penalty* becomes *penalty/corner*. This means that, whichever word is selected, the dominoes can be placed in an easy-to-read line. Competent readers can read upside down, but others may find it too challenging.

Sequencing loop for cardiac cycle – PE

vena cava	right atrium
pulmonary artery	lungs
tricuspid valve	right ventricle
pulmonary vein	left atrium
bicuspid valve	left ventricle
semilunar valve	aorta

Adapted from work by the PE department, Tuton Hall School, Chesterfield

Consolidating learning through linking *word loops*: The sequence of events, the idea of one thing leading to another, is relevant to a wide range of subjects like ICT, history, PE, geography, science and MFL (see example below). Anything that can be sequenced lends itself to being expressed as *word loops* and then, of course, it could be mimed. *Word loops* differ from dominoes because dominoes should be open-ended (there is no fixed sequence just a multitude of possibilities). Here is an example of sequencing vocabulary to match the order in which things would happen. In this example from PE of the cardiac cycle, all the stages of the sequence have been put onto domino-type cards. Each pair of students is given a set of these dominoes and the following two tasks:

1. sequence the information and explain what is happening in the sequence
2. mime how the cardiac cycle works.

Word loops for sequencing conversation

	Comment tu t'appelles?	Je m'appelle Jean-Michel.	Il y a combien de personnes dans ta famille?
Dans ma famille, il y a quatre personnes.	Tu as des frères et des soeurs?	J'ai une soeur mais je n'ai pas de frère.	Comment s'appelle ta soeur?
Elle s'appelle Christine.	Quel âge a-t-elle?	Elle a six ans.	As-tu des animaux chez toi?
J'ai un chat.	Il s'appelle comment?	Il s'appelle Felix.	

In this *word loop* for French, adapted from the work of Gaby Simons, Burnham Upper School, Buckinghamshire, the first task, in pairs, is to place the conversation in the right order. Once that's been sorted, one student becomes the questioner, the other Jean-Michel. They then read the conversation in role. They could then take it in turns to be the answerer but this time answer as themselves. In this way, the activity becomes a simple innovation.

Different subjects will be able to adapt these activities to suit their needs. The key thing, when devising vocabulary activities, is to keep the focus on the students saying the words.

Practical tips for all sorting activities:
- Keep the focus on maximising discussion – co-constructing learning is powerful.
- Remember to mix up the terms and definitions on screen before cutting them up so the matching pairs cannot be fitted together like a jigsaw.
- Try to ensure the words on the cards/activities only have a capital letter if they always need a capital letter or they are the first word of a heading. Your computer will love giving single words capital letters, so care needs to be taken. Correct use of upper and lower case will help students do the same.
- Store the sets in re-sealable plastic bags and the resource will last for years. If the sets get mixed up, do not despair. Most students will be more than willing to keep your resources sorted for you and, of course, they will help you make such resources.

Revisit never-heard-the-word grids at the end of units
The teacher says each word in turn.
The students write them down and then complete the grid.

Key words	Image	Use in sentence in context
1.		
2.		
3.		
4.		
5.		
20.		

Embedding understanding:
By the end of the unit, the students should have added all the key vocabulary of the unit into their working vocabulary so they understand the terms heard or read, can use them appropriately in context in discussion and, if they need to write them down, they can use the words appropriately and can spell them. A blank NHTW grid is an excellent way to do this. This could be an actual grid, or the students could just complete the task directly in their books. The teacher says all the words in spelling-test mode, so the class initially just writes all the words in the grid. Then they have to quickly sketch any supporting image and use it in context. If all the vocabulary is needed in a future unit, this could also be a good cold task to see what they have recalled.

A note on spelling for secondary schools:

Try to establish that each department builds in spelling activities throughout each unit focusing on key words from the unit, including setting spelling for homework and testing it. Then each department will be focusing spelling corrections on the key-terms list and any other words the students are frequently using to express their subject. You'll notice that all the chapters on subject areas from The John of Gaunt School use this sort of testing as lesson starters – an idea that underlines the centrality of vocabulary to learning, ensures a focused start to lessons and helps students recall what the lesson is about.

Doubtless some students will be misspelling a wide range of common English terms, for example, endlessly confusing *it's* and *its*. It is probably best to set up a coordinated approach to sorting out spelling problems so that each department deals with their technical terms and frequently used terms, and flags up problems with other words as appropriate, while the English department deals with the more general words. One useful idea is for the English teacher to inform the teachers of particular classes when it is having a blitz on careless errors so that these are flagged up by all departments. Being a little bit fussy works and saves hours as the errors are sorted. Practice only makes perfect if you are practising something perfect; otherwise it just embeds error. Also make certain that everything displayed in classrooms is spelt correctly. If you read the displays in classrooms or look at school booklets, there's a worrying number of spelling errors out there, including material that's come from teachers.

In addition to the video clips referenced in this chapter, these videos also focus on developing vocabulary:

Video clip 23. Nick Warren, Year 6 teacher at Briar Hill Primary, demonstrates how to help pupils develop a powerful vocabulary

Video clip 46. Science teacher Emma Lydon warming up vocabulary with her Year 10 class

Video clip 47. How Emma Lydon introduces her Year 10 science class to the terminology required to explain what they are learning to themselves and others

Chapter 5: Linking ideas coherently

The central role of generic text and particularly sentence signposts was introduced in chapter 2. It plays such a significant role in supporting students' ability to comprehend and write text coherently that this chapter looks at the issue more closely and provides a range of practical ways forward.

Small children, if they are lucky enough to have been read to a lot, will have been immersed in the language of story. Because they have the pattern in their heads, they quickly get to know how it works. They can then automatically say phrases like *Once upon a time, At that moment, Without warning,* in the appropriate voice and know what they signal. If they are taught in Talk for Writing style, they will very soon be able to start to make up their own stories using such language, and gradually both write them down and read them with ease. The primary curriculum initially, quite rightly, focuses on the language of story and recount; but we can also very much support children in developing the language of information and explanation through subjects like technology, history, geography, maths and science. If we don't, the pupils will be increasingly lost within the secondary curriculum. Look back at the typical Year 11 GCSE questions listed on **page 1** and you will see that various forms of explanation are king: the students are being asked to analyse and evaluate a wide range of information, and evaluation means different things in different subjects since it is subjective in some subjects and objective in others – familiarity with the generic text of the subject helps students negotiate the minefield.

As adults, most of us have had the experience of finding certain text hard to follow (for example, legal documents or information about tax). It is not just the technical vocabulary that holds us back: it is the phrasing and the way the text is linked that is often unfamiliar. We don't have the tune in our heads, so we can't comprehend it with ease. Often, we reread it and still feel befuddled. This is exactly how many students feel about text in many subjects. Every subject has its own tune: the more familiar you are with the tune, the easier it is to read about the subject and understand what is being said. And, once you have the pattern in your head, you will be able to write about it, too, if necessary.

When you look at much of the cross curriculum writing that students produce, the reader struggles to understand the text because it lacks the links that would give it coherence. It often isn't the lack of key information that stops the students from providing good answers, it is their inability to phrase their answers coherently so that the text makes sense as **video clip 27** illustrates. This is where the Talk for Writing approach can make such a big difference.

It is standard for teachers to think about the technical vocabulary of a unit but it is not so common for teachers to consider the generic text that underpins the subject, in particular, the joining phrases (sentence signposts) that are key to linking information about a subject – words or phrases like *consequently* (signalling the cause of something), *usually* (signalling generalisation), *whereas* (signalling contrast) or *equally* (signalling similarity). These linking phrases often take the form of sentence starters (sometimes known as sentence stems) that are frequently used to introduce points: *The main reason why … This leads to … Another problem is …* It is focusing on how to teach this generic phrasing of a subject that will help students express themselves clearly and make their work coherent. For subjects for which writing is key, this will lead to students being able to understand and write about the subject more effectively; for practical subjects, it will mean the students can talk more clearly about the subject which, in turn, will enable them to understand it better and put it into practice more effectively. For subjects based on logic like maths, being able to verbalise coherently the logic behind the reasoning, makes all the difference – see **pages 190–191**.

We need to open up the language of different subjects so the sentence signposts and generic phrasing that are typical of history, science, maths, art, PE, music, D&T, etc, are familiar to the pupils. Then they will know what is required by the word *evaluate* in different subjects just as they will know that causes have consequences and can express this clearly – see **page 243** for an excellent example in history of how to support students who haven't understood this. (It's a shame, though, that the children had somehow managed to get through their primary education without grasping this.)

Look at the generic phrasing and sentence signposts below: you immediately know which subjects they are liable to be found in because you're a reader.

- creates a feeling of …
- gives the impression that …
- makes me feel …
- almost seems to suggest …
- evokes a mood of …
- A key advantage …
- Another disadvantage …
- In comparison,
- On the other hand,
- Whereas,
- *The evidence suggests …*
- *Another possible cause is …*
- *Investigations have proven …*
- *A further significant factor …*
- *One theory suggests*

The green group lends itself to artistic subjects like English literature, art or drama; it is definitely not the language of science or maths. The middle group could be part of a discursive English lesson but would also be very much at home within comparative work in science, geography and D&T. The last group (in italics) very much suits the investigative, interpretive nature of history but could also be science or geography. If students are to become fluent speakers, readers and writers, they need to understand the power of generic phrasing and particularly that of sentence signposts in linking text coherently. Not being tuned into these signposts can leave students stranded within text, lost in a labyrinth of words.

This is why model text is so important. It gives students the key to understanding the tune of each subject: the typical generic phrases and vocabulary used to express the ideas and the typical sentence signposts and sentence starters that link the text together. Identifying these phrases is a key part of the imitation stage that helps students internalise the patterns of language they will need. The solution, in the end, is quite simple, as introduced in chapter 2. Every teacher who expects students to write should, when first introducing a type of writing:

1. Provide a model text of *what = good* so the students understand what they are trying to do.
2. Help the students internalise the tune of the text so they can say it.
3. Co-construct how to box up the structure of the text.
4. Co-construct with the students how to analyse the text, focusing on useful generic language and sentence signposts:

    - get the students to check the key ingredients of the text they need to write against the *plan-it, link-it, express it, check it* generic writing toolkit, to bring out any differences
    - co-construct banks of the key sentence signposts and stems that link the type of text they want the students to write, adding to the lists as more examples appear in additional text
    - devise activities that help students practise these phrases and recognise their centrality.

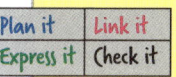

This chapter focuses on this fourth stage, particularly emphasising the signposts.

Identifying generic phrases in model text focusing on sentence signposts

As emphasised in chapter 2, **page 16**, first make certain your model text is a really useful model (i.e. it exemplifies the typical structure and phrasing that key text in your subject requires). Once you've reached the analysing-the-text phase, begin by getting the students to highlight key features like:

- the sentence signposts that link the text (e.g. *However, Furthermore, As a result*)
- additional generic phrases that feature in whatever the type of text it is (e.g. *extensive testing of a range of ..., the design brief ... a price that consumers felt was reasonable*)
- key technical terms (e.g. *magnetic fields, solid state devices, gigabyte*)

> **a. Phrases that are generally useful for ICT**
> **b. Sentence signposts joining the text together**

> Secondary storage is required to store data and programs that would otherwise be lost when power is lost to the computer system. These devices can be split into categories such as magnetic, optical and solid state. Magnetic devices, such as a hard disc drive, have a large storage capacity and are cheaper than solid state storage. However, due to the fact that they have moving parts, they are less reliable and are also susceptible to heat or magnetic fields. On the other hand, solid state devices, such as a solid-state drive, have no moving parts and are, therefore, not sensitive to movement. This makes them ideal when portability is important, for example, taking files from school to home. However, these devices are more expensive per gigabyte than magnetic storage and have a limited number of read/write cycles. Therefore, it is important to consider the characteristics of these devices before purchasing them to ensure they are suitable for their purpose.

If you look at the ICT model text for describing the characteristics of magnetic and solid-state secondary storage here, the students would have boxed up the paragraph and established it began with a clear introduction, followed by a series of points related to the question, and rounded off with a conclusion. They would have then analysed the ingredients of the text (e.g. by highlighting in green any generic phrases that would be generally useful for similar ICT questions and then highlighting in magenta any of this generic text that links the ideas together).

The highlighted text here shows that the model contains many useful generic phrases like *would otherwise be ..., are less reliable ..., and to ensure they are suitable for their purpose*, as well as some very useful sentence signposts:

- *However, ...*
- *such as ...*
- *for example, ...*
- *Due to the fact that ...*
- *On the other hand, ...*

Once the students have identified this generically useful language from the model, the sentence signposts could be displayed on a flipchart and additional phrases added as they are encountered in other computer science text. In this way, the students will quickly internalise the sort of language needed to express answers in this subject coherently.

The students could embed their understanding by matching the ingredients of the computer science model text against a copy of the generic writing toolkit (see below). This would be familiar to them because they would have initially co-constructed this in their English lessons and used it in other subjects.

LINKING IDEAS COHERENTLY

Ask the students to:
- tick all the features that are the same as the generic writing toolkit
- amend any features that need altering
- add any additional key features that are missing
- find examples of all of these features from the model text and annotate the grid.

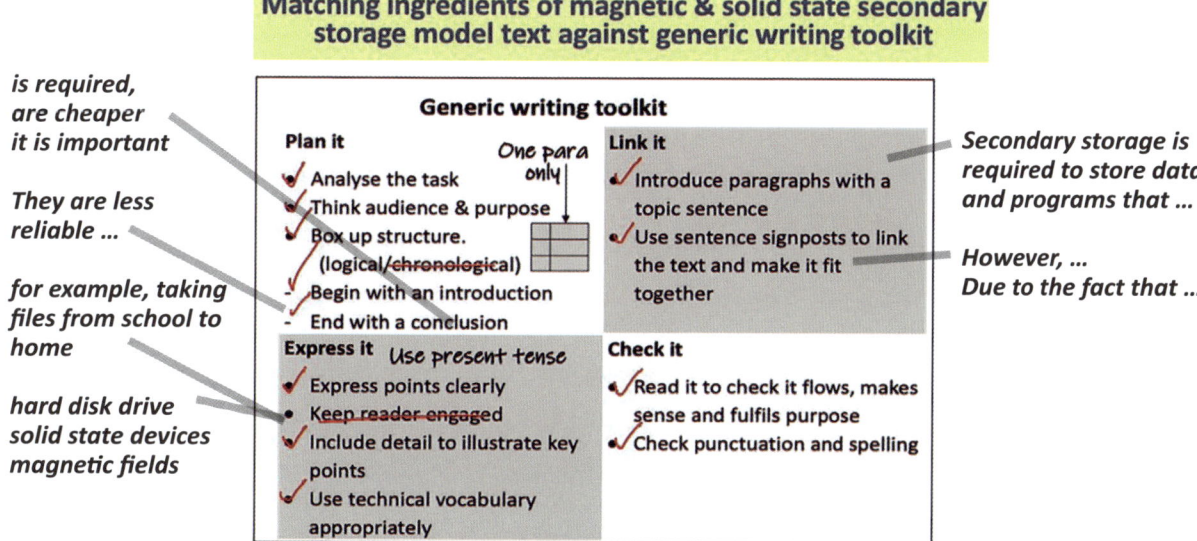

As you can see, the generic writing toolkit is a fairly good match for the model text for computer science. There is only one paragraph but that has been clearly structured and can be boxed up into its logically ordered sections. The big difference is that, just like science, *keeping the reader engaged* has been deleted and *using the present tense* has been added in, as this is an important element of information and explanation text.

Annotating the features against the generic toolkit will help the students internalise the features that are needed for this sort of text and help them transfer learning from one subject to another.

As soon as this has been done once for any subject, when additional model texts are introduced, they can be boxed up to establish the structure and analysed to check the key features. If any features differ from those identified previously, they can be flagged up to help students remember the difference.

In such a way, students will quickly build up a flexible writing toolkit in their heads which will enable them to adapt their writing to suit whatever task confronts them. They will no longer be doomed to fall back on some kind of endless recount style that staggers through bits of information in a disconnected way.

Highlighting key features of text really works

The good thing about work on signposting and generic phrasing is that it is easy to transfer from subject to subject. Primary teachers in TfW schools have

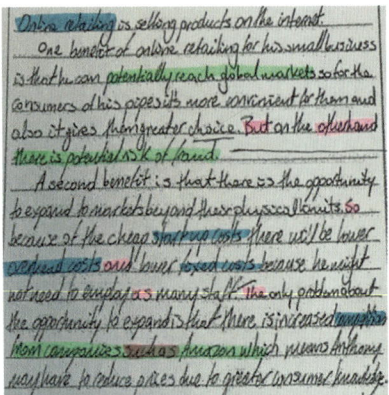 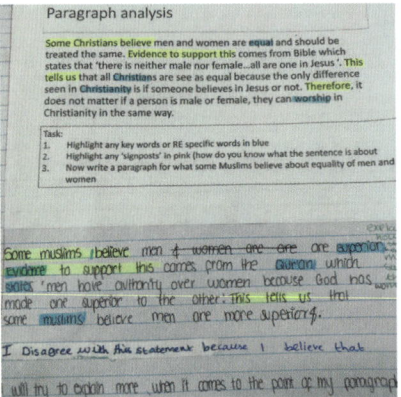 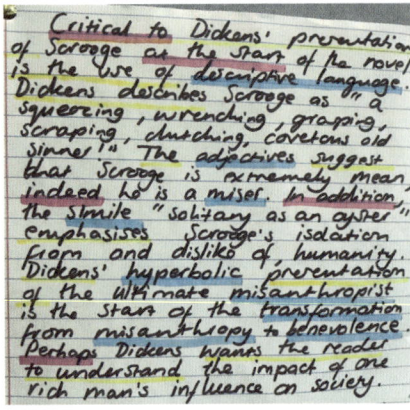

found that once pupils understand the role of signposts, they can easily transfer the skill to any type of writing and quickly build confidence in speaking and using the phrases. If you look at **pages 298–301**, you will see the transformational difference that model text focusing on sentence signposts and generic phrasing can make to students' ability to both annotate their artwork clearly and understand the underpinning art processes involved. If you walk round Wexham School in Slough, you will see that the students have understood the centrality of sentence signposts and generic phrasing to clear coherent expression. The images here show students identifying such features in business studies, RE, and English – the understanding was consistent for any subject dealing with text. The effect of this is powerful: the students' written work has improved across the curriculum. There's still a long way to go but they are on the right road.

This impressive piece of Year 7 writing about William's victory at the Battle of Hastings, from The John of Gaunt School, shows how focusing on the key linking phrases pays off. Here, the student has linked his text together expressing a series of related points well. The writer signposts clearly to the reader whether they are explaining how one thing led to another or if they are adding in a point. The student has highlighted the key linking phrases and, if you look at the text, it is correctly punctuated which helps the reader comprehend what is written. Expression falters every now and again but you feel confident that this student will become an effective writer.

Displaying the key signposts

Once subject teachers have identified the sort of generic phrases that are key to their subject, they should be focused on, as appropriate, in context, throughout every unit. Over time, the students will become very familiar with such phrases which will greatly help them express exactly what they are trying to say. There is a wide range of activities that can help students do this. Here are a few tried-and-tested ideas to choose from so that every unit contains at least one activity to warm up key phrases. These are excellent starter activities and can be used to build up a range of posters featuring these key phrases. Displaying such posters will support students in using the phrases so that they can magpie from them and begin to automatically express themselves coherently, as the image on the previous page of a magpie from The John of Gaunt School suggests.

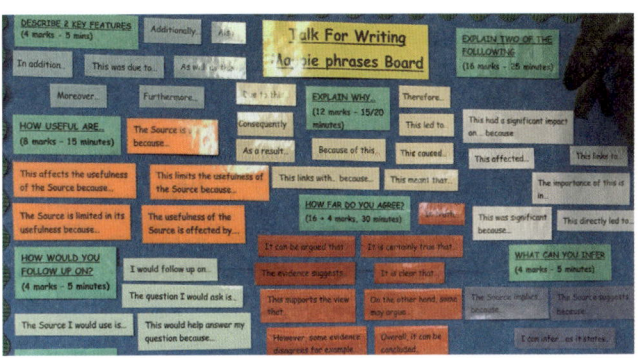

This next picture shows a very large display, in the same school, of the key history sentence signposts to help students answer the sorts of questions they will get asked in history exams. It has been colour-coded so that all the typical command terms and phrasing of history questions are in green, for example, *Explain two of the following: ... How far do you agree ...? What can you infer ...* The phrasing that particularly relates to this sort of question is then clustered around it in a particular colour. So, next to the infer question, the sentence signposts suggested are: *This source implies ... because ..., I can infer ..., as it states*. Since the students will have co-constructed their understanding of these phrases and how to use them over time, such a display is helpful because they understand its significance and can use it as an aide memoire. It also acts as a useful reminder for the teacher of what phrases to embed when different types of questions are tackled.

Don't forget the commas

You may have noticed that whenever I've given lists of sentence signposts that can begin sentences, I've included the appropriate punctuation that accompanies them:

- *However, ...*
- *For example, ...*
- *Due to the fact that* the speed of the wind increased, ...
- *On the other hand, ...*
- *Because* it hadn't rained for several weeks, ...

It's down to primary class teachers to teach the where and why of this and for secondary English departments to build on the fact that most Year 7s nowadays (at least those in England) will know a fronted adverbial when they see one, whereas many secondary teachers won't because these things weren't taught when they were educated. But what all teachers must do is make certain their model texts are properly punctuated and that they reinforce the punctuation when putting up lists of signposts. It's also quite common to see in primary schools that all these commas are in place when it comes to English lessons but disappear again when it comes to history or geography writing.

Games that support internalising signposts

Below is a series of sentence signpost games that have been devised to help students understand the power of the sentence signposts in linking text coherently and how they can help them become fluent speakers, readers and writers.

- **Reassembling text**
- **Sorting the paragraph starters**
- **Sorting the signposts**
- **Sorting activities that encourage being tentative**

All of them include these three key ingredients which will help students retain their understanding most effectively:

- doing it themselves
- co-constructing learning through discussion
- explaining to others.

Reassembling text

Text-sorting activity: Why vaccinations work

This allows your white blood cells to detect these type of micro-organisms **and** learn how to make antibodies to attack and kill them.

The harmful micro-organisms are, **therefore**, killed before they can make you ill.

When you have a vaccination, the doctor injects a weak **or** dead form of particular micro-organisms into your blood.

At a later time, you might be infected with a harmful form of the micro-organism. **Because** your white cells have already learnt how to defeat these germs, they can quickly detect the germs **and** make the antibodies to attack them.

One engaging activity is to cut up a simple model text into sections where the order of the text is clearly dependent on the sentence signposts. If you want to make it easier and clearer, then highlight the key linking phrases, as exemplified here. The students' task is to:

- reassemble the text in the right order
- read it through to check their chosen order makes sense
- be prepared to explain why their order is correct.

Here are a few useful tips for making this work:

- Write or find a short model text that is relevant to the topic you are teaching.
- Make certain it is a good example of how sentence signposts help make text coherent. If necessary, adapt your text to ensure it does this.
- Muddle up the paragraphs before cutting the text into strips. (In this way, the students can't put it together using the cut marks – like a jigsaw puzzle. This is important – human beings don't go for the long route if they think they've spotted a short cut.)

LINKING IDEAS COHERENTLY 81

When groups are feeding back, the important thing is to help everyone understand why the following order works and, in particular, why the only possible opening paragraph was the one beginning with *When*.

All the other paragraphs refer to something which has already happened and therefore can't be the introductory paragraph. Being a reader, helps you pick out such things automatically. Unskilled readers tend to wade without direction through text. Once the text has been reconstructed, you may want to *echo read* it to help the class hear the difference the signposts make.

Why vaccinations work

When you have a vaccination, the doctor injects a weak or dead form of particular micro-organisms into your blood.

This allows your white blood cells to detect these type of micro-organisms **and** learn how to make antibodies to attack and kill them.

At a later time, you might be infected with a harmful form of the micro-organism. **Because** your white cells have already learnt how to defeat these germs, they can quickly detect the germs and make the antibodies to attack them.

The harmful micro-organisms are, **therefore**, killed before they can make you ill.

You could add a drama activity that will serve to reinforce retention of what has been learnt. For example, in groups of 4 (and abiding by the no-contact rule), pupils have to see if they can devise a way of miming why vaccinations work. This will help them see how one thing leads to another. Or they could text map it to bring out cause and effect.

Most importantly, such activities engage the reader with the content of the text. They are much more liable to remember the significance of what they have read because they have worked first on ensuring it flows logically and then considered how to represent in action or image what the text has told them. Such activities are powerful because they strengthen reading skills, writing skills and knowledge and understanding of whatever the content is and, very importantly, the retention of that information. They are also engaging.

Sorting the paragraph starters

Sorting the paragraph starters

- **This was strengthened by realistic dialogue which …**
- **The staging helped make the scene work because …**
- **In conclusion, …**
- **In addition, the way the dramatist created credible characters …**
- **The scene was very effective because …**
- **The impact was built up by …**

In this example from drama (above right), the whole text has not been provided. Instead, the students have been given the key typical sentence starter signposts for evaluation in drama to place in a logical order. Activities like this help students to think about how text is structured and linked and will help fix the pattern of useful opening phrases in their minds. Again, remember to rearrange the order of the phrases before they are cut up so that they cannot be reassembled like a jigsaw. Claire Watson, RE teacher and TfW project lead at Dyson and Perrins C of E Academy, Malvern, decided to adapt this idea for use with her A-level class. She had noticed that the key weakness in her students' essays was their poor use of sentence signposts which resulted in their essays not linking together appropriately and failing to link back to the question clearly. She cut the students' essays up into paragraphs and then asked the students to reassemble each other's essay into the right order, as the picture above left illustrates. They found this hard to do and realised that this was because they hadn't sufficiently focused on structuring their essays properly or on linking the parts clearly.

Sorting the signposts

Sorting the signposts
In pairs, group the sentence signposts that signal:

- Ridicule — anyone who thinks like this is an idiot (persuasion)
- Neutrality — different viewpoints need considering (discussion)
- Being tentative — uncertain (discussion)
- Agreement — all sensible people think like this (persuasion)

On the other hand, …	Now is the time to stand up…	A counter argument is…	Surely, …
Are we going to let …?	This is just the sort of namby …	We are all united …	It's clear that …
Is there anyone who …?	Perhaps the answer is…	There can be no one who still thinks …	One probable explanation is …

If you are teaching English in a primary or secondary school, you can have fun getting the pupils to consider how different sentence signposts influence how the reader hears or reads the information. If you begin a sentence by saying 'Everyone knows that …' you are encouraging your audience to agree with you. Newspapers like *The Sun*, *The Mail* or *The Mirror* and politicians, particularly President Trump, use this technique all the time. It is important that the students are aware of these rhetorical tricks. Getting a range of contrasting sentence signposts that signal agreement, disagreement, neutrality and being tentative, as in the slide here introducing this activity, makes for a very engaging sorting activity that will help the students recognise the significance of the signposts. Get the students to read out their choices aloud using appropriate intonation and discuss how the intonation can change the meaning. Other subjects can then build on this or devise their own versions as suits their subjects, for example, signalling the difference between fact and opinion.

Sorting activities that encourage being tentative

If your subject requires students to distinguish between facts, theories and opinions, then helping them select the appropriate signposts will be useful. It is also an important part of students' education to help them be tentative about things that may be widely thought but are not necessarily proved to be true. Modern methods of communication like the internet increasingly present opinion or false information as fact since there is no editorial system to check the accuracy of what is stated – fake news and fake images haunt our existence today in many ways. So, it is useful to build up understanding of this. If you ask teachers if pupils like being tentative when answering questions, you will most likely discover that they don't. This could be very much our fault. Pupils want their answers to be right; they seek the nod of teacherly approval. If we are not careful, our teaching methods fail to encourage real thought and the weighing up of evidence.

Students should be encouraged to put forward ideas tentatively when they are suggesting information that is not known to be true or interpretations of ideas or texts. Encourage the use of this by modelling how to answer tentatively with phrases like:

- We think that it <u>might</u> …
- I'm <u>not sure</u>, but …
- <u>Perhaps</u> it could be …
- <u>Probably</u>, …

Praise students for their use of such phrasing so they learn that to be *good* you don't have to be *right*. Build on this, so students know that the intelligent way to answer is not to state a possible interpretation as if it were a known fact. Magpie tentative phrasing from all the texts that you use to support your subject. Visits to museums, etc, provide a good opportunity of seeing these phrases in action and of adding other phrases to the repertoire. All the phrases below were culled from one visit to a museum so it would be easy to create one relevant to any subject. For this sorting activity, ask the students in pairs to group a range of phrases into these three levels of certainty.

Tentative (uncertain)	Likely (highly possible)	Definite/certain (known to be true)

Initially, if the students are not good at this, provide them with very simple examples of phrases which signal these levels of certainty. All the examples below, relate to history, but it is easy enough to collect examples from science or geography or any discursive subject. When you do this activity, it's hard to place some of the phrases. This is good because it encourages thought and discussion and helps students see that these things are not simple.

Simple examples:
- One suggestion is …
- Another possible explanation is …
- It was probably …
- Perhaps, this was …
- It appears that …
- The evidence suggests that …
- Most experts agree that …
- Research has proved …

84 TRANSFORMING LEARNING ACROSS THE CURRICULUM

Over time, build up a wider range of such signals. Model and encourage their use, as appropriate, and create sorting games so that the students understand the difference between *tentative*, *likely* and *definite* information:

- This might have been part of …
- … that may have served as …
- According to …
- … provides the most extended evidence …
- Perhaps this was carried out by …
- This has been shown to be …
- They were experts at …
- This is thought to be …
- It was possibly destroyed …
- It was set up to commemorate …
- It is now clear that …
- Evidence has been found to suggest …
- Convincing evidence has now been found to show that …
- An alternative viewpoint is …
- According to an inscription found at …
- This was probably modelled on …
- This may be related to …
- … which are thought to be …
- … is claimed to belong to … It is more probable, however, that …
- Many scholars have identified the statue as …
- The site from where it is extracted is still unknown.

Cold to hot coherence in 15 minutes

- To improve the level of written literacy in a DT Year 9 lesson
- To build the pupil's confidence of writing longer pieces of work

Terry Wilkes, when Head of Design and Technology at Slough and Eton, devised a cunning cold-to-hot-in-fifteen-minutes activity focusing on students using the proper linking terms to make the text flow. You can see him explaining this on **video clip 27**. The objective of this part of the lesson is pictured above.

You will see that one pupil wrote the text pictured below (typed out to help you read it) as their cold task response to this question:

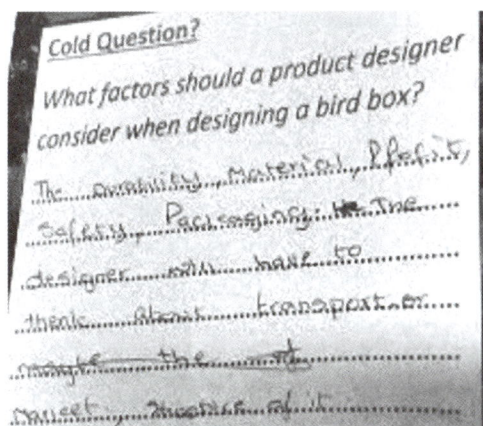

What factors should a product designer consider when designing a bird box?

The durability, material, Pfrofit, Safey, Packaging.

The designer will have to think about transport or market, structure of it.

This is a classic example of a student basically knowing what to include but having no idea about how to express it and, as Terry points out, the student knows he's no good at writing things down but wants to get better.

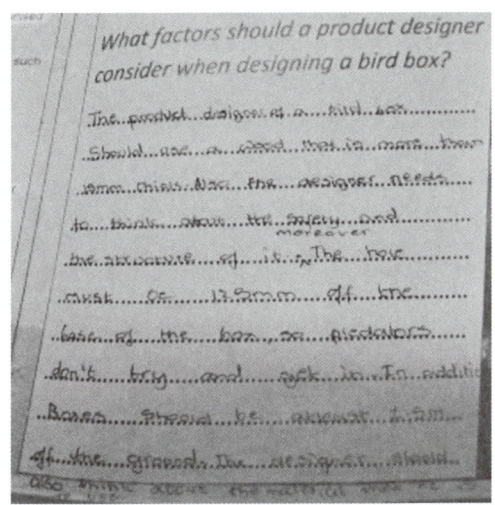

The teacher then provided the class with several paragraphs of *model* text from the BBC nature website about how to make bird boxes for the students to highlight key words, connecting phrases and user and manufacturer needs. As a result, 15 minutes later, the same pupil wrote this (see image to the left). Again it has been typed out because the quality of the screen grab is poor.

The product designer of a bird box should use a wood that is more than 15mm thick. Also the designer needs to think about the safety and the structure of it. Moreover the hole must be 125mm off the base of the box, so predators don't try and get in. In addition Boxes should be at east 1.5m off the ground. The designer should also think about the material that he is going to use.

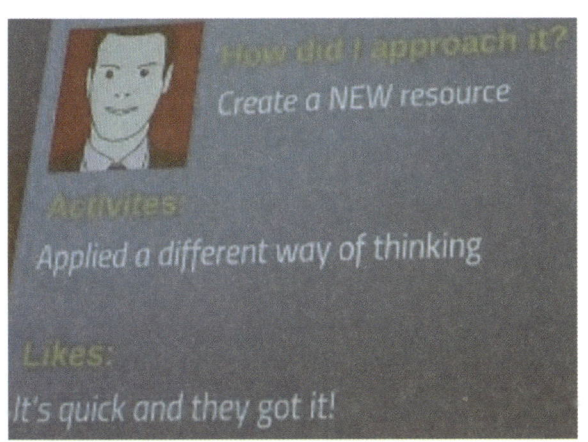

As you can see, the text is not yet perfect, but it is a great improvement on the cold task. Terry comments on how pleased the student was with the improvement and how much he laughed at his first effort. Importantly, this would give the student confidence when facing his next writing task. Terry's opening slide said: "Likes: it's quick and they got it." In a subject with as little teaching time as design and technology, this is important. And, as he points out, this was achieved through applying a different way of thinking.

The process leads to coherence

It all comes together to make a big difference as these three images of a

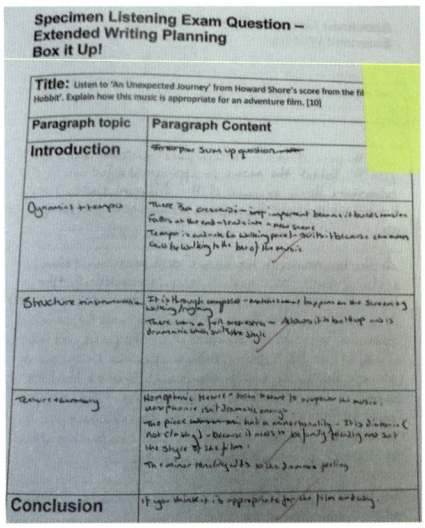
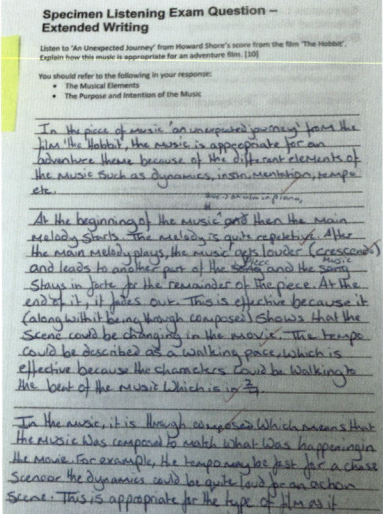
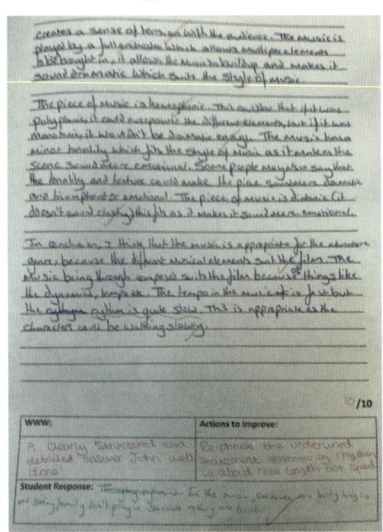

student's work in music at John of Gaunt show. Understanding structure through boxing up has helped him organise his points logically into *dynamics & tempo*, *structure & instrumentation*, and *texture & harmony*. He understands the role of sentence signposts that connect the text together making it coherent along with useful generic phrasing, for example, *At the beginning of …, it is through composed, which means that … This is effective because* … The process has helped this student write coherently using the technical language of music well. The marking process is also simple and effective: praise followed by something to improve – a statement near the end has been underlined because *rhythm* has been used as if it refers to speed instead of note length, a technical point that I, as a non-music specialist, would probably have missed. The student's immediate task when getting his work back is to rephrase it. The whole process builds towards effective writing.

Chapter 6: Co-constructing understanding

This chapter contains examples from subjects ranging from English, history and science to philosophy and accounting, illustrating the power of co-constructing learning through asking focused open-ended questions for the students to discuss. Not only does this lead to better results, but it also strengthens reading skills and leads to more interest and engagement with the work, a beam of light in our exam-obsessed times.

Pie Corbett recounts how he once saw a sad-looking, seven-year-old girl standing in front of her class's board of *I can* statements. The problem was *she couldn't*. She stared at the list and somewhat mournfully stated that she couldn't read them. She then pointed to the *I can* statement relating to similes and said, "I know what they are, but I can't do one." Her school was on the cusp of adopting the Talk for Writing approach.

A few years later, by chance, the girl was part of a short-burst, shared-writing session with Pie, focusing on a clock face. Pie had begun the sentence with: *It's smug face grins, mocking ...* Here he paused and asked the class, "What will the clock mock?" A girl suggested, "Mortals," in a somewhat tentative way. Her contribution is jaw-droppingly perceptive, as well as fitting both the menacing mood of the description and adding a touch of alliteration. Pie did not let this show on his face, since valuing all contributions is key to encouraging all the pupils to contribute, but inside he was cheering, even more so because he recognised who the girl was. And, of course, he chose her idea to add to the writing on the flip chart. You can watch this happening on **video clip 13**.

So, what had happened in between the two events to help the child make so much progress? Through Talk for Writing, she would have been bathed in a love of reading; she would have imitated model text internalising how stories and non-fiction work. She would have gained confidence in her ability to tell such stories herself and to write in a similar way by co-constructing how they were structured and the ingredients that made them effective. She would have been involved in booktalk (**see online handouts**) with the class discussing together the meaning of a text with the teacher acting as facilitator (see **page 125** plus online **Handouts 8 & 9**). She would no longer have been oppressed by a long list of success criteria that she didn't understand, but rather would have taken part in constructing the *what works* list herself, as a flexible writing toolkit that she could choose from when she wrote and when she commented on the writing of others.

Co-constructing understanding is key to effective learning. How to teach an understanding of structure through co-constructing boxing up text, so that students can box up a plan for any writing task, is explained on **pages 17 & 23**. Similarly, how to help students deconstruct the key features of any text they are writing through co-constructing toolkits and reflecting on how the text that they have analysed differs from generic writing toolkits is explained on **pages 25-27**.

Here are examples ranging from sorting activities to more extended work illustrating the power of co-construction, including dialogic talk in action.

1. Co-constructing understanding through reconstructing sheets of information (science)

Exam command terms activity (sorting activity – note: text below is muddled up)

Command word	Explanation of its meaning (in context of science exams)	Example answer to illustrate what the command requires
Compare	**Recount facts, events or a process in an accurate way (explain what happened).** For example, an experiment you have done. You may need to give an account of what something looked like, or what happened, e.g. a trend in some data.	• This trial involved large numbers so that would have given valid results. It was also a good trial of the general population because if poor uneducated women could make it work it would be reliable. However, the trial was not very ethical by today's standards because we don't know that the women gave informed consent, and they were not told it was experimental or that there could be side effects. The trial was not well designed as there was no placebo control group and they did not do pre-trials to find the best dose and check for side effects. I believe that this was an unethical trial.
Describe	**Describe (explain) the similarities and/or differences between things.** Don't just write about one.	• The particles might be small enough to pass through the skin and they might be toxic inside the body.
Evaluate	Apply your knowledge and under-standing to a new situation putting forward an idea tentatively, based on scientific knowledge and/or principles, rather than stating a proved fact.	• Generating electricity for an immersion heater burns fossil fuels, which releases carbon dioxide into the atmosphere but solar energy doesn't release any extra carbon dioxide. Solar energy is a renewable energy source, which also means that we are conserving fossil fuels which are in danger of running out. Solar energy does have disadvantages because it needs the daylight and some countries don't have enough hours of sunlight, like Scotland in the winter. This means there will be times when not enough hot water is available for the household, whereas an immersion heater can supply hot water all of the time.
Suggest	Use the information supplied (or your own knowledge and understanding) to explain the evidence for and against and draw conclusions. **This goes further than "compare".**	• In the beginning, dust particles and gases are pulled together by the force of gravity. As the atoms of hydrogen gas are forced together, the nuclei collide and nuclear fusion begins. The star becomes stable as the forces acting inwards and the forces acting outwards are balanced. Eventually it runs out of hydrogen so the star starts to cool and becomes a red giant. Then it starts to shrink under its own gravity and, as the material comes closer together, the temperature rises and the star glows much brighter as a white dwarf.

CO-CONSTRUCTING UNDERSTANDING 89

The simple example I often give on training days to illustrate the power of co-constructing understanding is to ask the teachers to reconstruct a cut-up, A4 sheet of paper containing key information about science command terms. The version pictured here contains all the text but not in the right order. The text is based on material from AQA, so it uses their definitions. The aim is to link the command term to its definition and to the example text that illustrates it. It sounds simple but, in reality, sometimes around half the groups of teachers working on it don't get it right, even though they are trying hard, because the word *describe* is used at the beginning of the definition of a different command term. Confusing? That's exactly what command terms are. See **page 67** for a demonstration of this looking at the 15 command terms from geography.

The main point is for the students to work out what fits with what for themselves through discussion. In this way, they will learn something. If you just gave them the sheet, they would probably learn nothing because it would remain meaningless to them.

Quick tip: For any text/process sorting activity, remember to muddle the text up on screen before you print it off and cut it up. In this way, you can't reconstruct the sheet like a puzzle just by using the cut marks or the size of the text boxes; you have to apply logic and understanding.

2. Co-constructing understanding in accountancy A-level

Marissa Bow, Head of Business Studies at Slough and Eton, told me that TfW had "even transformed accountancy". Text mapping had made the subject more engaging, boxing up had helped students structure their work and washing lines had helped to reinforce learning. But, most importantly, it was co-constructing learning that had transformed the students' ability to understand the more complex aspects of the subject (see **video clips 3 & 28**).

Traditionally, the students scored lower marks in the theoretical aspects of the exam. Following TfW training, she devised a number of co-constructing understanding activities to help the students engage more in the theoretical aspects of accountancy.

For example, to help the students assess their progress and know *what = good*, she devised this activity. For their cold task, each student answered a control accounts question (these were the ones they had the most difficulty with). Their scores were red/amber/green-rated with 6 students scoring green, 6 amber and 11 red, having scored less than half marks. She then:

- divided students into pairs
- gave out the mark scheme so they could mark each other's work
- handed each pair the moderator's report on the question
- asked them to box up the text into a table with what they understood the moderator wanted from the question
- asked them to discuss their findings in pairs and create a text table that they both agreed on.

In this way, they drew up an analysis identifying:
- what most students did well
- what they received the most marks for
- what the moderator identified as problematic
- why this was an issue
- where the moderators had awarded marks for good practice
- what their strengths were
- what they had done wrong and what they should do differently.

The students identified that they had to:
- know the format of the account
- label and date all adjustments.

They recognised that:
- marks were given for balancing the account (even if the balance was wrong)
- calculations should be shown in brackets in order to achieve part-marks
- marks were deducted for abbreviations.

All the students were then given another question to tackle with more complex adjustments. They had to do the question individually, using their newly acquired knowledge of the moderator's report. As a result, when their scores were RAG rated, no students were in the red category and only one in amber; 11 students scored full marks. Co-constructing understanding works.

The students had focused on accounting standards which, as Marissa explains, can be quite difficult because there's a lot of very complex vocabulary and rules that are difficult to apply. The activity she devised involved matching up information, boxing up and talking the text to help the students develop a real understanding of the topic. On the video, the students explain what they did and the difference it made.

Co-constructing understanding through focused discussion is also at the heart of embedding understanding of how to solve a range of maths problems as explained on **pages 189–194**.

3. Using focused discussion cards to transform understanding (history)

In July 2019, I received this message from Chris Davies, Head of History and enthusiastic member of Milford Haven Secondary School's TfW project:

> "Just an update report: my department and I created these cards that pupils could flip over and discuss sources with. We tried them out straight away with Year 7 before a *hot task* on sources and we have been blown away by the level of independence shown by pupils after completing the card task and annotating the sources. I have attached the cards which we laminated and placed into envelopes. Pupils have been using terms such as, *the source clearly infers that* and *However, this is a retrospective view.*"

CO-CONSTRUCTING UNDERSTANDING 91

KS3 history source key questions

Is the view VALID? Does it back up what we know?	Who wrote the source? Is the author biased in any way?
How might their job AND/OR religion affect the interpretation?	What does the source say about the topic? [What's the **gist**?]
What is their nationality? How might this affect their view?	What is the purpose of the source? What is the author trying to do? Why?
What is the title of the book? How does this affect their view?	What is the author's background? How does this affect their view?
When was the source produced? Is it a long time after? At the time? How may this affect their view?	Who wrote the source? What would you predict would be their interpretation? [Do they say what you expect them to say?]
Is the author VALID? Can we trust them? Why? Why not?	From what location was the author writing? How may this affect their view?
When was the source produced? Has the author had a long time to research? Is the work up to date or outdated now?	Where might the author have got their information from? What information might they have used to come to this view?

You can see the potential of relatively simple co-constructed group activities like this which led the students into interrogating and understanding the significance of the text effectively. They gained confidence by having the opportunity to discuss sources assisted by these cards which, in turn, has helped them ask the right questions and developed their understanding. This was followed up by an activity where phrases like *The source clearly infers that* were emphasised, discussed and flip-charted, which helped the students to formulate their responses clearly as this example of a student's work shows. Look at the phrases that the student has magpied:

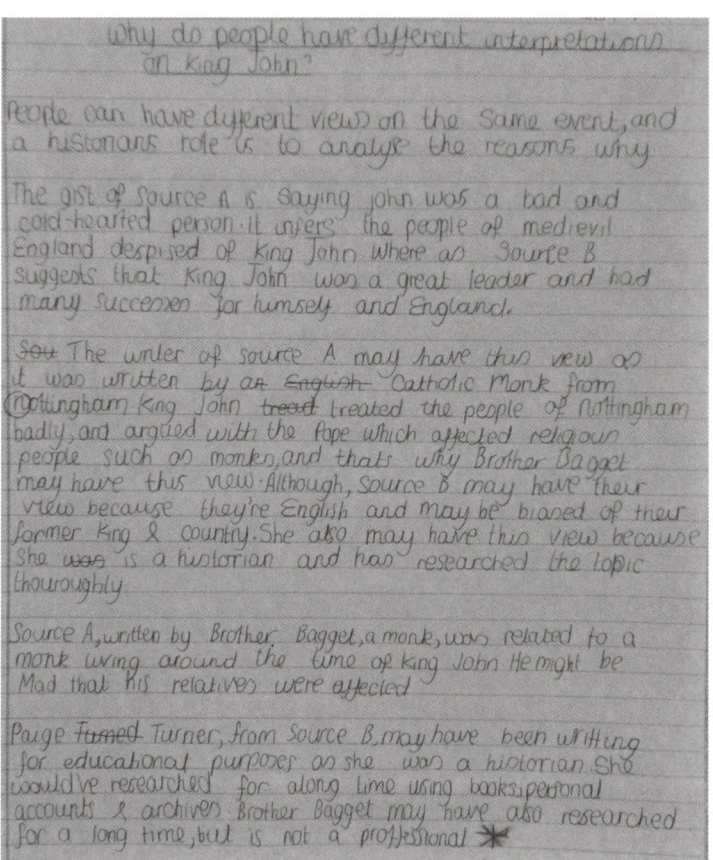

- The gist of source A …
- It infers …
- Source B suggests
- The writer of source A may have this view as it was …
- Although source B may have their view because
- She also may have this view because …
- … from source B, …

4. Co-constructing understanding through sorting key information and then talking the text (history)

A powerful way of helping students to structure and express discursive essays is to use sorting activities combined with boxing up, text mapping key points and talking the text. This helps them learn how to:

- select what information to use to meet the demands of the question
- structure that information appropriately
- link the information effectively
- express points and related evidence and comment clearly.

This technique is illustrated below by adapting Christine Counsell's excellent Fire of London activity*.

> *(Counsell first published these materials in the following pamphlet: Counsell, C. (1997) Analytical and Discursive Writing in History at KeyStage 3, London: Historical Association. Counsell's work has focused on how to integrate oral and written work to secure a strong relationship between thinking and knowledge-building within a disciplinary framework. The following publication sets out the most recent version of the resources, and models ways of using them in practice to secure historical argument: Counsell, C. (2011) 'Generating historical argument about causation in the history classroom: exploring practical teaching approaches', in Ghusayni, R., Karami, R., & Akar, B. (Eds.). (2012) Learning and teaching history: Lessons from and for Lebanon: Proceedings of the Third Conference on Education, Lebanese Association for Education Studies, 25-26 March 2011. Beirut: Arab Cultural Center.)

This approach can be easily adapted to meet the needs of any subject that requires discursive writing (as illustrated by the philosophy example **on page 103** which was inspired by this). The *Fire of London* example begins at the point where the topic has been thoroughly taught and you are now at the stage when you want the students to answer a discursive question. The class will already be familiar with the typical structure of history essays through boxing up model text on other topics. They will also have analysed various model texts, so they are aware of the typical language patterns that make up history text including the linking phrases that make it coherent. But different questions require different structures and the students have to be able to adapt their knowledge of the topic to the question asked: this is where sorting activities like *The Fire of London* are so powerful.

Obviously, such activities take up time but, as a result, the students will engage with the subject much more and will build up their analytical skills independently. If your subject is taught in KS3, ideally this approach could be developed before the end of Year 9 so that students begin Year 10 with these skills in place. But, as the A-level philosophy example later in this chapter illustrates, students will gain from these sort of co-constructing learning activities throughout their education, it's just that the material being co-constructed gets harder.

CO-CONSTRUCTING UNDERSTANDING 93

Co-constructing understanding of how to write coherent answers to discursive questions

- Stage 1. Analyse question so know what trying to do
- Stage 2. Select & sort info to match requirements of question
- Stage 3. Turn headings into sentences that intro the info
- Stage 4. Turn main points into icons and place them in order
- Stage 5. Talk the text to decide on logical order
- Stage 6. Work out an effective introduction
- Stage 7. Shared writing
- Stage 8. Co-constructing the toolkit for discursive writing
- Stage 9. Apply what have learnt: write own version and work in pairs to improve work
  (Teacher marks work)
- Stage 10. Embed learning & improve work
  (Teacher assesses next steps)

In this example, the students (working in pairs to maximise discussion opportunities) follow the 10 stages pictured here in order to help them understand the thought processes you go through to answer discursive questions like: "Why did the Great Fire of London get out of control and destroy so much of London?"

Stage 1. Analyse the question

First, analyse the question:
Why did the Great Fire of London get out of control and destroy so much of London?

1.	What's the question asking me? (highlight key words)
2.	What are the pitfalls to avoid?

It's essential that students get in the habit of carefully analysing the question they are being asked to answer. Echo reading questions with students (see **page 21**) should help them with this. Highlighting key words in the sentence and recognising pitfalls supports getting going in the right direction. So, the key word to highlight here is **why**; the pitfall is not answering the question but rambling on about what happened. This is where stage 2 comes in handy.

Stage 2: Select and sort information to match question requirements

Selecting relevant information is crucial. If faced with questions we don't really know how to answer, most of us fall back on some form of waffly recount, telling everything we know about the topic in an unstructured way. Professor David Wray graphically refers to this as, "the bed-to-bed style of writing".

94 TRANSFORMING LEARNING ACROSS THE CURRICULUM

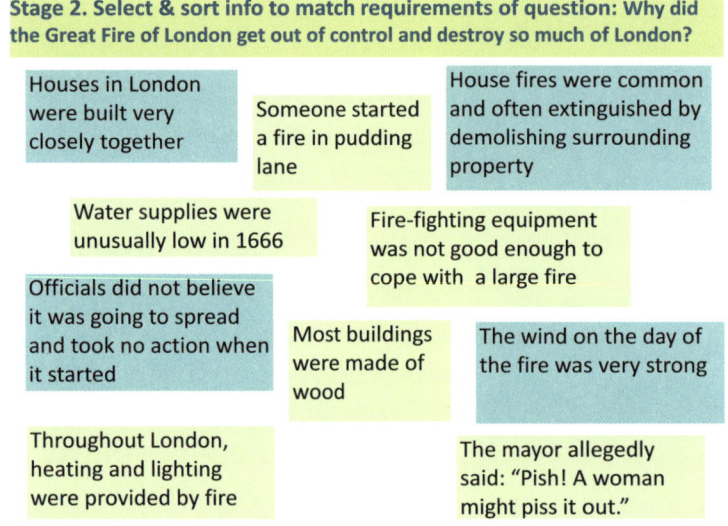

To help students avoid this trap, present each pair with some key information about the topic on cards (as illustrated here), including at least one piece of information that is relevant to the topic but not to the question. Then ask the pairs to select which of the statements is the **least relevant** to the question. Next, ask them to discuss their conclusion with another pair. Hopefully, groups will have selected *Someone started a fire in Pudding Lane*. Discuss why this is not relevant to the question and how it encourages you to recount everything you know about the fire rather than focus on the question asked.

Stage 2a. Identifying short- and long-term causes

Now ask the students to clump the remaining statements into short-term and long-term causes. Long- and short-term causes are a key concept in history. This will be central to their understanding of how to answer the question since the long-term causes are just that: they will have been around for a long time. So, ask the class to think up arguments for and against why each short-term cause could be the deciding factor and discuss these with another pair. Get groups to feedback their conclusions. If they are already very familiar with these concepts, understanding can be checked before quickly moving on; if not, time needs to be spent establishing this central understanding.

Stage 2b. Clumping the information into key points

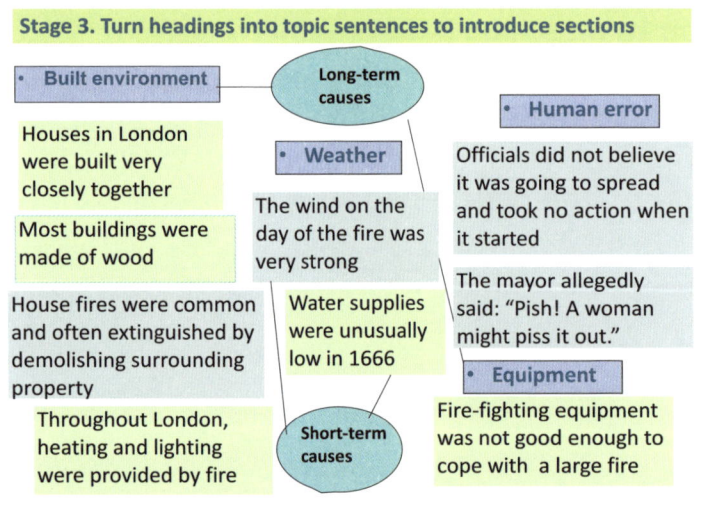

Now ask the students in pairs to clump the information into key points and give each clump a heading. Once this has been done, ask them to compare their headings with another pair. Get feedback from the groups and establish the most common key clumps – they will probably look like the clumps illustrated here. (When teaching an activity like this, by walking round the room you will know what clumps the groups are coming up with. If there are ones that are different from what you have selected but perfectly logical, tell those students they can continue the activity with their choices.) But it probably works best, once the students have

CO-CONSTRUCTING UNDERSTANDING 95

worked out their own clumps, to demonstrate the next stage using clumps on pre-prepared slides like the ones here. If several different ways of clumping the information are introduced when it is first presented, this will probably just cause confusion.

Stage 3. Turning headings into topic sentences

Now ask the pairs to turn their heading about the buildings into a good topic sentence that could introduce this point in the essay – providing pupils with whiteboards for this activity helps the quality of the feedback. Being able to write effective topic sentences is key to good writing. You have to know the point you are trying to make and devise a sentence that introduces it clearly. The more skilled the students become at this, the more coherent their writing will be; they need to have this skill modelled for them and to practise it.

You might want to take the first key point, the *Built environment* and model for them how to write a sentence that would introduce this paragraph. For example,

> *"A key factor in the spread of the fire was that most of the houses in London in 1666 were made of wood which was a serious fire hazard."*

Discuss with the class how the paragraph could then be built up from this point by evidence and comment to make a strong paragraph. The students could then, in pairs, draft a topic sentence to introduce why the weather conditions were key and several pairs could feedback their ideas so that the class becomes more confident about how to write the topic sentence that introduces a point clearly.

Stage 4. Using icons to decide the order of your key points and rehearsing your text orally

The order in which you organise your key points is central to building up a coherent argument. We have probably all experienced that feeling in an exam of only finally realising how to answer a question when you have finished answering it, but then there is no time to start again. The more we can encourage students to plan their ideas before they launch into writing, the more they will be able to write a coherent, discursive argument. We need to train them in boxing up their points before they start writing. Boxing up text that is in chronological order is easy – that's why recount is so popular – but, for discursive writing, the writer has to select the information they want to include and then decide on the most effective order in which to present it. One of the best ways of deciding on the key order of points is to use symbols to represent each key point and then jot them down in your boxed-up plan in the order that you want to use them.

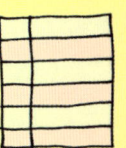

For this activity, provide each student with as many small bits of paper as there are headings and ask them to write an icon for each heading on a separate bit of paper. Then ask them to box up their headings in order, as illustrated here. It's important that, at this stage in the activity, everyone does this themselves, rather than working in pairs, as you only learn this by doing it yourself.

In this example, the writer has chosen to begin with the image for the built environment and end with the wind as the short-term killer factor. This, in effect, is their boxed-up plan. They could then jot down the key points they want to make in each section as symbols to help them remember what to say. Give them a short time to think in silence about what they are going to say.

Stage 5. Talk the text and finalise logical order

Talking the text before you try to write it is really useful as it helps you to formulate your ideas and arguments and polish them before you add in the further challenge of actually writing them down. Talking the text will help students to write with confidence as they will have clarified their ideas. It gets rid of the *I don't know how to start* syndrome.

Then model for the students how to use the images to help you present the arguments orally in a coherent, logical order. Next, ask them to take it in turns to talk their presentation to their partners as if they were a visiting expert come to tell everyone why the Great Fire of London destroyed so much of London. The pairs can then discuss how the presentations could be improved. They might find that they want to alter the order in which they presented their key points to help their argument to flow logically. This is a good point to discuss. Ask any students who did change the order to explain why they changed it to the whole class. (I had a boxed-up plan when I started writing this book – but I changed the order several times when I actually came to write it.)

You may want to select some budding professors to stand up and present to the whole class. This will provide an excellent opportunity for students to magpie goods ideas, words and phrases which they can then use in their own work.

A challenging activity, if you want to stretch the students further, is to encourage them to be tentative when presenting their points. After all, this is history. They need to make it clear if the information they are presenting can be proved or whether it is just an interpretation of the facts. Model for them a range of tentative phrases, for example, "It would appear that", "It is probable that", "One possible explanation is that", etc, and then ask the students to present their ideas again but this time more tentatively. For more detailed work on being tentative see **pages 82–84**.

In any situation where students have to make oral presentations, ban anything being written down and only allow them to have symbols for the key points. If it's written down, they will just read it out. Only having the symbols to remind you of the order and any key points, frees up your mind to be able to express what you are trying to say and leads to coherence. Try it – it works. This will not only greatly improve the quality of their presentation but also of any writing that follows.

Stage 6: Writing effective introductions

Now is the moment to focus on how to write a powerful introduction because it illustrates the fact that you can't decide on your introduction until you have some idea about how you want to answer the question. In effect, you have to plan the middle before you can plan the introduction. Now the students have established how they want to answer the question, use the *what = good?* technique for writing powerful paragraphs.

Which introduction is best given the question?

A. House fires in 17th century London were an everyday occurrence. The most logical reason why the Great Fire of London turned into such a disaster is that it was inevitable and just waiting for the right weather conditions to happen.	B. To answer the question why did the Great Fire of London get out of control and destroy so much of London I will start by looking at the long-term causes and then I will look at the short-term causes and then draw a conclusion.
C. The Fire of London started in Pudding Lane and spread in the most terrifying way so that just two days later most of London was destroyed.	D. Have you ever wondered why the Great Fire of London got out of control and destroyed so much of London?

Ask the students in pairs to

- Select which of the 4 introductions is the best given the question
- Establish what key ingredients help make it good
- Decide what lets the other versions down.

Once they have done this, ask them to check their findings with another pair and then get the groups to feedback on their how-to-write-a-good-introduction toolkit and build up a class version which may end up looking something like the one below. It is important that the class is involved in this process rather than just being given the toolkit. If they are just presented with the criteria, they will not have understood or internalised them and, therefore, are not liable to be able to apply them. Be aware that different subjects have different rules for what makes a good introduction – see the sorting activity of a model text for RE (**pages 47–48**) as an example of this, as the introduction reads like a conclusion to the eye of an English teacher. Different subjects have different expectations. Some want no introduction at all but just a clear topic sentence introducing the opening point. If introductions are important within your subject, then time will need to be spent on establishing *what = good* for your type of introduction.

The discursive introduction writing toolkit
Do
- analyse the question & work out the key points
- introduce the response clearly
- check the intro flows & addresses the question asked.

Don't
- try to put all points into the introduction
- bore audience by repeating question and saying how going to answer it
- just recount everything you know about the topic.

Then ask the students to use this toolkit to write their own introduction. Once they have completed their work, ask them to share their introduction with a partner so that they can discuss whether they have followed the class's instructions for writing good introductions. Allow time for them to read their work through and revise their work in the light of the discussions. Again, when you mark the work, check to see if they are all applying the ingredients of the toolkit appropriately and begin the next lesson with activities to secure these features, allowing time for the students to remedy errors when the work is handed back so the students are not only aware of the steps they need to take to improve their work but have had a go at putting them into practice. If this is not done, then all that time spent marking will have been wasted.

Stage 7. Using shared writing to show them how to do it

The teacher can now use the best of the students' introductions and the earlier presentations as a basis to model shared writing as the class should now be full of ideas about how to write this essay. If this is the first time the class has attempted this sort of writing, then you will need to model how to write the whole essay, so they understand how important it is to make ideas flow. If they have done this sort of work before, just focus on any aspects that have been causing the most difficulty. It may be that some of the class can be left to get on with writing their own version independently while those having difficulty could be grouped for the shared-writing session.

Display your boxed-up icons so they can see your planning and then, with the help of the group, craft the answer to the question involving the students with phrases like:
- *Which do you think would work best?*
- *Let's just read that and see how it sounds.*
- *We've got ... what else do we need? What could follow? You tell me.*
- *Which bits don't seem to fit?*
- *What would make it flow better?*

For more examples of useful phrases to use for shared writing, see **Handout 3 online.**

CO-CONSTRUCTING UNDERSTANDING

Throughout the process, the teacher would regularly read the writing out to the class so they can hear it and decide if it works. All the time, the teacher would model what a good writer does. This may include slightly moving away from your plan as often, in the actual process of writing, you refine your initial thoughts. You will end up with a shared writing example somewhat like the one below which can then be displayed, if necessary, when the students are writing their own essay to support them. See **Handout 4: The art of shared writing.**

Why did the Great Fire of London get out of control and destroy so much of London?

> House fires in 17th century London were an everyday occurrence. Perhaps the reason why the Great Fire of London turned into such a disaster is that it was inevitable and just waiting for the right weather conditions to happen.
>
> A key long-term cause of the fire was that, in 1666, London was a mass of narrow streets lined by closely packed wooden houses heated by fire. In such circumstances, it was inevitable that fire would often break out and, when it did, it would spread rapidly from house to house.
>
> Because firefighting equipment was not very effective, the main method of preventing the fires from getting out of control was demolishing neighbouring buildings to stop the fire from taking hold. Such preventative action could, perhaps, have limited the fire to a few buildings but the mayor rejected such action allegedly saying, "Pish, a woman might piss it out!" One probable explanation for what, in hindsight, appears to be serious human error, is the fact that the authorities would have to recompense property owners whose buildings were demolished and so the powers that be were often reluctant to select this solution. This contributed to the conditions for the Great Fire.
>
> However, it would appear that the weather was the deciding factor. Unfortunately, when the fire broke out, the wind was very strong so it rapidly spread from street to street with the wind fanning the flames. To make matters worse, there had been much less rainfall than usual that year so water levels were low, which made accessing water to douse the flames more difficult. Significantly, the fire was not extinguished until the wind subsided some two days later.
>
> In conclusion, it would appear that at some point it was inevitable that London would burn to the ground because of the closeness of the wooden houses. Human error alone, although a contributory factor, is not liable to be the main cause as it is reasonable to assume that the officials behaved similarly when other fires occurred

> *There is, however, much evidence to suggest that it was the strong wind that happened to be blowing at that time that was the deciding factor.*

Throughout the shared writing process, ask a student to act as teaching assistant and jot down on a flip chart all the phrases that will be useful when the students write their own versions (the dot-dot-dot solution for words they are unsure how to spell makes this a perfectly feasible task – see **page 14**). The resultant flipcharts can then be displayed as posters to support the class when they are writing. Below, some possible useful phrases that might have arisen from the shared writing have been divided into sentence signposts linking the text, other useful generic phrases, and tentative signposts. These posters can obviously be added to as more useful phrases emerge from discursive text including from the best of the students' work.

Poster A: Useful sentence starters and signposts

- **A key long-term cause of**
- **In such circumstances, it was inevitable**
- **because**
- **However,**
- **The main reason**
- **The main method of**
- **Such preventative action**
- **To make matters worse,**
- **It is therefore reasonable to conclude**

Poster B: Useful generic phrases

- an everyday occurrence
- has become known as
- just waiting for the right conditions to happen
- such destruction was inevitable
- helped create the conditions for
- was bound to happen
- the fact that
- the deciding factor
- helped create the conditions for

Poster C: Useful tentative sentence starters and phrases
- **Perhaps** the explanation for why
- **could perhaps** have
- One **probable** explanation
- **allegedly** saying
- It is worth **considering**
- for what, in hindsight, **appears** to be
- **probably** would not have
- It would **appear** that
- There is much evidence to **suggest** that

Stage 8. Co-constructing the toolkit for discursive writing

The good thing about having a whole-school approach to writing toolkits (see **page 26**) is that rather than starting from scratch, the students only have to consider if the writing they have just been involved in differs from the generic toolkit below. (They will be familiar with this because they will have been co-constructed in English and referred to in other areas). As they look through the ingredients, they will see that it is a very good fit. A few points will need amending, as illustrated in red below. It will be useful for the class to identify examples of the features from the shared writing, as exemplified here.

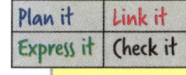

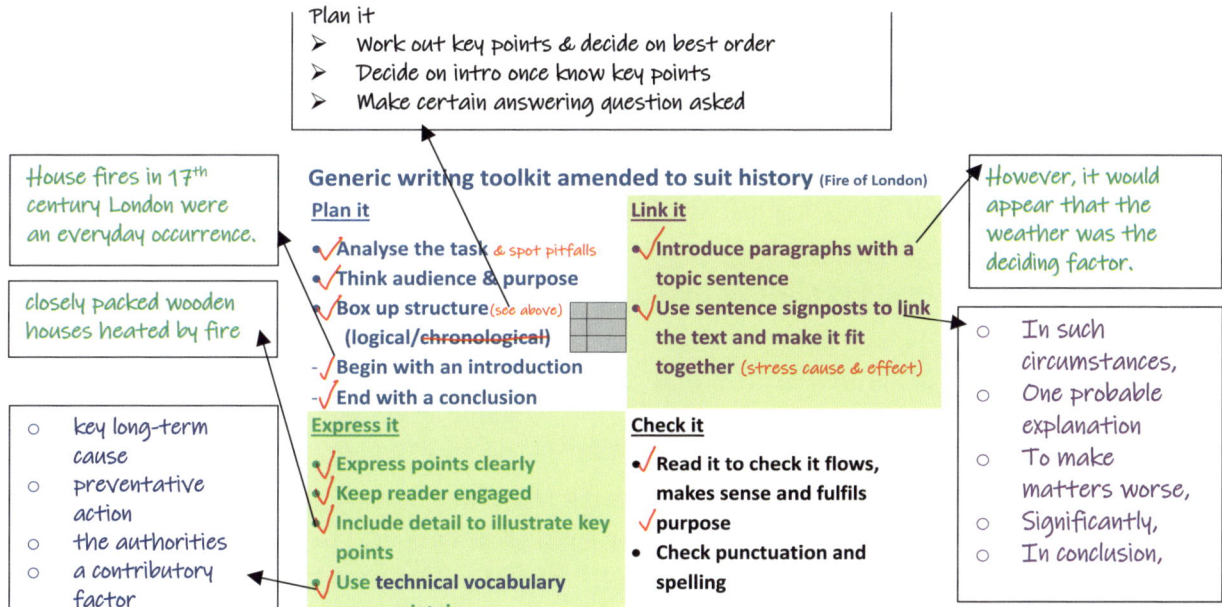

Stage 9. Write own version and work in pairs to improve your work

Each student then writes their own answer to the question, using their boxed-up points plus the annotated toolkit, the shared writing and the related phrase bank posters to help them. Once they have finished their first draft, they should read it through, correcting and improving it where necessary. Hopefully the shared writing process will have illustrated that good writers amend their work.

The whole point of teaching is to make yourself redundant, so the students have the skills to do the work without you. If the students become skilled at judging what works, then they will be able to self-correct their own work. So, it is useful at this stage for the students to share what they have written and discuss how to improve it together, with each writer making any changes that they choose to make.

When the teacher marks the work, apart from noting any deficiencies in the class's understanding of the particular issue being discussed, they can establish, using the toolkit as a useful guide, what needs to be focused on next to help the students answer this type of question. When the work is handed back is the best time to do work on rectifying any misunderstandings. If time is not set aside for this, again what was the point of doing all the marking?

Stage 10. Consolidate learning

One good way of consolidating learning is to select the best of the essays written by the students and to display them using a visualiser. Read the essay out to the class (or echo read it) so they can hear how the text flows and then ask the students in pairs to act in teacher role and pretend they were explaining to a class why this work was good. Encourage them to use the toolkit to help them with the phrasing they need, modelling it as necessary. For example, they might use phrases like:

- Good topic sentences have been used to introduce each point, for example, …
- All the key points are ordered logically so the argument is coherent, beginning with … and ending with…
- The essay begins with an interesting, relevant introduction that hooks the reader.
- Each of the points is clearly explained and backed up with evidence, for example, …
- Each paragraph is introduced by a clear signpost to guide the reader, for example, …

Go around the class listening to the pairs as they act in teacher role and ask one or two budding teachers to present their explanations to the whole class. The more the students become used to talking about what makes writing effective, the more they will be able to help themselves make their own writing effective. This process helps develop their inner judgment about what works – the voice in the head that prompts you to recast what you have written. At the end of this activity, allow time for the students to amend their work so they immediately put into practice what they need to do to improve.

A good hot task for this work is to set a slightly different question (for example: *"The reason why the Great Fire of London destroyed so much of the city is that the houses were built very close together and made out of wood."* Do you agree

CO-CONSTRUCTING UNDERSTANDING 103

with this statement?) and see if the students can independently plan and write their answers using the skills they have just developed.

5. Co-constructing understanding of complex ideas in A-level philosophy and A-level psychology

It is interesting to see how the following section on philosophy shows how this sort of content-based co-constructing understanding activity can transform students' ability to understand complex topics and write about them coherently.

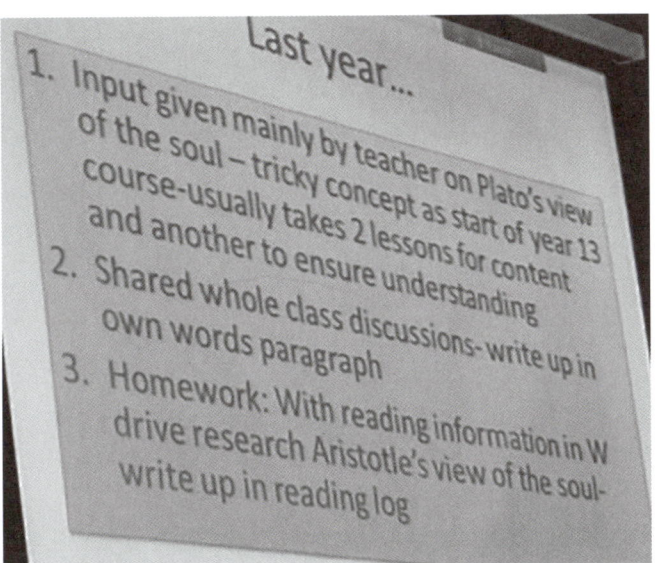

An A-level philosophy teacher, and member of the Rainham Girls' School Talk for Writing project, explained to the whole staff the difference using the TfW process had made to the quality of her students' work. She began her presentation by stating: "I thought it would be a good idea to show you what I did last year, which I actually thought was quite good at the time, and then show you what I achieved this year using Talk for Writing."

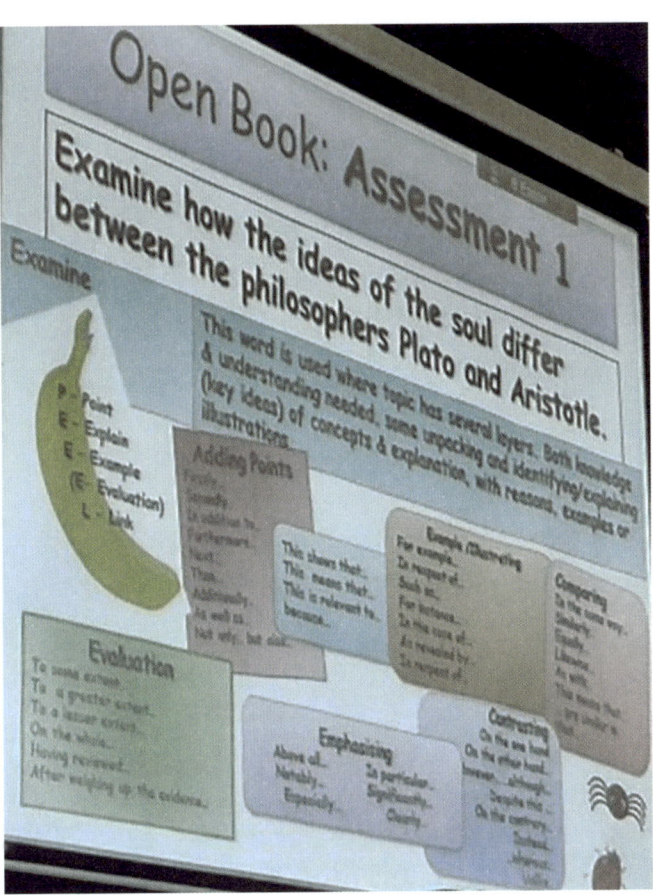

The topic she presented to bring out the difference was *philosophical ideas about the soul*, which required the students to be able to analyse and evaluate different philosophers' views on this issue. She then explained, as you can see in the first slide here, that the input on Plato's view of the soul in the previous year had mainly been from her. This was a difficult concept at the start of Year 13 and it usually took two lessons to explain the content and a third to try and ensure understanding. This was followed by whole-class discussions, plus students writing up a paragraph in their own words. Their homework was to access information in the school's drive and research Aristotle's view of the soul and then write that up in their reading log. The log included questions like this: *Aristotle's view of the soul: write key ideas and answer whether Aristotle was a dualist or a monist/materialist with examples to support your view.*

The work had included learning checks like reading through the last lesson's work, identifying key philosophical ideas and important vocabulary and then closing the book and testing yourself. This was followed by the *open-book assessment 1* pictured here. So, there was very little interaction; very little opportunity to engage in the learning process and co-construct understanding.

The difference using the TfW approach made

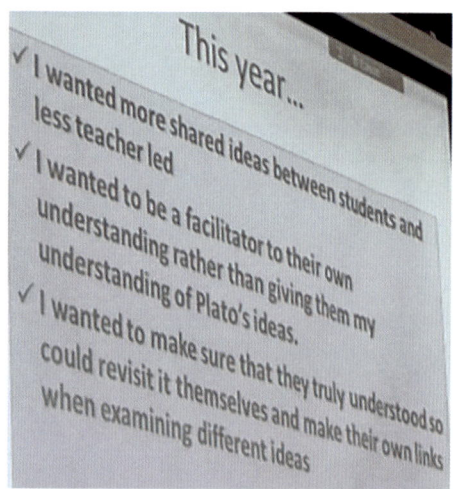

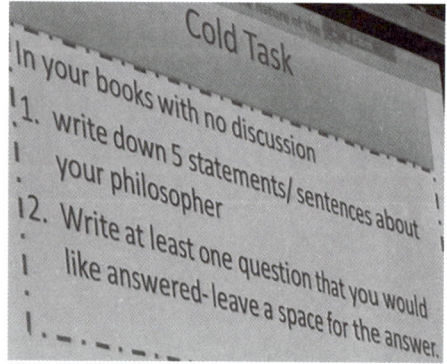

She then explained the difference it had made when she had adapted her teaching style using the TfW process with a particular emphasis on co-constructing learning. As you can see from the points on her slide, she put the focus on facilitating shared ideas rather than giving the students her personal interpretation of all the ideas, so they could truly understand the concepts being discussed and interrogate the ideas themselves. For example, students were asked to do paired research on Plato's or Aristotle's beliefs on the body and soul relationship. This was followed by a cold task. The activity selected is very interesting as it starts off in cold-task style but then develops into booktalk (**see page 125**) where students are invited to raise questions they would like discussed.

She then gave them a range of past exam questions to put their work in context and see why they needed to know such things.

For example:

1. Explain different ideas about the existence of the soul and its relationship with the body.
2. Examine differing ideas about the nature and existence of the soul.
3. "There are no reasonable grounds for belief in the existence of a soul." How far do you agree?
4. Analyse ideas about the soul that are found in both Plato and Aristotle.

This was followed by an understanding check where the students were divided into two groups – the Platos and the Aristotles. The Plato group then had to identify Plato's key ideas and explain them to the Aristotles, and vice versa. The groupings had been well selected so there was equal arguing power on both sides. This led to excellent discussion. Then, just to ensure full understanding, the Platos had to explain about Aristotle, and the Aristotles explain about Plato. This resulted in secure understanding. Moreover, the students were very fluent when explaining the ideas. And, of course, they were much more engaged in their work.

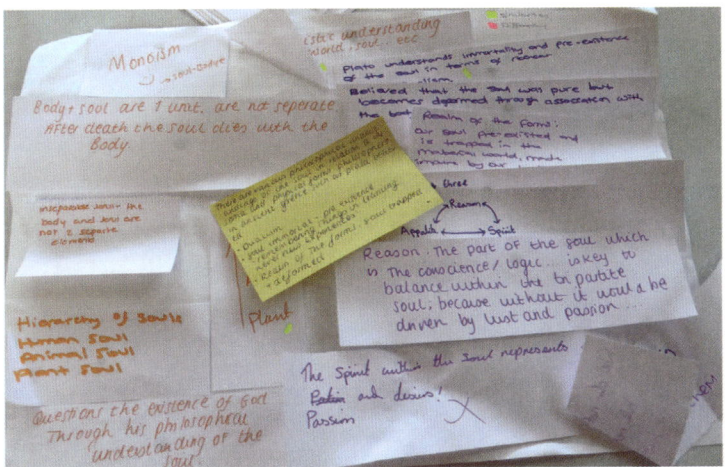

Next, she introduced an excellent activity where the students had to write down the key ideas of the two philosophers on little bits of paper using purple for Aristotle's ideas and orange for Plato's, as pictured here. Their understanding was then increased by being shown some key videos plus resource sheets on the topic. They magpied from these, adding to the points on the bits of paper and discussed the points moving from table to table, adapting their thinking as they went. They then looked back at the 4 questions above and reflected on how much more they knew now about how they might answer such questions.

The following lesson, the teacher focused on any key ideas that they had missed alongside explaining the more difficult ideas, addressing any misconceptions and consolidating the use of key words. All the time, the students were adding on more information on little bits of paper: orange for Plato; purple for Aristotle.

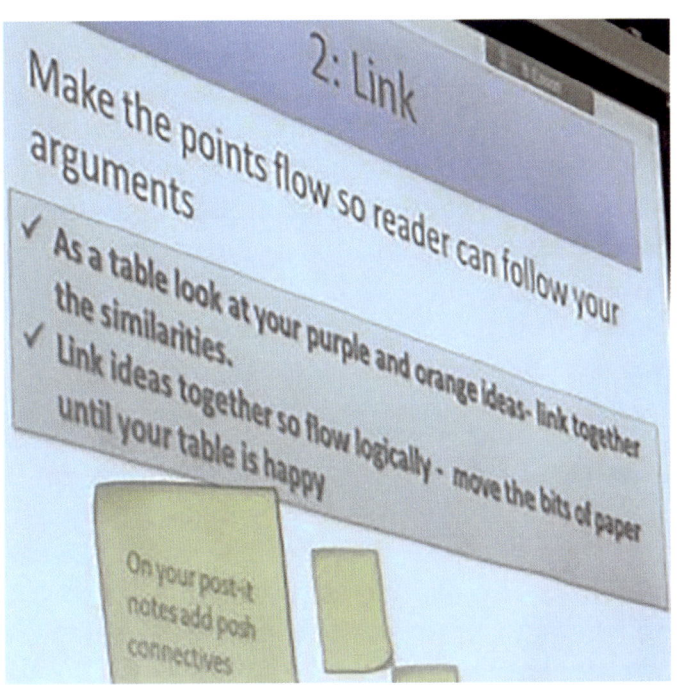

The class then had the task of working out how to answer one of the four questions. The teacher reminded them of the need to plan, link and express their work. First, they focused on planning their answer by deciding the best order in which to arrange all the key information they had recorded on the bits of paper. These were placed in boxed-up order on a sheet of A3 paper to plan and link their answer coherently, an echo of the Fire of London activity above. As you can see from the image of the screen, the groups then used Post-it notes to add the appropriate *posh connectives* that would link one point to another before moving on to consider how they were going to express it – having been reminded of the importance of following the key expression points from their toolkit. They then talked their ideas through to check that they flowed from point to point coherently. This prepared them for their hot task which was to answer exactly the same assessment as a similar group had answered a year earlier.

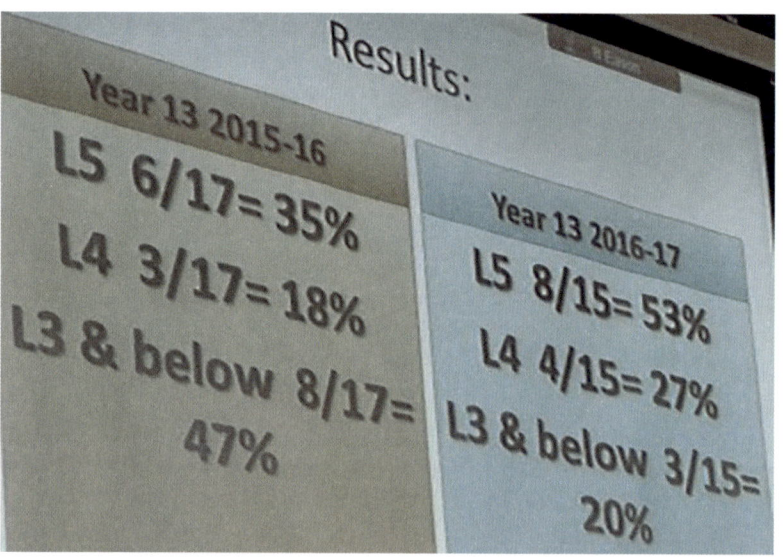

Look at the difference in the results. As you can see, those scoring the top level had increased from 35% to 53% while those performing at the lowest level had decreased from 47% to 20% – a very significant improvement, and the teacher felt they had got real secure understanding. Moreover, they had enjoyed the lessons much more.

Text mapping to support co-constructing understanding in A-level psychology

Video clip 29 is a fascinating explanation from Janine, who teaches psychology A-level at Beechwood School in Slough. You will see that she has combined text mapping of key concepts with co-constructing understanding of the psychodynamic approach.

6. Co-constructing thinking frames

In any discursive subject, co-constructing thinking frames can transform students' ability to understand complex ideas. These frames then support students in answering challenging questions. A thinking frame is just a grid with a series of headings selected to make you start to ask the right questions about whatever is being studied, as pictured below. The examples here suit English and could easily be adapted to suit the needs of drama. The whole approach can be adapted to suit discussion about any subject.

Which section	Key characters	Key events	Themes	Key stylistic techniques	Are they effective?	Writer's purpose & perspective	Key quotes

I first came across the essence of this idea when I took an A-level English class to some lectures at the Institute of Education in London many years ago. If I could remember the name of the speaker, I would attribute him. The idea was to use the grid to help students interrogate text and build understanding of the whole text. In this example, the focus is on author's purpose, this being the killer question at the heart of literature teaching. I gave it a go and developed it in my own way by putting the focus on co-constructing learning in a form of booktalk style (not that I'd heard of this at the time as Aidan Chambers' grand book that explains booktalk, *Tell Me,* hadn't been published then). It transformed the quality of the discussions, made lessons more engaging and gave students the confidence to deal with challenging text and challenging questions. This, in turn, led to much better essays being written and improved exam results, not least because the completed grids provided a marvellous way of condensing ideas for revising from. So, then I tried it with younger classes, and of course it worked a treat there too. Because the students could explain why the author may have made the choices they had made, meant they could comment effectively on any structure or style questions without reverting to mechanistic formula like PEEL (point; evidence; explanation; link).

The key ingredient is to use booktalk techniques (**see page 125**) to co-construct the thinking frames. So, with this frame the teacher might ask questions like:
- Tell me why you think the author chose to begin this novel/play with …
- Tell me why you think the first characters we meet are …
- Tell me what sort of imagery the writer has chosen to use …
    - Tell me why they might have chosen these images
    - Tell me whether you think it is effective and why.

As with all booktalk, the idea is to leave the discussion to the students so that they co-construct understanding. Your job is to facilitate the discussion by asking the right sort of open-ended questions and encouraging them to build on each other's ideas or challenge them. If a good point is made but seems to get lost, raise it again for further reflection.

I was teaching *Antony and Cleopatra* when I first experimented with this idea. I pointed out that most productions of the play miss out a lot of the little scenes, for example, where characters you never hear of again are gossiping about A &C in various parts of the Roman Empire. My opening question was this: *Did Shakespeare know what he was doing or was he having a bad day when he wrote the play?* I wanted them to justify, or not, all the scenes that he chose to include; the thinking frame was just the tool to do this with. We discussed whichever scene we were reading in booktalk style. Following the discussions, the students filled in the relevant section of the grid, completing their grids for homework. The next lesson, their ideas became a springboard for further discussion and then we decided what we wanted to put in our co-constructed grid. The slide here shows the very beginning of it.

Thinking frame for Antony & Cleopatra

Structure overview	Act & location	Key characters	Key events	Writer's dramatic purpose	Key quotes	Images	Themes
Sets scene	1.1 Egypt	Philo & Demetrius (only appearance) A & C & train	Philo intros A&C from Roman perspective: A = great general sunk to doting fool. Spurns messenger from Rome. Will never leave Egypt.	To intro A&C to audience from Roman perspective. Audience to get strong visual image of glory and decadence of A&C's lifestyle	"But this dotage of our general's … "Let Rome in Tiber melt …		
Intros dilemma	1.Ii Egypt	C's women & soothsayer. Enobarbus & A&C	Sexual gossip, punning etc. Then A hears news of wife's wars & determines to leave Egypt …	Series of clashing images contrast Egypt & Rome. Shows Antony in turmoil. Visually & thematically ever changing	"These strong Egyptian fetters …		

The transformation in the quality of the discussions is hard to recreate. Students who previously seemed to have very little idea, started to put forward interesting points or query ideas in a way that made us all rethink our interpretation of the text. The final co-constructed thinking frame, which I typed up for everyone, was about 5-pages long; the students treasured them because they understood how useful they were. And, of course, the frame, once completed, could be added to or challenged when the text was returned to at a later point in the course. They were very much the key to answering any question on the play. Instead of reading through what previously had often been somewhat half-baked essays when revising for the exam, suddenly they had a few sheets of paper which would help them grasp all the key information they needed to know. Having internalised this understanding, they could then select from it as necessary depending on the question asked. The discussion around the frames turned them into independent learners.

CO-CONSTRUCTING UNDERSTANDING 109

Line/Stage direction/Language	What it tells us about the characters and their relationship	Effect on the audience	Links to social/historical context	Links to the plays themes and ideas
"What keeps you so late? It's almost dark" ()	Elizabeth sounds suspicious of John.	The audience realise that this is a result of what happened with Abigail.	Although John has had an affair, the religious nature of society would not even entertain the thought of divorce. Elizabeth has to try to maintain her role as wife and get along with John.	*The Crucible* as trial – there is a trial within the Proctor's relationship – to do with trust and forgiveness.
Lots of short sentences, and questions at the start of the scene				
"I mean to please you " (John) ...He gets up, goes to kiss her. She receives it.				
(As gently as he can) "Cider?" "You ought to bring some flowers into the house"				

Here you can see an example of a thinking frame being developed around a discussion of *The Crucible* with a Year 9 class at Rainham Girls School. One of the columns has the excellent heading *Effect on the audience,* another is *Links to social/historical context*. The quality of the discussion taking place was excellent.

Thinking frame for artistic study on Surrealism

Surrealists	Method & technique	History	Subject – what work is about aesthetically	Influences	Individual inter-pretation	Artist's purpose
Examples	canvas; wire; paint; metal; Plaster; pastel	timescale; social/econ omic conditions; Personal background of artist	Composition; figures; portrait; narrative colour; abstraction; still life	Other artists; particular artistic movement; religion; reaction to events; political; romantic; commission; personal		(Fill in this column last)
Magritte						
Man Ray						
Ernst						
Dali						
Sources of info						

The image here is of a thinking frame for an A-level art project from a workshop session at Castle Hill School, Taunton. The approach can be introduced in KS3 and can be used for short extracts as well as whole texts.

A good way of introducing the approach in KS3, after the class has read whatever text is being focused on, is to create a series of around 16 dominoes with a significant event/point on the right-hand side of each domino and a related quote or comment on the left-hand side of the domino it links to. (The domino that opens the sequence should be blank on the left-hand side; the closing domino should be blank on the right-hand side so that you have created a sequence loop.) As illustrated here, the first task for the class in pairs is to see if they can put all the dominoes in order. The next task, since this is a play, is to try and explain who says the words along with the much more challenging task of why the writer would have chosen to include this particular speech. This provides a good warm up for a booktalk-style discussion on key moments within the text. If it had been a more factual text, the task could be changed to *What is the significance of this information?* or *What is the evidence for this statement?* etc.

Sequencing activity – dramatic purpose

1: In groups, sequence the cards into chronological order by selecting the quote that supports the event. Begin with the *Enter 3 witches* card.
2: Decide who says each speech and what Shakespeare's purpose was in including each speech.

[leave blank to indicate *This domino opens the sequence*]	Enter 3 witches	*Fair is foul Foul is fair.*	Macbeth defeats the rebels
Brave Macbeth - well he deserves that name.	Macbeth & Banquo meet the 3 witches	*All hail, Macbeth, that shalt be King hereafter.*	Duncan makes Macbeth the Thane of Cawdor

Co-constructing understanding through focused discussion is also at the heart of embedding understanding of how to solve a range of maths problems as explained on **pages 190–192**.

110 TRANSFORMING LEARNING ACROSS THE CURRICULUM

Using boxing up to plan exam answers

Boxing up applied to question analysis & planning

1.	What's the question asking me? (Highlight key words)
2.	Are there any pitfalls to avoid?
3.	How should I box-up my answer: – how many sections? – what is the focus of each section?
4.	Am I answering the question?

After co-constructing understanding activities in any subject, students should be in a good position to box up the answer to any question the exam process throws at them, using the example pictured here which, hopefully, is self explanatory.

If co-constructing understanding through dialogic talk doesn't underpin your teaching style, try it. You'll be amazed by the difference it can make. Useful resources to support what this means in theory and practice are *Exploring Talk in Schools* edited by Neil Mercer and Steve Hodgkinson, and *Transforming Teaching and Learning through Talk* by Amy Gaunt and Alice Stott, plus the EEF's evaluation of dialogic teaching – see https://educationendowmentfoundation.org.uk/projects-and-evaluation/projects/dialogic-teaching/

The key, as ever, is in the planning. Work has to be so structured as to enhance students' ability to build on each other's ideas so everyone is engaged in talking their way to understanding: getting the students talking about their learning underpins their learning. This can only be achieved by a skilful, well prepared teacher with a clear learning focus that enables them both to open up the discussions and to guide them meaningfully. Both of the books recommended above are full of practical explanations of how to do this backed by academic references. Interestingly, neither mentions Aidan Chambers' *Tell Me* which introduces how to do this in a step by step way in relation to reading. It's a useful starting point. **Video clip 31** shows Pie Corbett demonstrating this booktalk approach with a Year 6 class.

Chapter 7: Reading matters

If you are looking for evidence of the centrality of reading to progress in education, there can be no better place to start than *What Reading Does for the Mind* by Anne Cunningham and Keith Stanovich. Their fascinating research overview concludes with this message:

> *"We should provide all children, regardless of their achievement levels, with as many reading experiences as possible. Indeed, this becomes doubly imperative for precisely those children whose verbal abilities are most in need of bolstering, for it is the very act of reading that can build those capacities. An encouraging message for teachers of low-achieving students is implicit here. We often despair of changing our students' abilities, but there is at least one partially malleable habit that will itself develop abilities—reading!"*

Their research highlights what has become known as the *Matthew effect*: the rich get richer, the poor poorer, because the child who reads well can enjoy reading, and therefore reads more; the child who struggles with reading will not enjoy it, and will read less and less. In their words:

> *"Reading has cognitive consequences that extend beyond its immediate task of lifting meaning from a particular passage. Furthermore, these consequences are reciprocal and exponential in nature. Accumulating over time—spiralling either upward or downward— they carry profound implications for the development of a wide range of cognitive capabilities."*

In many ways, this says all you need to know about why reading matters – reading is the key that opens the door. To borrow A.C. Grayling's lines when reviewing Alberto Manguel's fascinating book *A History of Reading*: "To read is to fly: it is to soar to a point of vantage which gives a view over wide terrains of history, human variety, ideas, shared experience and the fruits of many enquiries." It gives children a gift that enriches their lives. We must ensure all learners have this point of vantage so that they can fulfil their potential through developing their minds. We must aim for every student who leaves our schools to enjoy reading.

Learners who read a lot find it easier to concentrate – they can sit, listen and think. This is because reading gives you abstract thought – the ability to think of things that aren't in front of you. Reading builds your imagination: as soon as you start reading to children, they have to start exercising their imagination – picturing what is being said in their heads. And, of course, it gives them a wide vocabulary – up to 90% of vocabulary is encountered in reading and not in everyday speech according to Ofsted's *Education Inspection Framework – Overview of Research*.

So, if students don't read, they don't have big vocabularies. This really matters as chapter 4 explained: there is a direct correlation between the size of your vocabulary and how well you will do in exams and thus how much you will probably earn in your lifetime. If you think about it, if you don't have words, you don't have knowledge, because words enable us to bring knowledge into being and sentences allow us to manipulate our thinking and discuss ideas. Reading also underpins writing. When you look at pupils' writing, you can tell immediately which ones read because their reading is reflected in their writing. The more we foster an understanding of how reading can really help pupils raise their attainment, the more likely they are to become avid readers. **Video clip 32** shows how a Y6 pupil from Selby Community Primary magpies ideas from her reading to use in her writing.

The bookseller and publisher Scholastic calculated the impact of reading based on Cunningham and Stanovitch's research, and came up with these interesting figures:

- A student who reads for 20 minutes a day will be exposed to 1.8 million words per year and scores in the 90th percentile on standardised tests;
- A student who reads for 5 minutes a day will be exposed to 282,000 words per year and scores in the 50th percentile on standardised tests;
- A student who reads for 1 minute a day will be exposed to 8,000 words per year and scores in the 10th percentile on standardised tests.

So, reading mileage really matters. What stops most students who don't read very much from reading is that reading for them is hard. The more you read, the more fluent you become at reading; the more fluent you become, the easier it is to read: but you have to reach that tipping point where reading starts to become easy and thus enjoyable.

The importance of reading and how to teach it effectively is the focus of a forthcoming book by Pie Corbett called *Talk for Reading*, so I will limit this chapter to a few key points that are of practical use to teachers across the curriculum, focusing on two key things:

1. Building a school community that reads
2. Integrating reading into teaching to increase reading mileage, understanding and fluency

1. Building a school community that reads

One glance at the statistics above, underlines the fact that getting all learners reading and wanting to read will be key to boosting attainment. This is very much a whole-school issue. What is your school doing to promote a love of reading? What image does reading have in your school? Having visited hundreds of schools over the years, primary schools definitely win hands down when it comes to creating a reading ethos that tells anyone entering the school that reading matters.

READING MATTERS 113

This is important because encouraging pupils to love reading and be interested in vocabulary can make a significant difference quickly. When the 2018 reading results arrived in England, some of our Talk for Writing primary training schools – who had been disappointed by the sudden dip in their reading results in 2016, when the national reading tests got much harder – had totally turned the situation around in two years. You can read the experiences of Burnley Brow, Selby and Montgomery Primary Schools at www.talk4writing.com. Focusing on getting the children to love reading, both in and beyond the classroom, through making the teachers enthusiastic about reading and creating an effective reading spine, made a big difference, as these comments from Selby Community Primary School suggest:

> *"I wasn't reading at home before and I didn't know any authors – but I started to get hooked into all the books we read. I couldn't even pick a favourite because I was so into all of them at the time!"*
> – boy, year 4
>
> *"I love the way we are taught; my teacher really engages us because she is so excited about our book. I have discovered so many new genres that I enjoy!"*
> – girl, year 5

St Matthew's Primary, Birmingham, has consistently achieved high reading results despite its extremely challenging intake. Walking round the school, it is easy to see where some of this success is rooted. Everywhere shows you, rather than tells you, that reading is what we do here: class groupings were based on famous authors, and those selected reflected the ethnicity of the school's intake. Book displays in the library were inviting, with covers facing out, and every teacher had created their own reading promotion display, inviting parents and children alike to borrow books

and widen their reading experience, alongside sharing with their children what they were currently reading. The pupils respected their teachers and wanted to be readers like them. The school has won national awards for how it promotes reading.

Here are a few extracts from an article by Headteacher Sonia Thompson explaining how to create a reading-for-pleasure culture in your school:

*"Purposely and purposefully plan for booktalk (**see page 125**). Children need time, space and support to interact with books. Deliberately using texts, which encourage children to see themselves, reflect on their own lives, as well as the lives of others, is crucial. Throughout our curriculum, we help the children to recognise the themes within books and through unpicking the affective nature of some books, we have provided a springboard for further storytelling, drama discussion and, of course, writing. This year, our celebration of National Empathy Day added to these opportunities.*

"Talk about quality books whenever you can. At St Matthew's, we regularly use assemblies to introduce new books and re-introduce classics. Our children are used to all teachers talking about and promoting children's literature, including their own favourites – all teachers and support staff have their own box of reading books, within their classrooms. We have found that when teachers do this, children are more willing to talk to and interact with each other about books.

"Widen and deepen children's reading choices but don't forget their agency as well. We are passionate about ensuring that our children read wide and deep. We want them to get lost in a plethora of books from a plethora of authors, both new and old. We also want children to own their choices and find 'their' author, book or series. Regular reading surveys help to locate preferences and the impact of changes. If, alongside this, they also indulge in a bit of Dahl and Walliams, it's not the end of the world! We, as reading teachers, will continue to read/share quality books, picture books, poetry and non-fiction with them and guide their choices. Daniel Pennac's popular Rights of the Reader declaration is a manifesto which we display around the school. We actively make time to discuss, enact and model it, so that our children understand that all reading has value and is valued at our school.

"Make dedicated time for reading for pleasure within the school timetable. Finally, at our school, whole-class reading, guided reading, independent reading, 1-1 reading, reading across the curriculum and, of course, reading for pleasure, are all part of our reading diet. Reading for pleasure has ring-fenced time, where children can read alone, with peers and across classes, using the library and reading spaces round the school. Whether it is interactive, solitary or social, this time is treasured and sacrosanct ... no matter what!"

Yes, it is easier in primary schools, but building a reading culture has to be central for all schools. In the first literacy-across-the-curriculum conference I ever organised, back in 1997 for the National Literacy Trust, there was one speaker who explained about an ex-merchant seaman/turned London taxi driver/turned teacher, named Arthur. He had finally turned to teaching because reading had changed his life and he wanted the new generation to benefit from what had so benefitted him. Apparently, he had been employed to help make the whole school read and that is, according to those who taught at the east London school where he got the job, exactly what he did. You couldn't walk past him, whoever you were, without him asking what you were currently reading. Arthur's enthusiasm for reading was contagious and he got the whole school reading and, of course, the school's results soared. One delegate left their notes behind and I noticed they had written down "employ Arthur". This got me thinking. Finding and funding Arthurs would definitely be hard but what about if we all contributed to the Arthur factor by all staff promoting reading, both as themselves as readers and related to whatever aspect of the curriculum they teach. So, I started looking for secondary schools as well as primary schools that had managed to turn their students on to reading and set up projects devoted to supporting this. What did we learn?

- **Involving all staff really pays** off because it raises the profile of reading and, in so doing, changes the ethos of the school.
- **You have to involve the students.** Your students will be most influenced by people like themselves so get some key students on board (most effectively the ones who other students want to be like) and get them interested in promoting reading.

So let's start by focusing on the first of these. If you ask teachers to score the importance of reading out of 10, most will immediately give it 10. But is this just a mantra that doesn't really impact on what we do in the classroom? In secondary schools, do we think it's the English department's job and we have no part to play? The key question is, what are all the staff doing to turn the students into enthusiastic skilled readers? Is reading highly visible in your school? When anyone walks into your school, would they know that reading was key?

READING MATTERS 117

Handout

Creating a school community that reads
a. Put yourselves in shoes of a student & consider what messages they receive about reading at your school.

Aspect	Yes	Some evidence	No	Not relevant	Bad idea
1. School publicity promotes importance of reading					
2. Parental interview promotes importance of parental involvement in student's reading development					
3. Induction day promotes importance of reading					
4. Attempt made to find out what each student thinks about reading and what types of reading interest them					
5. Foyer & corridors celebrate/advocate reading					
6. Part of registration programme used to encourage reading					
7. All classrooms promote reading related to subject					
8. Wider reading relating to subjects/topics integrated into units of work					
9. Students encouraged to magpie useful words and phrases from wider reading					
10. Reading promotional activities throughout school year e.g. Book Weeks, World Book Day etc					
11. Reading profile in assemblies and school communication system					
12. System to encourage peer reading recommendations					
13. Students encouraged to read more widely in a range of genres including non-fiction					
14. Broad range of reading material that reflects interests and ethnicity of students					
15. Reading groups/activities exist to motivate students					
16. Good links to local libraries e.g. weekly visits/ holiday schemes/ competitions					
Questions relating to school library					
17. There is easy access to library which is welcoming with interesting displays and a good induction programme					
18. Registration in library on rolling basis for year 7 groups					
19. Use of library integrated into curriculum					

b. At primary/secondary transfer – consider this from a management perspective

	Yes	Some evidence	No	Not relevant	Bad idea
A. Secondary schools work with their primary partners to encourage a school community that reads					
B. Primary partners forward what each pupil thinks about reading and what types of reading interest them					
C. Year 6 pupils send their summer holiday good reads recommendations on to their secondary schools for display in new school					
D. Events involving pri & sec pupils passing on messages about reading as part of ongoing relations between main partners					
E. Reading journal follows pupil up to secondary school – make sure all feeder schools participate					

Here's a useful checklist to assess the reading ethos in your school (**Handouts 9a & 9b** are downloadable online so you can adapt it to suit your school). The one shown here is for secondary schools but there is a primary one as well. The list has been co-constructed with hundreds of teachers, including many that have led the way in successfully building schools that love reading.

This would be a good activity to do first with the senior management team asking everyone to be really honest in their answers, so you have a clear analysis of where your weaknesses are and possible ways forward.

Certainly, when I've done this with project teams in secondary schools, the analysis is often very revealing to put it politely. Then ask the staff to complete the checklist to get them thinking about reading as a whole-school issue to help you co-construct the way forward and set up a *Get the whole school reading* group of enthusiasts from across the curriculum to help plan a successful way forward – don't leave it to the English department. The more staff who really enthuse about the need to build a school community that reads, the more successful it will be. Some schools include *enthusiasm for reading* as a criterion for any post in the school because everyone working in schools should be helping to build a sense that reading matters.

Make reading highly visible

If you think that reading promotion in your school needs a boost, then you may find some of the ideas below useful.

Make reading look engaging in all the corridors and classrooms

The foyer of any school sets the tone so reading should be visible there. Try displaying large posters of staff, parents and pupils holding a copy of their favourite reads with a few words beneath in large print saying why they have selected their choice. The more you can involve the cooks, cleaners and office staff, etc, the more your display will declare that this is a reading school. If your staff is largely female, make certain you include as many male readers, especially dads, as possible and get boys to help with the display so that it appeals to boys as well as girls – beware excesses of prettiness! If you want to ensure that the display becomes a real talking point, then get each person to include a picture of themselves as a small child, preferably also with a book. Many schools now have screens in their foyers: include videos of pupils from your school recommending good reads.

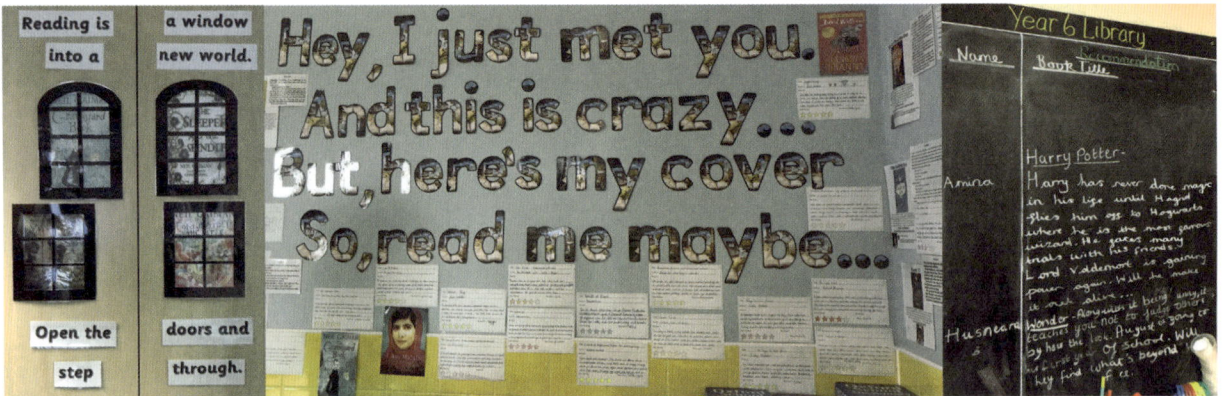

The corridors and classrooms of schools that promote reading are full of images that help pupils and their families see that reading is interesting and valued by the school. It is impossible to spend any time in Burnley Brow Community School, Oldham, without being aware of how the school places developing the children as enthusiastic readers at the heart of the learning process. Imaginative reading displays are to be found on the corridors and in every classroom, as these pictures from Year 6 classrooms illustrate. A boring cupboard has been transformed into a portal into the fascinating world of reading – who wouldn't want to open the door and sample the treasures inside? Alluring displays strengthened by pupil recommendations tempt you to look at the books, borrow them and take them home. A reading culture is being introduced into homes where it is not a traditional feature.

But is this focus built on in secondary schools? The contrast sometimes feels like moving from the oasis to the desert. Does the fact that teaching rooms become the dedicated space of subject areas, sometimes multi-occupied, mean that they can't promote engagement with the subject and the role of reading within it? Try walking into every teaching room in your school and decide what impression of learning the room gives. The photographs here do not do justice to the sense of walking into a scientific Aladdin's cave that you get when you enter

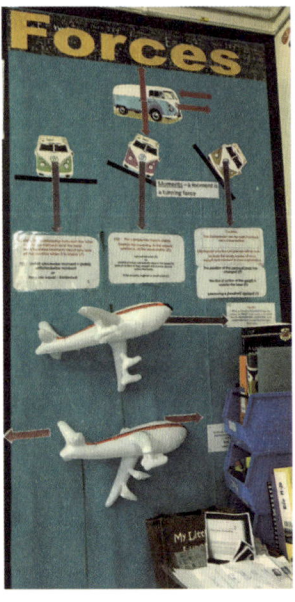

Emma Cooper's science lab, at The John of Gaunt School. Every wall space and much of the ceiling is used as a way of making the science curriculum come to life. It would surely make anyone want to learn and read all about it. If you look at **video clip 39** you will get some impression of the quality of the room. Yes, it is harder to use the walls effectively in secondary schools, but a lot of secondary teachers do and, if you are looking for help, many students will love helping you make the room look good. And the students really do notice the difference and respond well to rooms that are engaging.

Creating reading mileage across the school

Attempts to get the whole school reading, and thus extend reading mileage, have spawned a wealth of acronyms for when everyone reads (ERIC – Everyone Reads in Class; DEAR – Drop Everything and Read, etc). Do they work, especially in secondary schools? I've never quite been convinced, and I notice that the EEF isn't either. I remember when I was teaching that I could police these set occasions so that there was silence, everyone did have a book in front of them and pages were turned (often accompanied by that *look at me turning pages* smirk) but were they reading? Only some, and the atmosphere wouldn't have convinced many that reading was something they would choose to do. *Accelerated Reader*, on the other hand, seems to motivate a lot of KS3 students to keep on reading and certainly was causing a buzz when I saw it in action at Wexham School.

Tutor time offers potential for some dedicated reading time. The John of Gaunt School has recently started using this time to read novels aloud (for example *Cider with Rosie* for a Year 10 group) with the tutor groups. Every student has a copy of the book and is encouraged to follow what is being read with a ruler (something that definitely supports those who are not yet fluent readers). It seemed to be working. The atmosphere was good in the tutor sessions I visited, and the students seemed interested in the stories being read to them. When I asked members of the school council whether it was a good idea, they seemed to think it was: see **video clip 15**. Moreover, I could picture myself doing this with a class and it would definitely increase reading mileage, though some teachers will probably need a bit of training in how to read aloud in a way that brings the story alive; but that will be of great benefit to them whatever they teach.

Make the library the centre of the school

The library should be the learning hub of the school: a place that pupils love to visit because they know it is packed with treasure. But, in some schools, the library (if there is one) lurks in a dark and gloomy place or has been converted

into an ICT suite where books have little visibility. Is your library bright and engaging? Is there a great choice of reads (both fiction and non-fiction) with lots of covers facing outwards so the children can see what is there? Are there comfortable places to settle down for a good read? Wexham School has recently had new buildings – and the library is rightly impressive, as you can see here – but when I mentioned this to the project leader she commented, significantly, that it had always looked engaging in the old building because of the quality of the school librarian who cared and always created an area that students wanted to come to.

The power of peer-group recommendation

Research shows that reader recommendation is the most highly motivating reason for why someone chooses to read a particular book. You only have to think about how many books you have read because they were recommended to you by a friend or work colleague. An easy way to raise enthusiasm for reading is to have a star system where pupils can attach a star to the spine of a book they really loved, to draw pupils' attention to a good read. **A word of warning:** avoid the *write a review after every book you read* approach. This can be very tedious and can be counterproductive, encouraging children to read less and less to avoid the dreaded review-writing task. But if writing reviews is optional and is part of an engaging school initiative to raise reading across the school, they can be highly motivating. Maidwell Primary, a small rural Talk for Writing training school in Northamptonshire, found that the children just loved Pie Corbett's *Page Turners* (the Year 5 selection is pictured here) and loved to write reviews to promote books they had enjoyed as the pictures here illustrate.

You might want to try getting each class in the summer term to create reading recommendations for the upcoming class – everyone likes recommending books they have really enjoyed (for example, Years 5, 7, 8 & 9 could recommend good reads for the incoming classes; the Year 6 class could send recommended summer holiday good reads to be displayed in their secondary tutor room to cross the primary/secondary divide. It's all about getting the conversation going about reading.

It is important to separate independent reading from the more challenging texts used to explicitly teach reading. We must not to be stuffy about the reading material children choose to read. While series books may well be formulaic and not great literature, they do help children develop the reading habit and support children's development of fluency which is critical to understanding. Interestingly, Cunningham and Stanovich found that comic books contain many more rare words than prime-time adult TV programmes or adult conversations with college graduates. Stocking the reading corner with a selection of comics and magazines, and providing quality time to read, may well motivate some of the more reluctant readers to develop a more positive attitude to reading as well as exposing them to new vocabulary.

Integrating reading into teaching to increase reading mileage, understanding and fluency

Whatever subject you are teaching there will always be vocabulary and reading material of some sort related to it. If every teacher enthusiastically maintains a focus on extending vocabulary and encouraging reading related to the topic being taught, alongside devising activities that help bring this reading to life, it can make a huge difference; and not just to reading mileage but for students understanding of what reading is good for. Just think of some of the reading-related activities that have been mentioned in the preceding chapters outlining the TfW process:

Model text related activities
- Internalising and analysing the structure and ingredients of model text
- Selecting the best model text and explaining why it's the best
- Selecting the best introduction and explaining why it's the best
- Turning a text into images (text mapping)
- Providing a wider range of models

Structure activities
- Reconstructing text activities
- Attempting to reconstruct other students' essays
- Deciding on the order to place information
- Identifying key points made
- Sorting text activities
- Sequencing processes
- Identifying topic sentences

Analysing ingredients activities
- Co-constructing toolkits
- Understanding the function of sentence signposts including causal language

- Understanding the usefulness of generic phrases like sentence stems
- Focused discussion cards

Co-constructing learning activities
- Deciding what points to include in thinking frames
- Fine tuning thinking frames
- Co-constructing understanding from written extracts
- Annotating toolkits
- Creating coherent text from a list of bullet points
- Being involved in constructing coherent text
- Explaining which answer is best

Vocabulary activities
- Identifying words you are unfamiliar with
- Focusing on the meaning of words

Identifying content activities
- Identifying least relevant information
- Identifying long- and short-term causes
- Presenting different perspectives from text that has been read
- Giving the gist of text
- Summarising text
- Reading an answer and working out what the question was

Exam question activities
- Analysing exam questions
- Revising from *What have I learnt* text

Feedback activities
- Comparing cold and hot tasks
- Identifying error and how to correct it
- Discussing a partner's written work
- Reading work through to see if it flows, serves the correct purpose, makes sense and is accurate

Research tells us that if students are involved in some way in interrogating text, in reading for purpose, they will read it more carefully and gain reading skills. The more they are involved in dialogic reading – talking their way to understanding – the better their reading will become. This lies at the heart of what is known as directed activities related to text – the source of another ghastly acronym (DARTs). By integrating the approaches above into your teaching repertoire, the more practice students will have at these key skills and, if they frequently come across similar skills applied in different topics, the more skilled they will become at transferring their skills, and the easier it will become to read text for specific purposes. Understanding the role of sentence signposts, and slowly coming to know automatically which words tend to follow which words, makes a big difference to understanding and, in turn, to your ability to read such text fluently.

In the 19th century, many Cuban tobacco workers learnt to read because they had readers who read to them favourite stories as they worked. When some of them looked at the book from which the stories came, they quickly started deciphering the code because the pattern of language was in their

heads (though this will be easier in Spanish than in English because Spanish is phonetically consistent). The factory owners promptly banned story readers as they didn't want a literate workforce, but that's another story: the point here is, becoming familiar with the tune matters and every teacher can help make their students familiar with the tune of their subject, its disciplinary literacy. In addition, the more the students can begin to see why reading matters, the more motivation they will have to read. Watch **video clip 11** and reflect on why this Year 10 student thinks the TfW process has turned him into a reader. Interestingly, when we were first trialling the process for the Primary Literacy Strategy with teachers in the East Midlands, one primary teacher (who was the science specialist in his school) said that he had suddenly realised what reading was good for.

All of the above will also extend reading mileage. If every classroom promotes reading related to whatever is being taught, to hook and extend the students' interest and encourage students to read around the subject, the more chance there is of hooking the students into the reading habit. The picture below from the maths' corridor at The John of Gaunt School shows a few of the maths department's recommended maths reads.
There will be some great books out there about whatever you are teaching that can really make subjects come alive. Here's a few that could be dipped

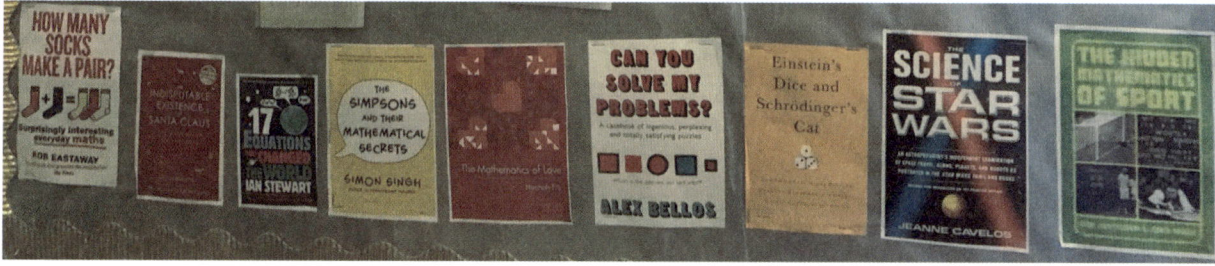

into from Year 5 upwards. They all have one thing in common: they are brilliantly written so you really engage with the concepts and want to read on. Interestingly, many of them, like *Longitude*, *The Map that Changed the World* and Bill Bryson's wonderful science book have relevance to history, geography, maths, science, sociology and English; with *Outliers* you can add in music, computer studies and D&T as well: *Outliers* provides statistical evidence

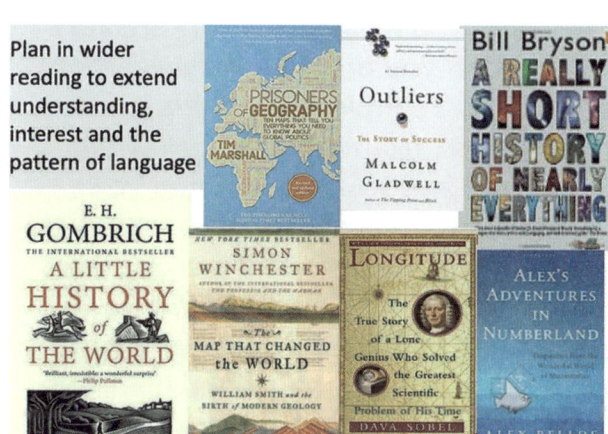

which backs up the great quote pictured here. It's also worth considering this interesting statement from Ofsted's *Education Inspection Framework – Overview of Research* overview of research:

> *"Boys in particular tend to read material appropriate for those below their chronological age. Non-fiction texts appear most likely to use overly simple language, and on average are two years behind readers' chronological age (Topping, 2018)."*

There is a tendency for publishers to dumb down school textbooks so it's important to choose textbooks and non-fiction books that will challenge the learners and teach in such a way that helps the learners meet the challenge. And, of course, every lesson across the curriculum will extend world knowledge, which is essential if you are to broaden your vocabulary and hence your reading skills. The one grows the other: references to the Titanic or Hiroshima are meaningless when you don't know what they signify. And words are tricky things since phrases may be meant literally or metaphorically: at around the age of 15, I inadvertently spent a long time drawing my own conclusion in a physics exam having misinterpreted the phrase, *and draw your conclusion*, probably because I had been told I was careless and should read the questions carefully and do what they said.

Focus on fluency and oral comprehension

In the days when the KS3 science SATs existed, I got bored with hearing the excuse from many secondary teachers that the reason why so many students did badly in the exam was because of their reading ages (the English department's fault again, clearly), so I decided to have a go at answering the exam questions myself. I don't know what my reading age is, probably not quite as old as I am but something high, but I didn't do too well in the exam – some sections were fine; others hopeless. Why? It was nothing to do with my ability to read and everything to do with the fact that I didn't understand some of the words and concepts I was being asked to comprehend. Familiarity with the tune of what your subject looks like on the page, and the technical vocabulary it spins around, is vital. Of course, reading age matters, but every teacher can contribute to helping the pupils become better readers.

Comprehension matters. This is where echo reading and dialogic reading are very useful teaching techniques to add to your repertoire if you don't already use them. Echo reading, already briefly explained on **page 21**, is a simple way of helping all students hear the tune of the text. Here's a typical D&T exam question: *How did your solution fulfil the original brief?* Read it out loud and you will find that you have probably stressed four words, as well as made your voice rise at the end of the sentence to indicate that it is a question: **How** did **your** solution **fulfil** the **original** brief? When you ask students to look at exam questions, model for them how to read the question aloud so that your intonation helps to bring out the meaning of the sentence. At first it might help if the students hear you read it and highlight the words that you stressed and then everyone reads it together – echoing your

intonation. After a bit, you won't have to model how to do it, as their fluency will increase, and they will automatically be able to read the questions with the appropriate intonation. The potential in secondary schools for increasing reading fluency is significant if all exam questions and model texts, at the stage when the students are shown the written text, are echo read together. No sensible teacher asks students with poor reading aloud skills to read aloud to a class, so the fluency of poorer readers is liable to decrease, but if we are all reading together, the weaker students will be supported by the pattern of the language about them and their fluency will increase. If they like football, suggest they play *the intonation game* when the football results are being read on the radio. You can usually tell whether the first team named for each game has won, lost or drawn from the intonation the reader uses to signal what is coming next.

It's useful to remember that oral comprehension questions are the best way to develop comprehension skills. The research which is probably the most useful for teachers who want to support students' comprehension when reading is the *York Reading for Meaning Project*. This was a large-scale randomised controlled trial carried out with 20 primary schools in the north of England, to evaluate three intervention programmes designed to support reading comprehension: one focused on text level only; another focused on oral work only; the third was text and oral combined. Interestingly, the approach that was found to be the most effective was the purely oral one (including dialogic reading) which suggests that all those hours pupils spend endlessly writing answers to comprehension questions is not time well spent; open-ended discussion activities that help students co-construct understanding (see the philosophy example on **pages 103-6**) will be much more effective. – *Reading for Meaning Project,* Clarke, Hulme, Snowling & Truelove.

Booktalk (also see online Handouts 7 & 8)

That leads us to what is the best way to make oral comprehension count. The book that explains dialogic reading best is Aidan Chamber's *Tell me* which is all about how to do booktalk. Every teacher of English should read this book and everyone else can use the approach to help students interrogate text effectively. The problem with a lot of oral questioning is that it becomes a tennis match between the teacher and the few students who choose to volunteer answers to questions, while everyone else opts out. Moreover, it is often a kind of game to work out what the teacher wants you to answer.

Through booktalk, the students themselves start to raise significant points about what the passage is saying and discuss significance themselves without seeking teacher approval. The important thing, and difficult for all teachers because we are used to being centre stage, is to stay neutral and show no reaction to people's contributions however brilliant or off the point. Just facilitate the discussion with interventions like:

- Is there more to say there?
- Can anyone build on that?
- Does anyone see it differently?

The key ingredients of booktalk are as follows:
- Read the text to the class clearly, sentence by sentence or paragraph by paragraph may work best, and show any relevant images
- Facilitate discussion. Do not give your opinion or suggest anything is right or wrong
- Hold back and be neutral – let the students talk
- Ensure all ideas are accepted and are open to challenge
- Only ask open questions
- Be a good listener and encourage thought.

What sort of questions to ask to get the ball rolling: Obviously, this will depend on the text being studied but, whatever the focus, it must be an open question that will start to get the class thinking. *Tell me why ...* is a good way to introduce what the question is. The best way to understand booktalk is to see it in action: watch Pie Corbett on **video clip 31** and then discuss in your subject area how you could apply this technique to interrogate text in your subject including what questions you might ask.

The six points above are vital. Without these, it will become just another round of *can we work out what's in the teacher's head and tell them the answers they want to hear*. Once these key points are in place, then the points below are useful:

Supporting thinking
- Encourage students to discuss in pairs before contributing
- Allow students to chip in – not hands up
- Allow pauses and thinking time – encourage deep reflection
- Probe for more ideas
- Invite students to suggest what they want to discuss

Supporting expressing ideas clearly
- Help students construct their thoughts coherently – e.g. *Because?*
- Model sentence stems to provide students with the sentence starters they will need to say the sorts of things they are trying to say
- Repeat thoughts that are worth sharing and invite more comment
- Encourage students to build on points

Supporting the flow of ideas
- Prompt and pause
- Re-look at the text as necessary and focus on any relevant images
- Refer back to the question asked and refocus discussion as necessary
- Help people see links
- Draw threads together and recap but don't say what is "right".

Handout 8 is a useful list of the sort of phrases to use to encourage effective booktalk. Praise the manner of people's contribution, for example if someone says, T*o build on that point,* or *From another perspective.* Build up banks of good phrases like these on posters but don't praise contributions as this a) tells people what to think and b) discourages other people from joining in. It's a really powerful teaching tool, so it's worth getting your head round it if you are not familiar with it.

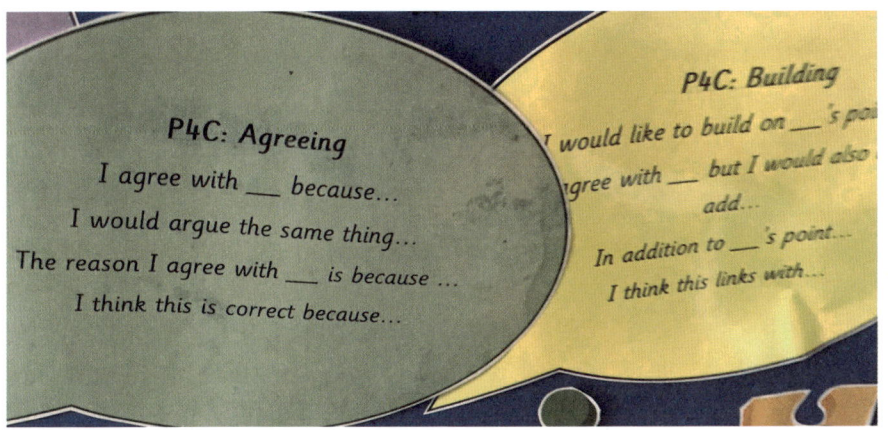

Schools that use the *Philosophy for Children* approach to teach reasoning and argumentative skills will be very familiar with the book-talk techniques explained above. The approach encourages asking the sort of questions that help learners to develop a logical approach to discussing problems/issues. It encourages children to use the sort of sentence stems that promote rational debate, as illustrated above by this poster from the Year 2 corridor of Briar Hill Primary School in Northampton. The pupils greatly benefit from gaining familiarity with the language of logical argument and this is very much in evidence when listening to class discussions throughout the school. And, of course, after several years of supporting the children to think and speak in such a way, the reading results are excellent. There is research evidence to suggest that including philosophy on the curriculum pays significant dividends. In the words of Angie Hobbs, Professor of the Public Understanding of Philosophy, at the University of Sheffield:

> "Increased philosophy provision in both primary and secondary schools can do so much to help young people from all backgrounds actualise their potential and live fulfilled, flourishing lives.
>
> "In addition to clarity of thought and reasoning, it has been shown to assist with both literacy and numeracy, and is being tested in respect of imaginative creativity, empathy, and resistance to various forms of indoctrination. It helps provide the training in mental rigour, flexibility and resilience that the 21st century so clearly requires."

Three documents that are very much worth looking at in relation to developing skilled readers are Ofsted's *Education Inspection Framework – Overview of Research,* the EEF document *Improving Literacy in Secondary Schools* Ofsted's *Overview of Research.* This last document includes these paragraphs:

> "In addition to explicit vocabulary instruction, there is clear evidence that teachers can support comprehension by modelling how expert readers read actively, including by monitoring their understanding, asking questions, making predictions and summarising (Rosenshine, 1997; Oakhill et al., 2014; Davis, 2010; National Reading Panel, 2000; Stuart and Stainthorp, 2015). However, it is important to note that the effects of any type of strategy instruction will be limited if pupils lack the requisite vocabulary or background knowledge to engage with a text (Education Endowment Foundation, 2017).
>
> "Another central, but often underestimated, aspect of reading comprehension is prior knowledge about the topic of the reading. The more knowledge readers have about the topic of a text, the better they will understand it (Willingham, 2012; Lipson & Cooper, 2002). This may appear just common sense, but in some cases educators have focused on developing generic reading comprehension strategies rather than the subject knowledge required for understanding."

The EEF document also has an excellent section on reading which is worth considering carefully and will be equally useful to teachers in upper KS2. It includes this paragraph:

> "Effective readers of informational texts continually draw upon a complex wealth of prior knowledge about the world and language, as well as their awareness of subject specific genres and vocabulary. As students tackle a challenging text, they make sense of it by constructing a rich mental representation (called a 'situation model') that goes far beyond a simple, literal interpretation. Drawing on their language skills, relevant background knowledge and ability to infer, readers develop their understanding, which is refined and adjusted as they learn more."

This is exactly what is happening in Tracey Adam's Year 6 class at St Matthews as they battle with a very challenging text about heroism – **see video clip 30**. It's worth analysing exactly what she is doing and thinking about how it might include aspects we can all learn from (see the teacher's notes accompanying the online video clips). Similarly, the explanation of how the philosophy students gained real understanding of the perspectives of Aristotle and Socrates on **pages 104-6** illustrates how we can support students in becoming effective readers of challenging non-fiction texts.

The forthcoming book on *Talk for Reading* will focus on how to build up the integrated skills that develop good readers rather than turning the teaching of reading into a series of isolated skills that just match the exam assessment domains.

Chapter 8: Useful research overviews

Rather than repeat the research roots of Talk for Writing that are already available, this chapter focuses on three useful research overviews related to language across the curriculum.

- Rosenshine's much-acclaimed *10 Principles of Instruction*
- EEF's very useful document *Improving Literacy in Secondary Schools*
- Ofsted's *Education Inspection Framework – Overview of Research* focusing on sections that are relevant to this book.

This chapter has been included at the end of the opening section because it makes more sense to read this once you have understood the Talk for Writing process.

1. Rosenshine's *10 Principles of Instruction*

The grid below illustrates how Rosenshine's 10 principles have, coincidentally, long been embodied within the Talk for Writing process; this is followed by an additional list of features that underpin Talk for Writing and which go beyond the 10 principles. These features are significant because they add together to make a powerful learning process that can be applied to any subject rather than just a list of good things to remember to do in any subject.

10 principles of Instruction	How they are reflected in Talk for Writing
1. Daily review	• Use of working wall/washing lines to make learning so far visible – this integrates revisiting learning into process • Warming-up activities at beginning of each lesson to revisit earlier learning before introducing the next stages • Ongoing review of toolkits – lessons reinforce understanding of key tools and add additional ones
2. Present new material using small steps	• Learners move from imitation, through innovation to independent application using small steps and embedding learning before moving on – key new features introduced at the imitation stage are consolidated through innovation • The cold task is used to help the teacher know what support to give which pupils and size of the steps • Warming-up activities at the beginning of each lesson introduce the next stages as well as revisiting the prior learning that they build on

3. Ask questions – to help students practise new information and connect new material to their prior learning	• Open-questioning processes including dialogic talk underpin interrogation of text • Co-constructing understanding through discussion and questioning are central to the process • Explaining to others is a regular feature
4. Provide models	• Modelling text or process is at heart of approach • Tune of subject modelled by teacher • Key sentence signposts & phrasing for topic focused on • Modelling the thought processes underlying writing thinking, calculating – making the implicit explicit
5. Guide student practice	• Guiding practice is central to imitation and innovation stages. In the first stage, the students understand the processes; in the second, they are shown how to apply and innovate on them
6. Check for student understanding	• Warming-up activities at imitation and innovation stages check progress as units develop and help reduce error • Feedback from co-constructed learning provides good check on understanding • Independent application stage applied flexibly to support different levels of progress
7. Obtain a high success rate	• Process based on helping students succeed. Levels of support and difficulty of tasks vary at each stage depending on differing levels of student progress to ensure high rate of success
8. Provide scaffolds for difficult tasks	• Process is based on scaffolding learning which can be varied to suit need so students are challenged but not presented with tasks beyond their current competence, so success is built into the process
9. Independent practice	• The process is structured to build towards independent practice; the independent stage is flexible to meet needs of different ranges of attainment
10. Weekly and monthly review	• Use of cold to hot process places review of progress at heart of learning • Use of working wall/washing line to make learning visible integrates revisiting learning into process • Peer review of work built into innovation stage • Explaining to others built into process • Teacher review of work & immediate follow up of key area/s that need strengthening is central

Additional features of Talk for Writing that help make it so powerful

In addition to these 10 principles of instruction, there are several key features of Talk for Writing that are not included within these principles and, in many ways, it is these additional features that help it to be so powerful.

- First and foremost, Talk for Writing is a **coherent integrated process that reflects how human beings learn in general and specifically in relation to how they learn language, rather than a list of useful points.** The whole approach adds up to a very powerful way of supporting the linguistic development that is key to learning alongside engaging students. It leads to success which builds confidence and motivates learners to keep learning.

- **Each unit should begin with a hook to motivate students** and help them see why they would want to learn whatever the focus of the unit is.

- **Understanding the oral tune of the subject being focused on** is central to the approach so students become increasingly familiar with the underpinning vocabulary and language patterns that make up the literacy of each subject discipline. These patterns are introduced through warming-up activities, modelled throughout by the teacher, and illustrated in action through models. **At the early stages of understanding, orally internalising the language of a model text in the imitation stage is key before seeing it in written form.** Understanding is further developed through innovating on the model through shared writing/calculating/thinking and shared practice.

- **Making learning visible.** One problem with interactive whiteboards is that everything flashes past very quickly. Talk for Writing promotes the use of flipcharts alongside electronic whiteboards so that key learning points can be co-constructed and displayed on washing lines or learning walls and returned to regularly to support the review of learning.

- **Text mapping is key throughout.** Personalising understanding by turning text or processes into images not only helps students understand the meaning of words and recall the pattern of the language but it also helps them remember key information.

- **Boxing up the structure of a text or a process is central to progress.** This simple device helps students plan their ideas and present information or processes in a logical order. It helps learners form their own mental model of whatever task they are confronted with.

- **Co-constructing a toolkit of the key features** of whatever text or process is focused on is key. In this way, learners understand the ingredients that they will need to successfully complete whatever work is set.

- **Finally, bookending units with a cold/hot task** helps students reflect on their progress which motivates them and helps them see the steps they need to make further progress.

In effect, Talk for Writing is a spiral of progress which not only helps students build their skills and understanding from unit to unit within subject areas but also enables them to transfer these skills across the curriculum. This enables communication skills learnt in one area can be adapted, applied and developed in another.

A useful short book on applying Rosenshine's principles is Tom Sherrington's *Rosenshine's Principles in Action.*

2. Improving Literacy in Secondary Schools

https://educationendowmentfoundation.org.uk/tools/guidance-reports/improving-literacy-in-secondary-schools/

In July 2019, the Education Endowment Foundation (EEF) published *Improving Literacy in Secondary Schools.* Like all its publications, all the points are well supported by research into what works; it provides a very useful outline of the steps secondary schools need to take to support literacy across the curriculum. If you look at the headings of the first 6 of its 7 main recommendations, you can again see that it covers much of the same key ground as this book:

1. Prioritise disciplinary literacy across the curriculum
2. Provide vocabulary-targeted instruction in every subject
3. Develop students' ability to read complex academic texts
4. Break down complex writing tasks
5. Combine writing instruction with reading in every subject
6. Provide opportunities for structured talk.

As with Rosenshine's findings above, the key difference is that the Talk for Writing approach joins all these elements into an underpinning teaching process that can both be applied to any curriculum area and joined together to make a coherent whole-school approach that supports learners in transferring learning from one subject to another. The following points are the key additional aspects of the TfW process:
- bookending units with cold and hot tasks to support learners in reflecting on their learning
- internalising the tune of each subject (disciplinary literacy) by internalising model text, using text mapping and actions to support this process
- co-constructing understanding of the ingredients of this text
    - first by boxing it up to establish the structure
    - second by analysing the underpinning features and creating a toolkit of features which supports learners in recognising the similarities and differences between the different sorts of writing required.

If you look at the comments from teachers and students on the elements that have most helped them, it is these that are most frequently mentioned. Moreover, this book contains a wide range of practical examples of how to put the approach into practice so that teachers of all subjects can see how they could adapt their units of work in line with the approach.

Literacy interventions

The final area the EEF publication covers is 7. *Provide high quality literacy interventions*. This book has not covered this area in any detail, though **chapter 9d** provides an example of how one school tackles this issue. We would strongly endorse the following statements from the EEF document:

> *"High quality teaching across the curriculum will reduce the need for extra literacy support. Nevertheless, it is likely that a small number of students will require additional support—in the form of high quality, structured, targeted interventions—to make progress …*
>
> *"While providing additional support should not be an alternative to investing in efforts to improve the quality of teaching in the classroom, preparing a strategy that offers tiers of support to struggling students is recommended."*

This final section of the EEF document covers a whole range of useful points. As they emphasise, this is an area where it is hard to assess the claims of the various literacy intervention programmes, so we feel it best to refer schools to the EEF findings.

In this book, we wanted to focus on what every teacher can do to support the literacy of their students. Successful TfW primary schools have found that as the quality of the teaching improves, fewer and fewer children require special needs support, a point emphasised by the EEF above. At the heart of this success has been ensuring that all children are given access to the curriculum so that the curriculum is differentiated by output not input, with layers of scaffolding to support those with additional needs.

The EEF document provides a very wide range of research references related to literacy across the curriculum.

3. Education Inspection Framework – Overview of research

https://assets.publishing.service.gov.uk/government/uploads/system/uploads/attachment_data/file/813228/Research_for_EIF_framework_100619__16_.pdf

In January 2019, Ofsted published an overview of the research evidence underpinning its new education inspection framework. This draws on a range of sources, including both their own research programme and a review of existing evidence bases and, as such, will be of significant interest to all school managers, not only those in England who are inspected within this framework. Given the focus of this book, the most relevant part is section 1: *Quality of Education*. It begins with four inspection grade criteria which very much emphasise the importance of having a broad curriculum that is not diminished by the pressures of high-stakes testing, alongside teaching the curriculum in such a way that the most disadvantaged can access it: sentiments that we would strongly endorse. This section of the overview provides an extremely useful insight into curriculum design, memory and retention, as well as teacher effectiveness and assessment.

Not surprisingly, it reiterates the centrality of reading and vocabulary to educational success. The key research findings it emphasises in these two key areas have been integrated into the related chapters above.

For those interested in the wider research roots of Talk for Writing, this is explained in Chapter 3 of *Talk for Writing across the Curriculum*. Of particular practical interest is the *Transforming Writing Project* in 2013 conducted in partnership with the National Literacy Trust and advised by Shirley Clarke. This action research shows the benefits of putting formative assessment at the heart of the process. A document summing up the key practical findings can be downloaded from the Talk for Writing website (click on *Baseline assessment* in the *Resources* section – the second document listed is *Formative assessment: the key to progress.* You can also download the full research report here:

https://literacytrust.org.uk/research-services/research-reports/transforming-writing-final-evaluation-report/

Chapter 9a: Warm up key skills with short-burst writing

Short-burst writing activities

- Encourage creativity/enthusiasm – play with words to create
- Remove fear factor
- Encourage personal expression
- Challenge and develop thinking
- Engage everyone
- Strengthen observational skills
- Encourage different combinations of words
- Increase vocabulary
- Focus on quality of language
- Teach key writing skills

If you're an English teacher and you want to raise your pupils' confidence in themselves as writers, alongside raising the quality of their writing and their ability to comment on the quality of the writing of others, one sure-fire quick win is short-burst, poetic writing. If your pupils are poor at creative writing, they will immediately see progress in their ability to write; if they are pretty good at creative writing, they will quickly be able to hone their skills even more. One deputy head on a Talk for Writing project in Aylesbury, who was teaching a Year 6 class, explained to me that it was short-burst writing that had made the biggest difference to the quality of her children's writing quickly. It's also the fastest route to turning around Year 11 students who are underperforming.

The secret behind the success of short-burst writing is that it is short, engaging and very focused. It can be practised regularly with the whole process often taking up no more than 10 minutes (and sometimes only five once the process is established) – so it is the perfect lesson warm-up activity. This dispenses with the blank-page syndrome: not only is a page not required but, when the pupils write, they know exactly what they are focusing on and how to do it. It also means that writing can be practised in weeks that focus on other aspects of the English curriculum.

Through the process, you can build up every single writing skill that helps hook and maintain a reader's interest. In this way, over time, learners build up a flexible hook-your-reader toolkit in their heads that they can select from depending on the type of writing required or the type of writing they want to create. They can also use this understanding of how writing works, to comment on the writing of others. Warm-up activities should be exactly that. The idea is to warm up skills that will be used later in the unit. The more this is done, the greater the impact will be because the short-burst activities are built on throughout a unit so that the best of the phrases that the learners have crafted can be used/amended to enhance later, longer-writing tasks, and the skills introduced can be practised, as illustrated in this chapter – see **pages 145–146** and **chapter 9b**.

One word of warning before beginning: remember to tell your class not to try to make their poems/descriptions rhyme. It is the curse of teaching poetry writing that learners tend to think that poetry has to rhyme. Most probably they, like practically everyone (probably you included), are not good at writing anything powerful that rhymes. Obviously, if you happen to have a rhyming genius in the class, let them loose on rhyme.

Warming up creativity – random association games

A good way to begin with short-burst writing is through games that warm up creativity and get the students thinking/seeing/writing in a more imaginative way. Display an image that lends itself to a range of different interpretations and ask the class to brainstorm as many ideas of what it looks like as possible (never including what it actually is). Flipchart all the suggestions, push pushing for as many ideas as possible and including all suggestions however obscure – if you reject suggestions, you reject creativity:

- *spider – tanrantula*
- *stick insect*
- *dragon*
- *dinosaur*
- *a running man*
- *gnarled fingers*
- *cracker*
- *stick man*
- *octopus*
- *scorpion*
- *praying mantis*
- *Medusa*
- *motorway flyover*
- *eruption*
- *lightning striking sand*

One useful trick, if someone uses a generic term like spider, is to immediately ask them to name what sort of spider – tarantula. **Name it** is a very handy writing technique that students need to have in their writing repertoire to help them to make every word count. It is the difference between, *The man entered the building* and *Donald Trump blustered into The White House*.

You could then, through short-burst shared writing, show the students how to *spin a simile round to make a metaphor*, another very useful writing technique to add to the students' toolkit of writing skills. *The dead tree looked like a tarantula* becomes *the tarantula tree* or even just *tarantula tree*. The advantage of the metaphor as adjective over the simile comparison is that it tightens the writing. The more the students come to understand that usually in writing less is more, the better writers they will become. This helps defeat the long = good myth.

Warming up creativity – random juxtaposition games

> **The city of sighs**
>
> In pairs:
>
> Person A: Jot down the name (common nouns not proper nouns) of 5 places e.g., *shed, stable* etc.
>
> Person B: Jot down the name of 5 things or feelings e.g., *joy, anger* etc.
>
> Now join your ideas to make the most interesting/imaginative links:
>
> The … of …

Another excellent warm-up game is *City of sighs*. This time, the purpose is to help students see the creative power of the random juxtaposition of ideas. For this game, divide the class into pairs so one is A and the other B (if there is a group of three, create one A and two Bs). Ask the A group to secretly jot down five concrete nouns naming places, giving them examples like *cellar, garage, riverbank, loft, bus station*. Ask the B group to secretly jot down five abstract nouns, for example, *hate, love, dread, courage, boredom*.

Then ask the pairs to join up the results (as in *the something of something*) and select the most entertaining/interesting results, for example:

- *the stadium of sadness*
- *the school of despair*
- *the cellar of hope*
- *the supermarket of boredom*
- *the carpark of joy*
- *the post office of regret*

> **Stadium of Sadness**
>
> Gloominess engulfs the stadium of sadness filling it with misery. With each passing moment, sorrow and despair hangs in the air, swallowing the last glimmer of hope as it evaporates into the dawn of time.

The randomness of the resulting ideas can spark off all sorts of interesting writing. Select one of the ideas and show, through brief shared writing, how to develop the ideas and then allow the learners to take any of the ideas that captured their imagination and give them a few minutes to paint a picture in words based on this image. You can see from this writing from a child in one of Pie Corbett's classes how the idea can grip the imagination and produce powerful writing.

If you want to arm yourself with a wide range of these sort of games that help build writing skills in an entertaining way, *Jumpstart! Literacy* by Pie Corbett is an essential resource.

Warming up dormant vocabulary

Another great activity, based on Pie's book, helps learners develop confidence in their ability to generate a wide range of vocabulary by plumbing the depths of their ideas through focusing on the five senses. Select a scenario that all learners will be familiar with (as appropriate for your intake), for example bonfire night, and tell the students to jot down quickly as many words as they can in one minute associated with bonfire night (tell them not to worry if they can't spell a word). At the same time, have a go yourself. At the end of the minute, you will probably find that you can jot down far more words than any of the pupils can. Then ask them to shut their eyes and imagine the scene – describe for them typical bonfire night experiences moving through the senses: sounds, tastes, smells, sights, feelings.

Once the learners' imaginations have been warmed up in this way, give them another minute in which to jot down as many words as possible associated with bonfire night. Normally, everyone greatly increases the number of words that come to mind. In such a simple way, you can teach the key writer's tool of picturing a scene in the head before writing about it and thinking of the five senses to help bring a scene to life. This is an excellent activity to do to warm up a descriptive writing unit.

Spine poem short-burst writing

If learners are to be successful writers, they need to be able to generate a wealth of ideas then select just the right word for the job. Short-burst writing trains them in these skills in an entertaining and confidence-boosting way. Pie's spine-poem technique allows every student to succeed rapidly because they are supported in what to write and how to write it. Select a powerful, simple image to help learners develop their observational skills. Display the image and ask the class to suggest which key features to describe. Given this image, they would probably suggest the *eye*, the *beak* and the bright red *comb* and matching *wattle*, plus the orange *feathers*. List these down your flipchart beginning with the feature that first grabs the attention. If it is an image of a creature, it is the eye that will draw the viewer in.

Always have a clear concept of the features you want to focus on and stick to your prepared order as this will help you demonstrate the writing features you want to illustrate, but welcome every suggestion the class makes to encourage contributions. Having a save-it box at the bottom of the flip chart is a good way of acknowledging ideas. For this image, I would suggest focusing on the following:

- *eye*
- *beak*
- *crimson comb*
- *orange feathers*

Before beginning the description, always ask the class to decide what mood is suggested by the image because this will determine the sort of vocabulary selected. It is not a question of throwing in fancy words (the concept of wow words! is not useful); it is more a question of what word will really help the reader picture what is being described. One glance at this image tells you that this is no cuddly, feathered friend and that you need to keep your distance if you wish to avoid being viciously pecked.

Then ask the class to describe the eye and brainstorm a wealth of ideas – flip-charting these as you go as a word bank ensures the students have no shortage of ideas to work with. Display these as a visual aid that students can magpie from.

> **Word bank**
> beady   glassy   marble   blind
> piercing   cold   cruel   dead   pinpoint
> sharp   peering   glaring

Push, push for a wide range of ideas before selecting the one you think works best, or ask a student to decide which one they would choose and why, and go with that, but only if it suits the direction in which you want to go. Then ask the class to consider which verb will go best. Explain what sort of sentence you are trying to achieve. For example, if you want to keep the opening line short and tight, when someone suggests, say, *glared*, ask them if they think *glares* or *glared* sounds best – demonstrating both versions orally for them. The chances are they will choose *glares* because it is immediate and ever present. This is a good moment to underline that the use of the simple present tense can make things seem more threatening. You will probably end up with a list like *glares, stares, pierces, bores, threatens, challenges, peers*. Now point out that all the verbs can be changed into 'ing' verbs (present participles) as in *glaring, staring, piercing* etc and can then function as adjectives so that a word you chose for the adjective can be the very word you want for the verb or vice versa. Reading aloud the opening line is the best way to decide which word works best where: is it, *The glaring eye pierces* or *The piercing eye glares*? Somehow, the latter seems more powerful, so that would be my choice. Now discuss whether to begin with *Its* or *The* and help the class see that you have chosen *The* because it makes the creature more distant. The whole idea is to make the thoughts behind a writer's choices explicit.

Then move on to the next line explaining that you still want to keep the language sharp and tight. Ask the class to look carefully at the beak and say what it looks as if it is about to do. Someone will probably say *peck* as this obvious cliché word is the one that somehow works best here, perhaps because there is no other word that so aptly describes exactly what birds do. Discuss what verb would go well with *peck* and someone will probably say *poised to peck* alongside *ready to peck, as if to peck, waiting to peck* etc. If they don't suggest *poised to peck*, then suggest it yourself and discuss why it works.

Read your two lines now and see if they work:

The piercing eye glares,
Beak poised to peck.

Now discuss whether the alliteration works or is it too much? Would it be more powerful if you changed **piercing** to **marble** or would that weaken the alliteration and harshness of **poised to peck**. It is important for the class to see how, in reading through, you adjust earlier decisions in the light of later choices, in order to create the effect you really want, making every word count.

Once you get to the **comb**, here is the perfect opportunity both to extend vocabulary relating to *red* and to teach the skill of turning a simile into a metaphor to tighten the effect of what is written (or embed the skill if you have already taught it). First, ask the class to come up with as many alternatives to red as they can think of and display them:

> **Word bank for 'red'**
> crimson, vermillion, blood-red, scarlet, ruby, cerise, cardinal, claret, wine-red, cochineal, flame etc.

Add in additional words yourself as necessary so that you are not just reviving dormant vocabulary but adding to the range of words they start to be able to recognise and use. Understandably, all words for red tend to have an in-your-face quality about them so choosing the word you want might come down to deciding which of the various words for red beginning with c you want to opt for, given that it will be paired with **comb**.

Then ask the class to come up with as many similes to help describe the crimson comb as possible:

> **Simile suggestions (looks like a ...)**
> saw,   crown,   jagged knife,
> gears,   halo,   punk hairstyle,
> party hat, lightning, serrated edge

Decide which one you want or ask a student to choose and explain their choice. Go with their suggestion, if it works, for example ***a crimson comb like a punk's hair***. Then show how you can spin the simile round into a metaphor: ***a crimson punk comb***.

Move through each of three or four features from the image before handing over to the class and inviting them to have a go themselves. They can magpie some of the ideas that you chose but the majority must be their ideas. They should now be bursting with their own ideas. Set a short time limit, like four minutes, and insist on working in silence so they get the discipline of observing something very closely, pushing for a range of choices and then deciding on just the right word to paint the picture they are attempting to recreate. Quickly, they will be absorbed in effective writing. Limiting the time to help achieve focus is one of the important points that Ted Hughes emphasises in his book **Poetry in the Making**: all English teachers should read this book because it teaches you so much about how to teach writing.

Always prepare

The tools used
- simple present tense adds to sense of threat
- alliteration to suggest threat
- short sharp description

- contrasting longer sentence including simile turned into metaphor
- use of harsh alliteration to stress threat
- drawing attention to clash of colour

The piercing eye glares, beak poised to peck.

Crimson punk comb crowns its kingdom, declaring control.

Orange feathers clash mirroring the harsh tone of eye and beak.

If you look at the example of shared writing here, you will see there is a margin listing all the features focused on. This is a very useful way of keeping yourself and the class focused on the skills you are trying to teach. When they come to write, you want them to show that they can use these skills themselves. It is a good idea to prepare for shared writing in this way so you have a prewritten example that you have crafted in advance, with the key features in the margin, as this will help keep you focused when shared writing. Obviously do not hold it in your hand and copy it – go with suggestions from the class as long as they fit in with the writing tools you wish to illustrate. The art of shared writing is to maintain the illusion that the writing has been co-constructed with the class while creating an excellent model that will help the class know what to imitate. It's not easy and is full of pitfalls, as Stu Gray honestly explains in his history chapter – see **page 244**.

Video clip 33 is a very useful video of Pie teaching the art of short-burst writing at a conference using the picture of a tiger's eye. Also look at **Video clip 13** of Pie teaching short-burst writing to a Year 6 class using a challenging image of clock cog wheels – some background to this is explained on **page 87**. You will notice in both examples that Pie is writing on a flip chart – a key piece of equipment for shared writing because it helps if the students can see the writing and editing process in action with all changes visible, a process that is masked if demonstrated on screen. Because the class is used to the short-burst writing technique, they rise to the challenge of this image.

As emphasised earlier, shared writing is absolutely key to teaching English. **See the online Teacher's notes** for suggestions of how to use these videos as part of training sessions on shared writing. Interestingly, when Warren Road Primary (a Talk for Writing training school in Orpington) held an open morning for secondary school English teachers to come and see what the children were achieving, the teachers were astounded by the quality of the writing that they saw in Year 6 classes – if you look at **chapter 9b** you will see what I mean. One local grammar-school teacher commented, "I think we're just giving the children opportunities to write; I don't think we are teaching them how to write." Another, from a different school, said that the Year 6 pupils were achieving higher standards of writing than her Year 11s. You may want to look at **handout 4 online** after watching these two videos and reflect on which of the aspects of shared writing you do well, and which need further development. The more skilled a teacher is at shared writing, the easier they make it look but it is a very significant skill. When done well, it greatly increases the students'

writing skills; done badly, especially if it is not interactive, it's like watching paint dry and will further discourage anyone from becoming a confident writer. One useful technique is to give the class whiteboards when doing shared writing so they can jot down lots of ideas and then use them when they come to write.

Short-burst writing practised regularly will quickly build the writing skills and related confidence students need to become effective writers within the discipline of English. To keep the hand in, every now and again begin a lesson with an effective image and tell the students they have say four minutes to craft a powerful brief description. Because they have been trained in the art, the class will immediately know how to focus on the image and decide which features they want to bring out and begin to write powerfully.

Using these techniques allowed 9-year old Rosannah to look at a close-up image of a bee and write so effectively. Just look at her opening image: **Aubergine eyes glimmer**. Shakespeare couldn't have described it more perfectly. Because Pie had taught her how to observe, she noticed that the purple, bloated eyes looked like aubergines and spun the simile into a more powerful metaphor. Read her poem aloud and you can immediately hear that this child knows how to focus and make every word that she writes count.

> The bee hovers.
> Aubergine eyes glimmer.
>
> Fragile wings quiver.
> Lemon pollen dusts his pencil-lead legs.
>
> Giant daisy petals curve back
> and wave like long lost cousins.
>
> Striped body shivers in the summer sunlight.
>
> The bee is a glistening jewel,
> sparkling in the spotlight,
> flitting effortlessly,
> from flower to flower.
>
> Rosannah – 9 years old

Equally, this technique could be used by art teachers, or anyone else who wants a class to focus on an image, to demonstrate the sort of annotations or other writing they want to model.

Using images to teach a specific skill

A useful extension spine-poem activity is to use an image to teach one particular skill. The art is to select a picture that will scaffold the learners in perfecting a challenging skill like personification (the attribution of a personal nature or human characteristics to something non-human). Here I have chosen a picture of a wild tortoise caught in the act of eating flowers in my garden, a *crime* much beloved by tortoises.

WARM UP KEY SKILLS WITH SHORT-BURST WRITING 143

What you can see	– verb that personifies	– extension
• The tortoise		
• Orange daisies		
• A flower victim		

Illustrate how to use personification by deciding on, say, three features that lend themselves to the technique. In this case, I have selected the guilt of the tortoise, the smiling witness flowers and the hapless flower victim and listed these in the *What you can see* column. Scaffold the activity by having two other columns, one for a verb that personifies and the final column for a phrase to extend the personification and make it more powerful by illuminating the image.

What you can see	– verb that personifies	– extension
• The tortoise	signals its guilt,	caught in the act.
• Orange daisies	sunnily smile,	smug witnesses of the robbery.
• A flower victim	appeals for justice	Pointing to the evidence

Then, through shared writing, devise some powerful examples of how this extension could be crafted. When complete, read through the three sentences to demonstrate to the class that you have to read your work through to check if you have built up a powerful description. (As always with shared writing, be prepared, so you have worked out the general flow of what you are going to write in advance.)

Now invite the class to have a go themselves using a different image. The most difficult aspect of personification is selecting verbs which personify so, before letting the class have a go themselves, support them by brainstorming potential verbs to personify the actions suggested by the image. Ask the class to look at this image of a tree, which invites personification because the trunk seems to have a face. They may choose to focus on

- *the trunk*
- *the branches*
- *the moss on the ground.*

Now brainstorm a range of verbs that personify:

- *the trunk* – *smiles, waits, captures, terrorises, stalks*
- *the branches* – *reach out, entrap, guard*
- *the moss* – *lures, deceives, invites*

Ask the class to discuss their ideas before they start writing so they have a chance to talk the text they are going to write. Then give them a short time (say two minutes) to write in silence crafting powerful extended personification on their mini whiteboards. When the time is up, ask students to present the sentences they are pleased with and display a few examples. If this is linked to an opportunity to use some of their ideas in a related piece of description (see the **I am** example below and the next chapter), they will immediately select the best of their ideas and integrate them into their work. Once taught, such skills can be quickly embedded if they are focused on in within the unit and embedded in later units. And, of course, when asked to comment on the techniques used in a particular piece of writing by someone else, they will be able to recognise such techniques and comment meaningfully on their effectiveness. Just because its personification, it doesn't make it good.

Embedding understanding through wider reading

To strengthen understanding, include short examples of whatever features you are focusing on from texts you are currently reading with the class. For example, if you want your students to understand the potential power of personification in action, look no further than Charles Dickens, the master of personification, alongside the skill of name-it. The names of his characters (Scrooge, Havisham, Deadlock, Uriah Heep) like the images associated with them, immediately tell you a lot about their personality. Perhaps his greatest use of personification is in *Great Expectations*. Use booktalk open questioning techniques, for example: "Tell me how has the author chosen to narrate the story" or, "Tell me how the author has made the reader feel that everything is against Pip" to help students understand how a story can reveal its moral message by showing how inanimate things take on human characteristics. Meanwhile human beings become dehumanised and identified with objects, like Pip's sister's obsession with portable property. Here, the terrified young Pip sets out to take the food he has stolen from this tyrannical sister (the aptly named Mrs Gargery) to the beleaguered convict on the marshes:

> *The mist was heavier yet when I got out upon the marshes, so that, instead of my running at everything, everything seemed to run at me. This was very disagreeable to a guilty mind. The gates and dykes and banks came bursting at me through the mist, as if they cried as plainly as could be, "A boy with Somebody else's pork pie! Stop him!" The cattle came upon me with like suddenness, staring out of their eyes, and steaming out of their nostrils, "Holloa, young thief!" One black ox, with a white cravat on – who even had to my awakened conscience something of a clerical air – fixed me so obstinately with his eyes, and moved his blunt head round in such an accusatory manner as I moved round, that I blubbered out to him, "I couldn't help it, sir! It wasn't for myself I took it."*

Short extracts of great writing like this are brilliant both as a means of improving writing and for helping students build their skills on how to comment on the writing of others.

WARM UP KEY SKILLS WITH SHORT-BURST WRITING

The line poem technique

I am the ...

In many ways, the line-poem technique is even simpler than the spine-poem technique. In this case, use repetition of a key line to bring out the potential of an image. The example here is a picture of Albert Einstein, a face identifiable by many students. Begin by brainstorming words that sum up the mood of the picture: *pensive, thoughtful, reflective, ponderous, entranced, tranquil, etc,* and flag them up as a flipchart, as pictured below. Then ask the students to focus on one feature and construct an interesting sentence on their whiteboards, giving them a couple of examples, for example, *I am the eyebrows deep in thought; I am the eyes trying to picture the solution*, so they are clear about what they have to do.

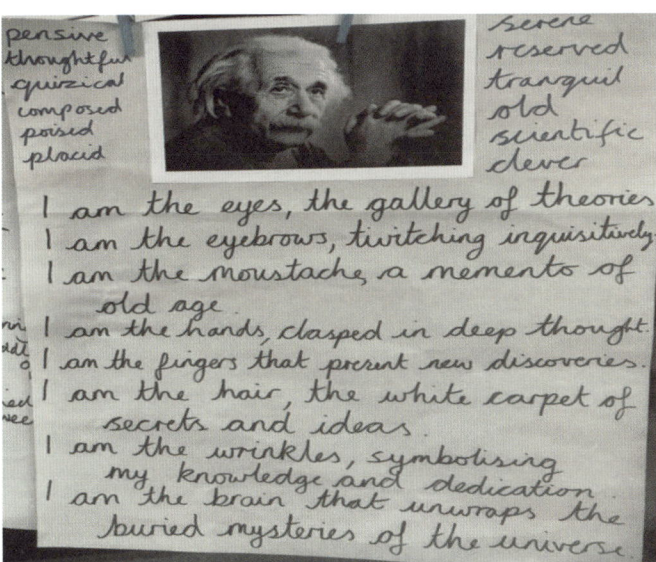

Then, through shared writing, bring the ideas together into an effective line poem, as illustrated here. Throughout, emphasise the importance of generating ideas then judging what works best through reading your work aloud and hearing what works and what doesn't quite fit in. When you read what Jamie Thomas's Year 6 class at Warren Road Primary co-constructed, you can see how this simple technique can lead to powerful writing.

I am the **eyes**, unveiling the deep mysteries of life.
I am the **eyebrows**, raised in surprise.
I am the **nose** that sniffs out the answers to scientific theory.
I am the **moustache** that twitches mysteriously.
I am the **wrinkles**, a souvenir of old age.
I am the **hair**, hiding all the answers.
I am the **brain**, controlling the inquisitive mind.

By Class 6PT (shared writing)

The elderly gentleman sat quietly in the corner of the room, his **moustache** twitching mysteriously as he read. As I approached, I noticed the heavy **wrinkles** upon his face, a souvenir of his old age. He turned and **sniffed** the air, almost searching for the scientific theory behind the page. Two **eyes** flickered in my direction and transfixed on me as I sat down opposite him. His book was no longer the focus of his attention: he was now beginning to unveil the deep mysteries of my life.
By Class 6PT (shared writing)

Now build their writing skills by showing the class how they can use the line poem as the source of ideas for a longer, more sophisticated piece of writing about a character of their own creating, selecting which ideas they want to use to bring the character alive. Show the class how to do this as illustrated by this shared writing from class 6PT. Here, the class had first been involved in co-constructing the *I am* poem above through shared writing, before being involved in turning the poem into a prose description of an entirely different character. They then wrote their own character description using the technique.

> **Co-construct specific toolkits that have a focus and a purpose**

Line-poems like spine poems can be used to build up a wide range of writing skills. In this case, it is being used to develop characterisation. It can then form part of a characterisation toolkit, so that the students know, when creating a character, the tools to choose from and how to make them powerful. If you look at the Warren Road characterisation toolkit pictured here, you will see that the *I am* technique has been highlighted. See **video clip 34** to watch Jamie presenting this unit of work to an audience of primary teachers interested in achieving greater depth in writing in KS2.

For more information on how to develop toolkits, see *Creating Storytellers and Writers* which contains all the key toolkits for fiction writing and how to build them up year on year. Short-burst writing related to image is also perfect preparation for Year 11 creative writing exams, for example, AQA's question 5: writing inspired by an image.

Making every word count – the art of pared-down writing

> *"Imagine what you are writing about. See it and live it. Do not think it up laboriously, as if you were working out mental arithmetic. Just look at it, touch it, smell it, listen to it, turn yourself into it. When you do this, the words look after themselves like magic."*

This is another important quotation from Ted Hughes' *Poetry in the Making*. The curse of so much writing, especially given a primary curriculum that often leads to an obsession with drilling extended noun phrases and fronted adverbials, is over writing. If we are not careful, the ladling on of adjectives and adverbs can be seen as good in its own right, regardless of the actual effect. Perhaps the best cure for this is to follow Ted Hughes' advice. Ask the class to picture something in their past that is significant to them. Ask them to think about the senses that they associate with it: the sights, sounds, smells, tastes and feelings that it recalls. Then introduce Pie's simple frame:

I come from the smell of …
The taste of …
The feel of
The sound of
I can still see

Tell the class to write about their memory using this frame and limit them to a maximum of three or four adjectives or adverbs. You may want to provide them with a personal example. Here's mine:

I come from the smell of strawberries sweltering in summer heat,
the taste of raspberries stolen from the fruit cage,
the feel of sawing wood on the bomb rack,
the sound of blackbirds staking their territory.
I still see that empty eye protecting the nest,
mirroring intermittent madness.
A lost love of reading, walking, nature –
staring blankly at birds, trees, flowers:
no longer determined her girls would
receive the education denied her generation.

It is a surprisingly empowering framework. Being prevented from searching out endless adjectives or adverbs forces you to select just the right noun or verb needed and makes you pare down writing powerfully. The focus of the framework makes you do exactly what Ted Hughes has recommended, and it works. Combine this framework with his short time limit and the results should be good. Remember to say that if the students want to keep their work entirely private, they are entitled to do so. Such writing may recall very painful memories. The right to privacy is important in creative writing.

Using a line from a poem as a way in

Another book about teaching poetry that is essential reading for English teachers is Kenneth Koch's *Rose, Where Did You Get that Red?* It is full of engaging suggestions that help students both appreciate the poems of others and be able to write more effectively themselves. One excellent suggestion is to use the opening line of a short, simple but powerful poem as a way in to inspiring students' own writing, for example William Carlos Williams engaging *This is just to say* (www.poetryfoundation.org/poems/56159/this-is-just-to-say). I adapted Koch's suggestions and have found it highly effective in achieving excellent writing from students and teachers alike. Interestingly, just one line from a short poem as a scaffold, combined with the reassurance that the poem need only be a few lines long, seems enough to get everyone writing.

First, ask the class to think of someone that they know, preferably not in their current class or school, whom they have felt humiliated or bullied by in some sort of way. Then read the poem aloud to the class so they can hear the rhythm and the sentiment of the poem. Then ask them to think what they would like to say to whichever person they have focused on, beginning with the line *This is just to say*…. Allow a minute's focused silence to give everyone a chance to concentrate their thoughts.

Now give your class three minutes in which to write in silence creating their own version, remembering to tell them not to try to make the poem rhyme. When the time is up, ask them to read through their work and amend as they think best. Ask if anyone wants to share what they have written – obviously don't pressure anyone, but usually a few people are keen to share their writing because it can be cathartic. Again, it is important that people can keep their writing private if they wish to do so. Such writing can be very powerful. I will never forget one training day when I noticed a woman who had arrived looking very upset, as if she had just had an argument with someone and had been crying. She remained very distant throughout the morning and I made the wise decision to leave her in peace. But when it came to this activity, she suddenly perked up. I noticed she had no hesitation in deciding the focus of her words and wrote swiftly almost grinding her pen into the paper. She read it through carefully, adjusted a few things and, for the first time in the day, smiled. She folded her writing carefully, hid it in a pocket and looked triumphant. She cheered up after that. Writing is powerful.

> **This is Just to Say**
>
> This is just to say,
> your endless memos
> used to haunt me
>
> but then
> I revelled in their receipt –
> even looked forward to the next.
>
> Forgive me, they reflect your inadequacy
> not mine.

At an earlier time, I had decided to write myself at the same time as my group. What I wrote in two minutes is on the left. And yes, I think, on completion, I shared the woman's sense of triumph. My memory of a fellow member of a school management team was from many year's back but the sense of defeating the monster was still very much alive. If you count how many adjectives I had chosen to use, it turns out to be just one. There had been no restriction but, of course, the model was very pared down, nudging me in the right direction. It is the choice of just the right noun and verb that makes the writing work.

Developing a hook-your-reader toolkit to support engaging writing

Once all the key writing tools that help a writer hook their reader and keep them engaged have been introduced through short-burst writing activities, an effective way to embed understanding is to use this transform-a-sentence activity. This shows the power of the different tools the students can choose from when writing, depending on the audience, purpose and form of what they are writing.

Choose a very basic, somewhat-boring sentence like, *The cat sat on the mat*, as the base from which to revisit the effects of different techniques as illustrated below. Then ask the students to transform a similar sentence like *The parrot perched in its cage*, using each hook-your-reader tool in turn.

This grid is also available as **Handout 10** on the website link. It is worth

WARM UP KEY SKILLS WITH SHORT-BURST WRITING

| The hook your reader toolkit: choose the tools that will create the effect you want |||
The tools	**How to do it**	**Examples**
Change words	a. Select precise words b. Name it c. Tighten the wording: d. Try something new:	a. The kitten curled up on its mat. b. The Siamese cat reclined on the Persian rug. c. The cat was purring sitting on the mat **becomes**, The purring cat on the mat … d. The skateboarding cat
Add in	a. Use adjectives & adverbs selectively b. Drop in phrases and clauses:	a. The cosy cat slumbered on the sofa. The cat slumbered cosily on the sofa. b. The cat, keeping a crafty eye on Rover's whereabouts, remained on its mat.

1. **Add on**
a. phrases and clauses
b/c. begin with:
d. images
	a. ed-ing-ly starters
	
	b. because, if, when, although, since etc
	c. In the/On the … etc
	d. similies:
		a. Vexed by Rover's sudden approach, the cat …
		   Seeing Rover approaching rapidly, the cat …
		   Instinctively sensing Rover's approach, the cat …
		b. If the cat sensed Rover's approach, it fled.
		   Although the cat sensed Rover's approach, it …
		c. In the doorway, the cat sat on the mat.
		d. as cosy as a slumbering cat on its mat

Show don't tell	Make the reader picture the scene and experience the emotions.	**Tell:** The cat sat nervously on the mat tensely watching Rover approach. **Show:** The cat tensed its paws on the mat, fur bristling, watching out for any sign of Rover.
Change sentence type	Use questions, exclamations and bossy sentences as well as normal sentences.	Is the cat on its mat? Sit on your mat, cat. That lazy cat's always sitting on its mat!
Vary sentences	Simple: Compound: Complex: Minor:	**Simple:** The hungry cat sat on its mat. **Compound:** The hungry cat sat on its mat and stared at the fridge intently. **Complex:** Staring intently at the fridge, the hungry cat sat on its mat. **Minor:** Cat.
Reorder sentence	Spin sentences to achieve the effect you want	On the mat, sat the cat. Selecting its favourite mat, the cat sat down.
Special effects	**Sound effects:** repetition, rhythm, onomatopoeia, alliteration **Imagery:** simile, metaphor, personification	How long has the cat in a hat sat on that mat? The hissing cat sat spitting on its mat. The kitten curled up comfily on the carpet. The black-as-coal cat sat on its mat. The coal-black cat sat on its mat. The cat cradled its kitten on the mat.
Hook reader in 1st paragraph	Move hook to front and jump straight in	Opening sentence: This is my big chance, thought Rover, seeing the cat oblivious in sleep on its mat.
Make every word, phrase, sentence earn its place -	Edit work carefully getting rid of overwriting and ineffective repetition	• The smug, self-satisfied cat purred contentedly on its much-loved favourite mat. versus • The smug cat purred on its beloved mat.
Slow down at significant moments		It was just then, when it seemed to sense Rover's presence, that the cat knew it was not the right moment to return to its beloved mat.
Change the writer's perspective	Instead of writing in 3rd-person mode (omniscient author/ author as God) write in 1st person mode (autobiographical mode)	Practically all the sentences above are in the 3rd person (someone writing about a cat). Here, the example above is rewritten in autobiographical style (narrator as cat): My cat's sixth sense told me that the dreaded Rover had just entered the house. I couldn't see, hear or smell him but I knew. Now was sadly not the right moment to return to my beloved mat.

displaying your version of this grid, once you've developed it with a class, for ease of reference, so that you can quickly refer to techniques as necessary and build confidence both in the students' use of such techniques and their ability to comment on such techniques when used by others. Short-burst writing, combined with dialogic talk analysis of short extracts of quality writing, are sure-fire means of both improving the students' writing and of helping build their skills so they can confidently comment on the writing of others. They will have something interesting to say and will know how to say it in an engaging way.

The Talk for Writing process when teaching English

The classic Talk for Writing process (see below) was developed to suit the needs of English teaching for both fiction and non-fiction. Short-burst writing is a key part of the imitation stage and enables you to teach all the key writing tools while integrating all the necessary grammar features in context, as exemplified by the following chapter. The key difference between this English version of the TfW process and the disciplinary subject version (**see page 11**) is that in English the key content is expression. This can usually be illustrated within the model text. However, in other subjects, the focus is on content along with how to express this content. This will be much wider than any single model text. Therefore, the process has been adapted to represent how TfW supports the content stages. In such a way, the students are helped to comprehend the content by talking about whatever topic is being focused on, before being faced with writing about it in any way.

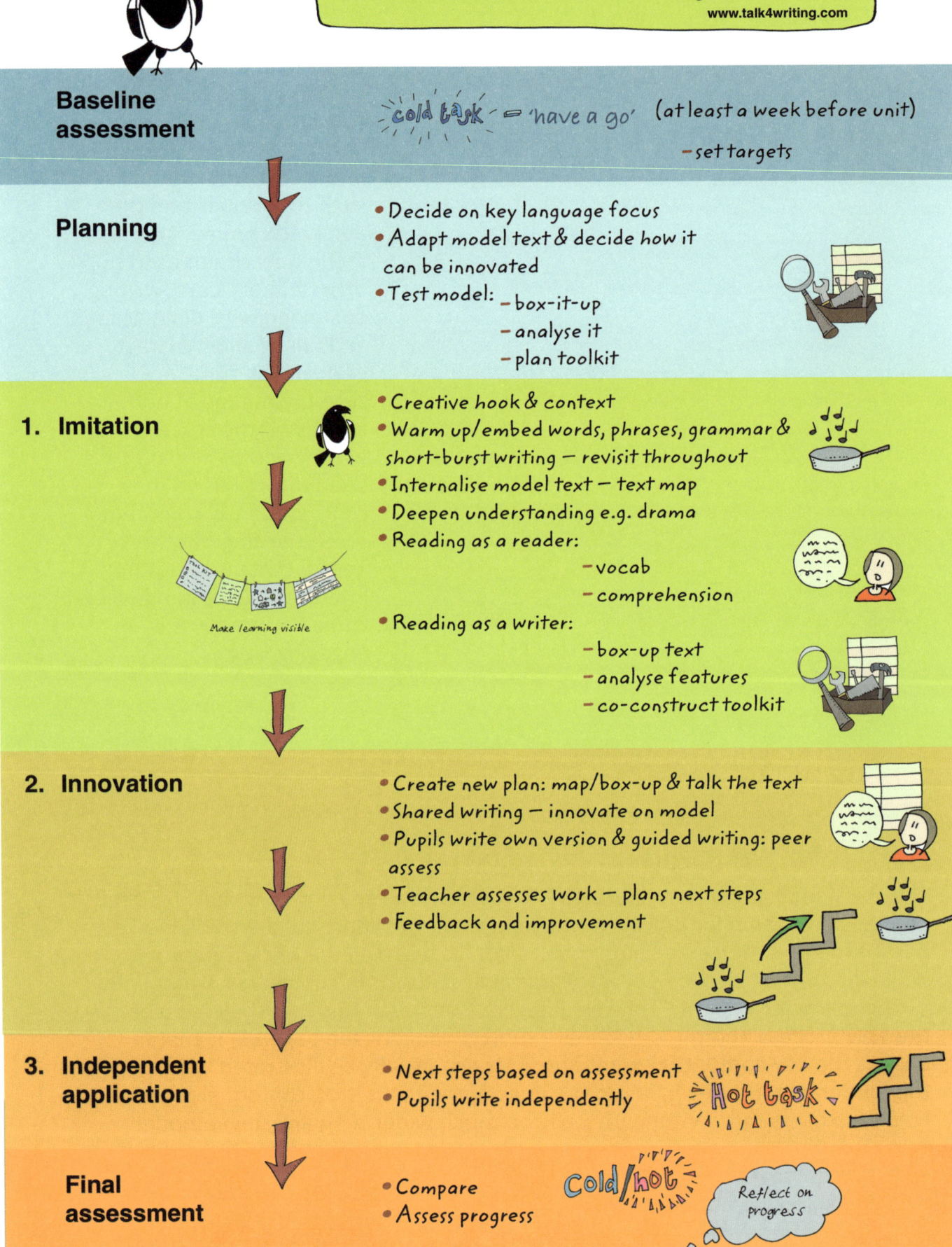

Chapter 9b: Transforming creative writing in primary schools

 Talk for Writing consultant Jamie Thomas explains how to craft a model text, supported by focused, short-burst writing that contextualises grammar activities, to help pupils understand the ingredients of effective action writing, embed existing skills and add a few more action tools to their repertoire.

Getting the model right

The model text below, based on a short, animated film by Josh Carroll and Scott McWhinnie, was written to explicitly demonstrate the variety of ways that action can be explored in narrative. Its initial purpose was to help Y6 pupils at Warren Road Primary School develop their use of action beyond the concept of creating excitement or energy. What lies at the heart of the unit of work is the way that action can be explored through a character's internal voice, their thoughts, and what they say, as well as what they do. This model was enhanced by the class book that we were reading alongside this unit: Malorie Blackman's *Thief*.

The Catch

Below the spidery knot of trees and bushes, I sat, staring at the murky water, a single fish in my bowl. The weight of the world leant on my shoulders, dominating my thoughts. How would we survive? What could I do?

SNAP! An ear-splitting howl filled the air, shattering the silence. Tentatively, I crept towards the dense copse that lay before me. My arms were trembling; my heart pounded like a bass drum. I did not know what lay behind the wall of leaves, but I had to find out.

Parting the foliage, I caught a glimpse of the victim: a fire-like coat of red filled with rage, panic and desperation. Man-made metal teeth held her captive. Without thinking, I took my knife, jammed it into the snare and prized it open. In an instant, the fox disappeared towards the lake … towards the bowl … towards my fish! Tearing after her, worry began to flood over me. What if she ate my only catch? Our eyes locked across the bowl, the fish in her jaw. Silence. Then she was gone.

"Come back you scoundrel! That's my fish!" In front of me, a labyrinth of thorns mocked me, daring me to enter – but rage spurred me on. Like a hunter, I bounded after my prey. Deeper and deeper I tunnelled in pursuit of the cunning thief, until I was blinded and alone.

"He...ll...o? Is...any...one...there?" As the fog lifted, I saw the jaw-dropping sight that lay before me: a glistening lake full of fish. The fox smiled. My prayers had been answered.

The thinking behind the models

In this unit, there are, in fact, two model texts. The one above is the model that the pupils story map and learn off by heart. It has been written to explicitly show how the tools for action can be contextualised within a short narrative. Each tool has been used to have an effect on the reader, whether it be to generate pace, build intrigue, advance the action or deepen their understanding of the events as they unfold. The text is deliberately short (258 words) so that the pupils can quickly internalise the key features and patterns in order to add these to their own repertoire as writers. As with all model texts, the teacher needs to adapt the sophistication of the model to meet the needs of their class: this class, having been taught in this style for 5 years, is on the way to achieving writing standards well above the expected level.

The second model text is an embellished version of the first that is later explored with the pupils during the 'Reading as a reader' phase (see stage 7 below). This model focuses on character perspective, with a second voice sharing the storytelling responsibility. This additional tool enhances the action by giving the reader an insight into the thoughts and emotions of both characters in the story as it unfolds. Balancing these two voices to ensure that the action is continually developed and not simply repeated through the second voice, provides a significant challenge for the pupils.

The stages of the teaching sequence

This section explains the logic behind how the unit has been structured – as you will see, it has been shaped by the Talk for Writing process as illustrated on **page 150**.

The imitation stage

1. The hook: A well-chosen hook can be a gateway into a child's imagination, allowing them time to dwell on something and consider a life away from their own. When I first began Talk for Writing, two of Pie's signature sentences stuck in my brain: "You can't create or imagine something out of nothing," and "Imagination is the manipulation of what you already know." This is so true! In a world where many pupils fail to stop and look at the amazing things that are all around them, it is our responsibility to open their eyes and help them take note. A cleverly manufactured hook will not only capture their imagination, it will also, potentially, provide a purpose and audience for their writing.

The wonderful thing about basing a unit of work around a wordless animation or picture book is that the story is already there for the pupils to engage with and develop. Therefore, in this unit, the short animation called *The Catch* (https://vimeo.com/47100690) acts as both the hook and the stimulus for the cold task.

2. The cold task: The point of the cold task is to provide the pupils with an opportunity to show how successful they can be within the focus of the unit, in this case, action. It is important to not see this as a test – we do not want them to fail. Before they write, spend time discussing what tools they have previously been taught about action (the latest edition of *Creating Storytellers and Writers* suggests what these action tools may be from reception to Y6. You may like to discuss books and stories that they identify as being rich in action and explore what makes these successful. Activating the pupils' memory is an essential element of the cold task as it will enable the pupils to give a true representation of what they can do, not just what they can immediately remember. However, it is also important that we do not start teaching at this stage as we want to use the written outcomes as an assessment tool for the unit that follows.

I often like to help the pupils activate prior learning by providing a simple model and asking them to discuss how effective it is. For example, for this unit, I devised this warm-up activity:

> He heard them coming. He ran. He got away.
>
> Is this a well-written piece of action writing? Explain your reasons.

Through discussion as a class, the pupils quickly recalled the key elements that develop action in narrative which tuned them in prior to writing. They then had a short amount of time, around 20 minutes, to demonstrate these skills. The cold task acts as an assessment for learning tool. Having read them, I was able to ask myself:

- What does my whole class need to be taught about action?
- What do different groups of pupils need to be taught?
- What individual skills and targets can I set for each pupil?

This assessment then drove the teaching that follows, so that I could plan short-burst writing opportunities to explore and practise the key skills and techniques required by the class. At this stage, it is sometimes necessary to tweak and adapt the model text to ensure that all of the tools being taught are contextualised.

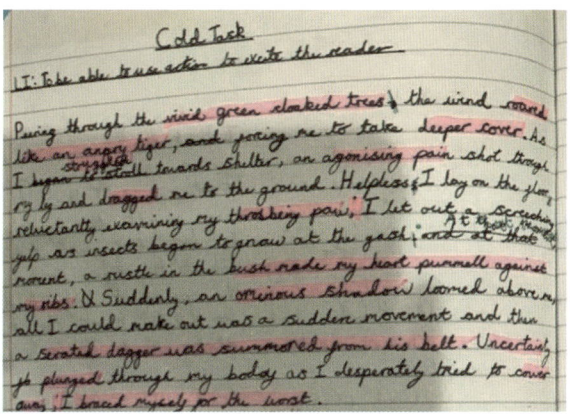

Here is an extract from one child's cold task: the pupil clearly demonstrates an ability to mirror the feelings of the main character through the setting, using vocabulary choice and personification to enhance the mood. They also demonstrate a strong understanding of how to show not tell – hinting at the character's feelings through their actions e.g. *peering, struggled, reluctantly examining, plunged through my body*, etc. This was fairly typical of the skills of the class.

In order to develop them further, I wanted to teach them how to manipulate sentence length and construction in order to affect the reader. This included skills such as the use of repetition to build tension and how short, snappy sentences can create an uneasy atmosphere. I also wanted to teach them how to use speech to advance the action and show emotion.

3. Story mapping and internalising the model

I began by reading the short story model aloud to the class, modelling how expression and tone enhances the storytelling, generating excitement and anticipation. It is essential that the pupils hear the model text in its entirety before they begin to learn it as this will enhance their own understanding.

In order to support the pupils in the internalising of the model, draw story maps and add in key actions. As you can see, the map I've drawn here is short and simple, focusing on key points. Remember – the map and actions are there as an aide memoire and should be kept to a minimum.

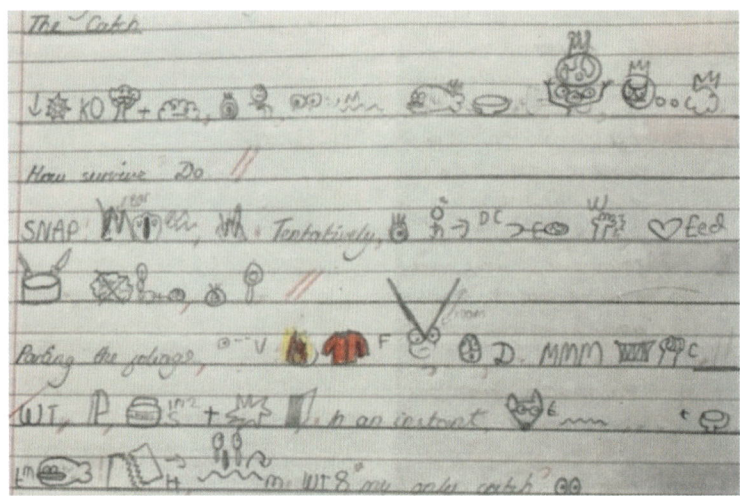

Getting the pupils then to quickly map the story themselves, as illustrated here, will help them to internalise and learn it.

Whereas younger pupils or less confident writers may benefit from learning a model word for word, by upper KS2 we want to get the flavour of the text into the pupils' storytelling repertoire and then encourage them to begin to retell it in their own words, embellishing and adding in detail to enrich the story. After all, this is what innovation is all about so, at this age, why not embrace this from the start? What is important is that they are developing an understanding of the structure of the model, as well as the language features and sentence patterns that drive the action forward.

4. Deepening understanding through drama: Drama is a key strategy to help pupils deepen their imaginative engagement with a story. It can also help to have pupils writing in-role as if they were one of the characters. Here are six drama activities that suited this text well:

- ***Freeze frames:*** working in small groups, the pupils take each paragraph in turn and create a freeze frame that captures the essence of the story. Focus on body position and facial expression to illustrate the power of show not tell.

- ***Hot seat MC:*** interview the main characters and explore their intentions, emotions, motivations and desires. Encourage the class to ask questions that delve deep into the character's backstory.

- ***Jump into a scene – see, hear, feel, think:*** as a scene is being performed, freeze the actors and 'jump in' to the scene, asking them to describe what they see, hear, feel or think at that precise moment.
- ***Eyewitness, on-looker or spy:*** in twos or threes, get the pupils to discuss what they saw from another character's perspective (e.g. the stable hand, livery boy or maid).
- ***Conscience alley:*** tune in to the emotions and feelings of a character.
- ***Rumours about the MC:*** like a game of Chinese Whispers, get the pupils to start spreading rumours about things they saw linked to the story. What may they have misinterpreted?

5. Short-burst writing – warming up the writing tools

Whilst internalising the model text, I had planned in opportunities to teach specific skills linked to the focus of the unit, in this case action. Each tool provided the pupils with another skill that they could draw upon when they came to write their own stories. A wealth of games and activities can be found in the Jumpstart books. In this unit, I used the following 5 short-burst-writing activities to warm up the tools needed for the unit.

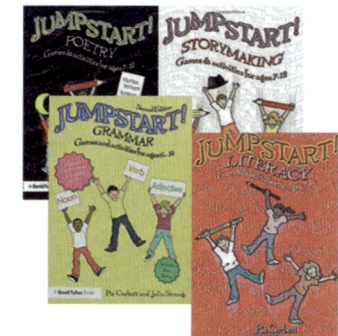

a) Vary sentence length to affect the reader

Either choose an extract from a class novel or write a brief paragraph that exemplifies the tools being explored, e.g.

> *Sid froze. He could hear their footsteps, heavy on the road, thudding along beside him. Without thinking, he spurted forwards, dodged into an alley and sprinted into the main road. He had lost them – the traffic roared past, but no one had followed him.*

- Talk through the model line by line with the pupils, identifying the tools:
    - Use a character's reaction in a short, punchy sentence to show an immediate impact and build tension (*Sid froze.*)
    - Build the intensity by revealing what they can hear or feel with added detail (*He could hear their footsteps, heavy on the road, thudding along behind him.*)
    - Use a dramatic fronted adverbial to advance the action (*Without thinking,*)
    - Generate pace with a sentence of 3 (*He spurted forwards, dodged into an alley and sprinted into the main road.*)
    - Connect ideas with punctuation that keeps the reader guessing (*He had lost them – the traffic roared past, but no-one had followed him.*)
- Through shared, short-burst writing, model how to use these tools in another context.
- Provide opportunity for the pupils to repeat the activity, exploring their own action scenes.

b) Mirror the character's feelings through the setting

Either choose an extract from a class novel or write a brief paragraph that exemplifies the tools being explored, building upon and contextualising previous tools. For this unit, I wrote:

> Later, she woke with a start. The sun had slipped behind the trees, casting charred shadows across the water's oily surface. A cold breeze whispered through the reeds. Jo shuddered. A twig broke, leaves rustled and something moved towards her! What was it?
>
> Jo ran. Branches whipped at her face and brambles tore at her feet. She was sure that she could hear something behind her, its feet thudding through the undergrowth – something breathing.

- Encourage pupils to identify the tools previously discussed but also identify any new tools connected to action, e.g.
    o Mirror the character's feelings through the setting (*The sun had slipped behind the trees, casting charred shadows across the water's oily surface.*)
    o Bring the setting to life through personification to intensify the scene (*A cold breeze whispered through the reeds.*)
- Give the pupils time to experiment with the tools, crafting short passages and analysing their effect on the reader. Here is an example from one Y6 child, practising using the tools identified:

> The eerie sound of footsteps curdled in her blood, tore through her skin, gnawed at her bones and jeopardized her soul. They thudded louder with every flaming heartbeat, targetting me amongst the towering, telescopic trees. A hair-raising shriek engulfed the trepid night, as a vortex of agony possessed her. A tremor of flamboyant fear surged through her mind. A cold breeze whispered to her within the woods which flanked her, as all remnants of happiness deteriated. Two white lights murdered the crepuscular night, shattering her heart – all of her attempts had been inept. They had found her...

c) Vary the adverbial to add specific detail to the action
- Begin by giving the pupils a simple sentence. Here I chose *Bertie dug a deep hole*.

- Explore a number of similar sentences (all of which use forms of adverbials) and discuss how they alter the initial sentence:
    - **_After_ _tea_**, *Bertie dug a deep hole.* (Use a fronted adverbial of time – when)
    - **_In_ _the garden_**, *Bertie dug a deep hole.* (Use a prepositional phrase – where)
    - **_Carefully_**, *Bertie dug a deep hole.* (Use an adverb – how)
    - **_As fast_ _as_ _a ferret_**, *Bertie dug a deep hole.* (Use a simile – *as* or *like*)
    - *Hop**ing** to reach Australia, Bertie dug a deep hole.* (Progressive – *ing* opener)
- Give the pupils another simple sentence, e.g. *Michu sat by the lake fishing.* Let them explore, adding in the different types of adverbial and discuss how it changes the meaning and impact of the sentence.

d) Balance description, action and dialogue
- Discuss the balance of description, action and dialogue and identify how dialogue can be used to reveal something about a character or advance the action.
- Through shared writing, model how to incorporate the three elements effectively, drawing on any previous toolkits around character and dialogue if taught. Here you can see the shared writing I produced with the class to help them understand what these tools looked like.

Give pupils time to explore the tools for themselves. The example below shows a Y6 child's short-burst writing paragraph, balancing description, action and dialogue:

e) Use poetry to strengthen creativity and connect with a character's inner feelings

- Using a visual stimulus that has a deep metaphorical meaning, discuss and brainstorm any language or emotions that it evokes. Encourage the pupils to capture and magpie these ideas for themselves. The image here shows the brainstorm in a pupil's magpie book.

- Explore how action is not only what is happening on the outside but also the host of emotions and feelings that are evolving on the inside.

- Using the vocabulary generated, create short poems that focus on the words and their effect. Ensure that the pupils do not get hung up on writing narrative as this will take away from the impact the poem holds.

- Once the poem is complete, model how to turn this into a piece of prose, raiding the poem for vocabulary and content, whilst filling in the narrative.

- Then give the pupils time to create their own poems and turn them into their own pieces of narrative.

Here is the shared writing of a poem that I created with the class alongside the prose that it was turned into. The pupils then wrote their own poems and used them as a source of inspiration for prose. **Video clip 34** shows me demonstrating how to do short-burst writing with a Year 6 class.

Bottled up

Swallowed within the
desolate vortex of her loneliness,
lost in a labyrinth of decision
all hope was shackled.
Shame...
Guilt...
Regret.

Lydia sat in isolation, swallowed within the desolate vortex of her loneliness. An innocent tear trickled down her cheek, tumbling into the emptiness of the world that surrounded her. Hundreds of questions entered her mind, taunting her thoughts. Why? How? Who? Staring out of the window, she could see the purity of the world outside and knew all hope was now shackled; she would have to live with her shame. Guilt was painted across her face for the world to see. How she regretted her actions. A gentle cough interrupted her thoughts...

6. Warming up grammar and punctuation in context

Plan into the model text a handful of key grammar focuses that the pupils can imitate and develop through short-burst writing. Here are some of the elements that are contextualised in *The Catch* and then warmed up in the imitation stage.

a) Fronted adverbials:

A selection of adverbials has been used to add in extra detail linked to when, where and how an action takes place. Positioning the adverbial at the start of the sentence emphasises how the author has choices available to them other than the subject-verb sentence starter, which can be repetitive and laborious for the reader.

- **Where?** (prepositional phrases) *Below the spidery knot of trees and bushes, ... In front of me, ... Deeper and deeper, ...*
- **When?** *In an instant, ... As the fog lifted, ...*
- **How?** *Tentatively, ... Parting the foliage, ... Without thinking, ... Tearing after her, ...*

b) Rhetorical questions:

Throughout the story, a series of rhetorical questions is used to connect the reader to the internal dilemmas that the main character faces as the story unfolds. This is not only an excellent tool to build suspense, it also acts as a cohesive devise, providing a moment's pause to gather one's thoughts before the action continues.
How would we survive? What could I do? What if she ate my only catch?

c) Use of repetition to build tension whilst advancing the action:
In an instant, the fox disappeared beneath the verdant quilt <u>towards</u> the lake … <u>towards</u> the bowl … <u>towards</u> my fish!

d) The use of colons and semicolons to create coordinating sentences that intensify the action:
- Semicolon used to separate two independent clauses, while still demonstrating that a close relationship exists between them:
  My arms were trembling; my heart pounded like a bass drum.

- Colons used to separate two independent clauses, where the second is an elaboration of the first and is being given additional emphasis:
  Parting the foliage, I caught a glimpse of the victim: a fire-like coat of red filled with rage, panic and desperation.
  As the fog lifted, I saw the jaw-dropping sight that lay before me: a glistening lake full of fish.

e) Adding additional detail by extending the sentence using a non-finite clause (a sort of incomplete subordinate clause that has no tense):
In the following examples, the added-on clauses act almost as an afterthought, showing you the thought-process of the character as they observe the action unfolding before them.

- *Below the spidery knot of trees and bushes, I sat, <u>staring at the murky water, a single fish in my bowl</u>. The weight of the world leant on my shoulders, <u>dominating my thoughts</u>.*

- *An ear-splitting howl filled the air, <u>shattering the silence</u>.*

- *In front of me, a labyrinth of thorns mocked me, <u>daring me to enter</u> – but rage spurred me on.*

f) Manipulating sentence length for a desired effect:
Short sentences are used to break up the flow of the story, creating an edgy atmosphere.

- *How would we survive? What could I do?*
- *SNAP!*
- *Silence. Then she was gone*

In contrast, patterns of three are used to create pace and fluidity to the action.

- *Without thinking, <u>I took my knife, jammed it into the snare and prized it open.</u>*
- *In an instant, the fox <u>disappeared towards the lake … towards the bowl … towards my fish!</u>*

7. Reading as a reader – embellished version
Once the pupils have internalised the model, read it with them as a reader, focusing on vocabulary and oral comprehension. Should your pupils be ready for some additional challenge, explore the embellished text as this offers greater complexity, as illustrated here:

The embellished model text

The Catch

Beneath the forest's looming canopy, I sat staring at the murky water that lay dead before me, a single fish in my bowl. The weight of the world leant on my shoulders, dominating my thoughts. How would we survive? What could I do?

I could tell that he was troubled right from the start. Out of the corner of my eye, I spotted poor Michu despondently fishing beside the half-drained pool, his confidence slowly evaporating. Watching the boy intently, I willed for him to catch something, but as his rod burst to life and the catch was reeled in, disappointment masked hope. A tiddler dangled before his eyes, relentlessly mocking his futile mission; all confidence disappeared.

SNAP! An ear-splitting howl filled the air, shattering the silence, tearing me from my daydream. Tentatively, I crept towards the dense copse that lay before me. My arms were trembling in anticipation; my heart pounded like a bass drum. What lay behind the wall of leaves, I did not know, but I had to find out.

Parting the foliage, I caught a glimpse of the victim. A fire-like coat of red filled with rage, panic and desperation. Pressing in on her from all sides, it seemed that the forest was trying to trap her in its thorny grasp. However, man-made metal teeth had held her captive.

Fatal jaws tore into my leg, holding me captive. I yelped in pain and thrashed out to be released but, to my dismay, it only made the agony more unbearable. Suddenly, I realised I was not alone. Two mischievous eyes were transfixed on my desperate struggle, ominously standing over me, blade drawn.

Without thinking, I unsheathed my knife, jammed it into the snare and prized the trap open. In an instant, the fox disappeared beneath the verdant quilt towards the lake … towards the bowl … towards my fish! Scampering after her in hot pursuit, worry began to flood over me. What if she ate my only catch? Our eyes locked across the bowl, the fish in her jaw. Silence. Calculation. Anticipation. Then she was gone.

I knew what I had to do. Charging from the undergrowth, I grabbed the pathetic fish in my teeth and darted into the forest, the boy close behind me. I sprinted past glowing leaves, quivering yellow petals and magnificent green cloaks. I jumped over piles of emeralds, thinking only of the joy that would be painted on Michu's face when he saw what lay in wait for him; joy that would dissipate his current rage.

"Come back you scoundrel! That's my fish!" The dark forest enveloped my words, issuing no reply. In front of me, a labyrinth of thorns menacingly mocked me, daring me to enter – and but rage possessed me, spurring me on. Like a hunter, I bounded after my prey, thorns tearing at my skin. Deeper and deeper I tunnelled in pursuit of the cunning thief. Deeper and deeper I chased her into the gnarled maze. Deeper and deeper I rampaged, until I was alone.

A padded quilt of fog masked what lay before me. Blinded, exhausted and alone. Already I could feel my chest tightening as panic set in. "He…ll…o? Is…any…one…there?" A faint glimmer of light began to creep out of the gloom. As the light intensified, I masked my eyes to shield them from the utopia that lay before me. I was surrounded by a curtain of dancing water, cascading into a simmering cauldron of opportunity.

I looked at him and smiled.

My prayers had been answered.

a) Vocabulary

Read the embellished story through, underlining challenging or unfamiliar vocabulary and discussing any words or expressions that might present a barrier to understanding. Provide simple, child-friendly definitions. Generate synonyms/antonyms and discuss 'shades of meaning', i.e. how strong one word is compared to another. Provide opportunities to use these words in context through word play and writing creative sentences. Here are the words and phrases I focused on:

> **'Tier two' words/phrases:**
> *forest's looming canopy; murky; weight of the world leant on my shoulders; dominating my thoughts; troubled; despondently; half-drained; confidence slowly evaporating; intently; willed; burst to life; reeled in; disappointment masked hope; dangled; relentlessly; mocking; futile; all confidence disappeared; ear-splitting howl; shattering the silence; tearing; tentatively; trembling in anticipation; pounded; parting; caught a glimpse; victim; rage; panic; desperation; thorny grasp; captive; thrashed; released; to my dismay; agony; unbearable; mischievous; transfixed; desperate; struggle; ominously; unsheathed my knife; jammed; prized; verdant quilt; scampering; in hot-pursuit; worry began to flood over me; our eyes locked; calculation; anticipation; darted; quivering; magnificent; painted on...face; dissipate; rage, scoundrel; enveloped; issuing; labyrinth; menacingly mocked; daring; rage possessed me; spurring me on; bounded; gnarled; rampaged; padded quilt; masked what lay before me; daring me to enter; exhausted; a faint glimmer of light; creep; gloom; as the light intensified; masked my eyes to shield them; utopia; a curtain of dancing water; cascading into a simmering cauldron of opportunity; my prayers had been answered.*
>
> **World knowledge & technical vocabulary:**
> *rod, catch, tiddler, dense copse, foliage, snare, undergrowth.*

b) Oral Comprehension

As a class, delve into the comprehension that lies beneath the surface of the story. Explore the text through oral enquiry, encouraging the pupils to discuss and share their thoughts, drawing on the evidence in the text to support their ideas. Whilst it is important that the pupils are empowered to steer their line of enquiry, it will be necessary to question them, deepen their ideas, ask for clarity and evidence and pose new lines of enquiry. The following list is merely a flavour of some of the questions that could be asked about this story to encourage dialogic talk. (For those not following the curriculum in England, the number references relate to the assessment domains for the Y6 reading exam.)

Paragraphs 1 & 2:
- Who is telling the story? How do you know? How does this change? (2b)
- Write down 3 words or phrases that are used to describe how Michu is feeling. (2b)

- What impression does the sentence: 'The weight of the world leant on my shoulders, dominating my thoughts' create? (2g)

Paragraphs 3 & 4:
- How was Michu feeling as he approached the copse? How do you know? (2d)
- What adjectives/similes/personification has the author used to describe the scene? What effect do they have on the reader? (2g)

Paragraphs 5 & 6:
- 'Fatal jaws ...' Why did the author use this metaphor? (2g)
- 'Mischievous ... ominously standing.' How do these words make the reader feel about Michu? (2d)

Paragraphs 7 & 8:
- 'Joy that would dissipate his current rage.' What does the word 'dissipate' mean in this context? (2a)
- What evidence is there of Michu being determined? (2d)
- How does Michu feel about the fox compared to their first encounter? (2h)

Paragraphs 9 & 10:
- Based on what you have read, what does the last paragraph suggest might happen next? Use evidence from the text to support your prediction. (2e)
- What is the main message of the story? (2c)
- The relationship of the two characters changes throughout the text. How does it change? Use evidence from the text to support your answer. (2h)

Below, you can see an example from a Y6 child's book, exploring the model for vocabulary, deepening their understanding through focused comprehension and identifying key tools and features that can be magpied and used in their own writing (see reading as a writer below).

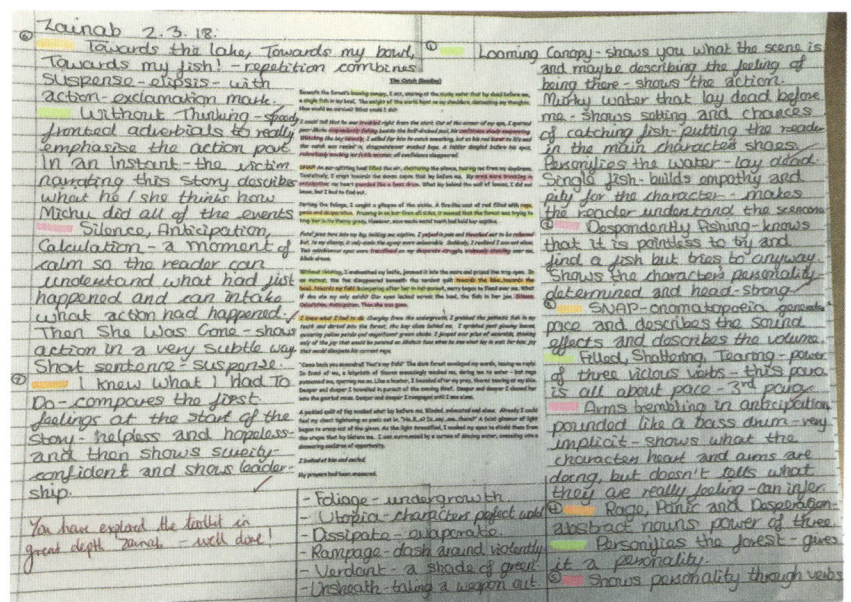

8. Reading as a writer
Now go back and re-read the text but this time as a writer. Identify the underlying sequence and pattern of the story and box it up with the class, labelling each section in sequence to capture its overall structure. Make sure that the underlying pattern uses generalisations as this will support innovation and breaking away from the model. In the example here, the class summed up what was happening in each

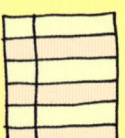

section before condensing that into the main idea or heading that would sum the section up. In the third column, we planned our innovation using our class novel.

a) Boxing up

	The Catch (key plot events)	Main idea	Possible innovation based on *Thief* by Malorie Blackman
OPENING	Michu sits fishing, staring at lake. Weight of the world on his shoulders – feels sad. Questions himself.	Main character (MC) wants something badly.	Lydia is desperate not to lose her best friend Frankie and seeks to be accepted by a group of girls, The Cosmics, in her new school.
BUILD UP	Michu hears something. He approaches and sees fox trapped in snare.	MC is having no luck. Something grabs their attention.	The Cosmics make fun of Lydia. Frankie ignores her. Lydia is told to steal a cup to be accepted into the gang.
PROBLEM	Michu sets fox free. Fox runs off and snatches fish. Michu and fox stare at one another. Fox disappears into forest.	MC is prevented by some sort of difficulty preventing their wish coming true.	Lydia battles her inner conscience.
ACTION	Michu hesitates but decides to chase fox. Chase through forest, up mountain to empty location (the lake).	MC battles/overcomes the difficulty.	Lydia dreams about the prospect of stealing the cup. She sneaks into school and is chased.
ENDING	Michu sees lake filled with giant fish. Fox and Michu form friendship and fulfil Michu's wish. Fox disappears	MC gets what they wished for.	Lydia wakes up and is thankful it is all a dream. Frankie hears about the dare and turns her back on Cosmics.

b) Create the toolkit (linked to the focus: action)

Having identified the underlying pattern and structure, read the text to identify the writer's tools. It helps if you slow the reading down, almost looking at it line by line. Tease out the tools that lend themselves to action and capture for future use. The toolkit must be co-constructed and can begin from the start of the unit, constantly being added to and developed through the reading and writing process. The purpose of the toolkit is to give the pupils a 'menu' of tools that they can pick from. The more this skill is practised with the pupils, the more they will begin to do it independently, raiding their own reading for great words, turns of phrase and writerly tricks. Remember, in creative writing we are creating tools not rules. If we want pupils to perceive themselves as writers, it is essential that we treat them like writers.

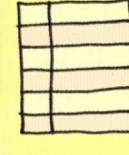

Here is an example of an action toolkit once it has been co-constructed. Note the fact that the pupils are presented with the sentence, 'To engage the reader through action I could ...'. This celebrates authorial choice and focuses on developing writing to create a desired effect. As you can see, the toolkit is colour coded: each tool is headlined in navy blue, ways of doing this are listed in green, and all examples are in brown (just like the examples in this chapter). Including examples is essential if the pupils are going to understand what is needed. The toolkit presents skills that influence the reader, underpinned by the grammar that is instrumental in their construction. In creating this, the teacher has asked two key questions:

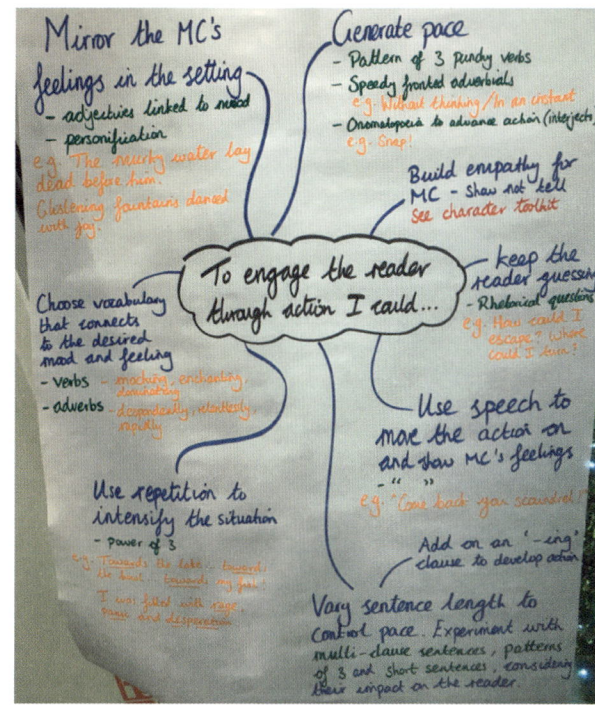

- What effect is the writer trying to create?
- How do they do it?

As you co-construct the toolkit with the pupils, add in examples and then practise the skills through short-burst writing opportunities like those explained earlier.

Here are the some of the tools that are contextualised in our model text, *The Catch*:

Action Tool	Examples from *The Catch* (embellished text)
'Show' not 'tell' – reveal or hint at a character's feelings through their actions.	despondently fishing; tearing me from my daydream; Tentatively, I crept; my arms were trembling in anticipation; thrashed out to be released; darted into the forest; bounded; tunnelled in pursuit; rampaged; my chest tightening as panic set in; masked my eyes
Mirror the character's feelings through the setting. Use personification to bring the setting to life and give it energy.	• … the murky water that lay dead before me… • … the forest was trying to trap her in its thorny grasp • … quivering yellow petals… • … a labyrinth of thorns menacingly mocking me, daring me to enter … • a curtain of dancing water, cascading …
Use short, punchy sentences to build tension and atmosphere.	• How would we survive? What could I do? • Snap! • What if she ate my only catch? • Silence. Calculation. Anticipation. Then she was gone.

Use a wider range of dramatic fronted adverbials to advance the action.	• *Without thinking,* • *In an instant,* • *As the light intensified,*
Generate pace with a sentence using a power of 3. Use repetition to build tension whilst advancing the action.	• *Without thinking, I unsheathed my knife, jammed it into the snare and prized the trap open.* • *… towards the lake … towards the bowl … towards my fish!* • *Silence. Calculation. Anticipation.* • *I sprinted past glowing leaves, quivering yellow petals and magnificent green cloaks.*
Use a character's reaction, internal thought or the author's comments to show the effect of a description.	• *How would we survive? What could I do?* • *I willed for him to catch something …* • *… worry began to flood over me. What if she ate my only catch?* • *Already I could feel my chest tightening as panic set in.* • *I masked my eyes to shield them from the utopia that lay before me.* • *I looked at him and smiled.*
Choose vocabulary that connects to the desired mood and feeling.	• *looming, murky, lay dead, dominating, despondently, half-drained pool, confidence slowly evaporating, disappointment masked hope, relentlessly mocking his futile mission, all confidence disappeared, ear-splitting howl, shattering the silence, tearing, tentatively, dense copse, trembling in anticipation, victim, rage, panic, desperation, thorny grasp, faint glimmer, simmering cauldron of opportunity.*
Use speech to advance the action and show emotion.	• *"Come back you scoundrel!"* • *"He..ll…o? Is…any…one…there?"*

c) Drawing upon other reading – expanding the repertoire

Whilst the model text is rich in character tools and writerly techniques, it is essential that we also explore a wide range of other examples to enrich and deepen our repertoire. Draw upon your own knowledge of quality pupils' literature to share an array of extracts that have depth in character. Encourage pupils to raid the reading, looking for additional skills that can be added to the toolkit. If they have magpie books, encourage them to jot down key ideas, language and turns of phrase.

The innovation stage – shared and guided writing

Before writing, make sure that you brainstorm lots of ideas and possibilities for story writing. I like to spend time creating lists of characters that we could use and their potential desires and wants, e.g. a wizard wanting to know how to cast a spell, a child seeking social acceptance, or an archaeologist seeking a hidden artefact. To strengthen the brainstorm, I usually encourage pupils to draw upon their reading, using characters they adore as an inspiration for their own story. This is where the stimulus for our innovation came from – our class book *Thief* by Malorie Blackman.

Below is the class boxed-up version and a pupil's innovation plan.

In the planning stage, it is also important to explore additional levels of sophistication with the pupils so that, over time, they would have seen how to:

- Genre switch: change text type, e.g. switch a story to a newspaper report, etc. Change story type, e.g. to sci-fi, fantasy, etc.
- Change time/person, view: past/present, etc.
- Reorder the text, e.g. flashbacks and time slips
- Write in the style of different authors
- Sequels and prequels
- Blend story types.

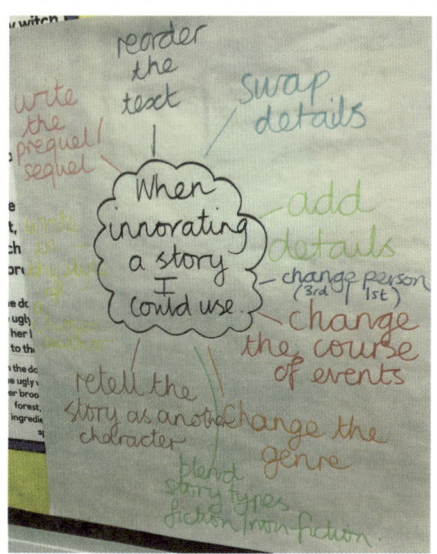

During the shared writing, ensure that it is pitched suitably high for all the pupils in the class. By upper KS2, they should be leaving the model behind and working off the basic plot idea and toolkit, as well as drawing on previous toolkits, their reading and their short-burst writing.

Below, is a transcript of the shared writing I constructed with my Y6 class for this unit over five days, allowing time to draw upon the short-burst writing and previous learning. As we co-constructed the class story, the children also drafted their own versions, adding in their own ideas and embellishing the story to suit their taste. The purpose of the innovation stage is to ensure that all children are accurately using the toolkit with great effect. It is during this stage that the children received in-depth marking and feedback, addressing any misconceptions and also developing their authorial voice.

Thief by Year 6
Chapter 1: The Dilemma

Have you ever felt trapped, confronted by the impossible choice? No matter what you decide, someone loses, someone gets hurt, someone suffers. Staring at my reflection in the mirror, the pitted lines of worry seemed to mar my face, reflecting my inner turmoil. Should I steal the cup or lose my best friend?

Chapter 2: The Betrayal

"Frankie ... wait! Frankie ... I don't understand ... please ..."
Turning to face me, I could see that my final plea had affected her, although she refused to look me in the eye. "I'm sorry," she whispered, "I really am, but there is nothing I can do." Frankie's bottom lip seemed to quiver as she spoke. "I ... I ... explained everything in the note. I've got to go." Wiping back the tears with the sleeve of her cardigan, I could see the pain that was eating her up from inside. Slowly, she looked up, shook her head, then turned and ran.

I looked at the note that was now crumpled up in my hand. Had she really meant it? Gazing in disbelief at the words on the page, a solitary tear fell.

You're not one of us.
Leave us alone.
You are not wanted here.

Watching Frankie run across the playground in tears, I knew that she had followed my orders. Lydia seemed to be frozen in disbelief, lost in her own pathetic self-pity, her confidence slowly evaporating. Part of me wanted to see her collapse in a heap on the tarmac, to hit rock bottom. However, I had worked too hard to miss this opportunity; she was vulnerable and it was time to strike.

Brrrriiiinnnngggg! The shrill of the school bell silenced the playground, bringing all activity to an immediate halt. Screwing the note into a tight ball, I flung it into the bin and trudged back towards class.
"Hey Lydia, wait up!"
Anne's words caught me off guard. I was certain that she was the reason Frankie had written the note – who else could be so cruel?
"I want to show you something. Come with me."
Grabbing my arm, Anne hauled me through the double doors and marched me across the empty gym to the school trophy cabinet.
"See that? The big one? Steal it and you're in."
Her tone was calm yet firm and somewhat menacing – I knew she wasn't joking. Eye-balling the trophy, floods of worry began to surge through me, instantly making me feel nauseous.
"I can't ..." I muttered, the words burning my throat as they forced their way out.
"Yes, you can. You can, or you can kiss goodbye to Frankie, and you can kiss goodbye to ever being anything in Tarwich. It's up to you." With that, Anne swept out of the room, slamming the doors behind her.

Chapter 3: The Dilemma Revisited

Staring at my reflection in the mirror, the pitted lines of worry seemed to mar my face, reflecting my inner turmoil. Should I steal the cup or lose my best friend?

Confronted by the impossible choice, I reached out to my only true friend...

> Dear Diary,
> Today has been the worst day of my life! I don't know what to do. Is it wrong to steal if I intend to give it back? I only need to prove to that cow Anne Riley that I am brave enough to do it, then she will get off my back. She is such a nasty piece of work! But if I don't do it, I will lose Frankie forever. I don't know what she sees in Anne, but she is so manipulated by her – it's ridiculous. If I get accepted into The Cosmics, I can get her to see things from my perspective – I can save her. So, does that make stealing the cup acceptable? Please help me make the right decision. xx L

Chapter 4: The Vision

Prizing open the janitor's door, I tentatively enter the school that lies deathly still, enveloped in darkness. An icy blast of air rushes in, suppressing any last warmth I feel inside. Tiptoeing along the maze of corridors, I can hear voices plaguing my thoughts: "Thief! Coward! Loser!" but determination spurs me on. I silently slide from room to room, in pursuit of my only goal – the trophy. Arriving at my destination, panic sets in. Questions begin to uncontrollably spiral inside my mind – questions that I thought I had answered. My heart is pounding like a machine gun, sending palpitations through my body; beads of sweat roll off my forehead; my breath quickens. Then silence. Contemplation. Action.

Grabbing the trophy, I turn and run, ignoring the deafening sirens that have engulfed the building. Screams of hatred chase after me, hunting me like a rabid animal. The corridors are now claustrophobic, glaring at me with condescending eyes. Bursting through the doors, I stream into the night, a thief on the run.

Chapter 5: The Reality

"Lydia, get up! We're going to be late for school!" My brother's words hauled me out from my nightmare. Sitting up in bed, I scanned the room for any traces of the heist – nothing. A relieved smile spread across my face.

Entering the playground, I had no idea of the fate that lay before me. Out of the corner of my eye, I spotted Anne with her precious Cosmics, laughing and fooling about. I was unsure why I ever wanted to be part of their gang as the mere sight of them now repulsed me. But it was never about Anne: it was always about Frankie. Frankie had been my best friend since I had arrived and I was not going to give her up without a fight.

Gazing back over at the giggling hyenas, I realised that Frankie was not with them. But where was she? Frankie was never late. Another wave of anxiety rushed over me – what had happened to her? What had Anne done?

A gentle tap on my shoulder snapped out of my world of insecurity. Turning to face Frankie, I saw that once again, she was unable to look at me in the eye. Slowly, she reached into her pocket and withdrew a small piece of paper that had been carefully folded and handed it to me. As I opened the paper, I noticed her feet, nervously shuffling. At the sight of the words, my eyes filled with tears. I flung my arms around Frankie and gave her a hug she would remember. "Of course, I forgive you," I sobbed, "you're my best friend."

Independent application

The final stage is where the pupils independently plan, draft and edit a new story of their own, drawing on all of the short-burst writing, poetry, rich reading and story writing they have been immersed in. Because the entire unit of work revolved around the needs of the class, identified from the initial 'cold task', the written outcomes all showed significant improvement. All the pupils demonstrated more confidence in applying the action toolkit within a story, many manipulating the tools for a desired effect on the reader. The following is an example of a pupil's independent action story writing, using Wolf Brother as the inspiration for their writing.

Wolf Brother by Connie Horgan

For a whole moon, we've been feasting on salmon. The herds of boar have migrated further South, leaving the Open Forest with hardly any prey. Fin-kedinn chose me to hunt for the clan, but even with my tracking skills, I've failed. Renn has tried to help, but the crunch of thick snow underfoot tells the Woodgrouse they're being hunted. So, they fly away. I remember the anger in Aki's voice: "Well done, Torak. I guess we'll have to starve thanks to your failure." I wish the boar would return.

Through the dense vegetation, the wind carries the scent of Forest-pig. In the Up, the wrath of the Sky-bear eats up the warm, bright Eye. My howl echoes in the darkness, bouncing off the trees, telling the forest that I'm hunting. The Thunderer throws his spears of light at the forest; as they feed on my surroundings, they turn into fire. Perfect. The crackle of flames and the applaud of the Thunderer will mask my scent as I tense my muscles, ready to pounce on the unsuspecting Forest-pig that has trotted into my cunning trap. My cubs shall feed like the Sky-bear tonight, because a Wolf shows no mercy...

Whoop! The alarm calls of a thousand monkeys pulled me out of my daydream. I jumped up, narrowly missing the flames that danced fluidly around me, blocking any escape route. "Think, Torak. Think!" A single vine hung from the treetops. I tore off my boots, flung them over my shoulder and began to climb, swallowing lungsful of smoke as fear choked me. My fist clenched around my Clan-guardian feathers. Surely, they'd protect me, wouldn't they?

Then, almost as abruptly as it had begun, the storm stopped. A shadow flew across the forest, leaving the land steaming and wet. A wave of relief washed over me. My eyes latched with the Wrens': 'Get ready. It is coming.'

As I shimmied down the tree-trunk, the foliage shook wildly. A deafening squeal pierced my soul. Thank the Spirit! It was a boar – but unlike any I'd seen. It exploded from the undergrowth, nostrils flaring: cries of terror tore through the forest. The whites of its eyes were bloodshot and lined with puss. They darted around, searching for an exit that wasn't there. Foam bubbled on its lips; ivory hooves threw week-old saplings at the sky; deadly tusks protruded from a gaping mouth. Its power flung me to the ground. I scrambled to my feet; I couldn't miss this chance! We couldn't survive much longer. I equipped my bow, drew my arm back and fired.

Even though the boar lay dead, joy soon dissipated into realisation. Realisation that the kill was not mine to take. A lone wolf entered the clearing. My arms trembled with fear. My heart pounded in my chest like a bass drum. His eyes suddenly flickered to life: two ebony flames that ate away at my heart. I couldn't outrun a wolf – I shouldn't even try. But he was padding closer, almost as if he knew I could escape…

He shot my Forest-pig. The little wretch did it on purpose so I couldn't toy with it. So much for my cubs feeding like the Sky-bear tonight – I was going to give them a live Forest-pig so they could rip its limbs off and hear it sequel in pain. But the boy ruined it. The boy made me fail. Now he would pay.

Our eyes locked over the Boar carcass. I shouldered my bow, ready to sprint. I tensed. The wolf unsheathed its claws. The chase was on.

Most people ask what happened next. I wish I could tell you, but only the Thunderer – perhaps even the World Spirit – saw what became of me. Although I was blinded and shrouded in darkness, I could still hear the crunch of snow under foot. I could still feel the hot, meaty breath of the wolf on my ankles. I could still hear that blood-curdling howl that reverberated in my mind. I could still survive…

Torak darted like a minnow through the waving trees. His lungs were heaving – in, out, in, out. His heart was pounding – boom-boom, boom-boom. He was sweating: his forehead and brow perspiring as his legs pushed him on. He wasn't paying attention; the Trees have never had their eternal meeting interrupted before. The Great Yew sighed. Oak glowered at Torak as he shot past. Willow whipped him with her long boughs, as I whipped them with my spears of lightning.

The wolf was gaining on him. Foolish mortal; why should I help him? I had given him a chance to save his clan, but he hadn't taken it. Now he was trying to outrun a wolf. He was more stupid than I thought. I, the Thunderer, rule the skies. I summoned the storm that melted the snow. I forced the sun behind my swirling mass of darkness and rain. I would never try to outrun a wolf – not that I couldn't; I'd beat a wolf any day. But a human couldn't. Torak couldn't. He would fail…

I could see the camp. I could see…the…camp! I had made it…I was going to live! Unable to go any further, my legs gave way beneath me. I felt sick. I arched my back and wretched. Suddenly, a wave of shock flooded over me, a realisation that I couldn't rest until I was safely in my tent – the wolf was still after me. Expecting to feel the fiery pain of fangs sinking into my flesh, I rolled over. The forest loomed over me. My pursuer was gone.

Jamie is Deputy Head and Head of English at Warren Road Primary School, a Talk for Writing Training Centre in Kent, where you can visit to see all elements of the process in action. He is an accredited Talk for Writing trainer and works both nationally and internationally offering inset, consultancy and school support in the implementation and integration of Talk for Writing and Talk for Reading as whole school systems.

To contact Jamie regarding training or to visit Warren Road Primary School, please email: jamie.thomas@talk4writing.com
Twitter: @JamieWTSA

Additional primary English video clips:

Video clip 20. *Mr T* shows his Year 6 teacher at Selby Primary that he does do poetry!

Video clip 23: Nick Warren, Year 6 teacher at Briar Hill Primary, demonstrates how to help pupils develop a powerful vocabulary

Video clip 31: Pie Corbett using booktalk to facilitate a Year 6 class discussion on Anthony Browne's *A Walk in the Park*

Video clip 32: A Y6 pupil from Selby Community Primary explaining how she magpies ideas from her reading to use in her writing.

Chapter 9c: Talk for Writing in English (secondary)

Sara Ambrose, Assistant Headteacher for Whole-school Literacy at The John of Gaunt School, explains how the Talk for Writing process is helping to improve creative writing in her Year 8 class.

My Year 8 group is very much a mixed-attainment group with reading ages varying from around 2 years below their actual age to five years above. Their combined scores in English range from 93 to 110 so some are significantly below the expected level and others significantly above. For this particular unit, the topic was Gothic genre and I was focusing on improving their ability to write descriptively.

Word	Never heard	Heard – can't use confidently	Know & can use in a sentence	Definition
ominous				adjective – creates a feeling that something worrying/bad is about to happen
sinister				adjective – giving the impression that something harmful or evil will happen
derelict				adjective – in very poor condition due to neglect or not being used
monstrous				adjective – having the ugly or frightening appearance of a monster
grotesque				adjective – repulsively ugly or distorted
menacing				adjective – threatening/suggests the presence of danger
obsidian				noun – a dark black volcanic rock – often used as adjective to describe dark-black
symbolism				noun – technique using symbols to represent ideas or qualities/ an artistic movement
pathetic fallacy				noun - technique giving human responses to inanimate things e.g. weather to reflect mood or atmosphere in art or literature

I knew that one of the weaknesses of this group was a limited vocabulary so, for the beginning of the unit, I wanted to make sure that all the class could understand and use some of the key vocabulary associated with the Gothic genre. Therefore, as well as using the never-heard-the-word grid as a diagnostic tool, I doctored it to include a simple definition, as pictured here. This meant the students had a clear definition upon which to build their understanding, one they could refer back to. Students were then asked to create a text map for the word, capturing either how the word made them feel or how they envisioned the word. To ensure they had complete knowledge of the word, they were asked to write a synonym and antonym for the word, as well as providing their own definition and using it in a sentence, as pictured here. We rehearsed the words orally and students were encouraged to speak their definitions and sentences before writing them down.

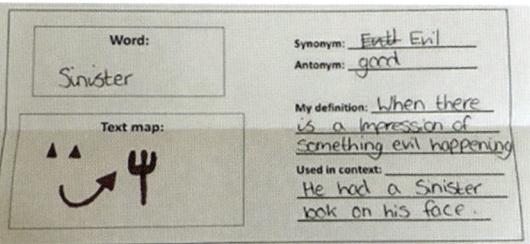

These words were then regularly referred to during low-stakes quizzes at the start of every lesson. On occasions, students were given a definition and then had to write the word; at other times, they

were asked to spell the word. To ensure that they were able to embed this vocabulary and use it independently, they were also asked to collage the mood of the word including any associated images, as illustrated above. These were then put on display in the room as part of our working word wall.

Previously, I would have taught vocabulary in a more ad hoc way, checking knowledge of words as they came up in a text or selecting words that I would think of as writing emerged. Teaching vocabulary in this more structured way has improved the embedding of vocabulary so that the students are able to use new and more ambitious language in their own independent work.

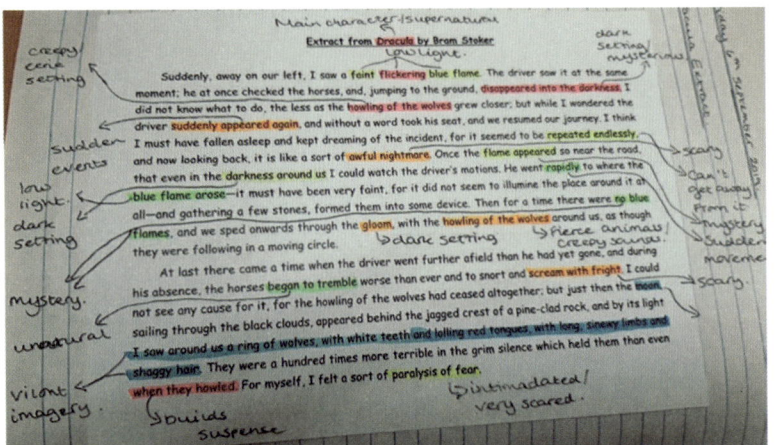

The next few lessons focused on warming up a Gothic writing toolkit to help the students recognise the key ingredients and underlying melody of a Gothic story. Extracts from Bram Stoker's *Dracula* were used to warm up the conventions of the Gothic genre and magpie descriptive writing techniques. Here you can see how one student has highlighted and annotated the ingredients.

Before their cold task, as a stimulus, students watched a short documentary-style video explaining what a séance is and why the Victorians were fascinated by them. A collection of images was also shown to help them visualise the setting and character types. I chose to provide this stimulus before the cold task to ensure that all the students knew what style of writing they were aiming for and were, therefore, able to write something. By making explicit what Gothic literature was, it also meant that I could assess any prior knowledge students might have – but not necessarily realise they had just by hearing the title. The work they generated also allowed me to focus more on assessing the way in which they crafted language and grammar for effect rather than their ability to generate an idea for a piece of writing.

Therefore, for their cold task, they were asked to complete a piece of descriptive writing about a séance that used Gothic conventions and descriptive writing techniques. Overall, this writing was too brief and lacked sophistication. Nevertheless, there was evidence that the warmed-up words were being used correctly to enhance the description and give the work a Gothic tone. Across the class, there were issues with technical accuracy and the sentence forms were often mundane, not being crafted for effect. In particular, some students needed to learn how to make their writing flow, and they all needed to think about making every word count, as these examples illustrate:

student 1

student 2

I've found cold tasks to be a really useful idea. They ensure that what you are teaching is focused on what students need to improve their work. It helps facilitate planning – actually making it far easier to plan a meaningful sequence of lessons – and enables students to see tangible progress.

From imitation to innovation

Given what I'd learnt from the cold task, the first aspect I focused on was common errors. This was differentiated. For example, some students needed to work on basic comma use while others were ready to explore using semicolons for effect.

Then the focus was crafting language for effect. A shared simile was created: the gnarled, leafless twigs were like spindly spider's legs. Ideas were then generated collectively and similes co-constructed before students innovated on these to produce their own, as illustrated here.

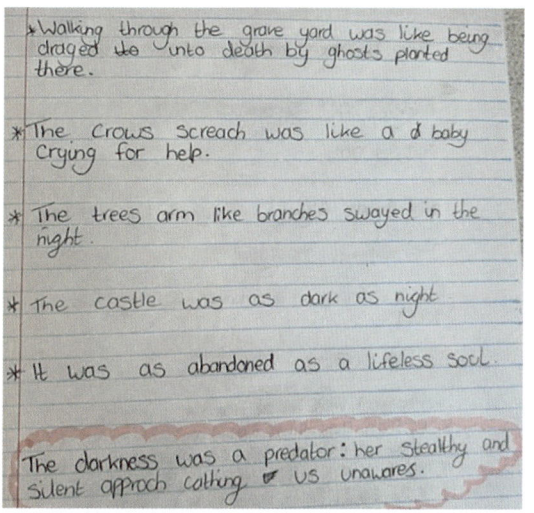

Following this, another extract from Dracula was selected (the first paragraph of which is shown above here. Students first highlighted specifically Gothic features in turquoise and descriptive passages that enhanced the atmosphere in red, before deciding on their own alternative descriptive passages. Using the framework of the model to substitute their own Gothic descriptions, enabled them to see how their phrases could be used for effect within the conventions of a Gothic text. They then produced another piece of Gothic writing that innovated on this model. The example below shows how the work of Student 1 had significantly improved: the scary atmosphere is generally well-maintained through selecting just the right word or phrase – though there is still some ineffective repetition

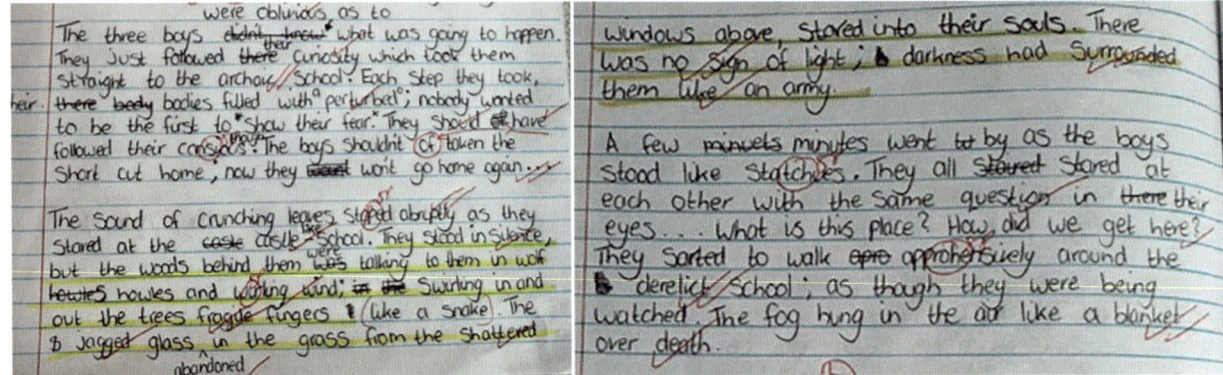

of words (for example, *took, stared*) which suggests the work hasn't been reread, sounding it out in your head thoroughly, to test if it works.

This task was marked using a key performance indicator grid. This identified that variety of sentence forms and sentence starts remained an area for development for many students. There is always a risk that grammar teaching can become detached from meaning, so another model was used to help illustrate that sentences should be formed to create a feeling or reaction from the reader. Students volunteered a range of Gothic appropriate verbs, adverbs and adjectives and, through shared writing, we co-constructed a range of sentences for effect.

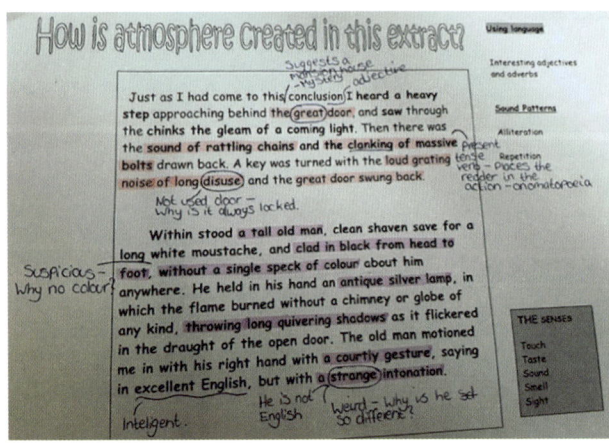

The final part of explicit teaching, before the hot task, focused on the importance of **showing the reader** how a character feels rather than simply telling the reader. The model selected to illustrate this was an extract from Susan Hill's *The Woman in Black*. We spent time as a class warming up the phrases by miming how the character felt. Collaboratively, the students highlighted all of the actions that the writer **showed** us that the character was experiencing and then mimed each of these actions before recording them on the washing line.

Finally, we were in a position to agree on a toolkit for our Gothic story and included examples to help us understand exactly what each tool meant:

- Show, not tell, the reader how a character feels – *The old man motioned me in with his right hand ...*
- Create an atmosphere by creating unanswered questions – *a strange intonation*
- Combine Gothic features with descriptive techniques to develop the setting and characters – *the sound of rattling chains and the clanking of massive bolts*

- Appeal to the reader's senses – *I heard a heavy step … and saw …*
- Use appropriate, Gothic style adjectives, adverbs and verbs to begin some sentences. *A key was turned …*

Together we planned how we could create a well-structured piece of Gothic descriptive writing and co-constructed the structure. I then typed this up into a boxed-up grid for the students to fill in with the elements they wanted to include.

Independent application

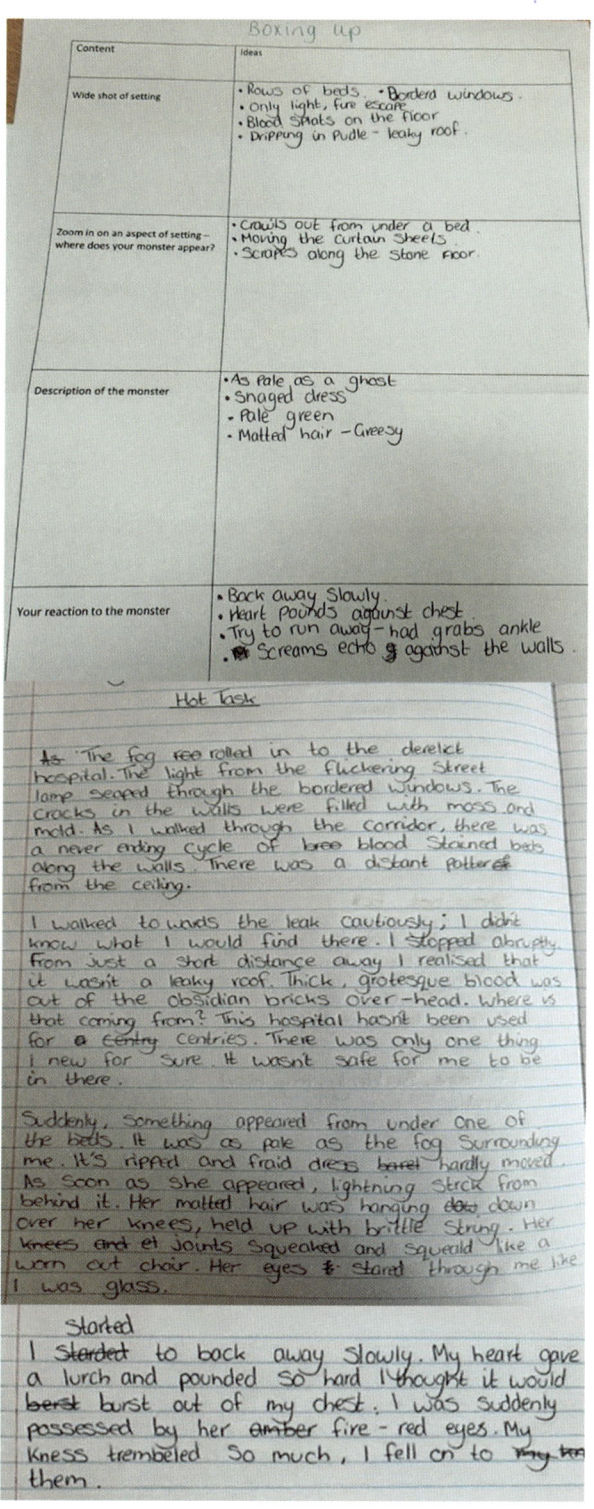

The students then boxed up their own stories independently, as illustrated here, using the toolkit and their own understanding. All students were able to do this confidently and with independence, something they had not been able to do with their cold task. During the boxing up phase, teacher support was offered, and live marking took place where necessary.

The following lesson, students independently completed their hot task without any intervention from me and the results were excellent. It is clear to see the shift in language use: many of the warmed-up words have been well used to create a threatening atmosphere; some of the phrases that had been warmed up and mimed during the final imitation stage prior to the hot task had been magpied and were now visible in the hot task, and the ability to craft language for effect is much more evident.

If you look at student 1's hot task here, you can see that both the quantity and the quality of the writing has improved significantly. The focus on Gothic-style vocabulary has paid off and the description builds up an atmosphere through showing not telling you; many words and phrases have been effectively selected, for example *brittle string* and *seeped through*. Moreover, it includes some good similes; the more

effective for their simplicity: *It was as pale as the fog surrounding me; Her eyes stared through me like I was glass.* And the punctuation is greatly improved: fronted adverbials have their commas and there is even a well-used semicolon.

Of course, there is room for improvement. Rereading the text aloud as the next step for improvement should help the student pick up on the overuse of *There was*, and help them hear that the first three sentences are too similar in structure and therefore don't flow as they should, along with noticing that the potentially good short question sentence in the middle of paragraph two is in the wrong tense. A careful reread would also pick out spelling errors of words they probably know very well like *knew*. And, all the Ss look like capitals – an error that should have been sorted way before leaving primary school and that will be harder to sort now. But, undoubtedly, the writing has significantly improved which is motivating for the student.

On marking all of the students' work, I could clearly see that the language of the models had been internalised and that the analysis of the ingredients that make Gothic writing effective had paid off. Students showed progress in areas such as showing not telling the reader how the character felt and using ambitious vocabulary. The mime of *show not tell* was especially significant in this – I wouldn't have systematically used mime before moving to the TFW approach. Thanks to the success of the process, all of the students' writing has been improved and very clear progress made. This understanding of what the Gothic style entails will also enable them to comment more effectively and confidently on any such text studied as part of the literature curriculum.

Additional secondary English video clips:

Video clip 25: Ruth Corrie, Assistant Deputy Head at Wexham, Slough, explains why her year 11 class's vocabulary is improving

Video clip 35: English teacher Alex Hamilton White using shared writing to help her Year 7 class understand how to comment on the features that make writing effective

Video clip 36: Rohan Cross's Year 9 English class demonstrating how the TfW process has helped them become better writers

Video clip 37: A Year 9 student from Slough and Eton explains how TfW has helped her class in English.

Chapter 9d: Helping lower-attaining secondary students

A few years ago, Claire Amor (who had worked in a TfW primary school) was part of the SEN department at The John of Gaunt School. The progress her SEN students made was highly influential in encouraging the school to seek training in the approach. This chapter begins with an explanation of SEN teacher Michelle Hickey's experience of how TfW has helped Year 7 students, who arrive with English results below the expected level, make progress. The chapter ends with SENCO Vicky Marshall explaining how TfW is helping Year 11 students with learning difficulties cope with the English literature exam.

Helping Year 7 students bridge the gap

As part of an initiative to improve the writing standards of students in Year 7, The John of Gaunt School has developed an intervention program targeting students whose SAT's score indicate their writing level to be below the expected standard. The intervention Michelle Hickey developed was based on fictional writing and was delivered using the Talk for Writing framework over a six-week period. *Creating Storytellers and Writers*, the Talk for Writing guide to how to teach fiction, was the perfect resource on which to base this initiative because there all the underpinning structure of the key story plots can be found along with all the key creative writing toolkits. For example, the key ingredients for good openings and suspense to co-construct with classes are provided for different levels of attainment, progressively gaining in difficulty.

An adapted version of Pie Corbett's *The Old Mill* was selected as the model text for this suspense unit. Instead of beginning by internalising the text orally, the students first read the text to themselves and then discussed it as a group; effective words and phrases were selected by the students to magpie.

A text map (the first half of which is pictured here) was then co-constructed through shared drawing with Michelle acting as illustrator. Students were given the opportunity to revisit this at the beginning of each lesson to see if they could retell the story just using the images. Michelle was surprised that this proved to be extremely successful as most students were able to tell the entire text within 2-3 lessons. It's easy to underestimate the ability of students to recall text when supported by a text map and actions.

Underpinning plot structure	Plot planner	
• Main character (MC) leaves safe space		
• MC in scary setting		
• MC sees something		
• Threat appears		
• Threat gets closer		
• MC escapes but promises to return & try again another day		

The structure of the model text was then discussed and boxed up to identify the structure used: each box representing a section of the story which could then be used to form the structure of their own writing. As you can see from the boxing up, the structure of the story is a slight variation on the classic suspense story structure.

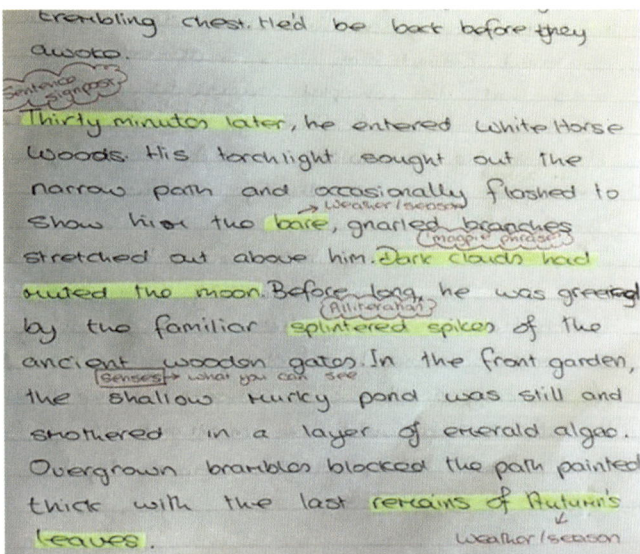

Next, the class analysed the text to establish all the key tools the writer had used to help make the story work and created a suspense toolkit of writing choices that they could work from. They could then move on to the innovation stage. The shared writing reflected the toolkit they had identified, and the class annotated the text together so they could see how these tools worked within the story. The image here shows the first half of this shared writing.

The students then wrote their own stories with subsequent feedback helping each student to improve any features that needed improving.

Independent application stage

In preparation for the hot task, the assignment at the end of this unit provided students a similar context on which to base their narrative but, this time, offering them a variety of settings to choose from for the location of their story. The planning phase of the writing involved students in producing a boxed-up plan. As students worked at this, feedback was provided by the teacher which encouraged students to utilise the model text, the shared writing and vocabulary from the word bank developed during the unit, as well as the various devices in the co-constructed toolkit. This planning phase provided students with a valuable opportunity to create their own ideas as well as a specific structure on which to base their writing.

HELPING LOWER-ATTAINING SECONDARY STUDENTS

Comparing the cold and hot tasks

When you look at the difference between this student's writing in the opening paragraph of the cold task versus the opening paragraph of their hot task shown below, you can immediately see the difference the approach has made.

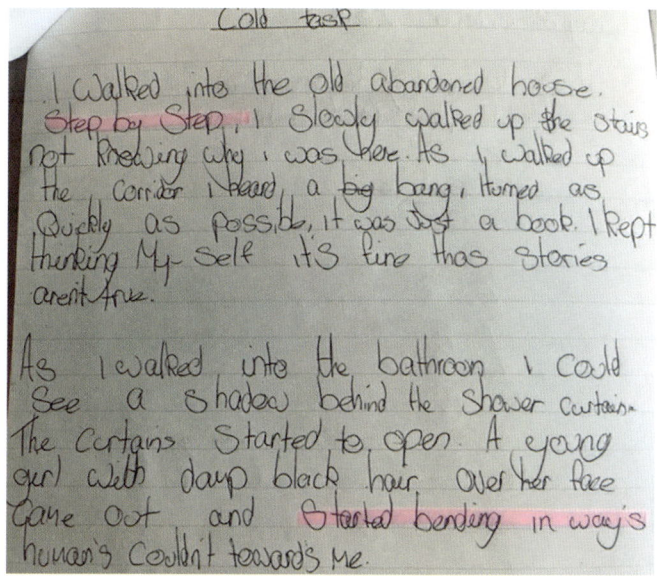

The cold task goes through the motions of being suspense, since the main character is alone in a scary place, but the writing lacks any atmosphere. The reader does not really want to read on.

Now read the opening of the hot task and you can see that the writer knows how to build suspense. The opening line immediately makes you sense that the main character is feeling edgy. The writer has shown us that, not told us. The reader is put in the place of Freya as she creeps down the stairs. Words like *headed softly* have been chosen very carefully to build up the tension.

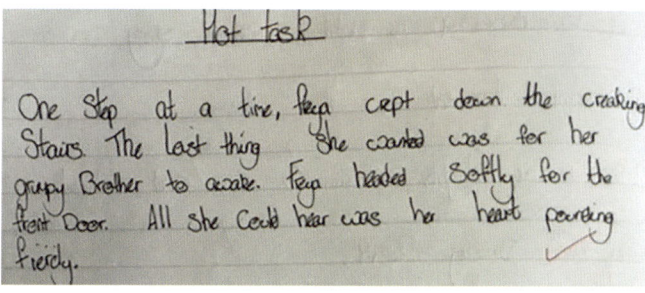

Could it be improved? Certainly. The writer needs to have a few weeks of a great fuss being made about capital letters – then she will quickly learn to show the difference between a lower-case s and a capital S and check a few other letters as well (again, it's a shame this wasn't picked up at primary school) but the handwriting in general has improved. The writer is starting to have a clear sense of purpose plus an awareness of the need to make every word count, and the suspense tools with which to do it. As her story develops, she shows an excellent use of empty words and other tricks of the suspense writer's trade. For a full list of the tools that aid suspense writing, see *Creating Storytellers and Writers* **pages 83–84**.

Helping low-attaining Year 11 students cope

Here SENCO Vicky Marshall focuses on how the Talk for Writing process is helping students succeed with that rather strange English literature exam requirement the comparative poetry essay, which often proves difficult for all students and is particularly hard for students with learning difficulties.

The aim of this Year 11 unit was to prepare students for the section of their English Literature GCSE exam in which students have to write a comparative essay based on two poems they have studied. This is hard because the question, rather than letting you focus on the effectiveness of each poem in its own right, wants you to compare them which means jumping from one poem to another. Moreover, the exam is closed book and, therefore, the students have to be able to recall quotations from a range of poems as well as be able to write analytically and comparatively, which is very challenging.

Once the students had studied several of the set poems, they were given an exam question to answer as their cold task to see how well they could cope with the tricky poetry comparison question they would face in the real exam. They were expected to write just two paragraphs rather than a full exam answer, at this stage. From this task, I could identify students' ability to:

- recall quotes from the poems;
- write analytically;
- make comparisons between the poems;
- make all their points coherently.

Here is a typical example of the work produced by students in the cold task. When you read this through, you can tell the student has some interesting points to make and is beginning to use some of the right sort of phrases, but the problem is they just can't make them clearly in coherent sentences and, of course, they have not backed up their points with quotations.

The imitation stage

Word	Never heard	Heard – not sure of meaning	Definition
alliteration			
sibilance			
repetition			
simile			
metaphor			
personification			
enjambment			
onomatopoeia			
rhyme			
half rhyme			
imagery			
juxtaposition			
pun			
Stanza			

Never heard the word grid - poetry

One of the things that makes comparative poetry essays particularly challenging is including relevant technical language – one of the exam requirements is for students to be able to know and use technical language when making comparisons.

The students had studied poetry units in previous years so they would have come across a range of poetic techniques prior to starting this unit. However, due to their learning needs, it was likely that their recall of this vocabulary would not be strong. As you can see, the vocabulary chosen for the never-heard-the-word grid here was predominantly centred around the techniques used when writing about poems, as opposed to writing about a piece of prose, to determine what the students could and couldn't recall from their previous learning. As suspected, the students struggled in recalling what these terms meant.

We then covered the meaning of these words in context as and when examples of these features appeared in the poems. These words and their definitions were repeatedly referred to throughout the unit, both in context when studying poems but also through low-stakes recall quizzes at the start of each lesson, for example:

What poetic techniques are used in the quotes below?
- "sneer of cold command"
- "sudden successive flights of bullets streak the silence"
- "My name is Ozymandias, king of kings"
- "The grim shape towered up between me and the stars"
- "Spits like a tame cat turned savage"

Providing the students with a model text to show how to answer a poetry comparative essay was key to helping them internalise the patterns of language they would need to succeed in the exam. We read the model text together and co-constructed how to identify two key features in it:

- the generic phrases that were being repeatedly used to structure the analytical aspect of the answer;
- the sentence signposts within this generic text which guide the reader.

We highlighted these generic features in separate colours:

> *In this essay, I will be comparing 'Storm on the Island' and 'Exposure' as they both focus on the power of nature and, specifically, the negative impact of the weather.*
>
> *In the poem 'Storm on the Island', the writer presents nature as being powerful, "forgetting that it pummels your house too". The writer's use of personification in "pummels" suggests the wind is physically punching and attacking the house. As a reader, we feel that people on the island must be being attacked by nature. By highlighting the theme of the power of nature, the author's intention could be to show that nature has the power to be destructive and violent.*

184 TRANSFORMING LEARNING ACROSS THE CURRICULUM

> *Whereas,* in the poem 'Exposure' *lines like,* "Our brains ache in the merciless iced wind that knives us", *focus on* how the weather can seem to cause deliberate pain to human beings *rather than* on its destructive side. *The writer's use of* the word "merciless' *suggests that* the wind is constant and his *use of* personification in the word "knive" *is very effective because it emphasises* the extreme pain that the cold wind is causing. *The writer's use of* the metaphor "ache" *suggests* the soldiers are in constant pain. *This highlights the theme of* the power of nature.
>
> In 'Storm on the Island', *the writer presents* the sea as aggressive, "spits like a tame cat turned savage". *The writer's use of* the verb "spits" *powerfully suggests that* the sea is deliberately attacking the houses. *The use of the* simile savage *also* suggests that the sea is out of control. *The writer's use of* sibilance in this quote *could reflect the* sound of the sea hitting the houses. *As a reader, we realise that* in a storm the sea is powerful and aggressive towards the island. *The author's intention could be to* show that nature can change suddenly and that the sea can go from being "tame' to "savage".
>
> *Similarly,* in 'Exposure', *the writer also represents* the weather *through using* sibilance, "sudden successive flights of bullets streak the silence". *The writer's use of* sibilance here *could reflect* both the noise of the wind and the bullets flying through the air. *The writer's use of* the noun "silence" *suggests that* the weather is almost a silent killer compared to the guns and bombs. *As a reader, we realise that* there was a lot of time spent waiting for things and that while they were waiting for the enemy, the real enemy was the weather. *The author's intention could be* to show that nature was just as deadly as the enemy.
>
> *Both* poems present the danger that nature can cause. *However,* 'Exposure' focuses more on the impact on humans and the pain it causes, *whereas* 'Storm on the Island' *focuses more on* the impact that nature has on the island itself and the property on the island.

We then co-constructed this text map to help students internalise the key analytical aspect of the model answer. I chose to focus primarily on this as it is something that could be applied to all sections of their English Literature exams. Hopefully, you can see that these images represent:

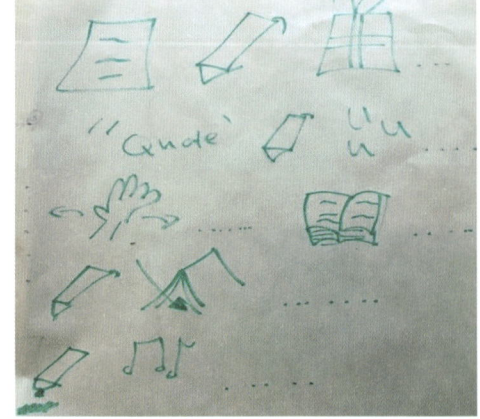

In the poem, the writer presents ……. [quote]. The writer's use of ……. suggests …………….
As a reader, we …………………. The author's intention could be to ……………… This highlights the theme of …………

We were particularly fond of our image to represent intention! We frequently revisited this text map and it stayed on our class washing line throughout the duration of this unit because internalising this sort of language was the key to the students being able to answer these types of questions successfully.

Boxing up the structure

In order for students to gain an understanding of how the whole essay is structured so that they would be able to apply this in their own writing, we boxed up the model answer together. These sorts of essays are particularly hard to structure because, as mentioned above, you have to jump from one poem to the next to bring out the points you are comparing as our boxed-up version shows:

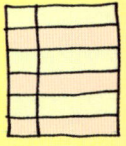

Introduction	In this essay, I will be comparing 'Storm on the Island' and 'Exposure' as they both focus on the power …
Analysis of poem 1	In the poem 'Storm on the Island', the writer presents nature as being powerful, 'forgetting that it pummels your house too' …
Analysis of poem 2	Whereas, in the poem 'Exposure' lines like, "Our brains ache in the merciless iced wind that knives us" focus on how the …
Analysis of poem 1	In 'Storm on the Island', the writer presents the sea as aggressive, "spits like a tame cat turned savage". The …
Analysis of poem 2	Similarly, in 'Exposure' the writer also represents the weather through using sibilance, "sudden successive flights of …
Conclusion	Both poems present the danger that nature can cause. However, 'Exposure' focuses more on the impact on humans and the …

The innovation stage

This underpinning structure meant that, as we moved through the unit and continued to study more of the set poems, we could innovate on this structure and build the students' confidence in using the language. We often did this through shared writing referring to our boxed-up structure and text map, both of which were on display in the classroom throughout the unit. Below is an example of the shared writing we did together as a class:

> In this essay, I will be comparing 'Ozymandias' and 'My Last Duchess' as both poems explore the power of individuals.
>
> In the poem 'Ozymandias', the writer presents a powerful leader by saying, "sneer of cold command". The writer's use of the adjective "cold" suggests that he was a cold-hearted, unfeeling leader.
> The writer's choice of the verb "command" suggests that he ruled like a dictator and gave lots of orders. The writer's powerful use of alliteration, "cold command", suggests he was a cruel leader as the 'c' sound in the quote is very harsh.
>
> As a reader, we feel that the writer is being critical of this method of ruling. The author's intention could be to secretly criticise King George 111, who was King of England at the time, through writing about Ozymandias. This highlights the theme of power.
>
> Similarly, in the poem 'My last Duchess', the writer also focuses on the idea of commands to demonstrate the power of an individual: "I have commands and all smiles stopped".
> The writer's use of ...

We completed pieces of shared writing like this together at least once a week: this repetition was very helpful for the students as they increasingly internalised the pattern of language needed.

Moving towards independence

After each piece of shared writing, I asked students to complete some independent writing. This allowed me to diagnose what areas to specifically focus on and make explicit reference to when we did the next piece of shared writing.

As you can see from the example here, the students highlighted any words/phrases used to compare, plus the sentence starters that they found in the model and based their text map on.

As we progressed towards the hot task, we repeated the process below:

- shared writing to answer question
- independent writing on the same question
- shared writing on a new question focusing on areas for improvement from the independent writing
- independent writing on a new question.

This obviously took place over a series of lessons with students having completed at least four pieces of semi-independent writing before moving to the hot task.

The hot task

For this task, students were given another practice exam question, this time with the expectation that they wrote the entire answer rather than the shortened version that we completed for the cold task. And, as in the cold task, they had to write this completely on their own. As you can see from this example, the essay flows well with the student clearly engaging with the poems and integrating the technical language of poetry appreciation into their work along with relevant quotations, although attention still needs to be paid to the appropriate use of capital letters. This work was two grades above the student's target grade. Most students achieved at least one grade above their expected target.

The hot tasks demonstrate that the students are now able to write answers that are well structured and show a good ability to analyse the writer's use of language. Internalising the structure of the essay, meant that students' working memory was freed up in the hot task, which allowed them to be able to write better analysis than they had done previously. In the cold task, many of the students would have felt overwhelmed because of having to think both of what to write and how to write it. In the hot task, they only had to think about the *what* as the *how* was now second nature to them. Talk for Writing works!

Chapter 10a: Talk for Writing in maths (Y6)

Tracey Adams, Deputy Headteacher of St Matthew's C of E Primary, Birmingham, and Y6 teacher, explains just what a difference the Talk for Writing process has made to the teaching of maths. Pre Talk for Writing, results were dire; now, although the intake is equally challenging (averaging around 88% pupil premium), the maths scores are over 90% along with all the other results. The picture here shows Tracey with Pie Corbett and the school's Headteacher, Sonia Thompson.

Integrating the pedagogy behind Talk for Writing into the way we teach mathematics has had a great impact on our children's ability to think and work mathematically, as it is a chance to encounter mathematical concepts and procedures through a successful strategy that they are very familiar with. Prior to this joined up way of thinking, teachers would not have a clear understanding of what children were able to do within a specific area of maths. This meant we needed a way to assess what children were bringing to the table and what they were able to do after a unit of work had been taught. The cold-to-hot-task process helped to bring real clarity to the data teachers had before beginning to teach and gave them the knowledge needed to develop connections as the teaching continued.

There were also key bits of knowledge we wanted the children to embed into their long-term memory but previously, somehow, once it was mentioned within a lesson, it would be lost. Creating texts maps means we now have a concrete way of getting children to embed and internalise bodies of mathematical knowledge, just like they would do for a model text. It is something we can use over and over again, as it can also support children's ability to make connections between different areas of maths.

Finally, we had seen the way that unpicking particular aspects of writing, through boxing up and co-constructing toolkits, had a powerful impact on writing, and we wanted to apply this to maths. It gives children a chance to see a teacher model a particular procedure: then we are able to unpick how this was achieved and identify the steps we need to take and the related tools we need to use to resolve a mathematical problem and achieve an accurate answer.

What this looks like in a unit of work

All of the features described above will be exemplified through this Year 6 unit on decimals, which focuses on these four objectives:

- Identify the value of each digit in numbers given to 3 decimal places and multiply numbers by 10, 100 and 1,000 giving answers up to 3 decimal places.
- Multiply one-digit numbers with up to 2 decimal places by whole numbers.
- Use the written division method in cases where the answer has up to 2 decimal places.
- Solve problems which require answers to be rounded to specified degrees of accuracy.

Establishing the base line: the cold task

Cold Task – Decimals

1. Identify the value of each digit in each number:
   a) 6.78
   b) 9.456
   c) 4.426

2. Multiply each number by 10, 100 and 1000

	x10	x100	x1000
53.42			
0.231			

   Fill in the missing boxes

0.5	x		= 500
33.56	÷	10 =	

3. Multiply decimal numbers

   4.32 x 5 =

4. Work out this calculation and show the answer, with up to 2 decimal places.

   9462 ÷ 8 =

5. Recall fraction and decimal equivalents

½	a)
b)	0.25
1/10	c)
¾	d)

In order to lay a foundation for this two-week unit, I present a cold task to my children (as illustrated here) with at least one or two questions linked to each objective. This is used to gather intelligence about what the children are already confident with (which will then be the focus of retrieval practice) and what is causing difficulties (which will then need explicit whole-class teaching supported by guided teaching).

It also helps me identify the specific gaps in knowledge (from previous year groups) which will need to be re-taught to give the children a firmer foundation on which to build current understanding and application.

This is a brilliant approach because, prior to using cold tasks, I would have been in the dark about what children were capable of doing. Now, both the children and I are clear about what they are good at and their next steps, and what will need to be covered in depth as the unit progresses.

Warming up the words

The vocabulary for each maths unit is developed alongside the teaching of each objective. To support children's understanding of key terms and to improve the quality of responses, a **talk frame** is used related to whatever the maths focus is. It includes two columns: one is a set of sentence stems to support children's ability to explain/reason; the second is the key vocabulary, with definitions, to ensure children's responses are specific and focused.

The use of this kind of talk frame has revolutionised my teaching. I am able

TALK FOR WRITING IN MATHS 191

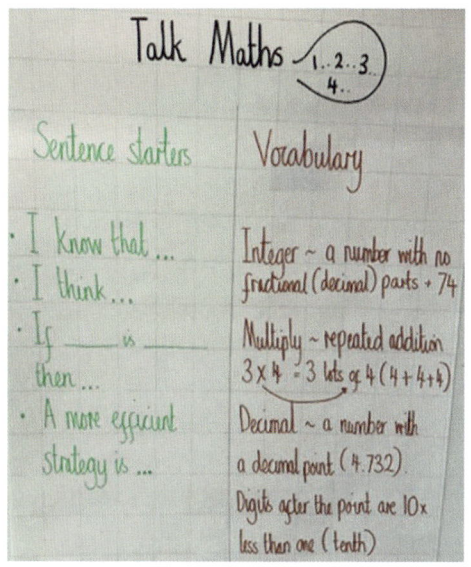

to prompt children to expand on their initial one-word responses. It gives me a frame to challenge their thinking and gives children the chance to structure their responses in a reasoned way. I have watched children's confidence increase as we have built the definitions, and this has meant that their conceptual understanding has increased.

Now, if I ask, "Tell me about the digit 4 in 4.346," I would expect children to respond with the support of the frame:

"I know that one of the 4s is worth 4 hundredths because it is in the hundredths' column, after the decimal point. I think the other 4 is worth more because it is before the decimal point, in the ones' column."

The imitation stage

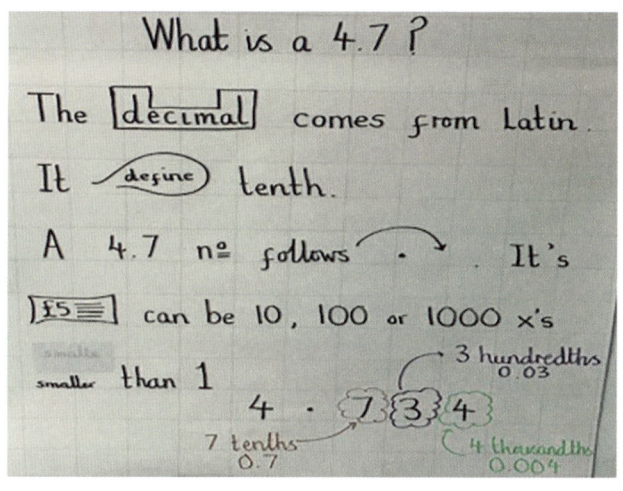

To help children internalise the key concept behind whatever maths is being focused on, I use a text map to tune children into the key vocabulary and ideas which we then refer to and build upon during the unit. So, for this unit, I focused on their understanding of the term *decimal* as the text map here illustrates. The use of pictures and text (dual-coding), supports children's cognitive understanding of this big idea.

Now the vocabulary is secure, the teaching focuses in on one particular objective: **Multiply one-digit numbers with up to 2 decimal places by whole numbers.**

In order to ensure the children understand the procedure behind this objective, I will model using both pictorial and abstract (written algorithm) representation, in a my-turn style question, as illustrated here.

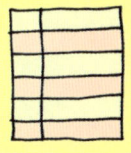

Once I have modelled this a number of times, both the children and I will co-construct a boxed-up toolkit of the key steps needed to complete a calculation in this way. This then become a supportive tool, which allows my children to begin their journey towards independence.

I write the boxed-up toolkit in full sentences because the discussions that we have had to co-construct the steps would have taken place in sentences. This is something I learnt during my Maths Specialist Teaching training (see below). Talking and writing in this way supports a child's mathematical thinking and conceptual understanding. I believe it gives them the chance to visualise the idea they are trying to communicate; constructing the sentences helps them to deepen and expand on that idea.

If you look at the boxed-up toolkit showing the procedural steps for multiplying an integer by a decimal, you can see how visually supportive it is because it is broken down into the steps you have to follow. It shows you clearly what to do and the order in which to do it.

The innovation stage

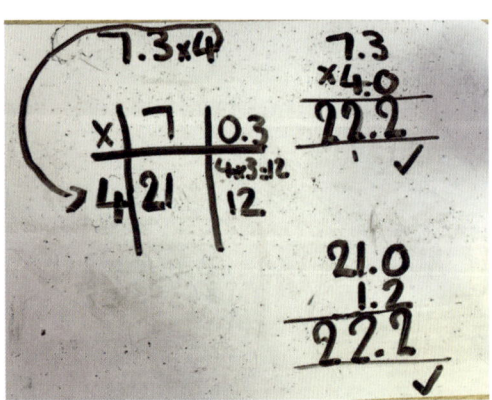

During this phase, my class are able to bring together their understanding of a concept (supported by the text map) and the procedure (supported by the boxed-up toolkit) and apply this to their our-turn questions, while we are still working together. This is an opportunity for my children to feedback orally, using the talk frame to explain coherently how they have answered a question and why they have used the particular steps they have chosen. If you look at the image to the left here, you can see that the child shows conceptual and procedural understanding of how to multiply integers by decimals.

The independent application stage

At this point, my class are given your-turn questions to complete and apply their conceptual and procedural knowledge independently.

This is then followed by a hot task, with questions linked to all four objectives. The purpose of this is to ensure that this learning has been embedded and can be applied in a variety of different contexts and question formats. This shows them how their understanding has developed across the two-week unit. They can look back at their cold task and see the progress they have made.

TALK FOR WRITING IN MATHS

The five-month later *Has the learning been embedded?* test

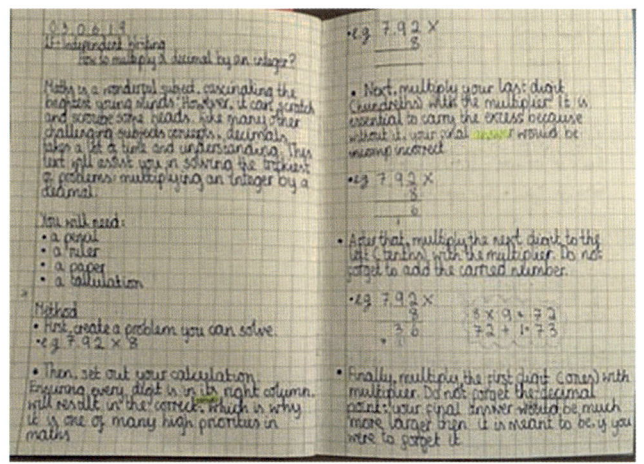

As a further extension to the initial teaching, and as a chance to deepen understanding, the children are asked to write a set of instructions around five months after the teaching took place to explain the objective in detail (in this example, multiply an integer by a number with up to 2 decimal places). The child's writing shows that their understanding of both the procedure and concept is extremely secure and flexible, as it can be applied within a completely different context.

Final reflections on why it works

It is not so much the linear sequence but the pedagogy behind Talk for Writing which I feel completely supports quality first teaching across a range of curriculum areas and, in this case, maths.

The big concepts which teachers are trying to explore with children can be greatly enhanced by embedding them within the pedagogy of Talk for Writing. It supports the teacher in breaking down the learning into small chunks of teaching, with quality modelling and models at the core of developing children's understanding and application. It enables both the teacher and child to co-construct how to box up structure and create toolkits of key ingredients, which can then lead to independent application. It is a brilliant tool for promoting quality dialogic talk within mathematics and, with thought, can be used as a vehicle for writing in maths, as children's subject knowledge is so secure, they can create their own texts from a place of real confidence.

It has taken a number of years to integrate the pedagogy behind Talk for Writing into the way we teach mathematics. When I first joined St Matthew's, I wasn't a specialist in maths so, when I was asked to lead this subject, I decided I needed some training, as this would help me carve out my vision for maths. One of my pet peeves is being led by someone who can't help me because they have no subject knowledge; I had seen this happen too many times. So, I did my Mathematics Specialist Teacher Programme, trained to become a Specialist Leader in Education and became a Professional Development Lead for the National Centre for the Teaching of Mathematics. All of this helped to shape my pedagogy for how to run maths, but it takes time. I would say, when you take over a subject, take some time (if possible) to develop your subject knowledge before making changes, understand where your teachers are at and think about the personal journey they will need to go on, as EVERY school is different. If possible, try to get a mentor who can support you with this initially, so you are making changes from a place of confidence, with a plan and focus.

Make links to other subjects: what pedagogy can you re-appropriate to support your subject's delivery? I began to unpick the pedagogy behind Talk for Writing. I talked to our English subject lead. I initially believed that you could just fit maths within the structure for TfW that suited English, but you can't. It took time to understand that maths is cyclical – you learn one element and make a connection and your knowledge spirals, whereas the TfW structure for English, though still cyclical in many ways, is more linear. With maths, you regularly repeat the process again, making connections across the elements. My advice here is to be your own guinea pig. I took time to trial aspects of TfW linked to maths in my classroom, then slowly disseminated the practice that worked throughout the school. This led to things becoming embedded securely over time because they had a real purpose and they really worked.

Finally, work with other curriculum leads. This allowed me to see the opportunities for creative and meaningful connections, which only enhance children's love of the creative elements of maths. An example of this is researching the Islamic civilisation – where many of our mathematical ideas come from. How do we use them now? What connections can be made to history, geography and science? This is a fascinating and developing area of our curriculum.

I aim to be a subject leader who has their finger on the pulse and always aims for excellence BUT, and it is a big BUT, this takes time. This is definitely a marathon, not a sprint and at St Matthew's we are still developing, but we feel we are now in a great place.

To see examples of Talk for Writing in maths, see the following video clips:

- **Video clip 38:** Alan Crozier, Year 6 teacher at Briar Hill Primary, demonstrates how the approach supports maths teaching. The picture here shows how this school is also getting pupils to write down the thinking behind the maths process they are using to help build their understanding and confidence.

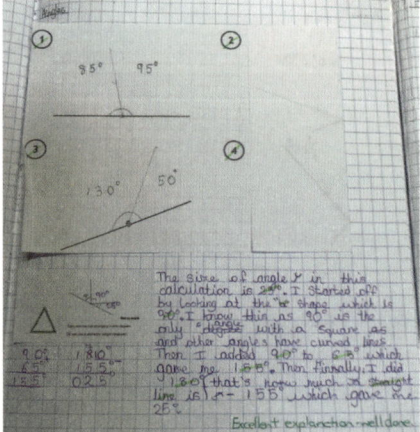

- **Video clip 40:** A Year 6 pupil from Yew Tree Community Primary, Birmingham, demonstrates how TfW is helping her with maths.

- Also, see the following chapter which focuses on Talk for Writing in maths in the secondary sector.

- To see Tracey teaching vocabulary, **see video clip 5**, and teaching reading related to RE, **see video clip 30**.

To find out when you can see Talk for Writing in action across the curriculum at St Matthews and related training, visit www.talk4writing.co.uk/train-with-us/st-matthews-ce-primary-birmingham/.

Chapter 10b: Talk for Writing in maths (secondary)

This chapter focuses on how a range of secondary maths teachers have found the underpinning principles of Talk for Writing help students understand mathematical processes – the key to progress in maths, including how the cold-to-hot-approach makes them much more confident about their ability to do maths.

At first glance, maths might appear to be the subject least likely to be helped by the Talk for Writing approach. After all, coherent writing is not key to success in maths since most of it is expressed in symbols, numbers or shapes. But one glance at the very high maths scores that the TfW primary training schools achieve (90% in 2019 achieved the "expected standard" as opposed to the national average of 79%) suggests there may be a strong link. The Talk for Writing process is all about moving from imitation through innovation to independent application, and maths, like any other subject, relies on that. And, of course, understanding the underlying mathematical concepts is key, as explained in the previous chapter where Tracey Adams illustrated how getting her pupils to write down the maths processes they use in sentences has really helped. This is touched on in relation to trigonometry later in this chapter, and it might be an area that secondary colleagues would find useful to investigate further. In this chapter, you will see that the emphasis has been on the power of boxing up, plus the cold to hot process, alongside students being able to explain the logic behind the maths they are doing orally – dialogic talk. In the words of Andy Lyon, when he was maths coordinator at Queensbury School, Bradford:

> "If students don't understand the underlying mathematical concepts, they are lost. Making them express concepts in words has significantly helped develop their understanding. They know they've made progress."

Following training in Talk for Writing, Andy discovered that if he spent much more time getting the students to comprehend what they were doing, more time unpicking what the mathematical concepts meant, then the students' understanding, and the quality of their practical application, greatly increased. There was less work in the books but much more mathematical understanding in their heads. Andy recently told me that he had just become Lead Teacher in Maths for a MAT in Wakefield and believes that his focus on getting students to explain their understanding of maths helped him get the job. He added, "You'll be pleased to hear that the first thing I did in my new classroom was to put up washing lines on the display boards and they are now covered in flip-chart paper!"

If you look at the slide here of how the TfW process can be adapted to suit maths, you can see that the main difference is that the focus on writing down

> **The Talk for Writing process adapted for maths**
>
> **Planning stage**
> - Cold task to establish prior knowledge & adjust planning
>
> **Imitation stage**
> - Hook: Why would anyone need to know this?
> - Warm up key vocabulary/concepts/formulae using actions & images to recall key processes. Use talk frames to help explain the processes used.
> - Model how to answer question/problem by **boxing up** the process to help students internalise the stages.
>
> **Innovation stage**
> - Model how to innovate by applying boxed-up process to a range of similar problems, increasing in difficulty
> - Students have a go
>
> **Independent application**
> - Use hot task to see if students can answer related questions/problems independently

ideas coherently shifts to a focus on understanding how to apply mathematical processes accurately. A model of *what = good* in maths is essential, just like it is in text-based subjects, but there is one big difference. In text-based subjects, you are trying to get the sound of the words and phrases into the student's heads to help them have the right tune in their heads so that they can express themselves coherently. Thus, in text-based subjects, it makes complete sense to start with orally internalising the written model and then actually seeing the model written down so that a class can work on co-constructing the structure of the model by boxing it up together and then analysing its ingredients.

In maths, however, you are not focusing on coherent sentences so much as trying to establish a logical thinking process in the head that enables anyone to solve whatever type of problem is being considered. This can then be supported by a talking frame, as illustrated in the previous chapter. If you look back at the models in that chapter, you will see that, unsurprisingly, they are mainly presented in mathematical symbols not words. So, the key focus in maths is a structure that takes you step by step to the solution, and that structure is boxing up. In effect, the teacher creates the mathematical model in front of the class, boxing up the stages and talking the students through the process logically as they go along (**see video clip 14**). This, then, provides the structure for the thinking that will enable the students to innovate on the model and then apply it independently. And later, when perhaps the class has been introduced to a range of possible models, students may be asked to select the one that will work best given the circumstances and carry it out independently. Tracey, in the previous chapter, explained how she embeds learning by getting the students to actually explain coherently in sentences the processes that they would use to solve a problem.

Planning your unit

Using a cold task as the baseline measure to bookend units

Are cold tasks useful in maths? Tracey is not the only one convinced of their usefulness. Maths teachers and students tell me that they are too. If you look at **video clip 6** from a Year 8 maths class in Slough and Eton, you will see that all of the students questioned didn't actually get anything down for the cold task because they didn't understand what they had to do – some of the words meant nothing to them. So does that make it a waste of time? Not according to the teacher or the students who, in different ways, all explained that it helped them recognise what they didn't know and what they needed to find out. Interestingly, one maths teacher commented that listening to the students on the video explaining why they couldn't begin had helped her perceive some of the misconceptions that students have. When we understand something very well, it is hard to see it through the eyes of someone who can't understand. Heather Brooks, who teaches maths at The John of Gaunt School, has come up with this effective model for the cold to hot process in maths. At the cold-task stage, the pupils are asked to complete an entry test as illustrated here. Since this Year 7 example on place value was typical of the class's understanding, the teacher then knew to particularly focus on building up understanding and confidence about pupils' basic comprehension of the number system (number size, the link between fractions with denominators that are powers of 10 and decimal numbers, and rounding numbers to decimal places and significant figures).

At the end of the unit, there is an exit test (the hot task) covering the same focus. As you can see, the student's understanding of place value has greatly increased. This student in the cold task only scored 4/25 but by the hot task they had achieved 16/25.

Y7 cold task on place value Assessment feedback Hot task on place value

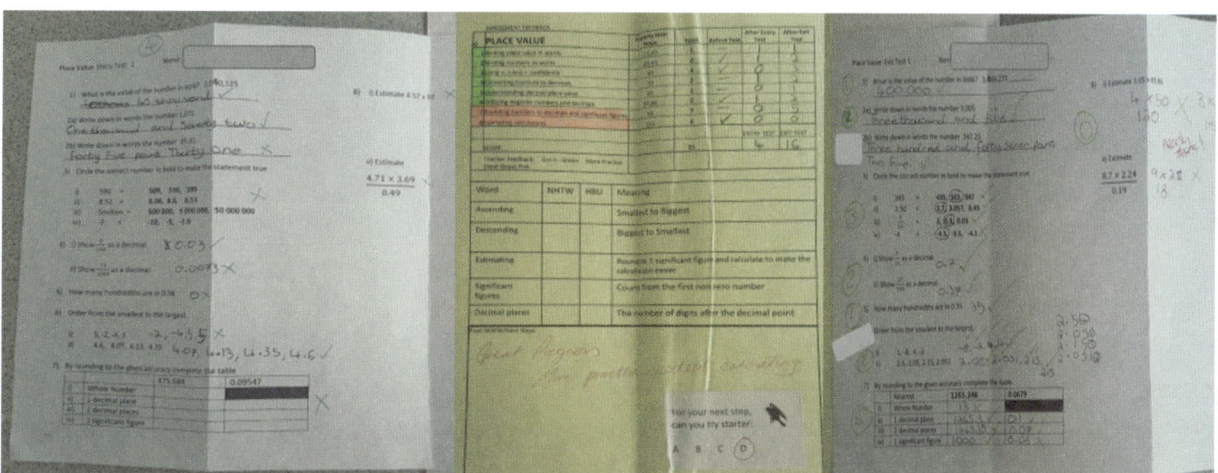

The teacher then fills in an assessment feedback sheet that helps the student see clearly what they now know and what is still proving challenging.

This sheet also reinforces some of the key vocabuary linked to the unit like *estimating* and *decimal places*. At the end of each unit, these three sheets are stuck together in the student's book (as pictured above) so the learning journey from cold to hot is very clear, alongside what the students need to focus on now to improve, as explained at the end of this chapter.

1. The imitation stage

Start with a hook

When focusing on the building blocks of maths, it can sometimes be hard to come up with a hook beyond the unalluring, "This will really help you with your maths". Fortunately, some topics lend themselves to a hook. For example, when starting trigonometry, pupils may be asked how could anyone work out the height of a tall building without climbing to the top. The teacher then goes through a few scenarios in pictures, as illustrated below, so that (hopefully) the pupils notice that when the angle between the ground and the top of the building is 45° it makes a right angled isosceles triangle and the height can then be calculated without leaving the ground.

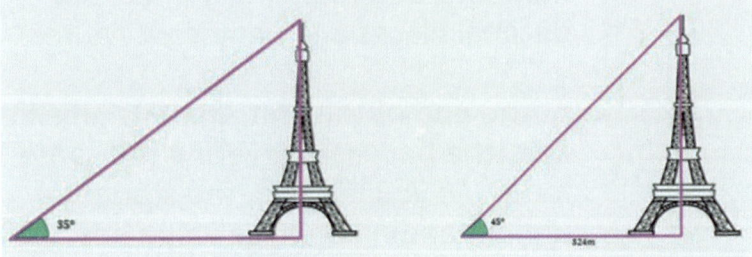

Warming up the words

Obviously, words are key to understanding. You may not often have to write the words down in maths but understanding the technical vocabulary of maths, so that you understand the processes you are using and can explain them coherently to yourself and others, is key to progress. I am still haunted by the 14 year-old-girl from a low-attaining class I was teaching at some point in the eighties who said to me one day, "We're getting good at English now, Miss. Why don't you teach us maths? You won't believe how bad we are at maths." All the class joined in the request. It was sometime before the coming of the National Curriculum; no one ever visited my lessons to check on what I was doing: so, I thought, why not? One Wednesday afternoon, I tried to find out what they already understood about maths. The girl was right: they knew nothing. They had no real understanding of what the words *add*, *subtract*, *divide* or *take away* meant whether in written, spoken or symbolic form, let alone anything more complex. Hopefully, all these years of a curriculum and strategies focused on raising the quality of teaching means that no students would find themselves in a similar situation today, but still we must remember the centrality of vocabulary to comprehension. The head of maths at Hungerhill School, Doncaster, said she had always assumed the pupils knew what *solve* meant, until she started using never-heard-the-word grids (**see page 58** and the page below). If you think about how many times a typical child would have heard the word *solve* by the time they reached Year 7, that finding is somewhat sobering.

Helping students become confident comprehenders and users of the technical vocabulary and processes of maths is key to raising standards in maths. If, by the end of a maths unit, the students can explain what they have learnt coherently and demonstrate how to do whatever aspect they have been concentrating on, they will remember what they have learnt.

Maths teachers at Slough and Eton found this to be true. A Year 7 unit on qualitative and quantitative data had begun with a never-heard-the-word grid to establish which words to particularly focus on. Interestingly, the child whose work is pictured here, feels confident about explaining tricky concepts like *mean*, *median* and *mode* and yet indicates that they are not sure about the meaning of *average*, on the surface a much easier concept but, because it seems easier, perhaps it wasn't focused on. If we are not careful, we assume that children understand words that they do not understand. Never-heard-the-word grids are a good way of tackling this problem along with creating an atmosphere where it is good to ask and say that you don't know the meaning of words. In that lesson on quantitative and qualitative data, every single child I spoke to could clearly explain to me what they were doing and what type of data they had chosen to investigate – all the more impressive when very few of the children would have had English as their first language. During the lesson, students were encouraged to write on the flip chart any terms or issues they wanted more discussion about – as pictured – an approach that was clearly paying off.

The image below shows how the maths department at The John of Gaunt School, Trowbridge, has adapted never-heard-the-word grids to suit their needs. The darker written text shows a student's initial attempt to fill in the sheet working from memory. The green text is the additions

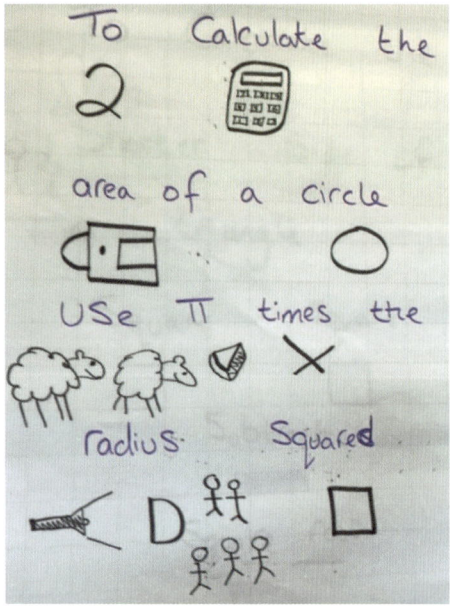

they have made following discussions in class.

Heather Brooks, stresses that making students explain what they are doing is key to learning in maths. All students are expected to verbalise the process every time they give answers in class: "In fact, little emphasis is put on the final answer. It is more about the process. This ensures pupils write down their full workings (the maths story) and allows those who are less confident with their mental arithmetic but more confident at verbalising the process not to worry about whether the answer to each stage is correct." They then work on ways to build in confidence and fluency with the mental arithmetic alongside building confidence with the process and being able to explain what they are doing.

Text mapping in maths

In maths, there isn't going to be a model text to text map like there is in most subjects because maths answers are not normally expressed in sentences and paragraphs. Why invent icons for something that is already in icons? But maths teachers have found that text mapping key formulae and coming up with entertaining actions to help remember mathematical concepts and technical vocabulary can be very useful. Here is a witty, dual-coded text map devised by Mr Roy from Royd's Hall, Huddersfield, to help his students remember how to calculate the area of a circle. Watch him demonstrate how to present this with actions to a class (**video clip 10**) and you will understand how memorable and engaging such an approach can be. Maths teachers have also found that making the boxing-up process memorable through rhyme, pictures and actions is a very good idea as illustrated earlier by **video 6**.

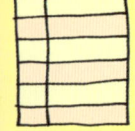

Introducing the model by boxing it up

The teacher, of course, models how to answer whatever problems are being focused on and this is where boxing up is so important because it sums up the best way to tackle approaching maths problems. There is such a wide range of maths problems it would be impossible to provide a model for all of them but the underpinning processes that will help students solve the problems should be modelled. What the students need is a way in to help them tackle problems.

TALK FOR WRITING IN MATHS (SECONDARY)

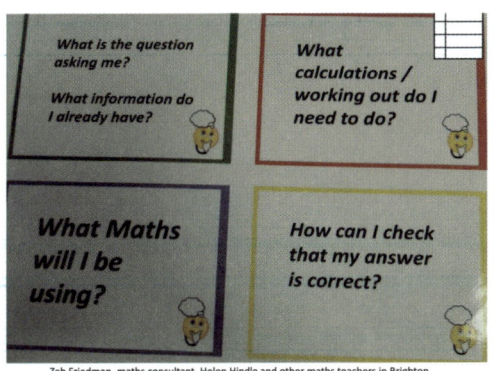

Adapted from work of Zeb Friedman, maths consultant, and maths teachers in Brighton

Zeb Friedman, when both a local maths adviser and a maths teacher in Brighton, was the first to develop this idea in 2010 when taking part in Talk for Writing training. Maths exam questions had just become much more problem based and, while listening to me explain how boxing up helped students understand how to structure coherent explanation text, she realised how the grid-planning approach of boxing up could be adapted to suit solving maths problems. In maths, instead of the written introduction of standard explanation text, the focus would be on analysing whatever problem had been asked and checking what information was provided to enable the problem to be answered. In place of explaining whatever the process was in written text, in maths you had to work out what maths to use and then use it appropriately to work out the calculations. When you had your answer, you checked that it was correct: and that was your conclusion.

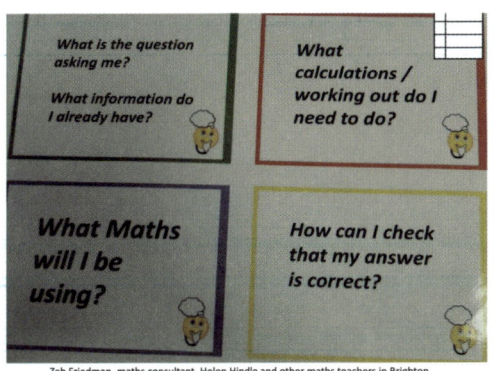

Zeb Friedman, maths consultant, Helen Hindle and other maths teachers in Brighton

Zeb converted her lightbulb moment into boxing-up mats (pictured left).

These were placed on the maths tables and, initially, students worked through problems in pairs, using this process to help them discuss the problem

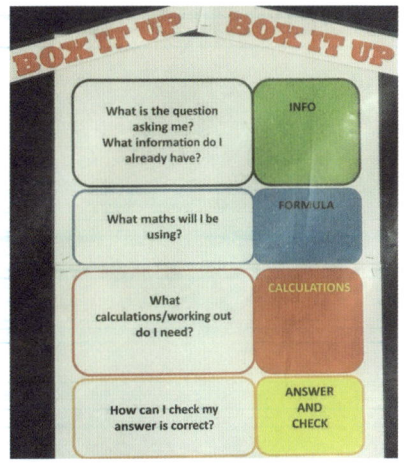

and establish what the question was asking, decide how to tackle it, carry out whatever maths was required, and finally check their answers were correct. Once the students were familiar with the process, they started to automatically use it when faced with problems and could therefore solve problems independently working entirely on their own. The image to the right is what boxing up looks like at The John of Gaunt School. On **video clip 39** you can see Uzma Southon, Head of Maths at Slough and Eton, explaining why boxing up works in maths.

The photograph here shows how Heather Brooks now has a permanent visual aid for how to box up understanding of 100s, 10s, units, tenths, etc. She had spent years trying to explain this by jumping from side to side, and suddenly realised that it would make the abstract more concrete if she physically boxed it up and literally moved from section to section as she explained.

Boxing up is also used effectively to model the different stages that you go through to answer specific types of maths questions. Below you can see how maths teacher Naomi Bell, when at Phoenix High School in Shepherd's Bush, London, used boxing up to make the 6 different steps required to solve equations in trigonometry crystal clear. Naomi explained at a whole-staff Talk for Writing feedback session how she had thought that she had always made the stages clear but, by boxing it up as a grid, somehow the students seemed to be able to really grasp the signficance of the stages, and their understanding improved alongside the quality of their work. It's the visual nature of the boxed-up grid that makes the difference. Below, Naomi explains why explicitly boxing up the stages you go through when answering mathematical questions made a difference to her students' ability to understand.

> "Now I would always have taught trigonometry in these stages but I never before made it as explicit as it is with boxing up. So, I compared it with two Year 9 classes. With one class I taught using the same methods as I had used previously when teaching trigonometry and, with the other class, I used the boxing-up method. And I would say that the boxing up method was much more successful.
>
> "I know as maths teachers often we think we don't really have to write anything in maths, so this isn't really relevant, but I think we really can learn something from this even if you don't have an essay-writing subject.
>
> "The first thing that I did was to split how you answer a trigonometry question into its six separate stages. The first stage was to label the sides of the triangle. Then choose the correct equation: whether they want sin, cos or tan. Then, when they are going to write down that equation, put in the numbers they already know from the question they had been given, and rearrange it so that they could solve it to find what they were looking for. And only at that point would they pick up their calculator to work out the answer."

Trigonometry: Boxing up the 6 stages makes the process clear

1.	Label the sides
2.	Choose the correct equation (Sin, Cos or Tan)
3.	Write the equation down
4.	Substitute in the values you know
5.	Rearrange the equation
6.	Now use your calculator to solve it

Naomi Bell, Maths department, Phoenix School

She was then brave enough to try using boxing up to teach trigonometry to all of the teaching staff – a few of whom initially seemed to display the terror of maths that somehow seems to plague this country, but you could see people who had felt daunted by the task quickly getting the hang of it if they actually tried to follow the steps.

Then she explained that she had run a little experiment to see if it worked by getting a class to copy down the six stages in their books, alongside referring to the stages frequently in subsequent lessons. She then asked the class to write down the six steps on the left-hand side of their books from memory and gave them three questions to answer that varied in difficulty: the first one being easy, the second more difficult and the final question being so challenging that it would normally have been beyond the competence of a Year 9 class.

The students who were able to write down the six steps on the left-hand side were much more capable of answering the questions, correctly answering the first two and having a good go at answering the advanced question or even managing to answer it, because the process had given them a route to use. Those who failed to remember the steps, struggled with even the easiest of the questions. However, students who normally struggled but had remembered the six steps were making much more progress because the process had given them the confidence to get going so they had some of the stages right. This experiment bears out Tracey's approach in the previous chapter of using writing out the process to help students remember it.

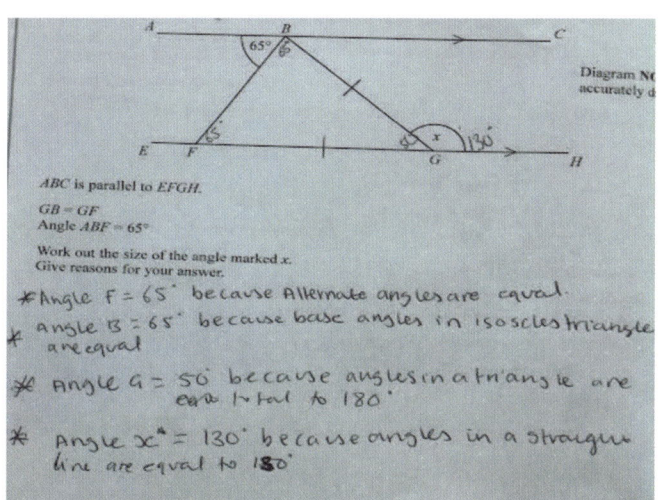

From this experiment, Naomi decided it would be useful to make the stages more memorable by using a rhyme, pictures or actions, to make it more explicit for them. If you look again at **video clip 6**, you will see that this is exactly how the teacher has helped her class do translations. As a result of boxing up the stages, students managed to grasp mathematical processes more easily and produced well structured answers, as illustrated here. Not only are the answers right, but the student can explain clearly how each calculation has been arrived at, showing that they understand the process.

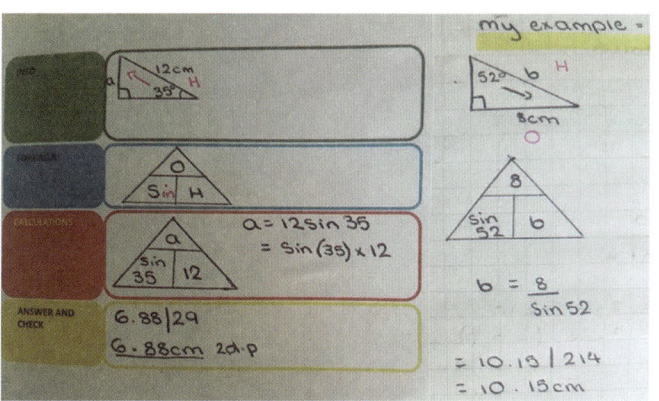

Heather Brooks has similarly found boxing up useful, again explaining that in maths boxing up is an effective way for the teacher to model the stages you have to go through to solve mathematical problems, so the students know what order to do things in. In effect, this is the **imitation stage**. They can then start to apply this approach to similar problems – the **innovation stage** – which then enables them to tackle similar problems independently, as illustrated here. To the left is the imitation stage, showing the boxing-up process as applied to trigonometry, and then what the teacher modelled to show how to innovate on this.

As you can see from this Year 10 student's independent work here on the right, students use the same layout and method that was modelled for them through boxing up.

Heather stresses that it is wrong, however, to give the impression that you are able to go from boxing up the process at the imitation stage to independent work seamlessly. In reality, this works for the more basic questions. However, when dealing with more complex problems, you have to spend more time as a class discussing what to look for, ways that may make it easier, and reminding each other of pitfalls to avoid etc.

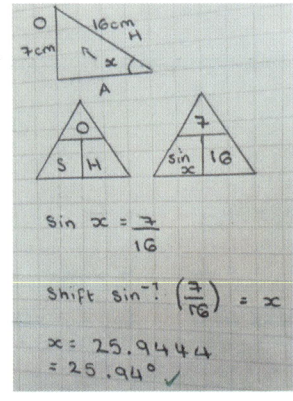

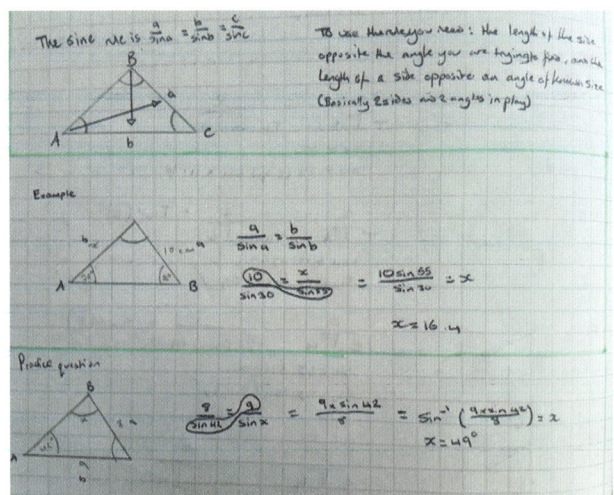

For example, in the unit of work pictured here, the Year 10 students were fairly quick on learning the formulae. However, they found it hard when problem solving to identify when to use it. This is why the teacher built in matching diagrams to the formula and the name of the formula. This shows the end of topic check on this: the teacher felt that it had definitely aided confidence.

If you look at this Year 7 work on rounding decimal places, you can see that the pupil has used the method illustrated by the boxed-up model answer at the top of the page to structure the thinking stages that they have to go through in order to handle the task. Because the boxed-up stages help to make the thinking process very clear, the pupil has been successful.

Importantly, the maths department at John of Gaunt have found that students who struggle with maths

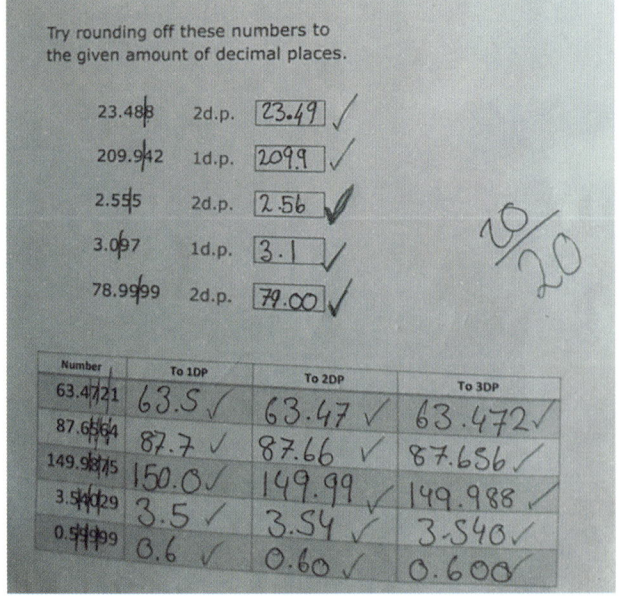

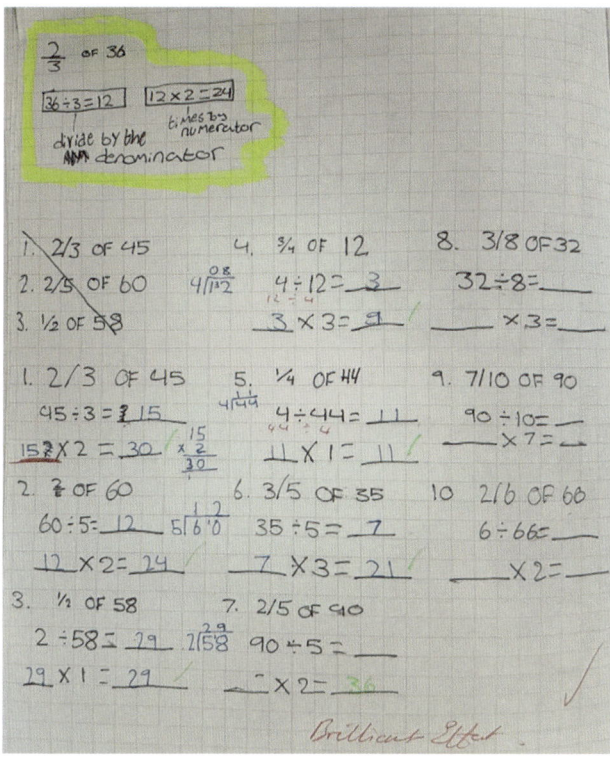

find the boxing-up process very supportive. They show more pride in their work than previously and can see the progress themselves. The image to the left here shows boxing up of fractions of amounts, followed by the initial steps to working out similar problems independently.

Because this class struggles with mental calculations, which really slows down the process, the teacher decided to just write out the stages of the calculations without completing them. This allowed for speedier repetition and helped the students remember the order of the calculation. On completion of the workings, the students could then concentrate their efforts on the calculations as illustrated below.

The idea here is twofold:

1. to help students remember the method
2. to help show the students there are stages to the workings.

With most students, if they can get the first stage down, they are able to complete more than first anticipated. Boxing up had enabled the teachers to scaffold the learning into manageable chunks. Because the process was clear, the students gained the confidence to handle the calculations.

Embedding learning

Dialogic talk is at the heart of building confidence in maths perhaps more than any other subject because of the abstract nature of maths. Consolidating learning through co-constructing understanding and explaining to others is therefore central to

206 TRANSFORMING LEARNING ACROSS THE CURRICULUM

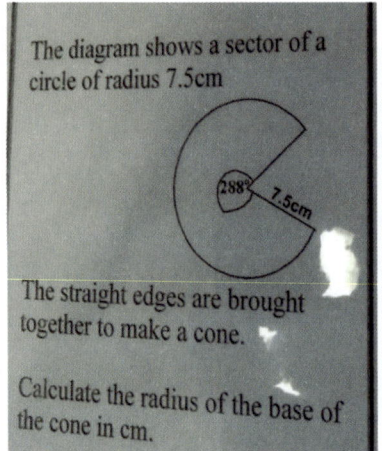

independent application. In this example, Uzma Southon, then head of maths at Slough and Eton, set up a consolidating-learning activity for her Year 11 class where the students, in small groups, were given a range of questions to consider (two of which are pictured here). They had to decide how to answer each of the questions and to be prepared to explain how to do so to the class. Once the groups had had sufficient time to discuss the problems, students were then asked to present their explanations to the rest of the class who listened and decided if they agreed with the suggested process or if they knew an easier route through to finding the answer. The resulting discussions were fascinating not least because sometimes you could see the class begin to query the method that was being suggested and then they offered different, more effective alternatives. There could have been no better way of embedding the students' learning and helping them identify the gaps in their understanding.

In June 2018, I was lucky enough to visit Royds Hall in Huddersfield on the day

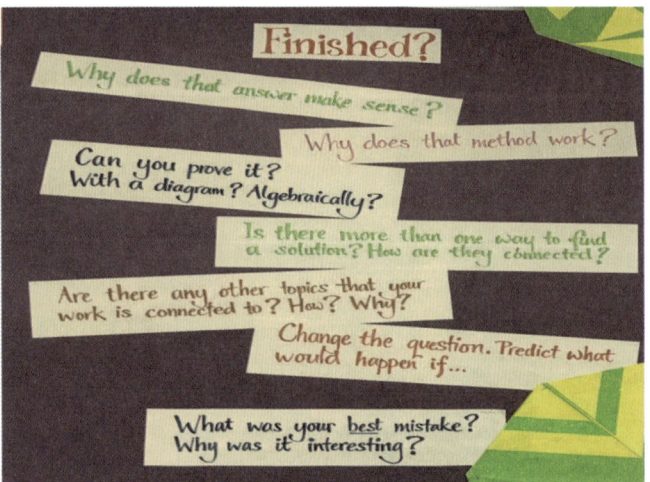

that they were having an after-school event celebrating the difference that Talk for Writing was making to student achievement. Maths classrooms showed Talk for Writing in action with great displays supporting the learning on the walls including this excellent poster. Each of the questions asked here encourages real thinking from the students, including asking them if there was more than one way to reach a solution. And the icing on the cake: What was your best mistake? Why was it interesting?

Comparing the cold to hot tasks

Bookending units with cold to hot tasks so that students can see at the end of a unit the progress that they have made, as well as identifying areas that are still causing problems, has proved to be a very powerful part of the Talk for Writing process.

As explained at the opening of this chapter, the maths department at The John of Gaunt School have included an assessment for learning grid which is used both pre the cold task and post the hot task. Pupils fill in their scores for

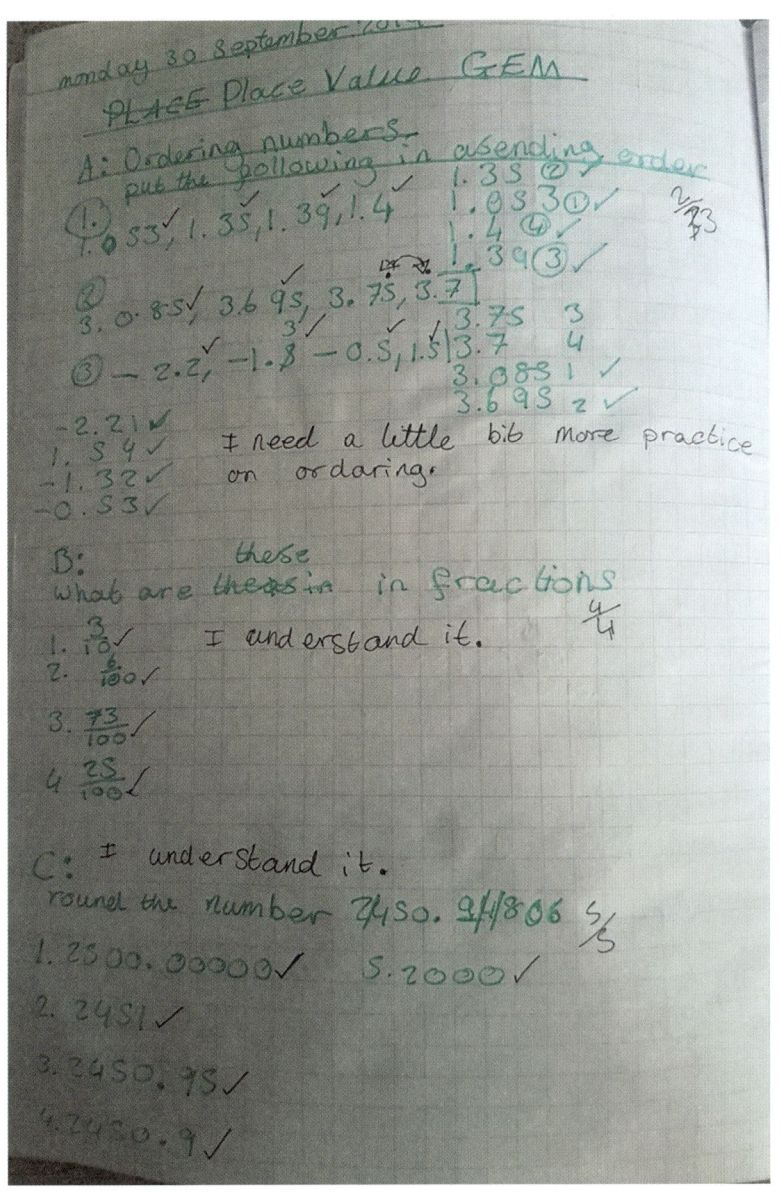

each area after the exit test. Marks can easily be compared from entry to exit, and the tests are kept together, so both pupil and teacher are able to check where the gaps are. This enables the pupils to more easily see progress, and recognise aspects that need improving. This is then followed up by whatever working towards *mastery work* has been identified from the hot task to push pupils' understanding a little further. The teacher establishes which areas need re-teaching to help the students progress further towards understanding the concepts. Individual students are then able to spend some time practising their personal next steps within class. The image here shows that this student had identified ordering numbers, changing decimals to fractions and rounding numbers as their next steps. After the re-teaching, the pupil has shown they have gained more confidence in these areas.

Students and parents are given a printed report which follows the same layout as the assessment-for-learning grid students have in their books (see **page 197**). This directs them to *Hegarty maths clips* that can be used for independent homework by students to help build up/consolidate understanding.

Maths teachers at John of Gaunt have found that students are much more positive about their progress now as they can easily see where their starting point was and can see in black and white where and how far they have progressed. Before this system, no matter what progress a pupil had achieved and the teacher could see and identify, pupils only saw themselves as having progressed if they got near to, or full marks, in an assessment. Needless to say, for the majority of students this was unattainable and therefore dented confidence. Now pupils feel much more positive about their learning.

Chapter 11a: Talk for Writing in science (primary)

Emily Ridge, Head of School at Yew Tree Community School in Birmingham, explains how Talk for Writing has spread from being the way Yew Tree boosted English to underpinning all subjects. Here she focuses on what this means for the school's science curriculum which has not only helped the children to understand the nature of science investigations but also to love science.

About ten years ago, Talk for Writing became the driving force to change how the school ensured that children enjoyed English, particularly writing and retelling stories. Most importantly, it impacted on children's confidence: it built up essential skills, such as developing speech, the use of correct grammar and the enjoyment of reading alongside developing a wider knowledge of vocabulary and understanding. We knew that vocabulary was key to successful learning, particularly for our children, as the majority have English as an additional language and many are new to English. However, the benefits for all the children were apparent. Armed with good vocabularies, the writing skills of all our children improved.

Securing real progress only happened when, as a leadership team, we ensured that Talk for Writing was strategically taught across the curriculum. The strength of this came from ongoing training, support and guidance for all staff. We were proud of our achievements in English, but we knew we needed to ensure the same passion for learning was embedded for all areas of the curriculum. We wanted to make certain that our pupils gained the subject specific knowledge they needed to prepare for their world tomorrow. Knowing how TfW had impacted all areas of English, we utilised its potential and took the strategy right across the curriculum. This provided opportunities for all to access the learning, making certain we developed all pupil's potential to learn and gain knowledge. Now, therefore, TfW underpins all teaching and learning at Yew Tree. This chapter focuses on what this looks like in science.

Adapting Talk for Writing to suit science

The following structure was developed for science lessons across the school which, as you can see, has been adapted from the Talk for Writing process:

Imitation stage

– Hook to engage pupils' thirst for knowledge and set a real purpose for learning
– Enquiry type related to unit recalled through actions and enquiry game
– Scientific scenario using an evaluation text map to structure scientific reasoning
– Review of prior knowledge
– Vocabulary game

Innovation stage

— Main teaching with practical investigation to drive long-term memory, knowledge and understanding
— Practise of skills

Independent application stage

— Application of skills
— Written outcome based on text map to structure scientific reasoning.

This consistent approach ensures teachers develop a good understanding of scientific concepts which can then be passed on to the children. Furthermore, children become confident in the skills required for carrying out investigations and proficient in recording their findings in a coherent way.

Laying the foundations: the imitation stage

At the beginning of each unit, teachers plan a hook. This acts not only as an exciting introduction to the unit of work, but also as a means by which the teacher can gather initial assessment of how much the pupils know about the subject. For example, at the start of Year 3's *Light and Darkness* unit, the children walked into a darkened room with window and door blinds drawn. The teacher asked the simple question, "Why can't we see?" This provided an opportunity to gather how much understanding the pupils already had. Hooks can take the form of a picture, video or scenario: anything to jog the children's memory of the last time they studied the concept.

Enquiry games

The strength of our science curriculum is that many of the Talk for Writing in science strategies are embedded and repeated throughout; these approaches not only support the understanding of science but also the wider curriculum. The key aspect of our science curriculum is to build up the children's skill in scientific investigation. The enquiry game is key to developing the children's understanding – **see video clip 42b** – to see an enquiry game in action. This is a very quick-paced introduction at the start of every session in which pupils identify the 7 key enquiry types, and link these to actions. A quick memory game ensures children know the enquiry type and can give an example of how it is used. This kinaesthetic approach supports our pupils in using the key scientific vocabulary of enquiry. The image here shows the actions that pupils have internalised from Y1-Y6.

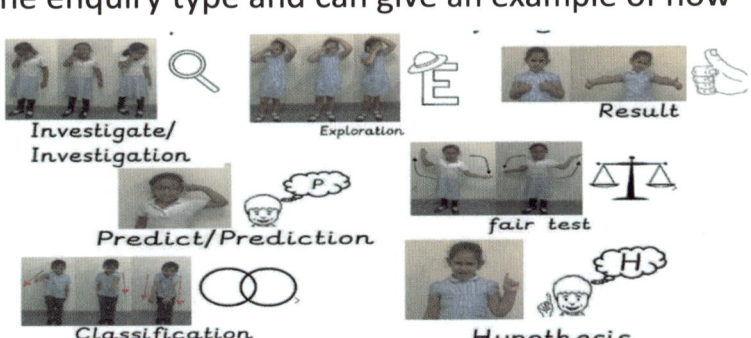

The enquiry type that is to be the focus of the lesson is practised in a quick game. This is all done verbally so that children can internalise the key concepts of the enquiry type. For example, for a fair test there would be a change of variables. Children will need to understand that in this investigation they must only change one variable and consider which variable they are going to measure. The teacher assesses whether the children understand the key concepts of fair testing. Following a brief discussion in pairs, ideas are fed back to the class with the teacher addressing any misconceptions. The Year 5 example here asks, *Which material would be most suitable for an umbrella?*

Children are then asked to suggest the variables.

Changing variable: _____
Controlled variables: _____
Measuring variable: _____

Science Question: Which material is the most suitable for an umbrella?

Changing Variable: type of material

Controlled variables: size of material, size of umbrella, thickness of material, umbrella is tested in the same climate or weather

Measuring Variable: Which material absorbs the least amount of water.

Following a discussion, the answers are revealed.

Warming up the words

Alongside the hook, at the start of a unit of work, the teacher introduces the never-heard-the-word grid. This contains 6-8 challenging words that are key to understanding the knowledge within the unit.

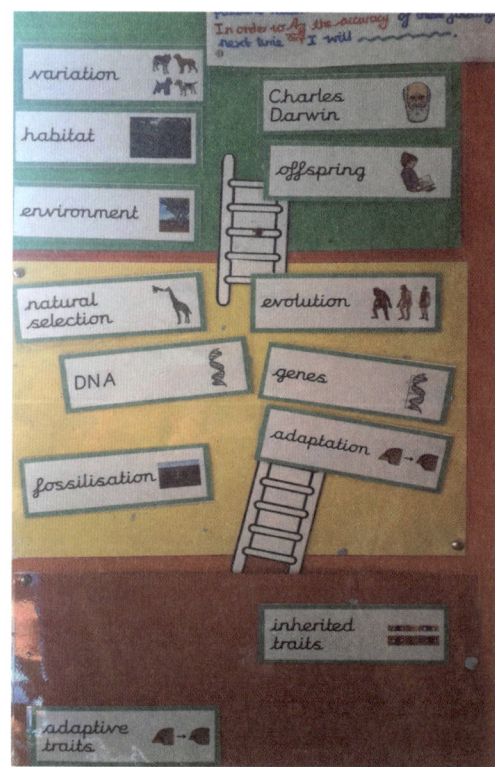

The words illustrated above are first taught following the suggested teaching strategies of Isabel Beck – **see page 19**. The scientific vocabulary is taught in different ways: through repeated verbal recall of a child-friendly definition, through examples within a sentence

TALK FOR WRITING IN SCIENCE (KS2)

from the reading extract, with a picture, and through a variety of games. A love of the language of science runs throughout all the years, as can be seen in two Year 1 videos (**see clips 21 & 22**) where the children use actions to help them remember key scientific words and are helped to use words like predict appropriately in a scientific context. In the example below, you can see that the children are asked to identify the correct use of the word conductor, following their direct instruction.

The vocabulary is added to the working wall and is referred to every lesson to help secure understanding in the long-term memory. The words are placed on a traffic light ladder (pictured above) and moved up as children use them in context as part of their writing.

Scientific scenarios to introduce the content

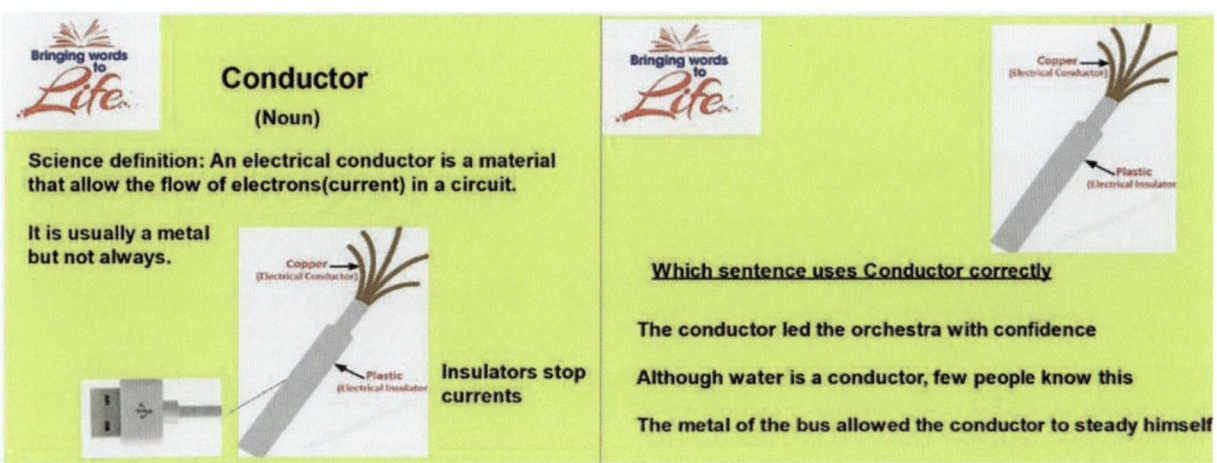

The following is an example of a scientific scenario, taken from Year 6. **See video clip 42a** to see a scenario in action. In this lesson, the objective was to classify plants in the local environment. First, the teacher checks children's understanding of tendrils based on their learning from the previous year. Then, the question is posed: "Which plant has the strongest tendrils?" Initially, children will use the photographs and prior knowledge to make their predictions in pairs or small groups. These predictions are then rehearsed verbally using the investigation text map. Then, the teacher reveals the results of the investigation. This is often in the form of a table or graph as pictured here.

Plant	Maximum weight held by tendrils
pea	300g
pumpkin	1kg
cucumber	500g

Children are then able to reflect on whether or not their prediction was accurate and pose reasons for the results. The children then use the text map to scaffold their verbal evaluation. Below is in an example of a text map for Year 6, followed by a transcript of a child's explanation.

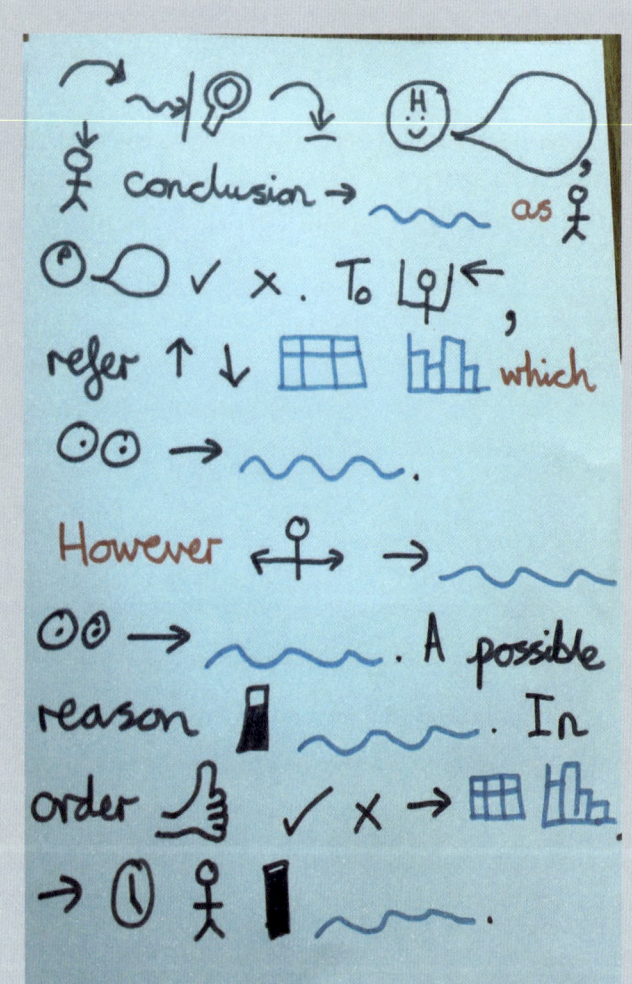

After conducting an investigation, based on the hypothesis that the plant that bears the fruit with the greatest mass will have the strongest tendrils, it is my conclusion that the pumpkin had the strongest tendrils as I predicted correctly. To support this, please refer to the table above which shows clearly that the pumpkin plant held a mass equal to 1kg.

However, if you compare this to mass held by the tendrils of pea plant, you will see that it only held a mass of 300g. A possible reason for this is that the pea produces very light pods and therefore has not evolved to withhold greater weights.

In order to check the accuracy of my hypothesis, I will repeat the investigation with three different plants that differ in the mass of the food they produce. – Oral explanation by Awaal, Y6

The innovation stage – application of skills

Now that the knowledge has been warmed up, the enquiry type consolidated and the structure of conducting an investigation internalised, the children are ready to move on to learning something new, innovating on their understanding.

Here, the teacher will use a range of strategies to deliver the subject knowledge (visually, verbally, kinaesthetically, through discussion, etc.) before asking the children to strengthen their understanding through a practical enquiry. Because the vocabulary, prior-knowledge and enquiry type have all been successfully 'warmed-up' at the start of the lesson, all children are able to access the learning and become secure in their understanding of the new scientific content. Again, text maps can be used effectively to deliver a scientific concept.

TALK FOR WRITING IN SCIENCE (KS2) 213

Knowledge organisers including key information (like the text on evolution below) are sent home at the start of units to strengthen learning beyond the classroom.

> **Evolution**
>
> Evolution is the way that living things change over time.
>
> The first person who explained how evolution happens was Charles Darwin with his scientific theory of natural selection.
>
> Charles Darwin observed that although individuals in a species shared similarities, they were not exact copies of each other; there were small differences or variations between them. He also noticed that everything in the natural world was in competition.
>
> The winners were those that had characteristics which made them better adapted for survival. These living things were more likely to reproduce and pass on their useful characteristics to their offspring.
>
> Over time, the characteristics that help survival become more common and a species gradually changes. Given enough time, these small changes can add up to the extent that a new species altogether can evolve.

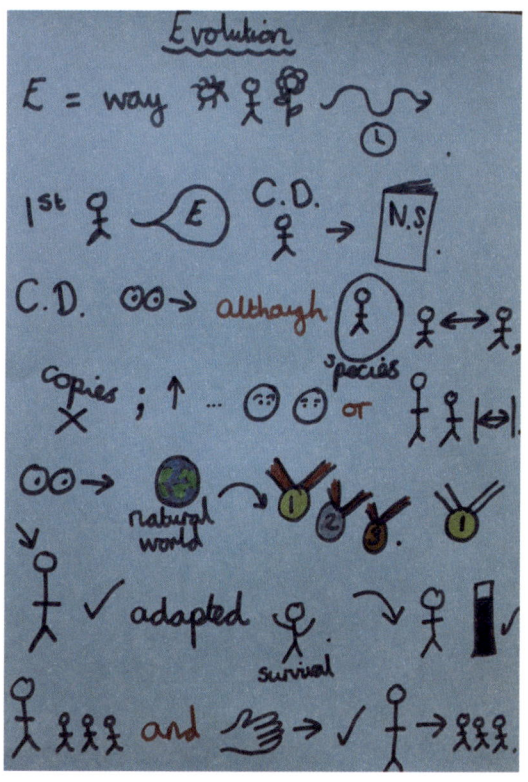

In school, reading activities related to this key information are a vital part of helping the children both understand the information and remember it. This includes a wide range of activities like text mapping (as illustrated here), simple retrieval questions and memory-strengthening games.

Reading extracts are also used in lessons to teach key concepts. Open-ended questions are posed before children begin reading. These questions are selected carefully to ensure that there is more than one possible answer. Children use sentence stems to discuss and debate their ideas using examples from the text to support and justify their ideas.

The knowledge organisers we have selected are visual with brief key information so that pupils have quick access to the main knowledge. They are

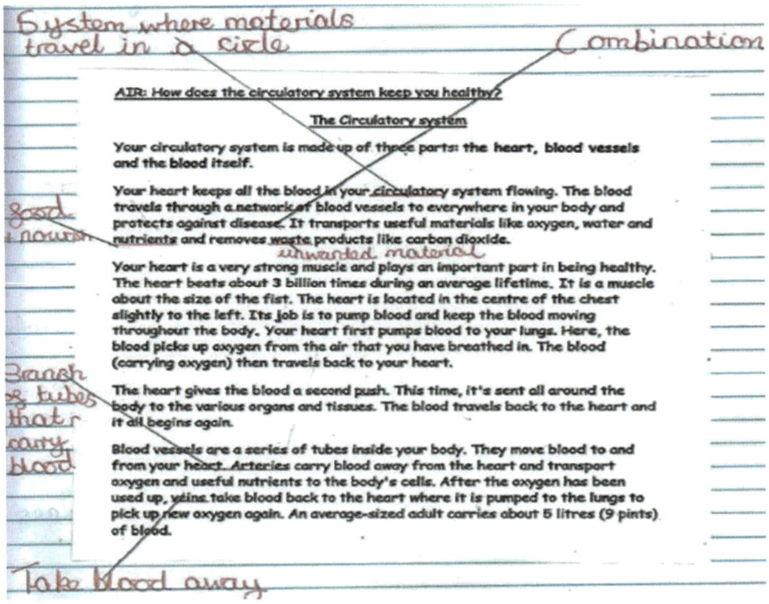

214 TRANSFORMING LEARNING ACROSS THE CURRICULUM

[Pupil's handwritten notebook page showing annotated text about the circulatory system, with annotations including "System where materials travel in a circle", "Combination", "good + nourish", "unwanted material", "Branch of tubes that carry blood", "Take blood away" around a printed passage:]

AIM: How does the circulatory system keep you healthy?

The Circulatory system

Your circulatory system is made up of three parts: the heart, blood vessels and the blood itself.

Your heart keeps all the blood in your circulatory system flowing. The blood travels through a network of blood vessels to everywhere in your body and protects against disease. It transports useful materials like oxygen, water and nutrients and removes waste products like carbon dioxide.

Your heart is a very strong muscle and plays an important part in being healthy. The heart beats about 3 billion times during an average lifetime. It is a muscle about the size of the fist. The heart is located in the centre of the chest slightly to the left. Its job is to pump blood and keep the blood moving throughout the body. Your heart first pumps blood to your lungs. Here, the blood picks up oxygen from the air that you have breathed in. The blood (carrying oxygen) then travels back to your heart.

The heart gives the blood a second push. This time, it's sent all around the body to the various organs and tissues. The blood travels back to the heart and it all begins again.

Blood vessels are a series of tubes inside your body. They move blood to and from your heart. Arteries carry blood away from the heart and transport oxygen and useful nutrients to the body's cells. After the oxygen has been used up, veins take blood back to the lungs to the heart where it is pumped to the lungs to pick up new oxygen again. An average-sized adult carries about 5 litres (9 pints) of blood.

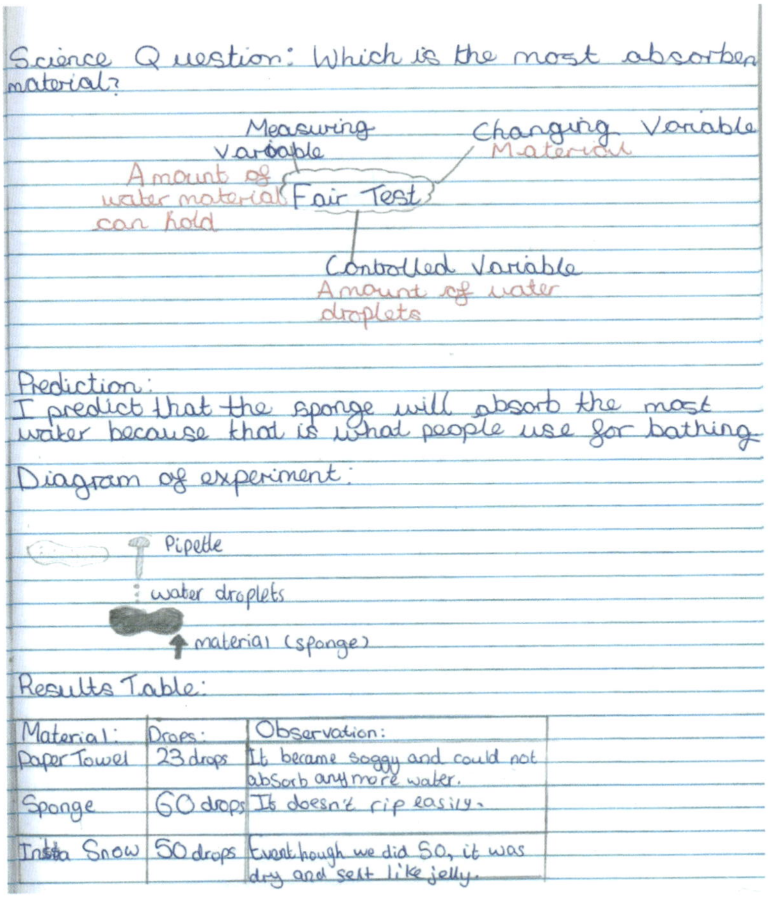

Science Question: Which is the most absorbent material?

- Measuring Variable — Amount of water material can hold
- Changing Variable — Material
- Fair Test
- Controlled Variable — Amount of water droplets

Prediction: I predict that the sponge will absorb the most water because that is what people use for bathing.

Diagram of experiment:
- Pipette
- water droplets
- material (sponge)

Results Table:

Material:	Drops:	Observation:
Paper Towel	23 drops	It became soggy and could not absorb any more water.
Sponge	60 drops	It doesn't rip easily.
Insta Snow	50 drops	Even though we did 50, it was dry and felt like jelly.

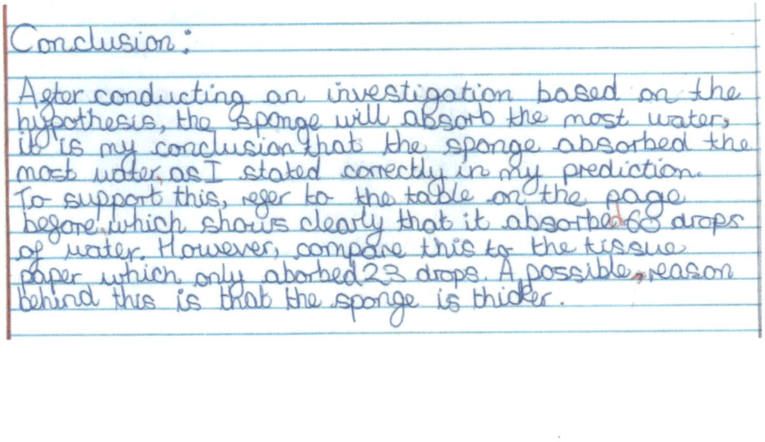

Conclusion:
After conducting an investigation based on the hypothesis, the sponge will absorb the most water, it is my conclusion that the sponge absorbed the most water as I stated correctly in my prediction. To support this, refer to the table on the page before which shows clearly that it absorbed 60 drops of water. However, compare this to the tissue paper which only absorbed 23 drops. A possible reason behind this is that the sponge is thicker.

---

differentiated so that pupils of all abilities can use them at their point of learning – then build on this.

These organisers are a working document for pupils to use as a point of reference, or annotate (written or pictorially), allowing them to make links with other areas in their learning.

After teaching the new concept, children explore their understanding through a practical investigation. At the end of every investigation, pupils write up their data and evaluation using the text map to scaffold their answers. This part of the lesson is supported throughout by the teacher, with independence being handed over to children gradually. For example, children begin to select their own variables, materials, presentation of data, etc.

In these examples from Year 6, pupils placed a variety of leaves in water and then measured the weight of each leaf after a specified period of time. After measuring and collating their data, children discussed what had occurred and why. Here, the child (Sama), having internalised the investigation text map, was able to write up her results (followed by her explanation) appropriately, using a clear structure. Children working at *greater depth* will naturally progress from using every aspect of the model text to using it only as a reference point. However, those less confident in their understanding of the scientific concepts, or those who are still new to English, will hug closely to the structure. After practising using the text map, children write their explanation.

Independent application

At the end of a unit of work, pupils are provided with a scientific question. They then devise their own hypothesis, prediction, enquiry type, method, data collection and evaluation. This challenges them to draw on all of their learning within that unit, as well as their understanding of scientific enquiries themselves. In the example here from Year 6, children were encouraged to think critically and make multiple decisions for themselves, all the while justifying their choices. Here you can see an example of how the investigation was structured, some of the evidence resulting from the investigation and, finally, the conclusion that was drawn.

For many teachers (and pupils), allowing this much freedom within a lesson can be daunting. However, because of the systematic teaching of the knowledge and enquiry-type throughout the unit, this lesson builds the knowledge and skills to

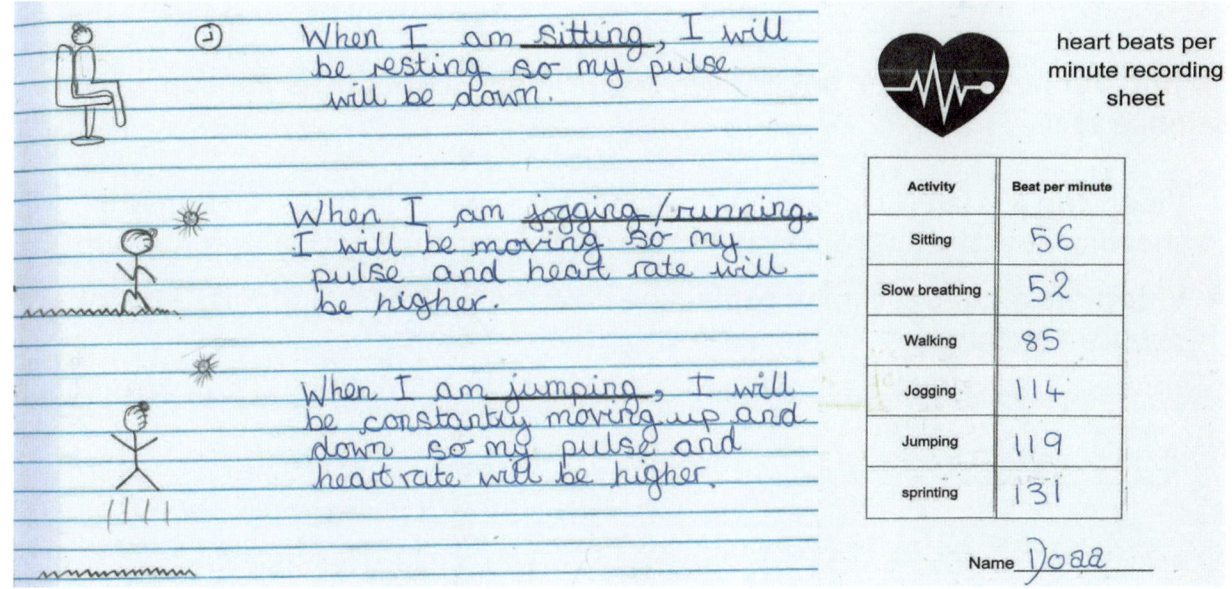

216 TRANSFORMING LEARNING ACROSS THE CURRICULUM

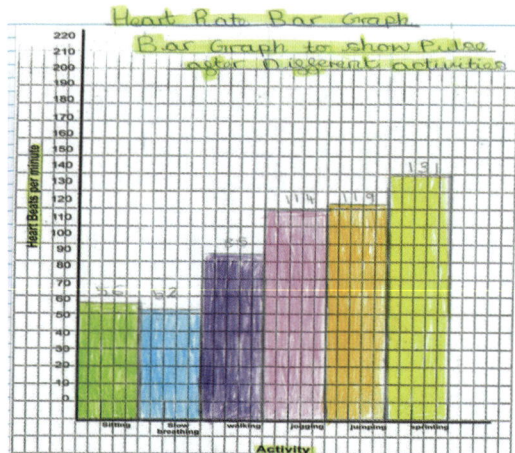

enable the children to rise to the challenge. Moreover, the very nature of the open-ended task provides a wealth of assessment opportunities for teachers. They then use this to plan their next unit of work, adapting their teaching to ensure any misconceptions are addressed (both in terms of knowledge and understanding of scientific enquiry).

Talk for Writing across the curriculum

Although the subject of science itself has its own pedagogy, we have found that the Talk for Writing process has significantly strengthened our teaching of science. The systematic structure for teaching allows less confident teachers to become secure in the delivery. Moreover, it allows pupils to routinely build on their prior knowledge, deepen their understanding of new concepts and – perhaps most importantly – commit their learning to their long-term memory. Consistently, we are able to see the impact on pupils' understanding of complex scientific concepts combined with their ability to pose questions, seek to find their own answers and reach their own conclusions in a sophisticated, scientific way. One of the most positive results has been the confidence and enthusiasm that flows from all of our pupils when they are presenting or explaining their ideas. Talk for Writing has transformed our teaching right across the curriculum ensuring that the children's love of learning is at the heart of every lesson.

To find out how another Talk for Writing primary school uses the approach in science see:

- **Video clip 41:** Ian Hickman, lead teacher for science at Briar Hill Primary, showing how the approach supports science teaching with a Year 4 group
- **Video clip 41:** Ian Hickman explaining how the approach supports quality science teaching

Chapter 11b: Talk for Writing in science (secondary)

Science departments from a wide range of schools have enthusiastically adapted the Talk for Writing process because it helps students engage with and understand the subject. Here, Emma Cooper, Deputy Director of Learning for Science at The John of Gaunt School, guides you through her planning on a GCSE science unit on atoms and isotopes to illustrate how TfW supports the learning of complex scientific topics. In her fascinating overview, the students move through the imitation to independent application stage several times, illustrating how the concepts covered within the unit build in complexity. Importantly, the class is having fun which, in Emma's words, "moves everything away from the exam factory". Emma's classroom is an Aladdin's cave of displays covering the whole science curriculum – it makes science come to life. The picture here shows her with one of the many displays.

Laying the foundations

There are many areas of the GCSE science specification where the Talk for Writing process can be utilised in full to support the students' understanding. I've chosen the topic *Atoms and Isotopes* to illustrate this because the key concepts within this unit feature in both GCSE chemistry and physics. A sound understanding of the model of the atom also underpins subsequent topics such as structure and bonding.

The planning process

Because of the success of the TfW process, my mindset has changed: I plan lessons differently now. So, as part of my planning, I mapped the topic against TfW strategies to ensure I made it as engaging and effective as possible. As you can see, every area of the specification was relevant to the process with many areas lending themselves to a wide range of aspects of the approach.

Key concepts	Possible TFW strategy							
	FACTS only	Warming up words	Using model text	Co-construct	Mime	Text mapping	Boxing up	Additional teaching e.g. modelling
The structure of an atom	✓							
Mass number, atomic number and isotopes		✓						
The development of model of atom (common content with chemistry			✓	✓	✓	✓	✓	✓
Radioactive decay & nuclear radiation		✓				✓		✓

218 TRANSFORMING LEARNING ACROSS THE CURRICULUM

Nuclear equations		✓					✓
Half-lives & random nature of radioactive decay		✓	✓	✓	✓	✓	✓
Radioactive contamination		✓	✓	✓			✓
Hazards & uses of radioactive emissions & background radiation (physics only)		✓	✓				
Nuclear fission & fusion (physics only)		✓	✓			✓	✓

Ref: https://filestore.aqa.org.uk/resources/physics/specifications/AQA-8463-SP-2016.PDF

The vocabulary of this topic is a significant challenge so, at the initial planning stage, I audited the topic focusing on unfamiliar key words and terminology, while keeping an eye out for the use of *everyday* language that may have a very specific meaning in a scientific context. I RAG-rated the words in the middle column as indicated below:

Red = unlikely to have used word/phrase previously
Amber = met previously within this topic
Green = met in previous topics

This grid demonstrates the range and complexity of the vocabulary within the unit and helped me plan how to best support the students' in becoming familiar with all of these terms and the key scientists linked to them.

Key concepts	Scientific key words/terms	General words used in scientific context
the structure of an atom	protons, neutrons, electrons, nucleus absorption of electromagnetic radiation energy level	emission
mass number, atomic number and isotopes	mass number, atomic number, ions isotopes	electrical charge
the development of the model of the atom (common content with chemistry)	protons, neutrons, electrons, nucleus plum pudding model, alpha scattering experiment, Ernest Rutherford, nuclear model, Neils Bohr, James Chadwick	theoretical calculations experimental observations evidence theory
radioactive decay and nuclear radiation	radiation, radioactive decay, activity, Becquerel, count rate, Geiger-Muller tube, alpha, beta, gamma, neutron ionising power, penetrating power	decay unstable random emit spontaneous
nuclear equations	alpha, beta, parent nuclei, daughter nuclei	emission decay
half-lives and the random nature of radioactive decay	half-life, nuclei, isotope, count rate, activity	random irreversible net decline
radioactive contamination	irradiated peer review	contamination hazard precautions
hazards and uses of radioactive emissions and background radiation (physics only)	background radiation, cosmic rays sieverts	man-made dose milli (i.e. 1/1000th)
nuclear fission and fusion (physics only)	fission, fusion, neutron, kinetic energy, chain reaction	absorb energy controlled/uncontrolled

Expected prior knowledge

Prior knowledge is always a key element within planning. For this unit, the students' prior knowledge varied enormously but, as an absolute minimum, the statements from KS3 Science guidelines reproduced opposite show the range of the content that the students should already know.

The cold task

All of this planning enabled me to construct a unit that would support the students in really understanding the topic. The topic starts with the development of the model of the atom which is a regular 6-mark extended writing question in GCSE examinations. A good quality answer requires the students to recall the names of specific scientists, the sequence of events and knowledge of the evidence that led to the changes to the atomic model.

Therefore, I designed the broad template pictured below to allow the students to build on this over a lesson or sequence of lessons. The students were encouraged to complete the first section (the cold task) in silence. I emphasised the fact that at this point there were no right or wrong answers. The students could decide to write in continuous prose or just list words that they associated with the topic. In this example, any facts they remembered from chemistry regarding atoms such as the names of subatomic particles would be relevant. Below you can see how this template has been used over the start of the unit to build up key understanding.

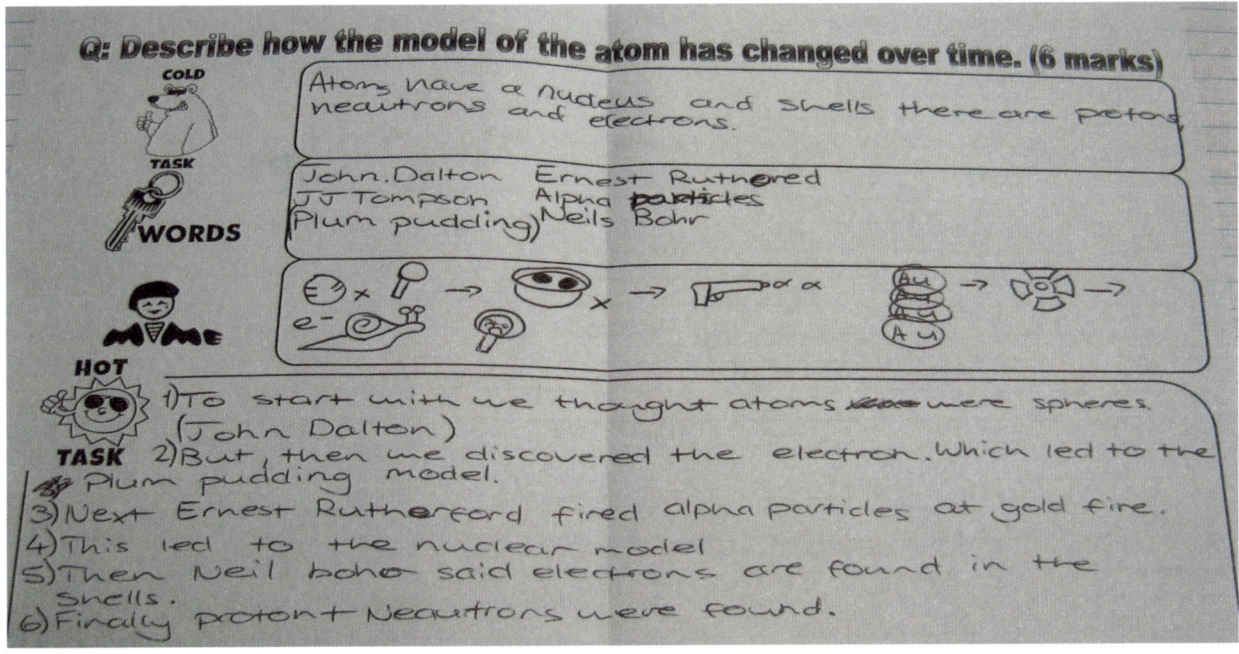

The importance of a good hook

Sadly, there was no problem in working out the perfect hook for this topic because all the students had seen the horrific film *Chernobyl*. To build on this interest and capture their imagination, I posed this key question:

If you could take an object and cut it into smaller and smaller parts, what would you end up with?

The students were encouraged to share their ideas regarding the smallest units of matter. Many students mentioned protons, neutrons and electrons (and some students had heard of quarks and other elementary particles way beyond the scope of GCSE science!). However, the key focus of this exercise is for the students to get a feel for the scale of the almost incomprehensibly small. Within this topic, students are required to look into the nucleus of an atom. The AQA specification states that:

> The students learn that atoms with very large numbers of protons and neutrons in the nuclei are particularly unstable and that there is a natural consequence of this in the emission of nuclear radiation.

Warming up the words

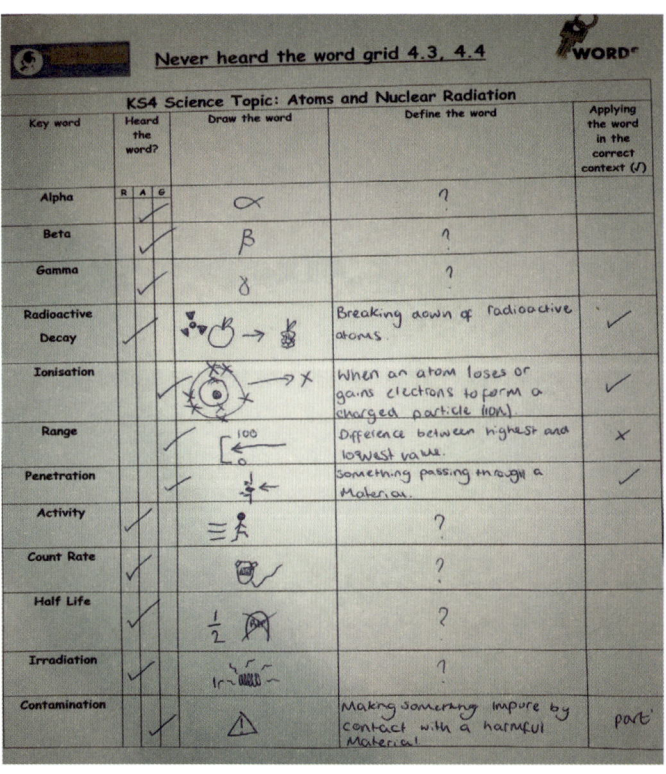

Using the RAG rating analysis of the vocabulary of the unit illustrated on **page 218**, I created an initial never-heard-the-word grid, which acted as an excellent diagnostic tool to confirm the starting point of the students.

The definitions for many key words in science are highly specific. Allowing students to embed poor definitions will damage their success within that topic. However, if students have correctly RAG-rated their familiarity with the word as GREEN, then they are encouraged to recall and develop links with other areas of the science course.

To warm up the words, I often ask students to go through a brief piece of information about whatever topic is being focused on and highlight any words they are unsure of. They then ask each other for clarification before I make certain they all have the right definitions based on the exam board's requirements.

Internalising key content

The early sections of this unit involve the recall of many significant scientists and their contribution to the developing model of the atom; this lends itself extremely well to the TfW process. Learning through storytelling refers to a process in which learning is structured around a narrative or story as a means of 'sense making'. The centrality of storytelling to learning lies at the heart of the TfW approach and is well researched (see Moon 2010).

This section of the *Atoms and Isotopes* unit was an appropriate point to incorporate mime. Surprisingly, Year 10 students were enthusiastic about getting on board with this despite some initial reluctance. This is partially because this idea of utilising mime is now used across the school and is no longer alien to them.

The delivery of new content is most effective when delivered via direct instruction (where the teacher stands in front of the class and explicitly teaches knowledge or skills or demonstrates the material). Consideration of working memory and cognitive load of the students should be at the forefront of the planning of this teaching – *What is the least I can say for the students to 'get it'?* ("The cognitive load involved in a task is the cognitive effort or amount of information processing required by a person to perform this task." Reif 2010.) Direct instruction is thought to limit the cognitive load of the students. During the teacher-led section of the lesson, students were encouraged to add important or key words to the proforma on which the cold task was completed. The students were then given time to sequence the stages of the developing model of the atom.

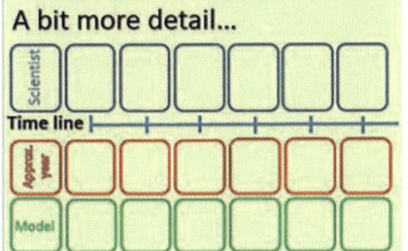

Following on from this, new information was given via an alternative medium – animations on YouTube – which can be highly effective. The aim of this was to further develop a sound understanding of the changing model of the atom. See TED-Ed at https://www.youtube.com/watch?v=xazQRcSCRaY

For some classes, it may be necessary to scaffold this task further by providing them with a template that allows them to box up each stage of the development of the model. Presenting this as a timeline, as pictured here, can help students organise their thinking.

Understanding the key ingredients

Prior to the completion of the initial hot task, the students complete two final stages.

1. Magpie from model text
The science GCSE specification is particularly detailed and descriptive. It is by far the best source of model text. Students are required to read and highlight any details that they had not picked up during the earlier stages of the task and

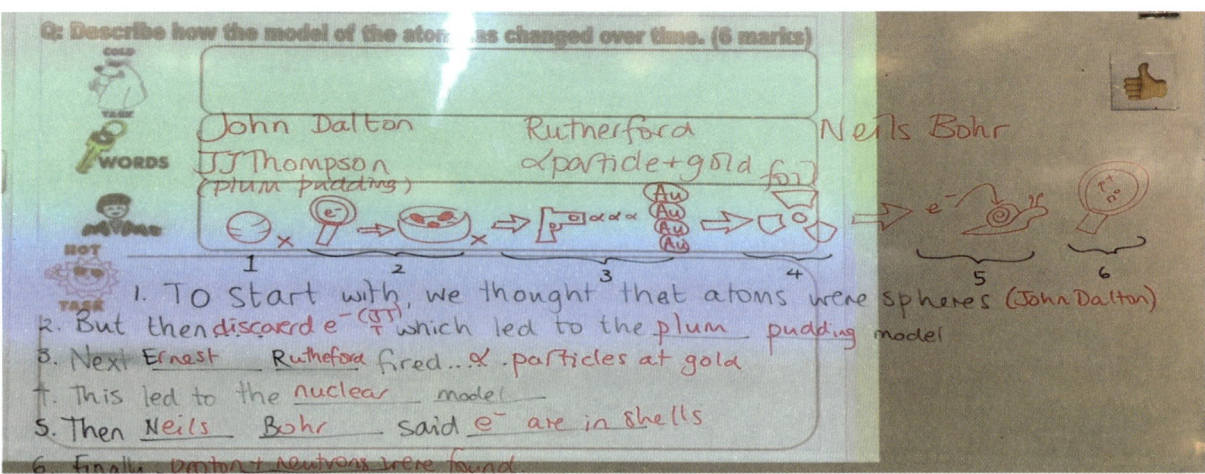

magpie useful phrases. This will then be incorporated into the final task.

2. Co-construct a model answer

For lower-attaining students, at this stage, significant scaffolding of the task may still be necessary. Sentence starters, cloze tasks and prompts could be used. The image below of my white board shows how the use of text mapping and cloze procedure has helped to support the stages of the 6-mark question.

The hot task is then completed with the expectation that students write a detailed account answering the 6-mark question asked at the beginning: *"How had the model of the atom changed over time?"* At this point, students have acquired a detailed understanding of the contributions of each scientist and of the main points that must be including in order to gain the marks. This then completes the initial stage.

The innovation stage

The teaching of science has always relied on the recall of many a definition and equation. However, in assessments, students are frequently thrown by the fact that the wording of the questions is slightly different from something they have met before, as illustrated here by the four different ways of asking questions about the model of the atom. This often results in confusion and a return to the "not knowing where to start" syndrome that we have been working so hard to address. This is where the innovation stage has proved so useful and has seen the greatest impact on students' confidence and resilience. By making a slight change to the command words and/or the focus of the exam-style question, we are able to assess the level of understanding in its entirety. This ensures that the students develop a concrete understanding of all aspects of the content and can adapt their understanding to suit the questions asked.

A repeat of the cycle – the challenge of internalising complex concepts

The GCSE science curriculum then moves on and requires the learner to build on this knowledge. This unit, in particular, takes students on a journey from the model of the atom, to focusing on the nucleus only, and then onto the nuclei of very large and unstable atoms, resulting in the ideas on nuclear radiation and radioactive decay. For our separate science students, this is taken further again onto the nuclear fission reactions that are fundamental to the nuclear power industry, and finally nuclear fusion – the reason our sun is able to provide us with energy on Earth. Clearly, there are some very BIG ideas here. It can be conceptually very challenging for students to internalise the process itself before considering how to internalise the type of language needed to explain such a concept. The greatest challenge as we move on through the topic is making an abstract concept relatable and story-like – just as the model of the atom section of this unit attempted to do.

Warming up the new words and concepts

As this unit progresses, many of the key words remain the same, e.g. *proton, neutron, nucleus* etc. However, we are now looking to incorporate additional words and phrases alongside these words and, therefore, developing the scientific language further.

For example, *activity, half-life, count-rate* and so on. As you can see from the AQA specification for GCSE Physics (to your right), precision is required.

> Required knowledge of the properties of alpha particles, beta particles and gamma rays is limited to their penetration through materials, their range in air and ionising power.

Check students know the meaning of this word

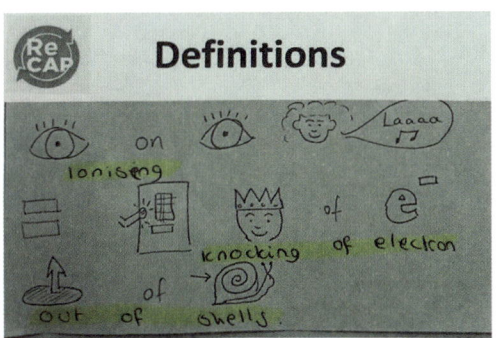

Text mapping and modelling have significantly helped students to make sense of such key words and really understand what they mean. Most science teachers at this point reach for the radioactive sources and demonstrate the clicking away of the Geiger-Muller tube. This will always be a fundamental learning experience for the students – the reality of the fact that alpha, beta and gamma radiation could be around us, yet we cannot physically detect it. The more actual experience can be included within learning, the more powerful it will be.

However, the internalising of a model is needed to facilitate accurate use of language in describing the process. For this, selecting something that the

students are already familiar with serves as an excellent support for developing a deeper understanding – popcorn! There aren't many students who haven't microwaved popcorn of an evening before settling down to watch Netflix! However, with careful planning and selection of language, the explanation of what is happening to the popcorn kernels can be transformed into an account of what is happening to the nuclei during radioactive decay.

Helping students understand by co-constructing understanding

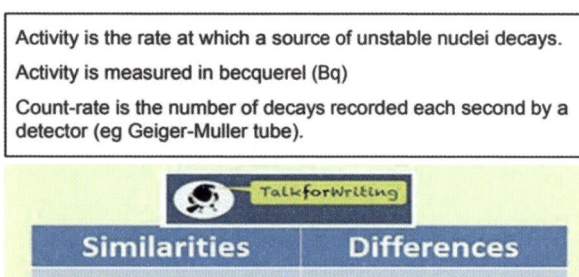

The key points from this modelling can be summarised within this simple similarities/differences table. Inviting students to contribute their ideas builds their confidence and resilience. By being a part of the co-construction of understanding, the students are helped to get their heads round such complex ideas. Throughout, the teacher has to ensure that there is emphasis on essential words such as *spontaneous*, *random* and *irreversible*.

Independent application

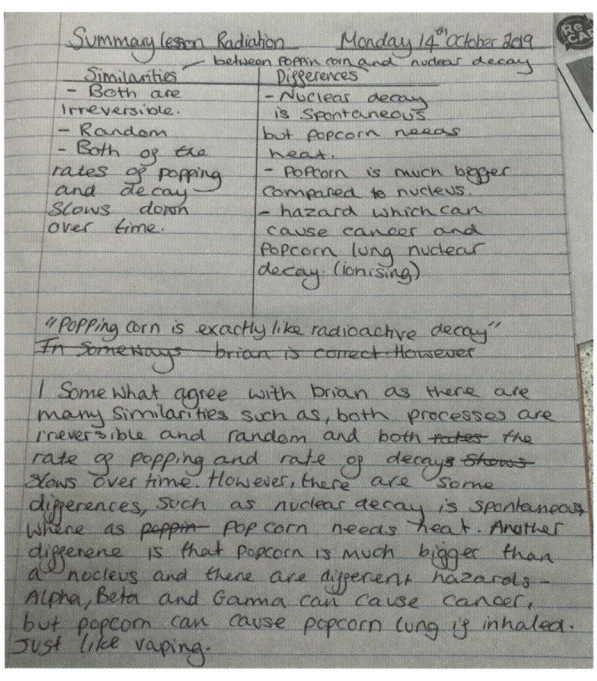

If you look at this example of a student's work at the independent application stage, you can see how they have effectively integrated what they learnt through the co-constructed table into their answer, using appropriate technical terms like *irreversible*. The use of popping corn to represent radioactive decay also serves as a good introduction to the idea of *half-life*. The students are only too aware that the popping of the corn is rapid at first but, over time, this rate of popping decreases. This involves a slight tweak of the teaching order described within the specification, but seems like the natural progression with regards to the ideas presented to the students.

Again, a fun way of embedding the definitions of keywords is by creating text maps like the one pictured below. These can be used in a variety of ways. For example,

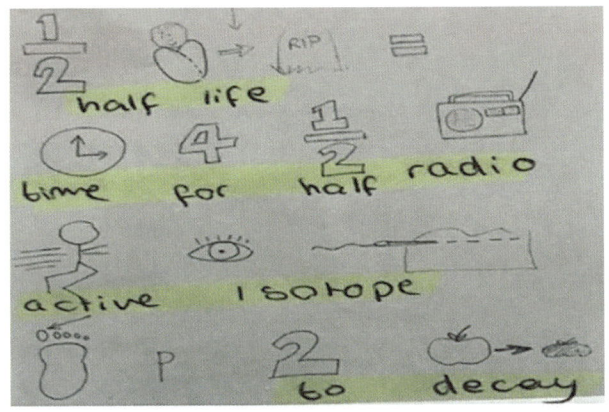

by asking the students to design their own, by co-constructing them with the class as a whole (often done by choosing the best parts of the students' text maps) or by the teacher creating one in advance with the students attempting to *decypher* the code. This choice always goes down well ... often causing hilarity at the poor quality of the art work!

Analysing the text

With the huge emphasis on recalling definitions, a wonderful quote that resonates is, *"Things may be made darker by definition"* – Samuel Johnson. Often, the concept is explained, and the student is able to visualise it, but the density of the language used in the definitions can hinder rather than enhance the students' understanding.

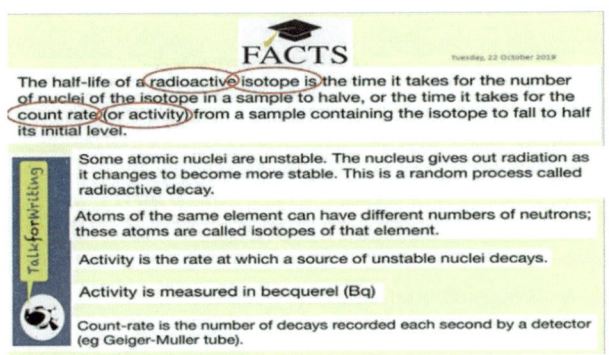

The use of analysis of text, even if the text is relatively concise, is invaluable. In the example here, the definition as set out by the exam board is used. The students are asked to read the definition and highlight any words they are unsure about. The students then circle the science-specific vocabulary.

From this, the teacher and students work on where they have met these words before and their meaning. The aim is to improve the fluency of scientific language and avoid the dumbing down approach to definitions.

The innovation stage (apply it)

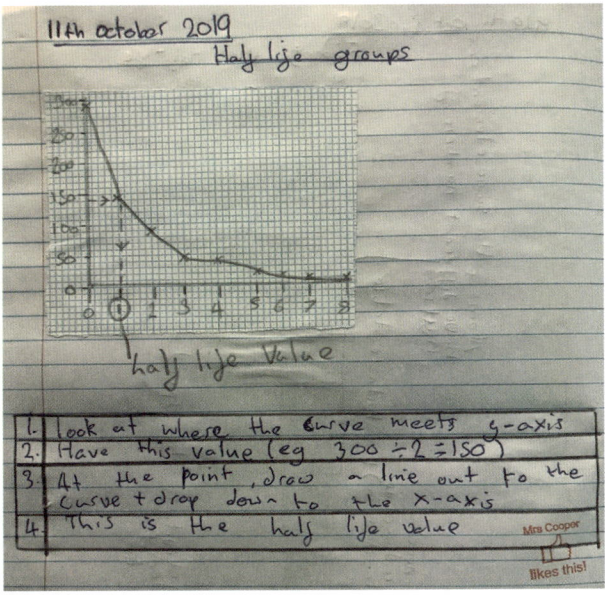

From this point, the students should feel confident when discussing radioactive decay and describing half-life. However, physics examinations frequently include the analysis of graphs.

The example here shows a typical half-life graph generated by a whole-class activity involving chocolate M&Ms! After each *throw*, the students collected data on the number of M&Ms with the letter *M* facing upwards. All other M&Ms are eaten each round. A simple task such as this produces a relatively accurate decay curve.

The technique for answering questions about half-life graphs can be approached by following clearly defined stages within the answer. In order to understand the structure of how to answer the question, students are encouraged to delve into their TfW toolkit and box it up – as illustrated above. The focus here is having a clear sequence and direct instructions. These instructions are fully transferrable to any question of this type, should the students meet it in future assessments.

The independent-application stage

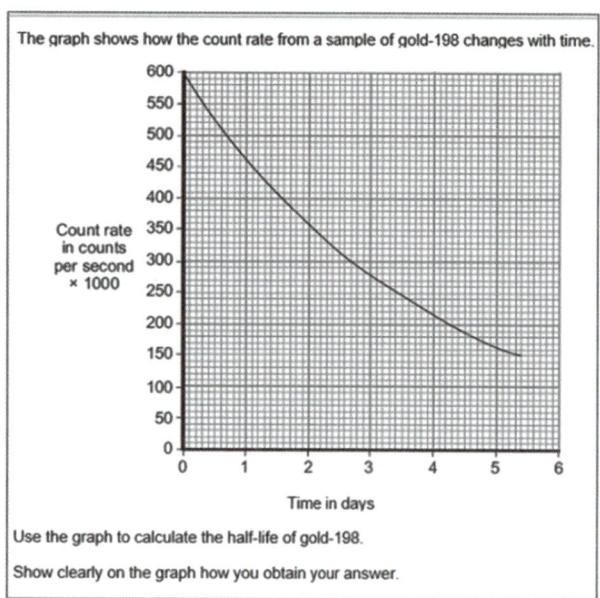

At KS4, the best source of hot-task questions has to come from past examination papers. The boxed-up stages can then be applied directly to answer the question, as illustrated below.

1	Curve meets y-axis at 600 (x1000 counts per second)
2	Half of that is 300 (x1000 counts per second.
3	See lines on graph
4	The half-life value of Gold-198 is 2.6 days

Nuclear equations

By now, the students have developed an understanding that these radioactive nuclei are changing in some way during the decay process. This is due to the emission of the alpha, beta, gamma and neutron emissions from the nucleus.

They are then reminded of the facts:

- nuclei contain only protons and neutrons
- the mass number of the atom tells us the total number of protons and neutrons within the nucleus
- the atomic number refers to the number of protons in the nucleus.

These facts should be familiar to them from both chemistry and physics. Making sense of what happens to the atomic number and the mass number during an alpha emission can be rote learnt – "mass number – decrease by 4, atomic number – decrease by 2". However, in the high pressure situation of examinations, without a concrete understanding of why this happens, there is a possibility of confusion and the dropping of relatively easy marks.

Although this example mentioned here may not be strictly correct – Nitrogen-14 is not a radioactive isotope – the decay process is the key learning point for the students.

Internalising the model

Finding concrete ways of helping students talk through the processes has proved key to helping them understand. The picture shows that by using plasticine to represent the protons and neutrons, students are able to effectively mime the process of alpha emission. Students must identify their *parent nuclei* and, following the emission of the alpha particle (2 protons and 2 neutrons), identify the *daughter nuclei*.

If students are allowed to access their mobile phones within the classroom, they may like to produce an animation using one of their many whizzy apps! The important thing in this task is the commentary – verbalising the process as opposed to providing a script; a list of buzz words that should be included. The sharing of their models with other groups in the class helps to further consolidate their understanding before the innovation stage and the opportunity to apply it.

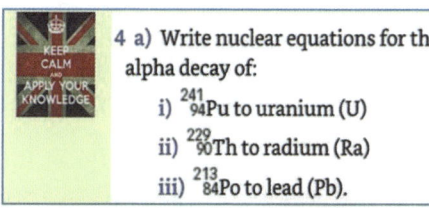

4 a) Write nuclear equations for the alpha decay of:
  i) $^{241}_{94}Pu$ to uranium (U)
  ii) $^{229}_{90}Th$ to radium (Ra)
  iii) $^{213}_{84}Po$ to lead (Pb).

Thanks to this hands-on approach to studying alpha decay, students should now be able to tackle questions like the one shown here with confidence.

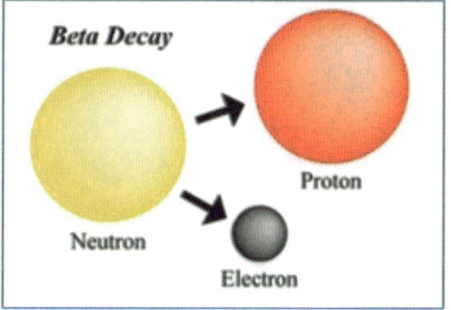

For beta emissions, the opportunity for the students to mime/text map the process is even more important due to the unexpected properties of beta emissions. For GCSE physics purposes, the illustration here is sufficient. Students are often confused when told that the mass number of the nucleus remains unchanged, but the proton number increases by 1. Frequently, student comments are along the lines of, *"How can the proton number go up by one if we are losing something?!"* or *"Beta is an electron. But there are no electrons in the nucleus"*. Both are valid comments and provide an insight into the misconceptions that need to be eliminated.

Building on the use of plasticine to represent the protons and neutrons, students are also able to mime the process of beta emission. However, they should be provided with a third colour of plasticine.

228 TRANSFORMING LEARNING ACROSS THE CURRICULUM

Students are instructed to essentially hide a green electron and a red proton inside the blue plasticine neutron. During the beta decay, this neutron breaks down revealing the proton and the electron. In simple terms, the electron shouldn't be in the nucleus, so it is ejected and the proton remains. Students realise that there is no net increase in the total number of particles within the nucleus (mass number remains constant) but the number of protons has increased by 1 (atomic number of the daughter nuclei increases by one compared to the parent nuclei).

Warming up the words and concepts for radioactive contamination

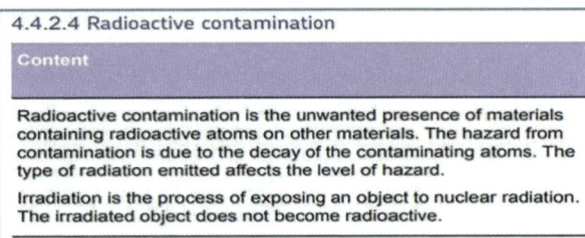

For combined science, our final section of the topic discusses the difference between radioactive contamination and irradiation.

Students often have a general understanding of the meaning of these words in everyday life. This was seen from our initial use of the never-heard-the-word grid at the very start of the topic. For example, one student described contamination as, "Making something impure by contact with a harmful material," which is a pretty good starting point. The language of the exam specification particularly emphasises the fact that this is an "unwanted presence" and that the level of hazard depends on the contaminating atoms. In addition, there is clear distinction between contamination and irradiation.

To help the students comprehend the difference, the students were given a model using Velcro hats and balls! The idea is that the students are asked to throw a ball at some brave volunteers, as pictured above. The ball represents the radiation/radioactive atom. If the ball is thrown and it sticks to the Velcro, the students in the class should shout, "Contamination". However, if the ball

passes near the volunteer but does not stick, the students should shout, "Irradiation". From this, students develop the idea that the "unwanted presence" of the balls (i.e. radioactive atoms) attached to the Velcro hat means that the hazard is greater due to prolonged exposure to these decaying atoms. However, the hazard associated with the irradiation is relatively low as the exposure is brief. For those students studying Separate Sciences, this can be extended to cover the idea of radiation dose in milliseiverts (mSv).

Triple Physics Only: fission and fusion

Finally, we are able to repeat many of the stages already described. A particularly efficient use of time is to provide the students with the exact wording needed to explain a process such as nuclear fission and fusion (as reproduced here). Students are given time to read and make sense of the wording. In this example, the student has tried to make sense of the final paragraph using a simple yet effective text map.

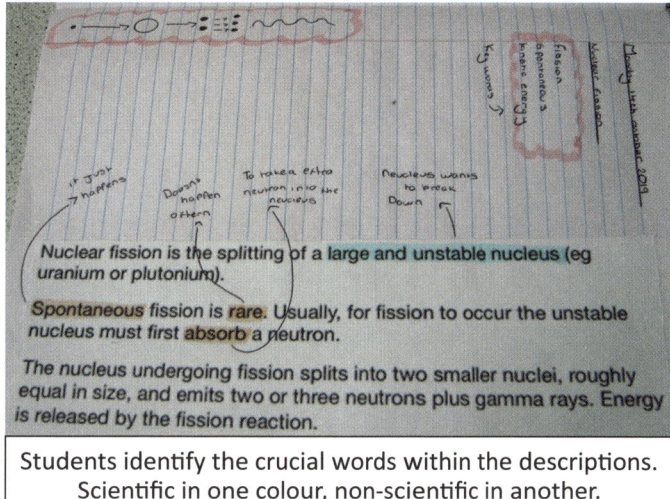

Students identify the crucial words within the descriptions. Scientific in one colour, non-scientific in another.

Changing the emphasis within a lesson from copying down a definition to making sense of a definition has had a significant impact on the fluency of the scientific language used by the students. They are able to confidently describe these terms and, interestingly, place emphasis on those essential words.

Checking students learning

Throughout the delivery of all topics, I believe that emphasis on knowledge recall – in particular of key vocabulary – is incredibly powerful. As a school, we routinely incorporate low-stakes quizzing into our lessons. The idea is that we ask 10 questions in total – 5 from the current topic and 5 from any previous topic. This interleaving of knowledge helps to keep key ideas and facts at the forefront of the students' memory. With our linear courses, anything that supports this is very welcome! This is one of the most effective teaching and learning strategies we have adopted as a school. In my opinion, the low-stakes quizzing has not only allowed emphasis of keywords/facts but the impact that this has at the start of a lesson on student confidence and engagement is impressive. The audible "Yesss!" that comes from the class when they have the correct answer is hugely motivational for both students and teachers! Here, you will find a selection of the type of low-stakes quizzing that I have incorporated into this sequence of lessons. Enjoy!

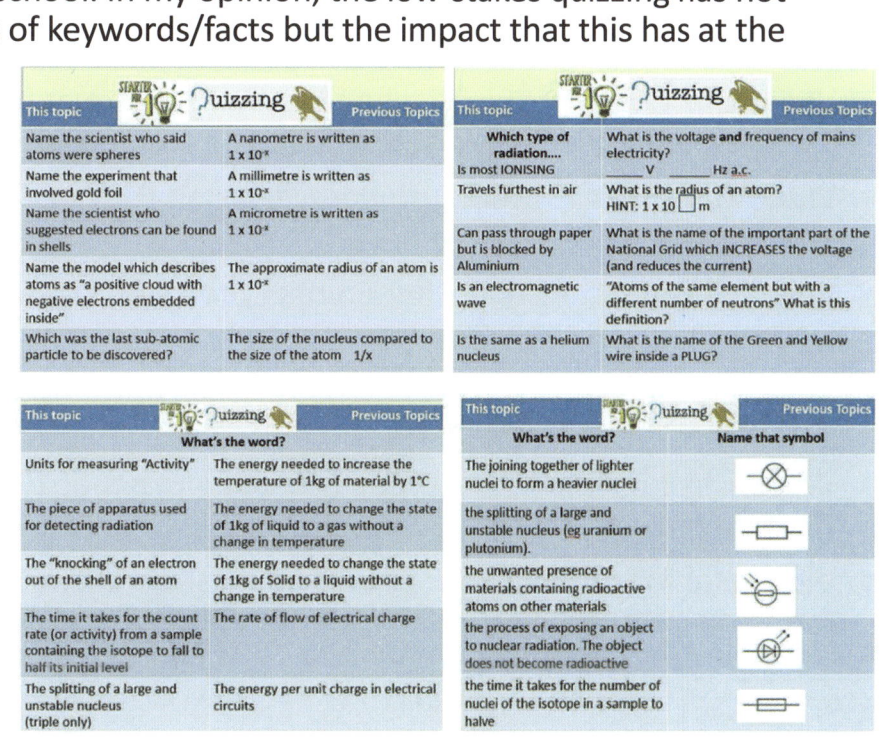

Has Talk for Writing made a difference?

It's literally filled my heart with joy. It's enabled me to award many more of my special PTMs (Proud Teacher Moment) awards and the students just love receiving these. With some activities, students you might have felt were the weakest kids have scored the highest marks – it's really making a difference. The great thing is that TfW helps them get there and it's fun. It works especially well for the lower and middle attaining students because it makes me think more clearly about chunking up information into manageable chunks and it makes you think about the format of what needs to be said and how to express it as well as the content. Step-by-step, boxed-up text mapping transforms their ability to express content clearly. And the text mapping is great – the dual coding just helps them remember. We laugh all the way through my text mapping and the kids can close their eyes and see the images of what they are trying to write and that's a really powerful tool. They'll remember nuclear fission when munching popcorn for the rest of their lives!

Initially, Emma was a TfW sceptic, who dismissed the approach. Through trialling the approach, she has come to appreciate its true potential – see video clip 43 which was filmed early on in her conversion!

To find out how other secondary science teachers have used the approach see:

- **Video clip 4:** science teacher Tom Killigrew feeding back to staff at John of Gaunt about how Talk for Writing just equals good teaching
- **Video clip 8:** A Year 9 science class at John of Gaunt using text mapping to help remember a scientific equation led by their teacher Tom Killigrew
- **Video clip 17:** Hiri Arungiri, when Head of Science at Slough & Eton, demonstrating the power of text mapping to support recall in science
- **Video clip 18:** Three Year 9 students from Hiri's science class explain how TfW has helped them
- **Video clip 44:** Science teacher Emma Lydon (John of Gaunt) beginning a lesson with a vocabulary quiz
- **Video clip 45:** Science teacher Emma Lydon warming up vocabulary with her Year 10 class
- **Video clip 46:** How Emma Lydon is helping her Year 10 science students have the terminology to explain what they are learning to themselves and others
- **Video clip 47:** Emma Lydon explains how she uses memory prompts to help the students explain complex scientific concepts

Chapter 12a: Talk for Writing in history (Year 5)

Tom Wriglesworth (a leading member of the Talk for Writing team at Selby Community Primary School in Yorkshire) uses a Year 5 unit on crime and punishment to illustrate the difference the Talk for Writing approach has made to the quality of history teaching and learning in the school, with the help of Year 5 teacher Beckie Reeve.

This chapter focuses on a Year 5 unit to inform the children about varying forms of crime and punishment throughout history. Whilst the unit follows the logic of the Talk for Writing process, it was adapted so that the key focus for the children's learning was to develop the following underpinning historical elements through:

- imitating and then innovating on these skills so that the children learn to think, talk, read and write like a historian independently
- in-depth subject knowledge including chronology
- the ability to make sense of the past through the skill of causation
- the ability to interpret evidence
- the skills of historical enquiry
- the ability to communicate understanding of the past.

This unit focuses particularly on the fourth element – the ability to interpret evidence.

Laying the foundations to our unit (what do we need to teach?)

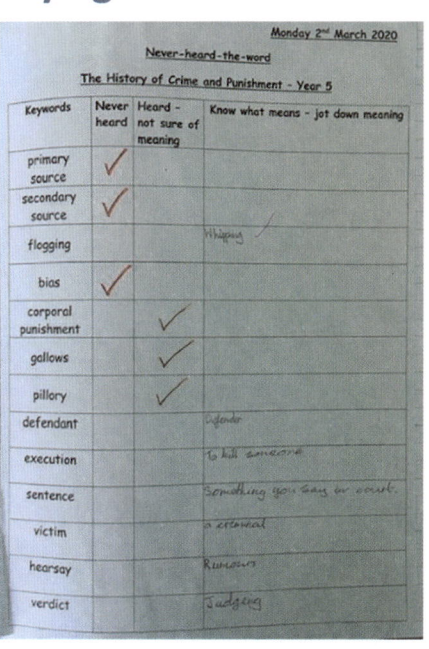

When conducting a **cold task** in our topic sessions, we always begin with a never-heard-the-word grid (NHTW) focusing on the key words that we know will be used throughout the unit. Certain pieces of vocabulary will be used within historical parlance (such as *verdict, hearsay* and *bias*) whereas others will be more 'third tier' words (such as *gallows* and *pillory*). The useful thing about this part of the **cold task** for this unit was that it only took a short time but served as an indication of what the children already knew about the subject of crime and punishment and pointed to where more detailed understanding would be needed. It also told the teacher which words needed to be worked on more than others, for example, the child here has indicated no understanding of *primary* or *secondary source* and *bias*.

THE WHIPPING POST.
Flogging is still a frequent form of "dicipline." The warden of Jefferson City, Mo., penitentiary strongly advocates it.
See page 141.

The children's ability to interpret evidence and communicate their understanding of the past also needed to be established and their start-point ascertained. This was done by giving them their first source with the title, 'How does an historian use a source to gather evidence from the past?' As the basis of this additional cold task, the children were presented with a drawing (the secondary source pictured left) of a person being flogged (as a representation of a punishment). We gave no suggestion of how to set out their written response to the source except to verbally ask them three questions:

1. What is the source?
2. What does it tell us?
3. What does it not tell us?

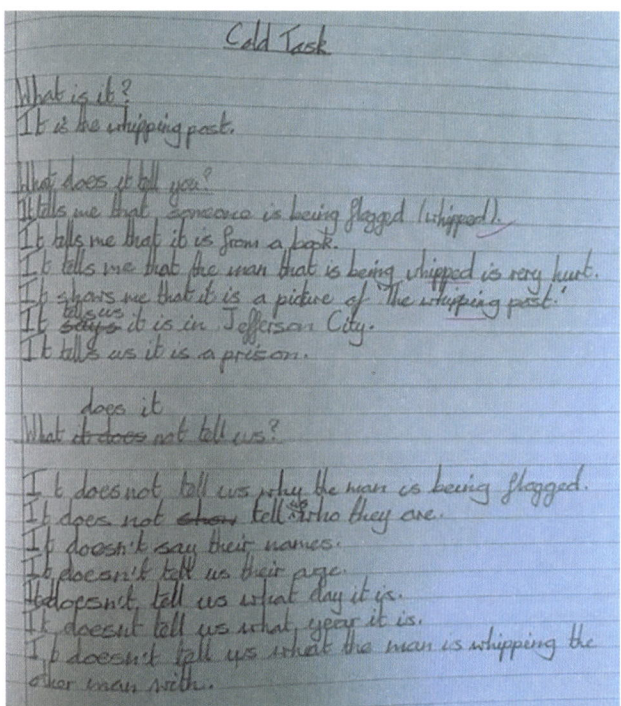

Here is a typical response to this task. The children were very interested in the subject of flogging, having never previously heard of such a punishment. So, it was decided to progress onto our imitation stage using this particular form of punishment as its focus.

The imitation stage

We began the imitation stage by showing the children a photograph of an actual flogging. We explained that this was known as a primary source, rather than a secondary source, as had been shown in the cold task, which was just a drawing. Primary and secondary sources were terms that needed to be warmed up and their meanings more thoroughly explained. The children repeated these meanings back to the teacher and recorded them in their magpie books – small books in which they record shiny pieces of vocabulary they can't wait to utilise within their own writing and independent conversational speech. A point to note in this session, however, was that occasional wild inferences

were drawn by certain pupils, with very little (if any) evidence for their thoughts: for example, *"I think the boy on the left is the man who is being whipped's son because he looks upset"*. At this point, an explanation was needed that, similar to when completing a reading comprehension, to allow a point to be valued, there has to be evidence to back up your suggestion and, in that case, a boy's facial expression could be taken as proof suggesting how he felt but not as proof of his relationship to the man being flogged.

After discussing what they could see, and what they did and did not know, the children were issued with their text map and began to internalise the related model text. They enjoyed creating key actions and, whenever they found a word from the NHTW, it was repeated with extra intonation and its definition repeated to reinforce their understanding of it. Children coloured their text-maps saying their sentences as they went, further internalising the vocabulary and the tune of the text, as illustrated below.

Understanding the structure and content

When the children were shown the model text, written by the teacher, they first highlighted the sentence stems that could be utilised across any piece of historical writing or discussion. These were written in their magpie books and stored for future use. The class discussed the structure of the model text and agreed that when looking at any historical source, these three questions must be asked:

1. What is the source?
2. What does it tell us?
3. What does it not tell us?

At this stage, the group decided that they should stick to the facts as presented and steer clear of inference unless substantiated by the source document.

Further, in this specific instance, information concerning the photograph, the crime and trial that led to the punishment, as well as quotations from witnesses and observers would need to be taught in order for the children to understand the historical context. After all, if we want the children to learn to stick to the facts, they must **know** what the facts are first.

Consequently, the children were presented with the two additional sources shown below concerning flogging. They were encouraged to highlight areas of interest, vocabulary they wanted to understand and facts about the case that they wanted to discuss. They now had supporting facts, enabling them to link it to the source of evidence shown earlier.

During the imitation stage, it was also clear that certain pieces of historical vocabulary were being used incorrectly and so needed warming up further. This image shows how the words *bias, defendant* and *sentence* were then taught. As you can see from the example sentences the pupil has written, some children needed more help in how to use some of the words appropriately in context.

Applying their understanding to a different context (innovation)

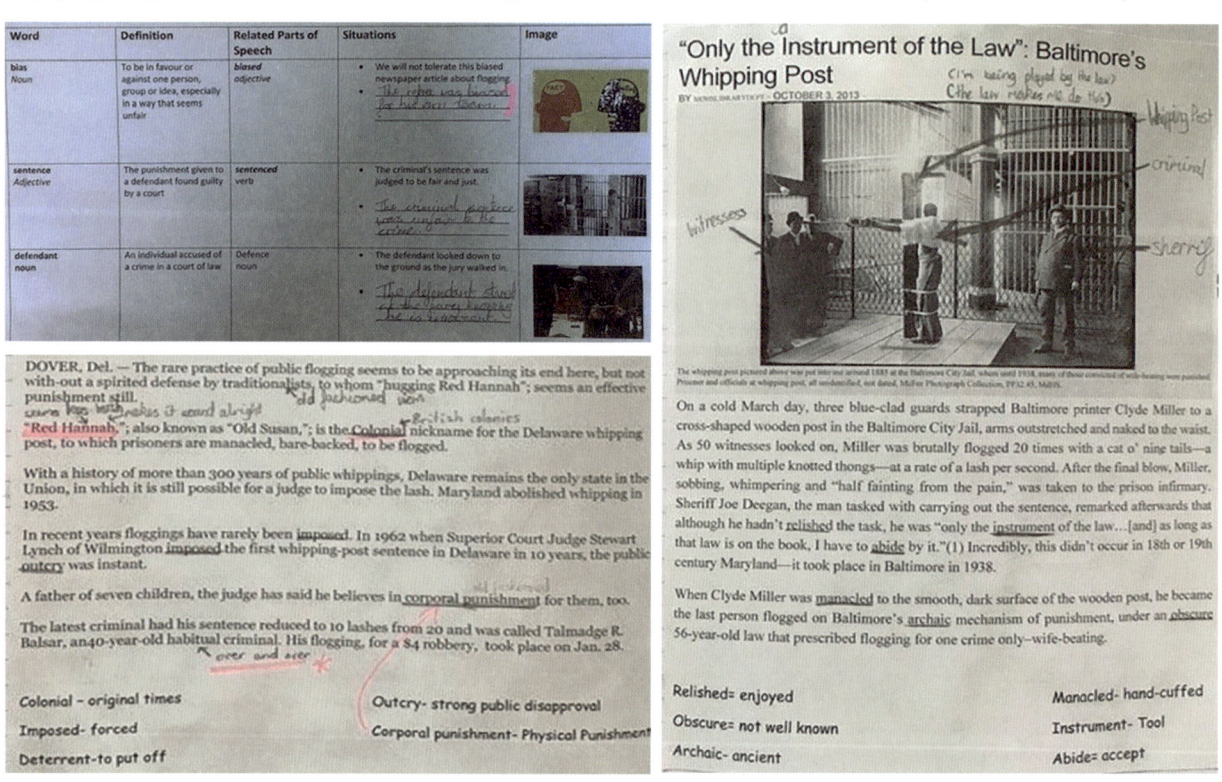

During the innovation stage, the teacher decided to focus on a different form of punishment and one which the children probably knew something about: hanging, drawing and quartering – the punishment for treason that awaited Guy Fawkes. To begin the unit, the children were shown the image on the next page, without any introduction or explanation:

TALK FOR WRITING IN HISTORY (YEAR 5) 235

The children were asked to study the image and again think about:
1. What is the source?
2. What does it tell us?
3. What does it not tell us?

Following discussion, the class agreed that the source was an artist's impression of an event – a *secondary* piece of evidence. They then discussed what it told them. Immediately, the children said that it was a depiction of Guy Fawkes being foiled in his attempt to blow up Parliament. Whilst this was actually correct, the children were reminded that, as historians, they must stick to what they know and what they do not know from the source and not infer anything. With this in mind, the teacher drew up a shared list of these *known* and *unknown* aspects of the source, which allowed the class to compose the shared writing below, summing up the children's observations of the image.

Year 5 – Shared Write – Guy Fawkes Cellar Picture

This **secondary source of information** is a drawing of a person who seems to be being restrained by a gang of men. **It tells us that the** man being held back by the gang of men is desperately trying to get away from them. **Furthermore, it tells us that** the men are armed with swords, are wearing armour and are wrapping a material around the man who is trying to get away. **Moreover,** in the corner of the source of information, there appears to be a large pile of wood and at least one barrel in the foreground.
Interestingly and a point of note is that the doorway is being blocked by a number of men. **It is also interesting that the** gentleman being restrained is facing into the room and not facing the way out.

However, this source of information does not tell us who the man being restrained actually was. **Nor does it tell us what** year it was when the picture was created or what year it was supposed to be in the image. **This source does not tell us** what the man had done to be treated in the manner that he is being treated or what punishment he will receive as a result. The barrel in the foreground is not open and therefore we cannot tell what is inside nor can we tell what is in the rest of the pile of wood to the left of the image.
This piece of evidence also can show bias as it is a drawing and therefore a piece of secondary information. The artist capturing this image may want to show the person being restrained in a certain way. Without speaking to the artist, it is unclear as to what, if any, the bias could be.

As you can see, the children were encouraged to structure it similarly to the model text from the imitation stage, alongside utilising their newly learnt sentence stems and vocabulary from their magpie book. Once completed, the children highlighted the sentence stems they could use within future pieces of historical writing and logged them in their magpie books. Of particular note is that the name 'Guy Fawkes' is never mentioned in this shared writing as this would constitute inference and cannot be corroborated from the source.

1840.—The Autographs of Guido Fawkes before and after Torture.

The children were then taught about the history of Guy Fawkes including the chronological difference between when Guy Fawkes was alive and the source of evidence from the imitation stage, plus his beliefs, his trial, his sentence, his punishment and so on. After acquiring and developing this historical subject knowledge, the children were given an additional source of evidence (relating to Guy Fawkes' signature) to write their own piece of historical writing. If you look at what one child wrote below, you can see that the child has successfully integrated the appropriate sentence stems into their writing.

To end the innovation stage and to further develop an in-depth subject knowledge of this event and period, the teacher asked the class if they now knew how Guy Fawkes had died. Immediately, they all stated that he died by the process they had studied: being hanged, drawn and quartered. It was, therefore, imperative to tell them that this was technically not the case and to always look further into the forensic evidence of history, as he actually died because of "cervical fracture" after breaking his neck following a drop from the gallows ladder, thus missing the gruesome punishment he had been dealt. A discussion then ensued as to whether he slipped or jumped …

The road to independent application

During the final stage of the unit, the teacher decided to focus on the crime of being a witch or warlock during the late 16th/early 17th century. Throughout the first two stages, the children's ability to interpret evidence and then to communicate their understanding of it was the main focus of the teaching and resource preparation. While the teacher needed to further inform the depth of their subject knowledge (correcting certain misconceptions that sprung up along the way), it was always the historical skills of enquiry and acquisition of facts that drove the sessions. Witchcraft is a subject the teacher knew would be of interest to the children but one where an element of reasoning and inference would need to be employed due to the lack of evidence from the time. This is something of a departure in approach from the earlier stages.

TALK FOR WRITING IN HISTORY (YEAR 5) 237

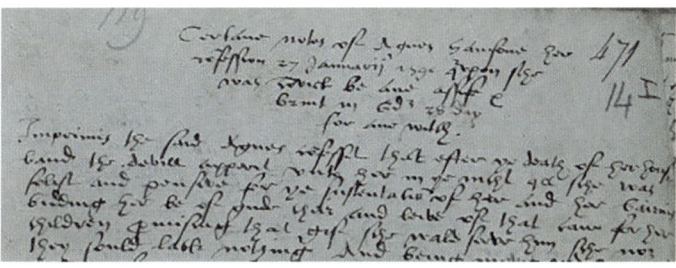

To begin with, the children needed to build a picture in their minds about what life may have been like during that time and how those accused of witchcraft may have been treated. They studied various secondary sources of information and took part in dramatised punishments from the time. Here, for instance, we can see a *witch* being burnt at an imaginary stake. The children also learnt about other punishments such as sleep deprivation, the dunking stool, pricking/scratching and also pressing.

They were then issued with the source of evidence that they were going to explore, question and, ultimately, write about – a small section of which is shown above. The teacher, therefore, issued them with a version that was easily readable (see left). Children were encouraged to make notes, highlight features and question certain aspects of the source. Discussions were had as to what specific sections meant and if they could believe all or any of the elements contained within the document. At all times, the children (almost automatically now) started their dissection of the source with the key questions:

1. What is it?
2. What does it tell us?
3. What does it not tell us?

From there, the children and teacher were able to discuss what the source of evidence showed, after which the children independently wrote for themselves. As the photograph below shows, the sentence stems learnt during the first two stages are being utilised correctly and allow the tune of the text to come through with confidence. The structure is suitable and has been orally rehearsed before being committed to paper. Towards the end of the piece of writing, the children were able to state what they wanted to know more about specific elements of this case, while suggesting informed and research-based conclusions concerning the actions of the people involved: "Upon doing other research and reading around the subject, I have found that there is not a great deal of evidence from the times witches and warlocks were tried and that, therefore, we struggle to form a factual picture of events".

Comparing this piece of writing to the cold task, shows huge improvements not only to the child's writing attainment, structure and subject-specific vocabulary, but also their grasp of what it is to think and write like an historian.

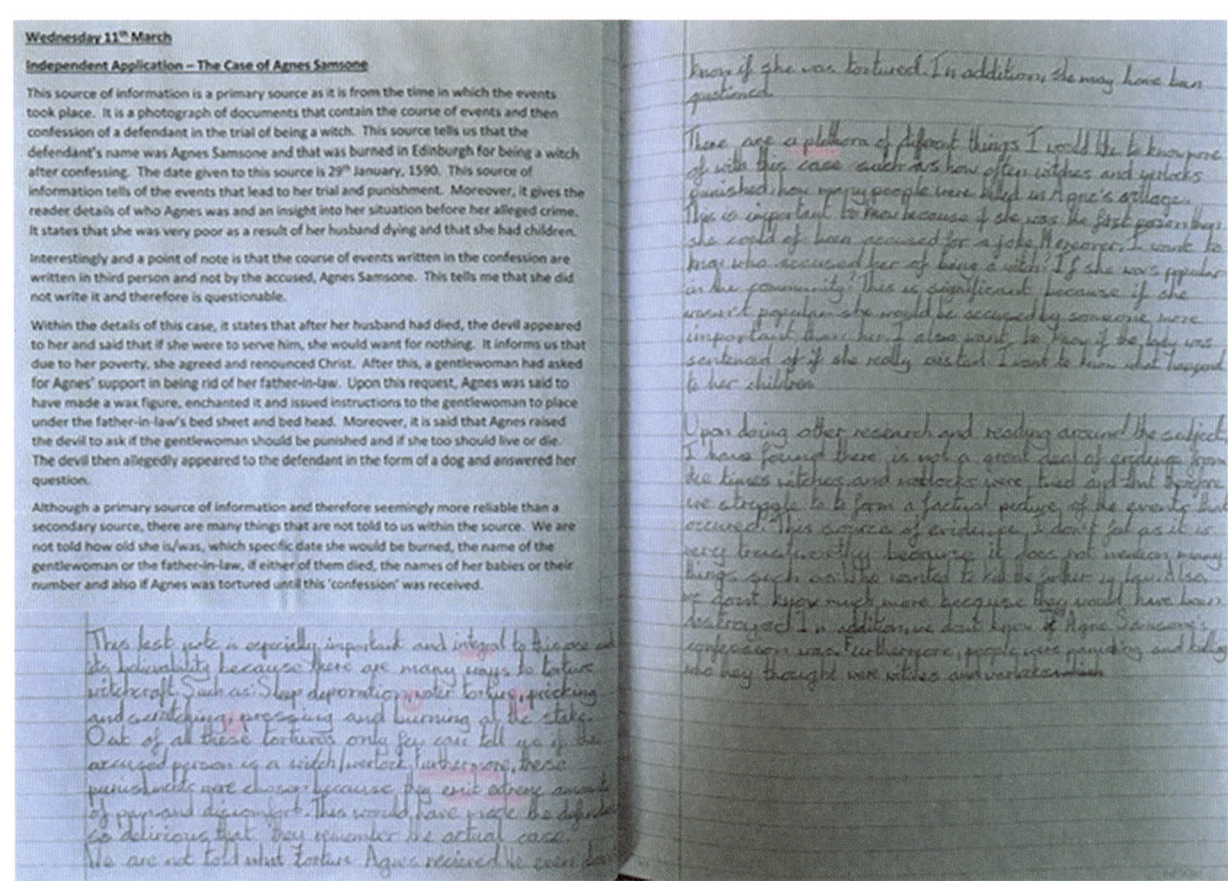

What the children thought

"I found it so much easier to write about the sources when we had the stems to help us organise what we could see and what we couldn't see. I also became really involved in thinking about the lives of others in different times in history."
– Olivia.

"I loved this unit because, even though I enjoy history anyway, this helped me look at sources and bias in a whole new way. It made me question whether we can really trust sources that we study. It became easier as we looked at more sources too because I knew how to look at them."
– Joe.

"I feel so much more confident with my historical vocabulary now like chronological, bias, primary and secondary sources. I feel like if I had to do a task like this again, I would know exactly how to tackle it. My hot task was so much better than my cold task, so I feel really proud about that too."
– Sofie

What the class teacher thought

"At the beginning, the children did already have an innate love of history born from a desire to know exciting (and often gruesome) historical facts! However, they hadn't developed the historical skills of enquiry and deeper questioning. Throughout this unit, they began to question history in far greater depth: asking why events happened and really striving to understand the time period and the lives lived within it.

"At the start, they would study a source and make up their mind about what was going on there from either previous (often grainy) knowledge or using wild inference to piece together the gaps without attempting to delve into the facts around the source. Now, they understand a piece of evidence needs to be researched and investigated fully before they can draw conclusions, rather than waiting to be told by a teacher. The children were excited to read around the subject, which gave me a lovely opportunity to read meaningful non-fiction during reading sessions, as they were desperate to know more about specific cases and time periods. Finally, they have come out of this unit with a much firmer grasp of the tune of a historical text."
– Beckie Reeve (Year 5 Class Teacher)

To find out when you can see Talk for Writing in action across the curriculum at Selby Community Primary and related training, visit www.talk4writing.co.uk/train-with-us/selby-community-primary-north-yorkshire//.

Chapter 12b: Talk for Writing in history (Year 8)

Stu Gray, Head of humanities at The John of Gaunt School, has chosen a Year 8 history unit on the Protestant Reformation for a mixed attainment class to illustrate how integrating the Talk for Writing approach into his history lessons has made them more effective. In his words, he wanted to "show the beauty of Talk for Writing".

Laying the foundations

I wanted to make certain that my 10-lesson unit focused sufficiently on introducing and embedding the vocabulary that would enable the students to access the content, alongside including a model text to demonstrate the sort of causal language that would really help them.

My experience with Talk for Writing had already taught me that I had not been putting sufficient emphasis on vocabulary, but had just fallen back on giving kids a list of key words and hadn't really checked if they knew what they meant. Now, the never-heard-the-word (NHTW) grid approach helps me establish what the students do and don't know. For this unit, I wanted to include a mixture of *tiered* words, plus those that are commonly misspelt. Research identifies that introducing 10–15 words over a two-week period is a nice balance between overloading students and insufficient filling of the word gap. I divided the words to focus on into Isabel Beck's 3 tiers:

Tier 1 (everyday words) – *divorce, Pope, Latin, criticise, Bible, heir*
Tier 2 (often encountered in text) – *Archbishop, altar, Catholic, Protestant, to pardon*
Tier 3 (subject-specific technical words) – *The Reformation, purgatory, Church of England, Act of Supremacy, Papal Bull*

I also planned to clarify the difference between *Church* and *church* (using *School* and *school* as an example), and the humorous idea that the Pope was in charge of *the church* (meaning the one down the road and only that one!).

My aim for the hot task was for students to be able to explain causation and consequence clearly. Many students (even at KS4) fall into the trap of narrative or descriptive writing. I therefore wished to model key causal sentence signposts to get the students used to using *explaining* phrases like: *As a result, This caused, Therefore, Consequently, As a consequence, For this reason, Due to this, Because of this, So, This led to, This meant that,* and *which led to.*

I decided I would co-construct the model text through shared writing as part of the TfW teaching process as opposed to using a model that had been purpose-written previously, but I knew exactly what I wanted the co-constructed text to include. This may have been a mistake for me to learn from, as you will see.

The cold task

I introduced my students to the historical content of the Protestant Reformation through a PowerPoint presentation supported by teacher explanation. We then elicited four or five key events, names, places and dates which led to the Reformation. I recorded these on the whiteboard so that the students had key information for their cold task but had not been helped in how to express it. I then asked my students to write a paragraph titled: *Explain why the Protestant Reformation took place in the 1500s*. There was no time limit and the information on the whiteboard was available for them to refer to. It was a *free* task which I told them would be read but unmarked and they could attempt the question in whatever manner they wished.

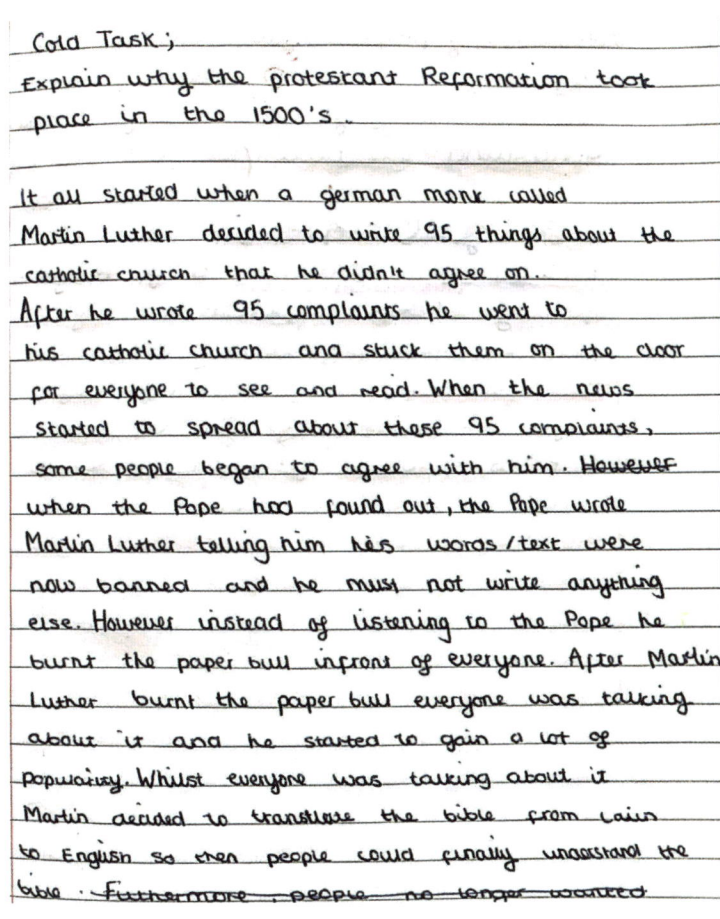

The example that you can see here was fairly typical of what was produced and allowed me to ensure my teaching was focused appropriately, as well as giving the students a baseline to compare with at the end of the unit.

The work clearly highlighted (as I had expected) a strong leaning towards using a narrative format (then X happened, after this Z happened), which resulted in a lack of 'explaining' phraseology being used, as recount style doesn't demand explanation. In addition, many students wrote in the present tense which told me they didn't have the tune of the text in their heads.

The imitation stage

The key vocabulary identified at the planning stage was introduced through a never-heard-the-word grid. The students completed these on their own then shared ideas at their tables, before finally resorting to using dictionaries or asking for help if needed. We then discussed and *said* each word as a class 3 times. Students had been asked to *use* or *draw* the word on their NHTW grid as

opposed to writing the definition. Some were deliberately left blank and then filled in as their learning progressed (e.g. the Protestant Reformation was filled in after we had watched the PowerPoint). **Video clip 26** shows me explaining to staff how warming up the words has made a difference.

The warming-up process was done through repeated use of these words in our *starter quizzes* which begin each lesson so that the children are ready to use them independently. Here are some examples:

- Fill-in-the-gap quiz – I say a sentence and ding my bell in the place of using one of the 15 words. Students must choose which word goes in the gap. The answer can usually only be determined by the context of the sentence. We repeat the words again afterwards as a class.
- Spelling quizzes – the students try to spell the word, then we say it and review its meaning.
- Comprehension quizzes – the questions are based around the meaning of the words and check understanding of say *The Act of Supremacy* or *a Papal Bull*.

Text mapping has really helped the students improve their vocabulary. When I'm asked what a word means from the NHTW grid, I usually text map an answer on the whiteboard. We co-constructed our class text map alongside the words for our model text on the Protestant Reformation by agreeing on the pictures to accompany these words. Similarly, many text-map ideas were put onto the whiteboard for students to use in the independent-text-mapping phase for the hot task on Henry VIII's *Break with Rome*. A diagram or picture can show clear understanding of a word or concept whereas copying out a definition from a glossary or dictionary does not. It is also very easy to check understanding and, importantly, students often enjoy trying to figure out how to text map new words and concepts. The image above is Hala's NHTW grid. **Video clip 49** shows me using images to help Year 8 students remember some technical language for history and then embed the terms.

Co-constructing a content text map and model text focusing on causal language

Students are often unsure about how to text map (the level of detail required for their drawings or the layout, etc), so I wanted to familiarise them or refresh their memories with the techniques and concepts involved. We talked through the process of the Protestant Reformation and drew a class text map as a flow chart of the key events and then the students drew

TALK FOR WRITING IN HISTORY (YEAR 8)

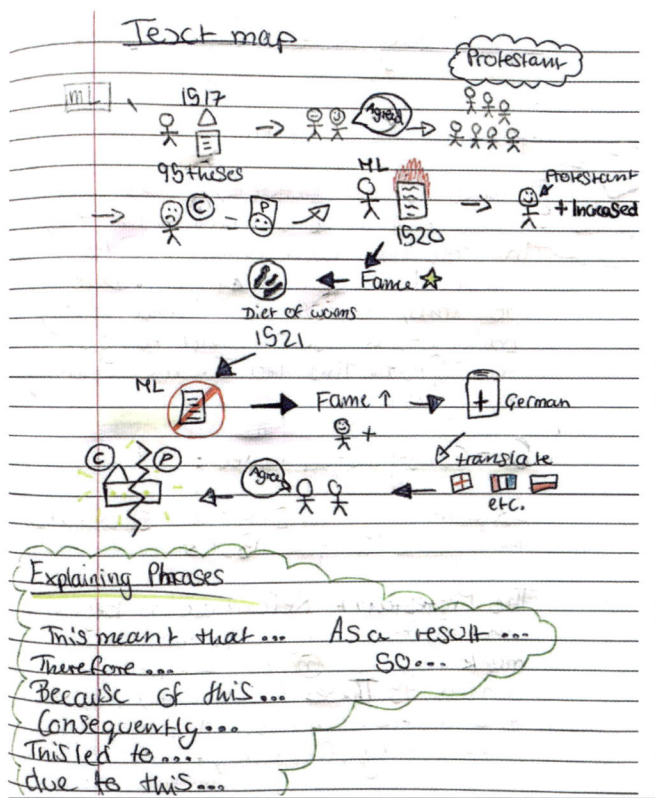

their own map: Kinga's map is pictured here. The focus of this was to illustrate causation. During this, I modelled signposting language – *What did this lead to? What was the result of this?* or *What was a consequence of this?* before drawing the next stage. We used dates and abbreviations to act as *aide memoires* for some events. You can have a lot of fun with this, too. Try to make the pictures entertaining for the students (a furious Pope, Martin Luther being a punk rebel, etc). They also can see how unimportant it is to be able to draw well or in great detail, which makes them more confident to have a try themselves – speed and clarity are the key facets. I always stress that the only person who needs to understand their text map is them. I often mock my own drawings which amuses the students too!

We used this text mapping process to discuss and clarify that an explanation of causation and consequence should always end with the consequence. I therefore drew my CONSEQUENCE (Protestant Reformation) first then my CAUSE (actions of Martin Luther) and said that we are going to need to show through our text map how one connected to the other.

Modelling generic phrases including sentence signposts

To model the language and phrases of causation, I chose to remove the historical context completely and give students an utterly free rein without complicating things with historical facts and concepts. I modelled this on the whiteboard as a flow chart about breaking my leg:

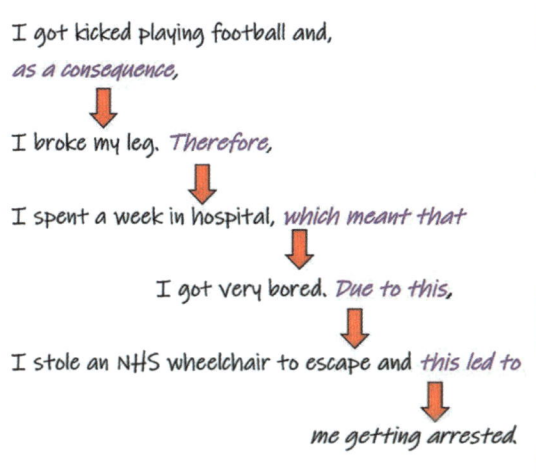

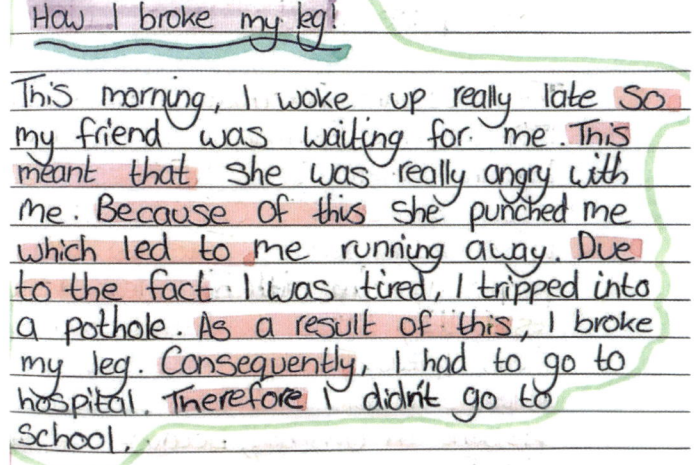

The students then produced their own *free* writing using 5 or more of these *explaining* terms and shared them with each other. The class heard the funniest ones and decided if the phrasing had been used correctly. This was very entertaining and helped them understand the function of the new language and phrases. Izzy enjoyed writing the example above. **Video clip 50** shows me familiarising Y8 with the key role of cause and effect signposts.

Co-constructing the model text

Students then used their text maps and the *signposts* activity to help me co-construct a model half-paragraph on the question: "Explain why the Protestant Reformation took place in the 1500s." If there were connecting arrows on the text map, then this suggested causes and consequences. The co-constructed model was done on a laptop being projected onto the whiteboard, and students were randomly chosen to add a sentence, improve a sentence or introduce an explaining phrase. Sometimes, students were asked in groups to discuss ideas and feedback their suggestions. All the *explaining* phrases were highlighted.

This was an excellent model of the writing process for students but the quality of the model produced could have been better in terms of modelling top-end academic language, something I blame myself for because of my desire to not be overtly nit-picky during the construction which could have prevented students from staying engaged. A solution to this might be to have prepared my own model text, in Blue-Peter style, and projected it at the end of the activity. The students could then have highlighted and magpied useful phrasing and vocabulary from the model before writing their own version.

The students then wrote their own version of the explanation highlighting the causal phrases used, as can be seen in Alisha's version here.

Moving from innovation to independent application

I stopped midway through writing up our text map to enable some independent application to take place to finish the paragraph – this supported students as they had already got started, they had seen in the co-constructed model how the text-map was being converted into sentences using the signpost language, and had all the content necessary on the whiteboard or in their text maps. The explaining causal phrases were also clearly displayed for them to use. The

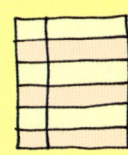

students' ability to write about cause and effect had greatly improved as Tom's paragraph illustrates.

We discussed our model and clarified again that an explanation of causation and consequence should always end with the consequence.

Independent application

The students were then introduced to the historical content of Henry VIII's Break with Rome through direct teacher instruction. Key dates, names and statistics were then simply listed on the whiteboard. Students scribbled notes, images and information under three boxed-up headings:

Wanted an heir	
Wanted money	
Wanted power	

Over time, this will become an embedded process which a class can undertake with very little teacher input. However, as a first attempt at a hot task, in the opening part of the academic year, I felt some support would be necessary.

Students were, therefore, given an A4 planning sheet boxed up into the 3 sections (Heir; Money; Power). I drew the CONSEQUENCE – **Henry VIII becoming Head of the Church in England in 1534** on a mini diagram and asked the students to ensure that their boxed-up, text-map explanation ended with this. I divided the whiteboard into 3-CAUSE sections and added my CONSEQUENCE diagram to the end of all 3 sections to model it. For the first paragraph (Heir) we didn't group text map but we did co-create images/diagrams for a selection of the required vocabulary on the whiteboard (*Pope, heir, Anne Boleyn, divorce, refuse, miscarriage, Act of Supremacy, Catherine of Aragon,* etc) for the students to use when they began to text map their explanations. Key dates, statistics and such were also on the whiteboard for students to use and we added sentence starters for each paragraph. Below, you can see James's text map for the paragraph on Henry VIII wanting an heir.

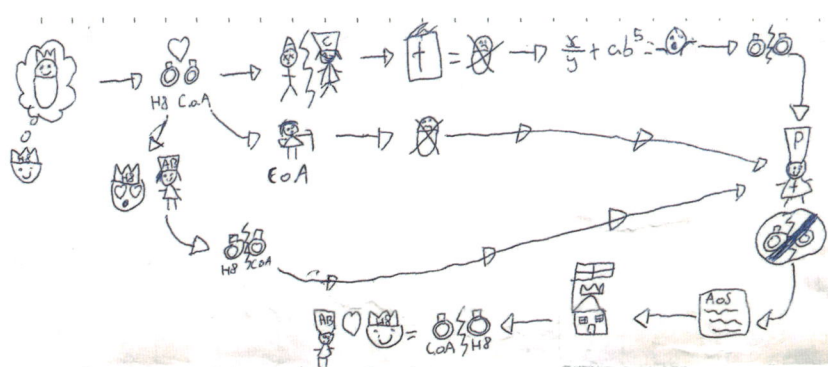

His text map shows Henry's desire for an heir, and his reasons for wanting to divorce Catherine of Aragon as she was unable to give him one; Henry felt the Bible stated he would remain childless as he had married his dead brother Arthur's widow. His relationship with Anne Boleyn is also included and the refusal of the Pope to grant a divorce. The text map finishes with the Act of Supremacy which makes Henry the Head of the Church in England enabling him to marry Anne Boleyn and try again for an heir.

I suggested that the students included a list of their explaining phrases to help them when they put their text maps into words – you can see such phrases encircled in Konner's text map here.

Plan it

Students were given the title, "Explain Why Henry VIII made himself Head of the Church of England in 1534". They then used the flow-chart ideas from our Protestant Reformation model, and a combination of their images and shared ones on the whiteboard, to illustrate how a range of factors led to Henry VIII becoming Head of the Church in England. For paragraphs 2 and 3 (Money, Power) students were given much less support with their text maps (unless specifically requested by individual students).

Konner's text map here for the *Power section* illustrates how the soft justice of the Church angered Henry, and the loyalty of the clergy (archbishops, bishops and priests) to the Pope, as opposed to Henry, led to, and was then resolved by, the Act of Supremacy.

Talking the text

I then gave the class 15 minutes in pairs to look at their text maps and tell their partner what they were going to write in each paragraph including their *explaining* phrases. This was noisy but students were keen to talk through their text maps and also share some of their diagrams and pictures.

The hot task

The students were given as long as they wished to turn their text-map planning into 3 paragraphs. There was a noticeable confidence about how the students attempted this work and, unusually for a mixed-attainment Year 8 group, no one was *getting stuck*. The questions I faced as they wrote were usually just to clarify historical details (which were mainly on the whiteboard anyway) as opposed to their lacking any understanding of the conceptual focus of the question.

TALK FOR WRITING IN HISTORY (YEAR 8) 247

> Another reason Henry became Head of the Church was because he wanted money. Henry needed because of "the The battle of Spurs" also "The battle of Flodden". For these battle's he needed needed: 80 warships, + Hampton Cout + 54 palaces also his lifestyle. As a result, all this costed a lot of Money. Additionally, the Church owned 30% of England land, and also the Church earned earned 3x more money than the king did. If Henry Henry became the head of of the Church he could make all of that money. As well as this he could sell the slate tiles, melt down the bells and get the taxes that used to go to the Church. This led to the Act of Supremacy being written and Henry became the Head of the Church due to this Henry got lot's of money.

> Due to this he saw that the Church made three times his salary and had 30% of Englands land Consequently this led to Henry

> Makei a law that makes him the leader of the church in England and after that he sold the church's land, gold and silver Makeing him even more Rich.

Here you can see extracts from Emma and Fred's hot tasks. These examples show impressive progress from the cold tasks in relation to the language and concept of causation, if still showing the need for the development of more grammatical sentence structures in some areas.

Check It
The students were instructed to
- highlight the explaining phrases they had used
- make sure that each paragraph ended with a CONSEQUENCE
- Check their use of capital letters (the students had been given a list of words which should have capitals: Act of Supremacy, Church, Henry, etc.)

Progress and embedding learning
Three areas of improvement were particularly noticeable:

a) The cold tasks had highlighted a lack of explaining language to deal with causation, even among the higher attaining students and more confident writers. The hot tasks showed a great deal of improvement with many students showing a confident use of a range of causal phrasing.

b) The cold tasks had highlighted a common approach for students to want to explain why something happened using a narrative or descriptive format. The use of the text-map flow charts, coupled with the focus on causal phrasing, meant that even the previously least-attaining students were becoming adept at actually illustrating the relationship between causes and consequences with appropriate phrasing. They were starting to sound like historians.

c) The level of confidence students had with their writing was clear. Several students who find putting pen to paper difficult, clearly used the support they had been given (text map, whiteboard info, etc), as well as their confidence from watching a model being constructed and talking the text, to produce several pages of independent written work, of which they were rightly proud.

Outcomes and reflections

I was very pleased with the academic level of work which arose out of this process, and the progress which was evident between the cold and hot tasks. Some Year 8 students who achieved 10 or 11 out of 12 when using a KS4 GCSE mark scheme, showed that they had a clear grasp of the requirements of the question and the concept of causation. Students for whom writing was a huge challenge were also able to provide a clear indicator that they could explain a cause and a consequence, although further embedding of the structural functions of the language would be needed.

The co-constructed models were not perhaps of the highest quality they could have been. Due to them being done quickly in a classroom and wanting to include the input of students, the quality and phrasing is of lower quality than I would have liked. However, interleaving co-constructed models with purpose-made academic models over the course of the year should help ensure that the students are exposed to the higher-level language and phrasing we are aiming to teach.

Pleasingly, I also felt that the content delivery had not been compromised as we had covered a great deal in terms of historical knowledge, signposting language for explanations, subject specific vocabulary and using our boxing-up toolkit for these types of questions.

Adapting the TfW process to meet the needs of history

I have adapted the TfW process to suit the demands KS3 and KS4 history because covering the content required by the National Curriculum/exam boards could be said to be a challenge at best. The key TfW tools I've employed are:

a) using the cold and hot tasks to bookend the students' journey from imitation to innovation to independent application;

b) warming up the words through text mapping followed by short, sharp, regular testing; plus speaking and use-in-context (as opposed to any specific dedicated classroom activities to enable this, aside from the initial NHTW grids and discussion surrounding them);

c) using model texts to signpost the language and deliver content. This may include using a co-constructed model as well as a chance for the students to imitate aspects of the model;

d) text mapping key ideas, content and sentence structures (text mapping extended writing would be too time-consuming);

e) focusing on one specific language signposting feature in each assessment – as the students have to wrestle with knowledge of content and historical concepts as well. Focusing on only *explaining* phrases, *adding* phrases, or *giving an opinion* phrases ensures they are not overloaded. These will, hopefully, become embedded, and they often begin to use them naturally anyway. (Some Year 8s now often confidently use *moreover, additionally* or *furthermore,* something which is being embedded in Year 7 through the TfW process).

Has it made a difference?

The Talk for Writing approach makes a huge difference: it is all down to the way it imbues confidence in the kids. I started using it two years ago and was enthusiastic from very early on, as **video clip 12** of me feeding back to staff near the beginning of our project shows. Now not a single student says, "Sir, I don't know how to start." Previously, there would always be at least one who just felt they couldn't begin. It's flexible: you can tweak it to respond to the students' needs and the needs of the subject so KS4 needs it as much as KS3. In history, the language facilitates the concept: the causal explaining phrases automatically lead to recording conceptual understanding – the word *because* forces you to come up with a reason. In this way, the language structures the answer. Text mapping is both really fun and really powerful: it bridges the gap between vocabulary and understanding. You can't begin to draw an image to represent the meaning of a word or phrase without understanding what the word means, and the picture stays in your mind, but you can write it down without any understanding. It's a great way of underpinning understanding and increasing retention. It's been brilliant and makes it a pleasure to teach, so I hope what I've written helps to explain the beauty of Talk for Writing.

Chapter 12c: How Talk for Writing supports religious education

Daniel Martin, Y6 teacher and Assistant Head Teacher at St Matthew's Primary in Birmingham, explains how the Talk for Writing approach helps him to help the children read, write and speak like theologians.

Psychology professor Daniel Willingham suggests that stories are psychologically privileged in the human mind. If this is true, then stories and a rich 'reading for pleasure' culture are the foundation to teaching any subject discipline. Storytelling is also the cornerstone of the Talk for Writing pedagogy. Religious education is rich with stories: those which stem from sacred texts and cultures, and those which tell us of the lives of magnificent people of faith. Religious education enables learners to be immersed in hearing and telling faith-based stories.

Reading for pleasure is at the heart of our curriculum at St. Matthew's and is very much a part of the school culture. Teacher's and support staff routinely make their books available to children and make recommendations (**see page 114**).

The unit of work I've chosen to illustrate how Talk for Writing helps children access religious education focuses on the core Christian religious concept of 'incarnation'. The children were introduced to varying faith viewpoints on Jesus being the Messiah. The answer that needed to be addressed by the end of the unit being, "Was Jesus the Messiah?".

What do they already know? (cold task)

The pedagogy of Talk for Writing can be applied across the curriculum and RE is no exception. The necessity to have a clear understanding of children's starting points is a crucial part of the teaching and learning process. This may not always be in the form of a written task: it could be to gain insight into the conceptual understanding of the learner by assessing their understanding of the key vocabulary (as seen in the 'heard before' word grid below). This not only requires the children to state their familiarity with the given word, phrase or idea, but it places a demand on them to demonstrate their depth of understanding by contextualising it with a sentence and illustration. When choosing the words to focus on, it was important that I selected the words that would:
1. Add to the children's theological vocabulary repertoire
2. Aid the understanding of texts that we would encounter
3. Relate to other words that the children were learning or would need to know, *e.g. transfigured (trans:* Latin root *– across, beyond, through, changing thoroughly).*

HOW TALK FOR WRITING SUPPORTS RELIGIOUS EDUCATION 251

Here you can see one pupil's attempt. It was clear that although some of the words hadn't been encountered before, there was still some understanding at a word level but not necessarily at a conceptual level. For example, some children could not demonstrate their conceptual understanding of *incarnation*, but they did understand that it had something to do with God and flesh due to their knowledge of the word *carna – flesh/piece of meat* in Greek.

The cold task also highlighted the fact that the children would need to see examples and non-examples of some of these theological terms. For example, you could demonstrate an understanding of *transfigured* in relation to the metamorphosis of a butterfly. It would be a perfect opportunity for the children then to see and read about 'The Transfiguration of Christ'. Raphael's romantic painting 'The Transfiguration' also provided some excellent talking points in order to directly address the meaning of the word and provide further evidence of the Messianic qualities of Christ. This also allowed us to address the disparities between religious art and sacred texts and the reasons why these exist. The picture here shows how one pupil annotated the painting to strengthen their interpretation of it.

Imitation stage

This was immediately followed by a session that focused on some of the key vocabulary that the children would need to successfully reach the 'end goal' of this unit of work. In the long run, exploring the etymology and morphology of these root words will support the children with their ability to use theological vocabulary effectively. It's also important to have in mind, when delivering lessons across the curriculum, that a disciplinary approach can be taken: "How can I get children to read, write and speak like a theologian?"

The pedagogy of Talk for Writing supports the internalising of texts. It was important that the children had a firm understanding of the biblical account of The Transfiguration. One of the key techniques to embed this was through text mapping. The children had previously heard the story read from the model text featured here. They then independently ordered the sequence of key events, as illustrated.

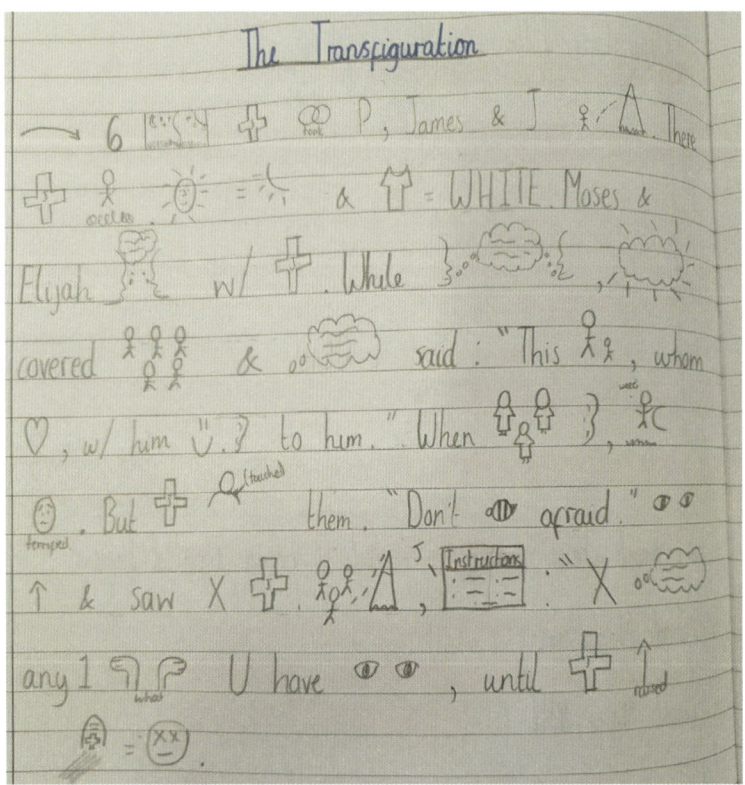

The text mapping allowed the children to discuss and evaluate the importance of what they deemed to be the significant events as well as identify the underlying structure of the text, as illustrated by one child's work here.

Having now mapped the text, children were then able to 'talk the text'. This was an important and necessary part of the unit as the key events that took place in this particular text would form a vital part of the argument for whether Jesus was the Messiah.

What can they do now? (independent application)

The culmination of the unit calls for the children to answer the question, "Was Jesus the Messiah?" Having recently completed an English unit on writing information texts, children were given the opportunity to choose their audience

HOW TALK FOR WRITING SUPPORTS RELIGIOUS EDUCATION

and form with the purpose of informing the reader of the Messianic qualities of Jesus and determining whether he was the Messiah or not.

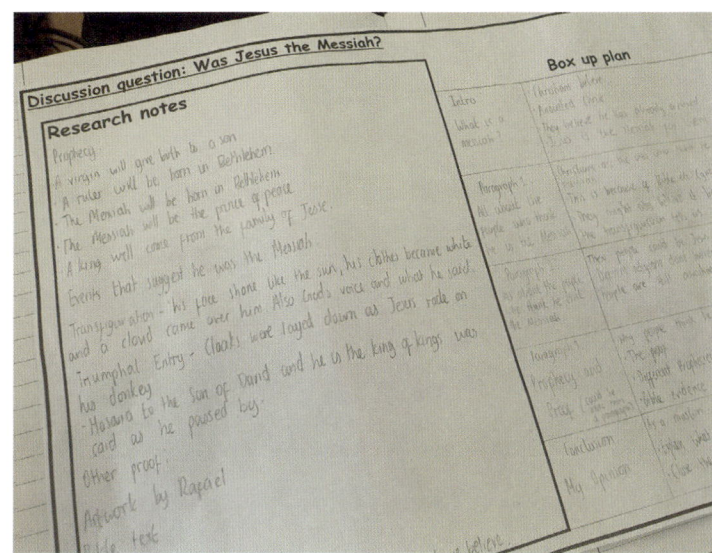

It's important to note that during the research and planning stage, all research came from the work completed throughout the unit. Boxing up was a straightforward and common task for the children as they are routinely familiar with the writing process and it is very much a natural prerequisite to writing across the curriculum. One pupil's research and planning is reproduced here.

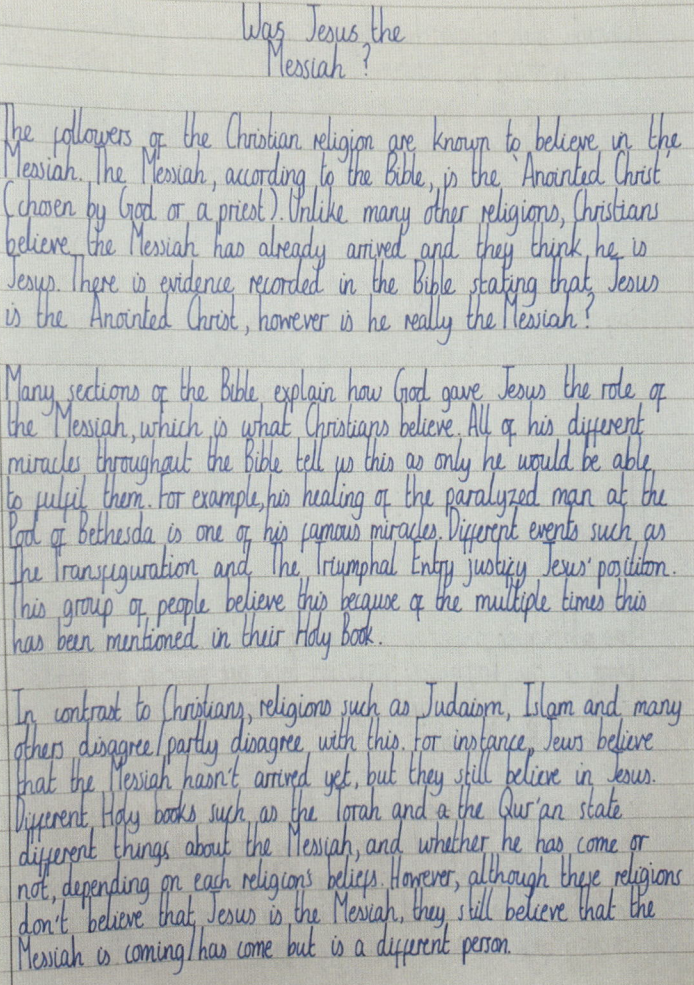

The example, which continues on the next page, exemplifies a written report that sets out to answer whether Jesus was the Messiah. There is mention of varying religious viewpoints as well as personal opinion and belief, which will be very useful for future work. The progress that was made here is encouraging for teacher and pupil alike – this piece demonstrates reference to various sources, opinions and beliefs. Additionally, vocabulary is used purposefully and effectively to inform the reader. All of this is underpinned by strong content knowledge, a sound conceptual understanding of key theological terms and the application of 'informing the reader' in another curriculum area.

Although religious education has its own distinct pedagogy and is an academically rigorous subject in itself, the Talk for Writing pedagogy is obviously applicable in a seamless fashion. It always makes sense to assess where children

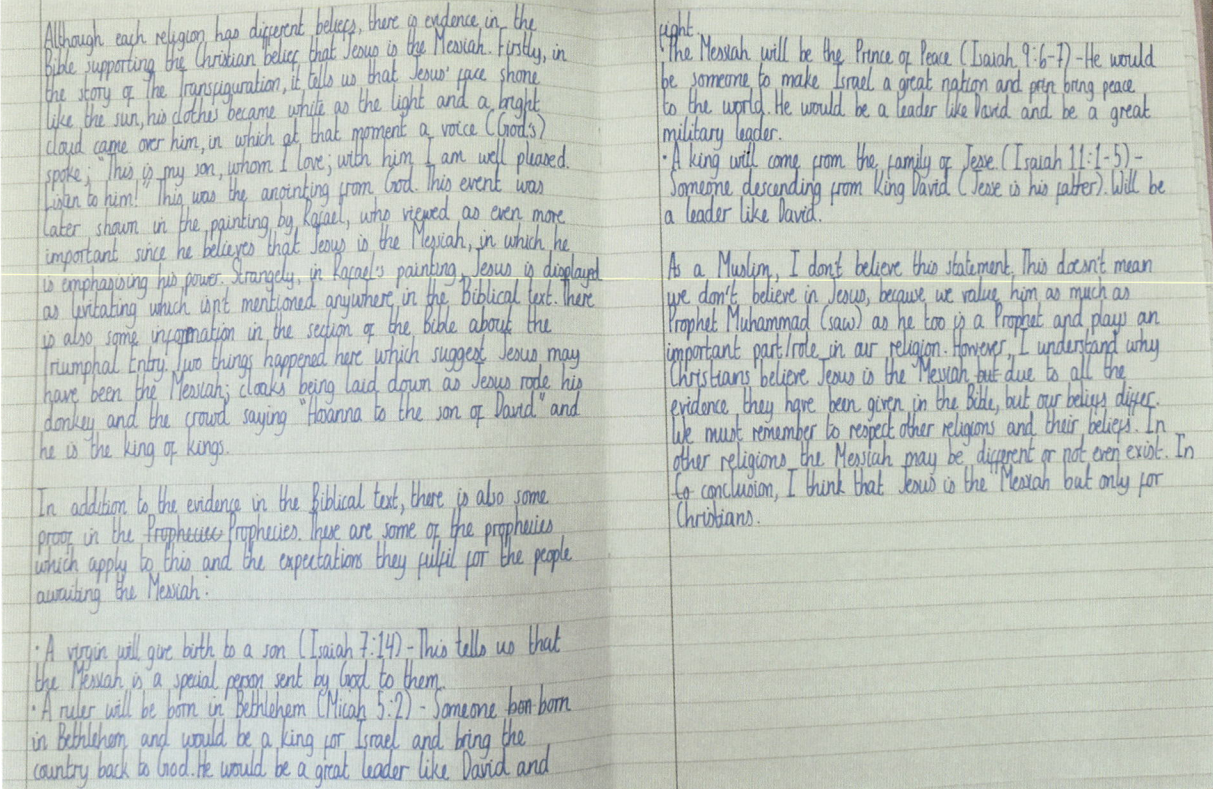

are, what they need, address those needs and then see what they can now do. When writing is not required, being able to understand the key vocabulary and concepts of the topic, so that the pupils can comprehend the issues and discuss them, is always essential. Moreover, when the end result of a unit provides an opportunity for writing to show the pupils' ability to independently express their understanding, the Talk for Writing process provides a very clear structure from which to work to.

To find out when you can see Talk for Writing in action across the curriculum at St Matthews and related training, visit www.talk4writing.co.uk/train-with-us/st-matthews-ce-primary-birmingham/.

The following video clips all relate to how Talk for Writing supports the teaching of RE in secondary schools

- **Video clip 7:** Two A-level RE students from Dyson Perrins Academy, Malvern, explain why text mapping helps them
- **Video clip 16:** Billy, a Year 10 student at Dyson Perrins, explains how TfW has increased his confidence in RE and beyond
- **Video clip 30:** Tracey Adams illustrates the power of dialogic talk when discussing heroism with her Year 6 class at St Matthew's Primary, Birmingham
- **Video clip 51:** Jess Martin teaching a Year 9 RE class at John of Gaunt, following the GCSE short course
- **Video clip 52:** An RE teacher from Slough & Eton explains the difference text mapping has made and how TfW has changed her way of teaching

Chapter 12d: Talk for Writing in geography

Since text is such a significant part of geography, the potential for the Talk for Writing process to support teaching and learning in this subject is immediately apparent. Here, Ella Wood, a geography teacher at The John of Gaunt School, demonstrates this is true even in the most practical elements of geography in KS3 and KS4.

The first geography topic facing Year 7s is map skills, alongside assessing the students' baseline knowledge of a wide range of geographical content. At first sight, map skills do not seem to lend themselves to the full Talk for Writing process, given the focus on skills rather than text but, on reflection, oracy will be very much a part of the skills. Students being able to explain how to do the skills is the key to them being able to complete the skills well themselves, alongside being able to answer questions like the ones focused on here. The key strategies from the TFW toolkit for learning can be applied throughout the unit, ranging from never-heard-the-word grids to imitating successful models to help the students build up their skills, so that, by the end of the unit, they can apply them independently.

10. Powell Construction wants to build 2000 new homes in Bath. He has 3 sites to choose from. Use the evidence from the map and the facts in the table below to advise him which is the best site.

Write a letter to Mr Powell where you tell him the advantages and disadvantages of each site then advise him which in the best site.

Site one Grid reference: 7763	Site two Grid reference: 7766	Site three Grid reference: 7168
3km SE from the centre of Bath and within walking distance of the university	3km NE of the city centre Located on the floodplain of the river Avon.	5km NW of the city centre. The hills allow beautiful views of the surrounding area

Sometimes an 'exam style' question on the topic is selected as the cold task to see what students' understanding is at the beginning of the topic. Not only does this prepare students for the demands of GCSE study later in their school career but it also helps them to begin internalising the process and the geographical language needed to answer such questions. This enables the focus, as they progress, to be on the innovation and independent application because they have the underpinning pattern of how to answer these type of questions in their heads. At the end of the unit, students reattempt their answer of a similar type of question as the hot task.

Dear Mr Powell, Needs a conclusion with overall judgement. Why?

The advantages of site one are: It is not far from the city centre, so people might want to live closer to the city for work reasons. It might be good for young adults starting university as it is ~~not~~ close to the university. However, you might get the crowds of students walking/driving back from uni, and as it is close to the city centre, there might be more tourists. The advantages of site two are: It's close to the city centre, therefore it may be appealing, however it is located on the floodplain and Britain rains lots so it may be flooded easily, causing it to be less appealing. The advantages of site three are: the hills make it a scenic and beautiful place, although it may be a little harder to get around. However, it is further from the city centre, but that also means there would be less tourists. Personally, I think site one or three would be good. Site 3 would be good, because of the scenic view you could charge more, and site one would be because of students, although they might not have the money to pay a lot so you might get less money out of it.

(Continue on separate paper 5 + 2 9 marks plus 3 spag)

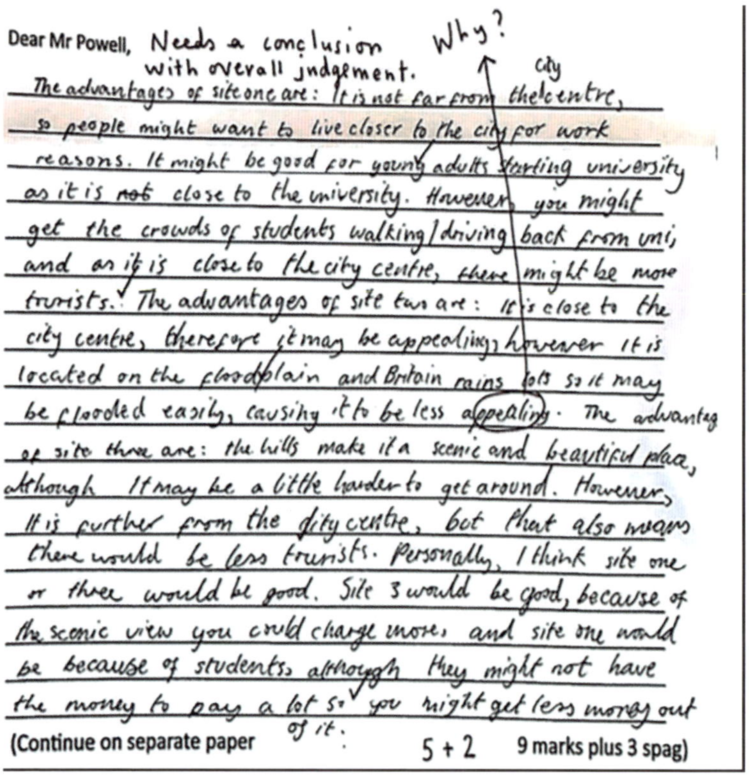

The cold task pictured here is the first attempt of a high-attaining Year 7 student at a 9-mark GCSE-style question. You'll note some signposting and connective use, but a lack of development. GCSE questions such as this are level marked and look for development over points – quality over quantity to use the cliché. Level one would be *basic*, level two *clear* and level 3 *detailed.* TfW lends itself well to all levels of geography.

The imitation stage

Students are provided with a NHTW grid for key words to help establish which terms they know and which they don't and to flag up the importance of these words to the topic. They are, therefore, encouraged to use and revisit these words throughout the topic. These words are tested through low-stakes quizzing each lesson on the key words encountered the previous lesson, for example, "What is a scale?", "What is a key?" to cement student understanding and encourage a range of *acceptable* definitions that each individual can remember and subsequently internalise so that they can use the terms appropriately in their writing.

Plan it	Link it
Express it	Check it

Q8) Explain some benefits and disadvantages of the main road near the village?

Firstly, a benefit of living near a main road is that villagers can leave and return easily, as a result travelling to work in a town or city would be much easier to do so people could earn more money. Secondly, an advantage would be that visitors could travel to the village more easily which might attract more tourists for activities such as the golf course.

On the other hand, a disadvantage of living near the main road would be the noise of cars and trucks travelling past, especially at night time, consequently, some villagers might not be able to sleep. Additionally, if children are playing close by and they run in to the road they may be injured or killed because will be travelling quickly.

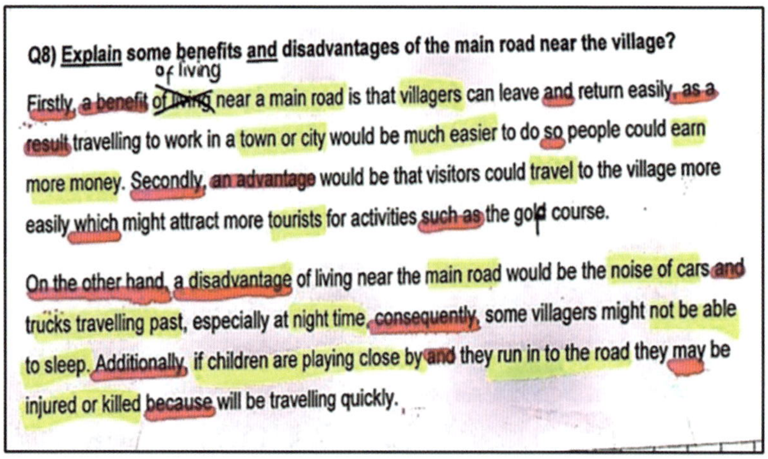

At the heart of the process is a range of model text which enabled the class to box up the structure and analyse the content. This analysis included the group brainstorming of sentence signposts which they are now becoming accustomed to looking for when the class deconstructs model answers. By using a visualiser to display the model text, students are helped with the deconstruction of the model. Through boxing up the model, they understand the structure; through highlighting specific features, they understand the ingredients: the typical language features required. Often,

TALK FOR WRITING IN GEOGRAPHY 257

students look for *key terms* – technical geographical terms and sentence signposts plus anything generically useful that can be magpied from an answer – which, of course, is dependent on the context. In the example here, the yellow highlights are regularly used (generic) phrases in geography; the red highlighting is the sentence signposts.

At this stage, students can sometimes misunderstand what key terms or signposting looks like, so the vocabulary may be revisited; adaptations are then made to better embed this.

The innovation stage – analysing for purpose

As a result of this groundwork, by the innovation stage, the students were in a position to co-construct their understanding of more challenging model text related to the topic. They discussed the advantages and disadvantages of a number of different sites that could be located on a map provided. To the left, are the annotations resulting from an activity where the students looked at information and discussed the positives and negatives of each site with a partner to develop their ideas. The oral nature of this activity allowed the students to verbalise their ideas as well as the initial structure and rhythm of their final answer: in effect they were talking the text and, importantly, it was an engaging activity. When you look at the annotations, you can see that they are analysing the material well, for example, site 1 is near to Bath University, which obviously means students will be seeking accommodation, but this group has astutely commented: "they might not be able to pay as much". They are very much engaged in reading the information provided for purpose to inform the points they can make.

The independent application stage

As a result of this process, the work of the students showed significant improvement. If you compare the hot task below with the same student's cold task at the beginning of this chapter, you can see that the hot task is much better structured with clear paragraphs in a logical order and the ideas are valid, well linked and clearly explained.

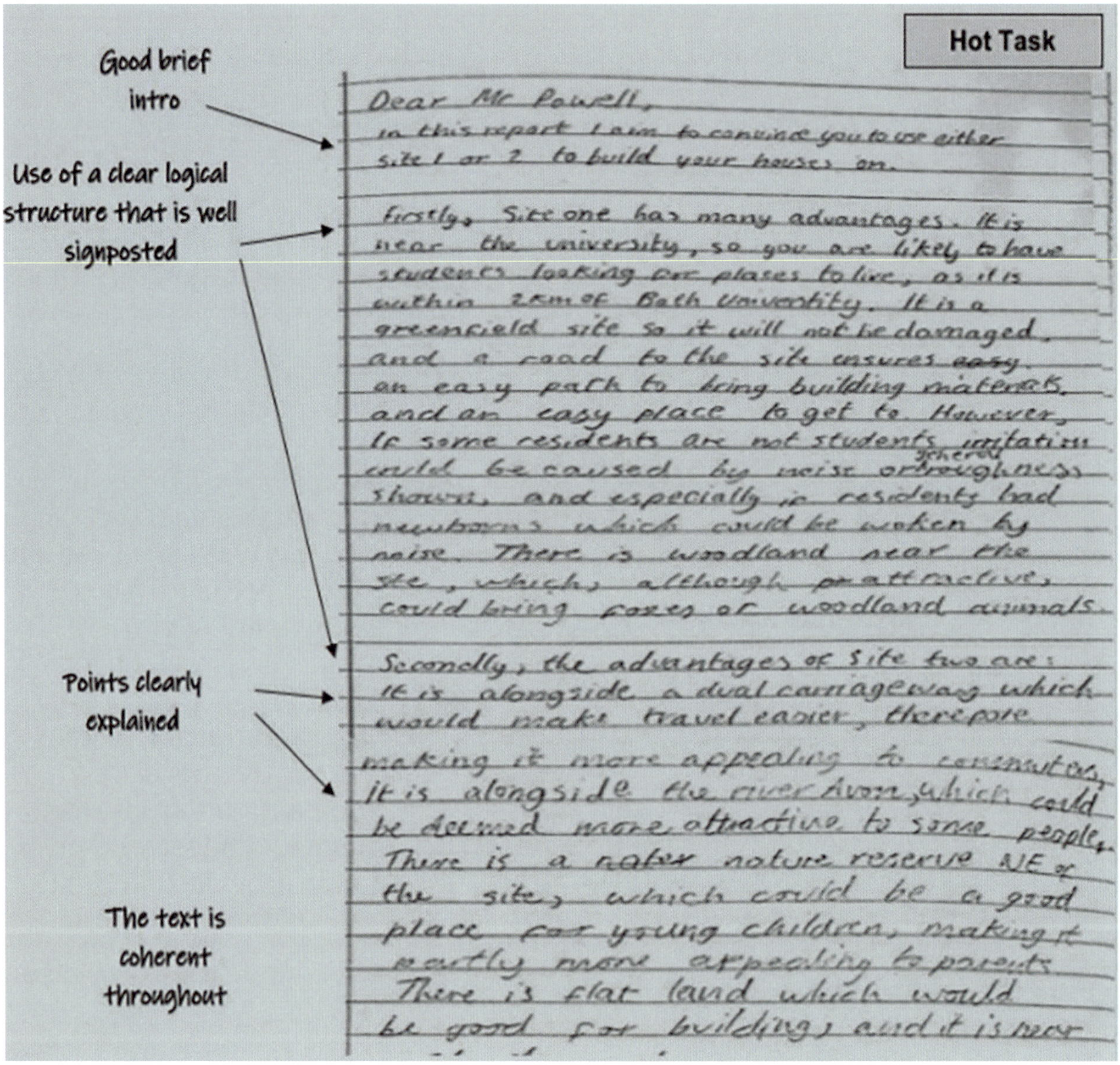

258 TRANSFORMING LEARNING ACROSS THE CURRICULUM

Hot Task

Annotations on handwritten text:
- Good brief intro
- Use of a clear logical structure that is well signposted
- Points clearly explained
- The text is coherent throughout

Handwritten letter:

Dear Mr Powell,

In this report I aim to convince you to use either site 1 or 2 to build your houses on.

Firstly, Site one has many advantages. It is near the university, so you are likely to have students looking for places to live, as it is within 2km of Bath University. It is a greenfield site so it will not be damaged, and a road to the site ensures easy, an easy path to bring building materials, and an easy place to get to. However, if some residents are not students, irritation could be caused by noise or general business shown, and especially in residents had newborns which could be woken by noise. There is woodland near the site, which, although pr attractive, could bring foxes or woodland animals.

Secondly, the advantages of site two are: It is alongside a dual carriageway which would make travel easier, therefore making it more appealing to commuters. It is alongside the river Avon, which could be deemed more attractive to some people. There is a nater nature reserve NE of the site, which could be a good place for young children, making it partly more appealing to parents. There is flat land which would be good for buildings, and it is not

How Talk for Writing supported learning in Years 9 & 10

Meanwhile, Year 9 were working on *Ecosystems and Hot Deserts* which forms the bulk of *The Living World* unit, while Year 10 were looking at *Coasts* as part of the wider unit *UK Physical Landscapes*. Both modules are part of the AQA GCSE geography course and lend themselves very well to the Talk for Writing process. In particular, never-heard-the-word grids are useful for laying the foundation. That said, the sheer volume of key terms per unit means I'll have to adapt these more next time so students can better embed the key terms/vocabulary in preparation for answering exam questions; just as the toolkit will need adapting to accommodate the difference in question stems and structures.

TALK FOR WRITING IN GEOGRAPHY 259

Here you can see an image of the NHTW grid for the *Coasts* unit for Year 10 taken at the start of the unit study, when students had limited knowledge and understanding of the key terms involved. The aim is to revisit this as the unit progresses to better embed this vocabulary. As with KS3, understanding of the key terms is tested regularly through low-stakes quizzing. However, the volume of key terms at GCSE makes appropriate and effective use of NHTW grids difficult at times and, as explained above, they would probably be better employed on an almost lesson-by-lesson or sub-topic basis. For example, in this instance, a *coastal processes* NHTW grid could be employed for the key terms and, once this has been embedded and assessed, new vocabulary could be introduced for the next sub-topic, such as coastal landforms.

The cold task was a practice exam question. The example here shows a Year 9 answer on the topic of hot desert animal adaptations. In this instance, students had been given support for their cold task in the form of an example paragraph which followed the *Point, Evidence, Connective and Explain (PECE)* structure often used in geography at KS4. This was co-constructed on the board before being written down by the students. Subsequently, both the example and the students' own work was deconstructed using colour coding to help with imitating the structure of the text required and then boxed up to show the PECE structure.

Often the imitation stage at KS4 includes the deconstruction of model answers to help with further embedding of the vocabulary, understanding the structure and rhythm of the answer and to prepare for co-construction of a new model, or an example paragraph, which also assists with understanding additional content. The example here shows how a Year 9 employed deconstruction of a model answer to look for key terms and signposting as well as anything they may wish to magpie for their answer.

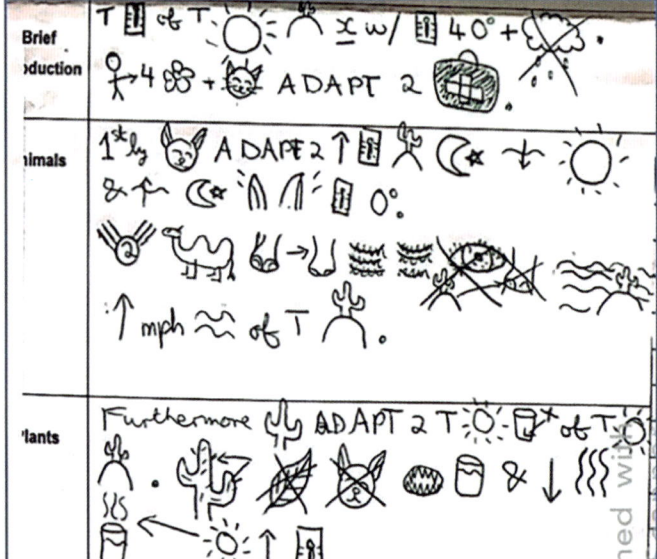

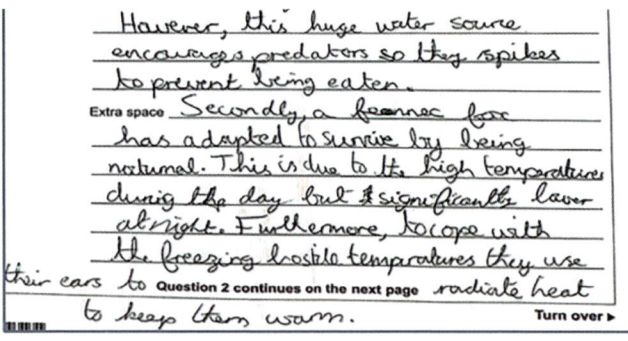

Students then boxed up and text mapped a possible answer for a similar question – the introductory sentence was text mapped together before the class was encouraged to continue independently with this, as illustrated here. Text mapping has turned out to be an engaging way of helping students remember key content.

The deconstruction of the model and the co-construction of the text map was used to help the students to:

- internalise the model
- understand the structure
- understand the content
- analyse the text.

These tools were then applied effectively to a new exam question from a GCSE past paper – the question was phrased differently but the content and structure remained consistent with what the students had been working on, as can be seen from the image of the text reproduced above. This shows a Year 9 student's work following the deconstruction of model answers, co-construction of a plan and text mapping. Students were also provided with a boxing-up grid on the board in which key text map items e.g. *first, secondly, animal, vegetation* were provided in the correct order to support their understanding of the importance of a good structure. *Live marking* means feedback is provided during the innovation stage leading students directly to the independent application stage.

We have found the process not only supports the structure and expression of the text but also the understanding and recall of content which is key to success. The image here shows how we co-constructed the text to support both content and structural understanding, first by focusing on images to help the students recall the key vocabulary and then by showing how these terms fitted into a text explaining how a sea stack is formed. This enabled the students to complete answers to questions that made well-structured, clearly explained and supported points, using technical terminology appropriately. When the students then attempted an exam question, the average score was 4 out of 6, which is a top level 2 answer, with some students achieving 5 marks as in the example below.

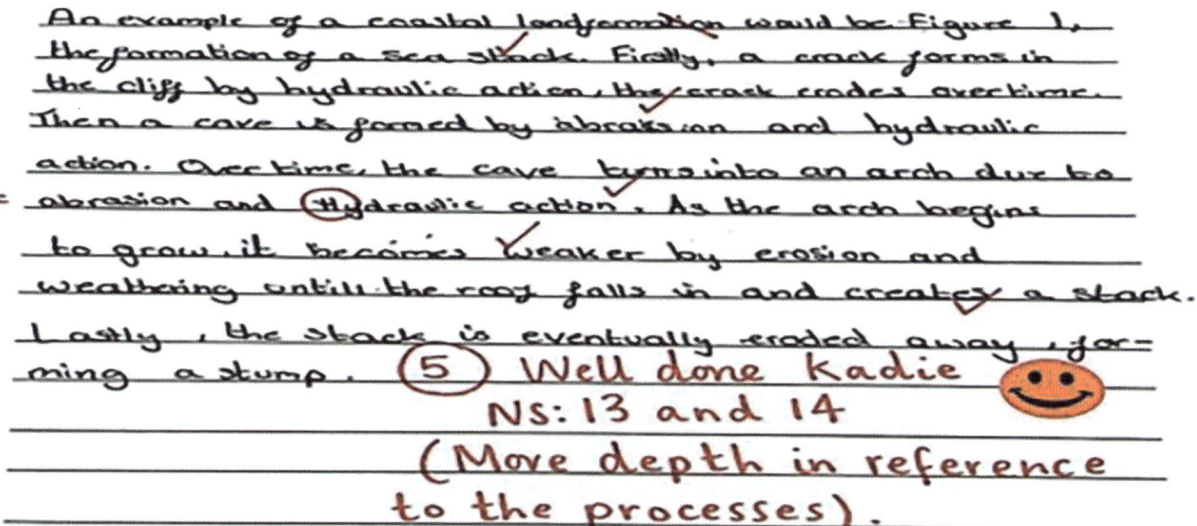

When you read this *hot task*, you can see that the process of erosion is clearly outlined with technical language like *abrasion* and *hydraulic action* being well-used to help to explain the process. The whole text flows coherently using time signposts like *firstly, over time* and *lastly* effectively. With a little more depth explaining the processes of erosion, this would have won full marks. I was pleased with how the students had gained in confidence as a result of the scaffolding processes used to develop their understanding of what to say and how to say it.

Now, I'm planning to provide more feedback ahead of further innovation in preparation for the independent application, which most likely will come in the form of a Year 10 mock exam. As you can see, I've tweaked the process to make it fit the demands of geography and it has enabled the majority to reach level 2, and some level 3, which is pleasing for the students and myself. Moreover, teaching the unit in this way has enabled me to reflect on the teaching and learning process and come up with ways in which I think I could adapt what I'm doing to make it more effective next time.

Significantly, the students tell me that the TfW approach has been helpful, so I want to end with a few comments from some Year 9 students:

> *"I find boxing up the structure strips useful because it breaks things down into understandable and useful chunks."*
>
> *"I find deconstructing model answers helpful in my writing because it allows me to visually see content ratios and gives me the ability to have a template where I can substitute information."*
>
> *"I find boxing up and deconstruction useful as I can look back and see what I missed. It also helps me with my future work as I know what to look for and what to write."*

This geography chapter should have been followed by a chapter on Talk for Writing in A-level sociology, by Jess Martin, who teaches RE and sociology at The John of Gaunt School. Due to lack of space, this chapter is now available online. Go to www.talk4writing.co.uk/access-csw-video and follow the instructions 'Code: 1224'.

Chapter 13: Talk for Writing complements PE

Ben Rhodes, Deputy Headteacher (School Improvement) and PE teacher, was on The John of Gaunt School's Talk for Writing project team. Here is his excellent explanation of how the process reflects how you teach PE, illustrating the way it can be easily adapted to suit the practical and theoretical demands of physical education for all ages.

Introduction – *Pre-amble before kick-off*

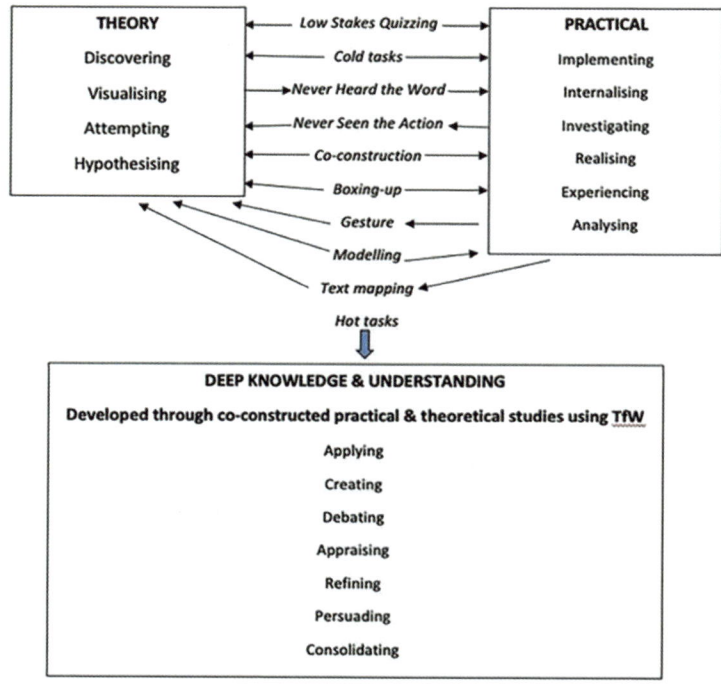

If you think Talk for Writing is just a classroom-based approach to developing language and literacy, then think again! The broad range of TfW strategies complement and enhance learning within the practical context, fitting in with the *rhythms and tunes* of the subject. The cyclical learning process TfW brings allows the cross-pollination of learning between theoretical study with practical performance and investigation. It provides the scaffold to create descriptive and analytical text, drawing from the student's primary physical evidence and experiences. Gesture can be a powerful, but awkward, tool for the self-conscious young adult. Using valid movements from specific sporting techniques provides learners with a justified reason to use gesture and text-mapping to recall key theories, rules and their explanations. Cold tasks of hypothesising outcomes of tests and visualising performances leads to independent physical discovery, providing purposeful application of findings in scaffolded written work that can lead to higher-order analytical and evaluative text.

This chapter aims to illustrate some of the TfW approaches that facilitate these outcomes.

Laying the foundations

High performance cannot occur without a proper warm-up: warm-up the body – warm-up the mind – warm-up the words.

A familiar TfW approach is warming up the words via never-heard-the-word grids. This enables students to attempt to describe a range of technical terms in a low-stakes task, simply to ascertain their depth of knowledge.

Word familiarisation table

1. Rate your knowledge of the words below by ticking one of the 'Don't know', 'Have a go', 'Nailed it!' boxes
2. Text map and describe the words that you have ticked, 'Have a go' or 'Nailed it!'
3. Research ALL the words so that you are sure your descriptions are correct. ANY BLANK DESCRIPTIONS OR CORRECTIONS SHOULD BE COMPLETED IN GREEN PEN

Term		Don't know	Have a go	Nailed it!	Text map it	Describe it
Skeletal muscle	Short term responses Muscular skeletal system					
Long bones						
Synovial joint						
Mobility						
Elasticity						
Osteoblasts						
Metabolic rate						

This can also be carried out in a practical form. *Never-seen-the-action activities* set students the task of performing the technique or action of a key term, allowing the teacher to observe whether a student understands a particular term or has had previous experience in a particular topic area. Students **SHOW** what they know as the teacher **S**ets the tasks, **H**ears the responses, **O**bserves the attempts and questions **W**hy students responded in the way that they did. Students then reflect on these attempted techniques and movements that have been verbalised through carefully structured discussions with the teacher. They then feel more able to create descriptions and explanations in written form.

Recall and copying – demonstrating and imitating technique

Modelling within the classroom is based around text mapping, reviewing model answers, magpieing words or phrases and co-constructing written text. The model text below explains what reversibility is following the *define, explain, exemplify, compare and conclude* process. The annotations and highlighting help draw attention to key factors.

What is reversibility?

DEFINE – EXPLAIN – EXAMPLE – COMPARE - CONCLUDE

Performance and physical adaptations can deteriorate if training stops or slows[1] (also known as regression). The body will return to its natural state or worse if it is not overloaded regularly[2]. You lose the fitness you gain quicker than the time it takes to progress[3].

Reversibility/regression — *How?* — *What does this mean?*

All reversibility is basically if you stop training then the improvements you have made will be reversed and you can actually go backwards. This means you go back to where you started from or you could become less fit than when you started. So if you do not train for a period of time as little as a week you may not be able to restart training at the point where you left off. — *Why?* — *After competition*

Sporting examples – Jessica Ennis stopped training for a couple of weeks after she won her Olympic gold medal. She started training lightly again after having a couple of weeks off so that her body retained some of its fitness or she would have to start from a lower level when she gets back into full training. Phillips Idowu wanted to do well in the Olympics but he was injured for a few weeks just before he had to do the triple jump in the Olympics. This meant he was not very good at the Olympics because he had missed a lot of training through being injured and it affected his performance.

Before competition — *Why?*

The same approach can be taken in a practical context:
- Images can be used to copy techniques
- Clips can be watched to analyse techniques, specific plays or tactics
- Adaptations of basic techniques and tactics can be replicated in personal performances
- Techniques can be co-performed by teacher and student with variations of technique and alternative sequences of drills or plays suggested by students.

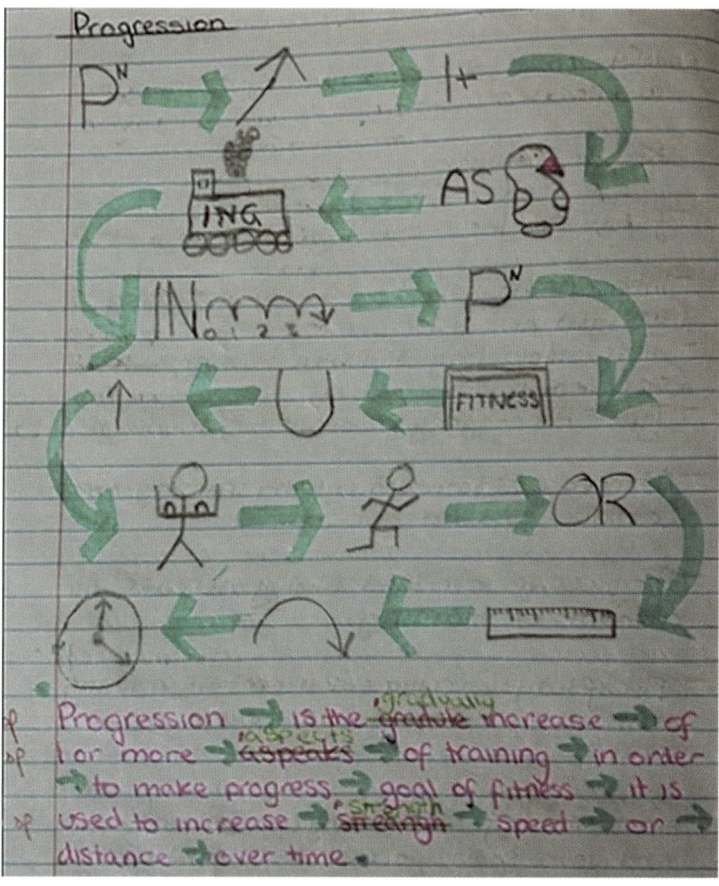

Realisation through the experience of practical performance, whilst regularly referring to key terminology, normalises technical words, embeds knowledge and internalises understanding of theories and concepts. This enables students to verbalise their knowledge and understanding and hence apply this in the specialist written form required at Key Stage 4.

Here you can see how text mapping has helped a student sort out a clear explanation of what progression means in PE.

This has enabled them to write a clear explanation. With a little attention to spelling, they will have sorted this one.

In this example, you can see the student has first been involved in co-constructing an explanation for why we need progression and overload, using golf as an example.

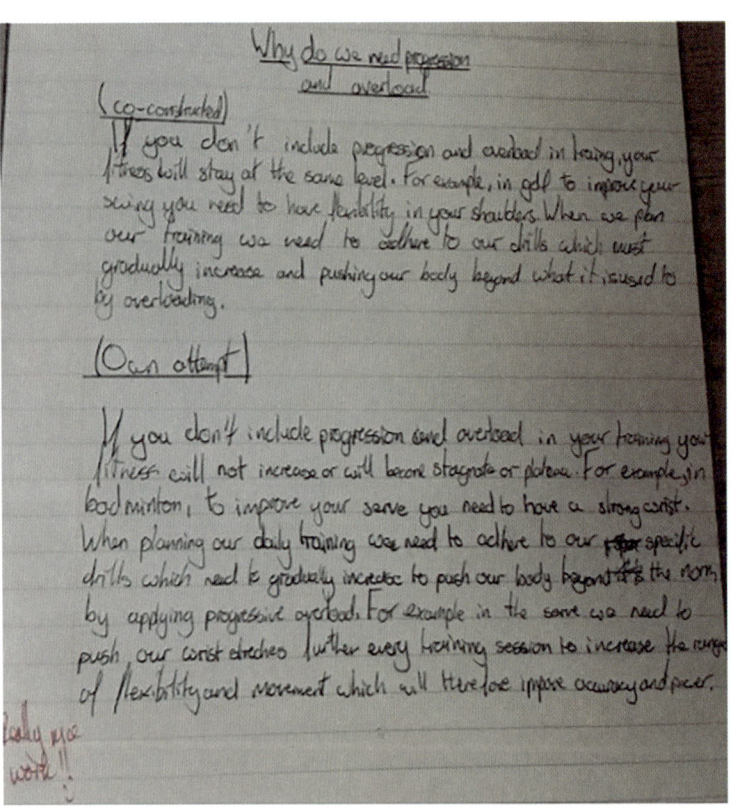

The student has then written their own very clear explanation, this time giving badminton as the example. When you read it, the sentences all flow clearly, integrating the examples into a coherent explanation.

Setting the structure, stepping back and facilitating extended writing and technical performances is a powerful TfW tool.

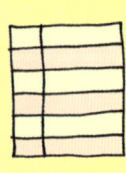

Boxing up allows students to structure their work so that they can plan how they will create a well-balanced, extended piece of text that flows and builds on the information and opinions that they have acquired. The image here shows simple boxing up to build student understanding of how to plan their writing, accompanied by useful sentence signposts to introduce the stages of the text. Initially, students may be shown examples but then they analyse them themselves. Once they have internalised how to structure their work, they can link it independently.

Boxing up also supports students in improving performance techniques since these require fine motor skills, playing with tactical astuteness, developing sequences of movements or training in a progressive and effective way.

A technique should be performed at a super-slow pace; it can be played out by the teacher or it can be a co-constructed performance between teacher and students. This process allows take-up time and internalisation of what is required to perform the technique correctly. Breaking down a technique is crucial for regular, accurate application and performance.

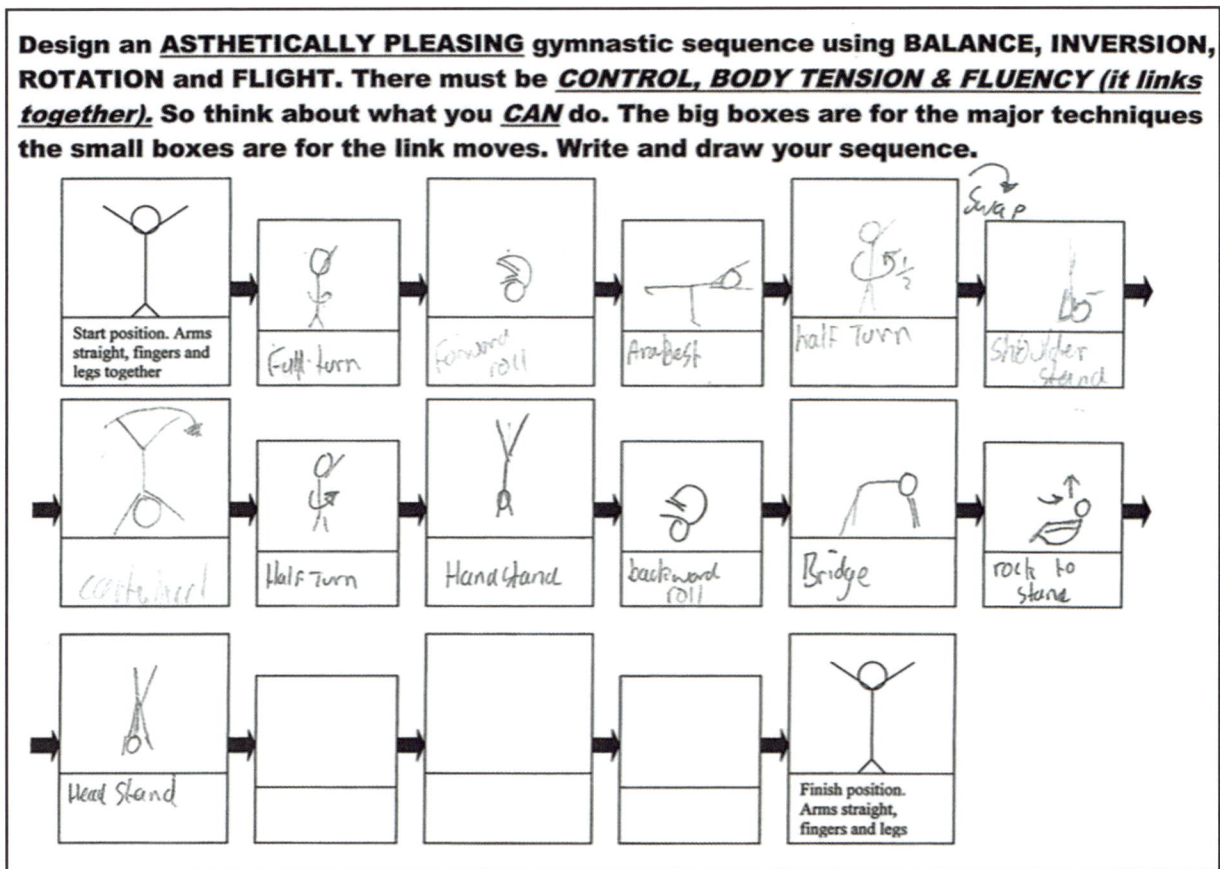

Boxed-up images of a technique (broken down into the base, the legs, the torso, the arms and the head) allow students time to reflect and work on one section of a technique at a time until they can be put together section by section. Using a boxing-up table for each section of the body, allows students to make notes of each part of the technique.

In the top boxed-up image above, the students are being asked to use the boxes to demonstrate a gymnastic sequence by writing and drawing it.

Feedback from students on this approach is very positive:

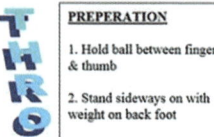

- *This has helped me by keeping track of my routine – it helped me remember. I could focus more on skills like my balance, body tension, and other things like that. It has also helped me by letting me look at all of my routine at once.*

- *Using the sheets has helped me put together my routine because it helped me visualise the different skills I had to do and in what order. This then led to my movements having a better flow to them. It also helped me remember what to do so I could make my sequence as clean and aesthetically pleasing as possible. It has also aided my drawing skills in a way, as I can put my own movements on to paper in a legible way.*

- *It has helped me because it isn't just words. It has pictures to help me remember what to do in the right order. Also, it has helped me with the small and larger boxes, which link moves and major techniques.*

- *It has helped me remember the routine and also to imagine what I am doing. It has also helped me to plan the routine easily.*

- *Because I can remember my moves and can be creative with how I design them. By choosing on your own, you know what you can do and what challenges you have.*

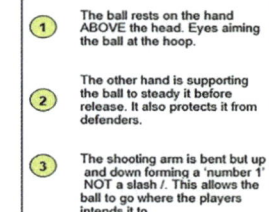

The basketball images have the sequence of each stage numbered beside them. In the set-shot image here, the numbered paragraphs link to the numbers on the pictures to help students understand what the images are illustrating.

Boxing up, linked to mime, enables the student to create their own gestures to support their ability to recall technical terms or explanations of the terms. These gestures also support text mapping of extended pieces of writing by using icons of the gestures.

As a result, students are more able to plan out, and then write, coherent descriptions of techniques that are multi-layered, including the effect of a technique on the performer, the equipment or an opponent.

Innovation of the technique – coaching & personal training

The ability to adapt moves the student towards mastery of a technique but, to nurture this, controlled situations need to be set. Conditioned games, steering plays or providing processing time allows the student the opportunity to take basic techniques and manipulate them to generate the outcome they are seeking. For instance, developing a scenario where an overarm throw needs to be performed on the run after picking the ball from the floor, or performing a set-shot whilst attempting to create space against a defender.

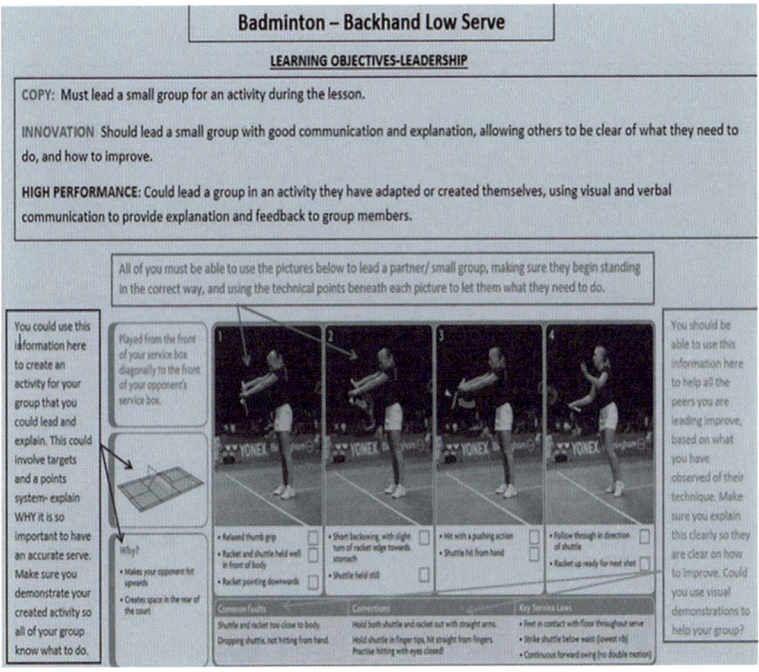

The key to this is moving from the copying (imitation) phase to the coaching phase (innovation). Once students have successfully boxed up the basic parts of a technique, they need to understand how and why to adapt their technique for a particular scenario. Once they have established this, they can start to work out the best way of doing it. The opportunity to attempt this physically is a real benefit before the teacher attempts to encourage the student to explain their modifications. Through shared discussions between peers, teacher designated thinking time and open questions, students are able to attempt explanations in the analytical written form phase-by-phase. Providing opportunities to adapt training drills provides an excellent way for students to challenge their understanding of techniques and tactical play. Allowing time to write up sequenced sessions, using modelled examples and the boxing-up structure, ensures students' explanations are detailed. This deepens understanding of what, how and why adapted techniques work. It also provides students the opportunity to develop leadership skills through planning and evaluative writing tasks. The activity pictured above provides guidance for students on creating an activity to improve the quality of a backhand low serve in badminton. Students are challenged to do this at 3 levels moving from imitation through innovation to independent high performance.

Independent application – *high performance & freestyling*

Gradually taking away the support of TfW, is like helping someone learn how to ride a bike. The teacher pushes the students with the TfW stabilisers on, they then take away some of the scaffolding, like removing one stabiliser and then both, whilst still giving a little balance but not over pushing the student and, before they know it, the student is off writing independently, moving forward finding their own way.

The crucial part is knowing when to take away the support and what aspects of TfW to withdraw at the appropriate time. There is no set rule; each student is different. Some students are more reliant on the physical structure to support their writing and others require the text-based scaffold. The key to high-performing independent writing is knowing when to start withdrawing the TfW approaches and which ones to take away on a personalised, student-by-student basis.

The end game is for the students NOT to need the support of TfW approaches as they perform, investigate and write-up their knowledge, findings and conclusions independently. Their high literacy performances come as second nature and are a natural reaction. They have internalised the processes. This is when improvisation or freestyling occurs. The addition of pressure in the physical application of sport (say through time limits or due to the addition of an opponent) is similar to the written form where difficulty can be increased (for example, through giving challenging scenarios where a student has to respond with evidenced-based justifications or use persuasive writing to convey their opinions about the most effective techniques or programmes).

For me, Talk for Writing hasn't been about re-inventing the wheel. It has been about refining a number of my approaches with clarity about how and why the strategies of support work. To this end, I have been able to predict more effectively the outcomes of the students' work and therefore plan further TfW strategies to help students overcome their personal barriers and realise they can rise to the challenges I set them.

The following videos show how Talk for Writing supports the teaching of PE:
- **Video clip 53**: Olly Harrison, when Head of PE at Slough & Eton, explaining how the TfW approach supports PE in KS3
- **Video clip 54**: Olly Harrison again (but this time with the help of some of his 6th form students) shows how the TfW process supports a Business Environment & Concepts PE assignment
- **Video clip 55**: Tom Mair, PE teacher at Briary Hill Primary, Northampton, demonstrates why the approach suits PE perfectly with a Y3 class
- **Video clip 56**: Tom Mair explains why the approach suits PE

Chapter 14: Talk for Writing in modern foreign languages

The TfW process was initially developed as a storytelling initiative to support young pupils in learning another language, so its oral-based approach naturally lends itself to teaching languages and many of its features have long been embedded in the teaching of MFL. This chapter illustrates how modern language departments from a range of schools have found TfW supportive, with a particular focus on work with a Year 7 class as they start to learn Spanish with their teacher Meredith Callaghan at The John of Gaunt School.

Laying the foundations: the cold task

Teachers of MFL are often confronted with a blank page when setting out to teach a new language to Year 7s. This was certainly the case for Meredith's Year 7 Spanish class. So, when planning the first unit, she concentrated on the words and phrases that would begin to enable the students to introduce themselves in Spanish and hold very simple conversations expressing basic information. There was, therefore, no role for a normal cold task since there was no prior knowledge. In its place, a very practical cold task was devised by introducing a sentence builder exercise for taking the register. This consisted of answers of various length to the question "¿Cómo estás?" (How are you?) to which the students responded while the register was being taken. This cold task allowed the teacher to see how at ease the students were with expressing themselves in the language. As the term developed, she was able to gauge the students' growing confidence and experimentation in an immediate manner as, by the end of the term, many were using complex sentences and asking questions in return.

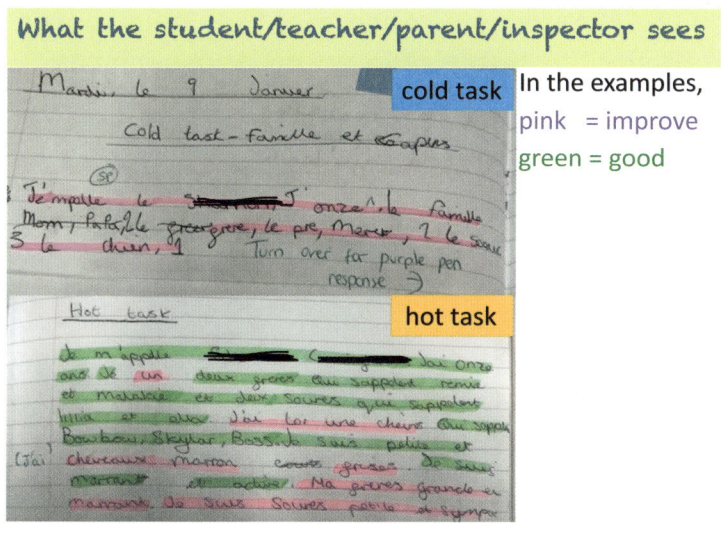

In the examples,
pink = improve
green = good

If the Year 7s had been continuing with a language that they had already started at primary school, a cold task like the one here would have been a good way to establish what the class already knew. Here a student in the spring term of Y8 at Royd's Hall, Huddersfield, had been set the cold task of writing about her friends and family. There is some sign of her knowing what to write but nothing has been written correctly. It has, therefore, all been highlighted in pink, (the colour the school was using to indicate problems). Whereas, by the hot task, the student and anyone else looking at the work, can clearly see progress as well as the areas that still need attention. Practically all of the first 5 lines have been highlighted in green for good, while pink dominates the last three lines here. The student proudly showed me her work; the progress she had made clearly gave her confidence and boosted her motivation.

KFL grids to frame learning

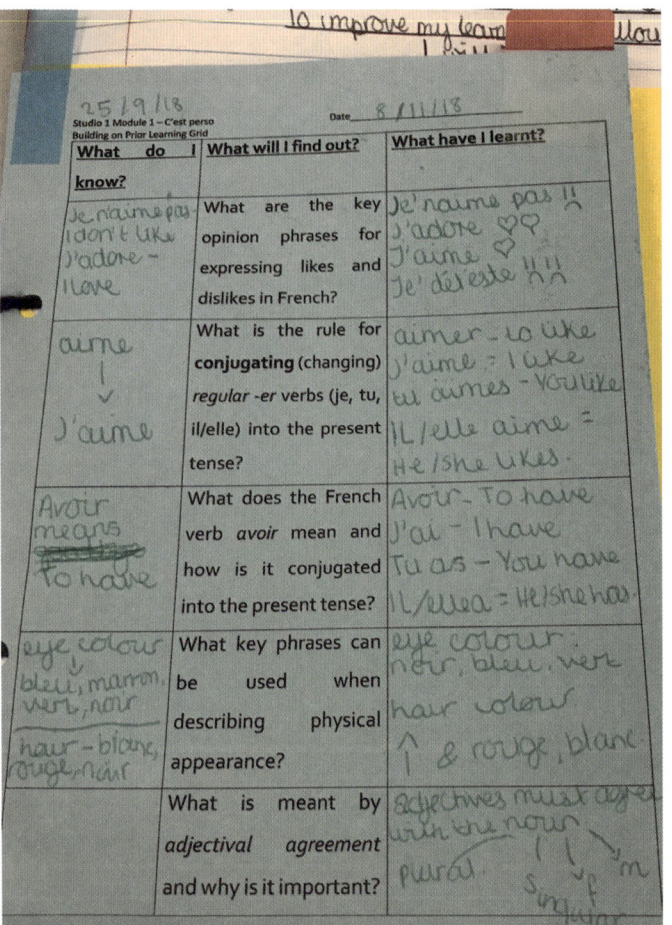

Another useful resource at the beginning of units, which can both act as a cold task and be used as a way of framing learning, is the *KWL grid* (What do I **know**/What do I want to **know**/What have I **learnt**) see page 15. If you look at the example here from Wexham School, Slough, you will see that it can act both as a form of cold task and, at the end of the unit as a form of hot task. At the opening of the unit, the students had written examples in French of the various phrases and grammatical features that the forthcoming unit was going to focus on that they already knew. They understood clearly which aspects to focus on because the teacher had already filled in the *What will I find out column?* in the middle of the grid. At the end of the unit, the student has written the features in French that they have learnt. At the end of this chapter, is an interesting example of how this approach can be developed across a whole unit.

The imitation stage (recall it)

Warming up key phrases

It's essential to find a good way to help the students quickly build confidence in their new language. So, as Meredith explains, vocabulary focuses around the words to express personal information, along with everyday useful words like dates, numbers and classroom vocabulary. These words, along with the verbs for *to have* (*tener*) and *to be* (*ser*), give the students a way into the language and enable them to apply basic ideas in a meaningful way. It allows the teacher to move from simple vocabulary (words for days and months) to the implementation of such in sentence form, for example, saying when your birthday is. The introduction of grammar is implicit, with the modelling of forms within the question and response routine. And, of course, YouTube simple videos in the target language are invaluable: the students can hear the vocabulary in songs, etc and jot down words they can identify from video clips.

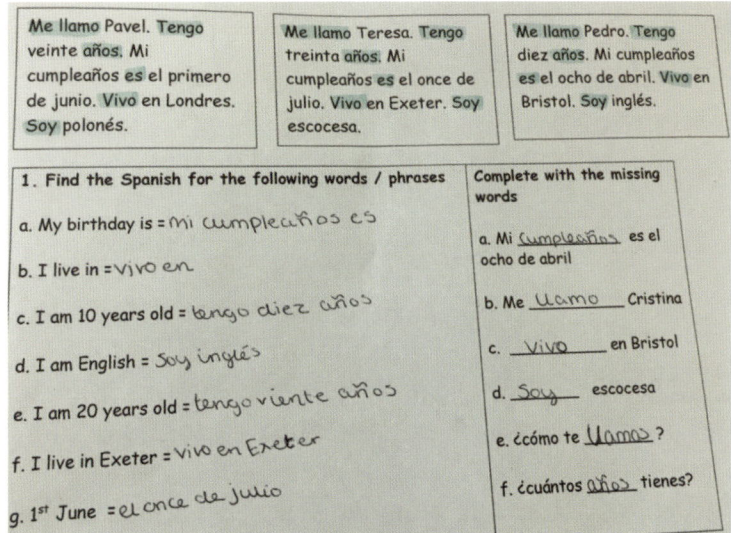

For all the key stages, Meredith uses *cold call* (randomly asking students to answer) and *pass the bear*. Students initiate the practice of vocabulary by throwing a soft toy around the room and responding to either teacher or peer questions. When learning the dates or numbers, they start with the traditional patterns (1 to 31, January to December) and, as they progress and students take on more responsibility for their learning, they begin to question each other with more randomness. Repetition in this way – particularly of questions regarding personal information which requires longer phrasal answers – allows students to internalise the inherent patterns in the language through listening and speaking. Internalising these individual words, then questions and responses before writing, is particularly beneficial. It also allows students to develop at different paces. Some will respond with one-word answers – "¿Cuántos años tienes?" (How old are you?) – "once" (11) – but, through listening and mimicking the answers of others, they will develop fuller answers – "¿Cuántos años tienes?" –"Tengo once años."(I am 11 years old).

As the words and phrases are warmed up before writing, students are more comfortable with the language. At the writing stage, the students colour code their work to distinguish questions and answers and more advanced aspects like verbs and identifying articles. By the time they write the words, as illustrated here, they understand what they mean and have begun to internalise the pattern of how they fit within sentences. This is generally more successful in getting the student to think about how and why the patterns emerge because they have internalised the tune. With teacher-directed questioning, a student can identify the patterns, which leads to a better understanding. The short reading passages are used to highlight a correct response to typical questions that you may be asked. Students work through the texts, usually highlighting key words and ideas that they will repeat or magpie for their own response.

These can also be used as a listening activity with the key information being swapped out and students being asked to identify what is different from what they are reading. With this type of exercise, you are providing the students with a model text that will equip them with the skills to replace and personalise information.

Text maps to support content

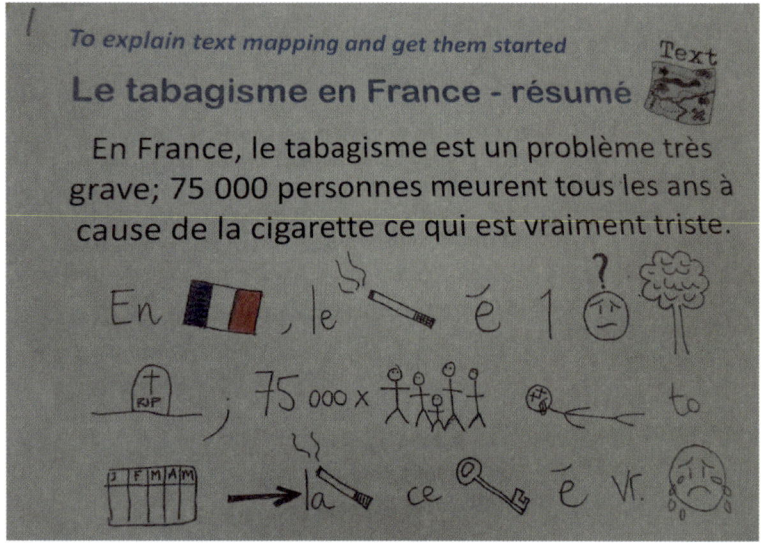

Text maps are not always straightforward in MFL as you want the images to help the students remember the words and phrases in the target language, not in English. If you look at the entertaining text map here from Rainham School for Girls, you will see that some of the images (the flag and the cigarette) just help you recall the content as usual but images like the key are to help you remember how the word *qui* sounds in French, rather than being related to its meaning. Very sensibly, *le* and *la* are written as words to help the students recall the gender of the words they relate to. Meredith explains that once Year 7 has developed their knowledge base, she often employs text maps for developing sentences. For example, when talking about school, they start with pictures of subjects, then add in images reflecting opinions (likes and dislikes) and further images for reasons. The students then swap maps and use these as a starting point for speaking or writing activities.

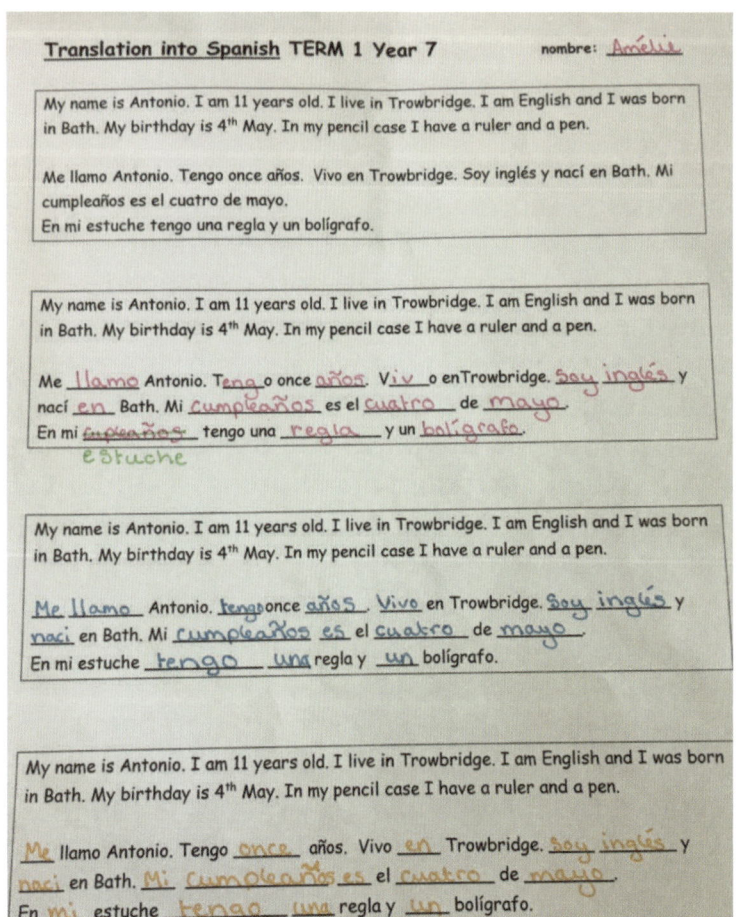

One teacher of German from Rainham told me the entertaining story of how text mapping using pictures to replicate the sound of the word rather than its meaning led to a breakthrough. One girl had been particularly insistent about not saying any words at all in German but, having discovered that the German for something to do with libraries sounded remarkably like *whore*, she delighted in a quick image to help her recall the sound. That was practically the first German word she had ever spoken, and after that she was willing to try and speak German.

Analysing the text

As mentioned above, the reading exercises are invaluable tools for having the students analyse the text for key vocabulary, and phrases. As students develop their language base, they can move on to identifying different parts and aspects of speech – pronouns, verbs, masculine and feminine, etc – which allows the students to internalise the patterns inherent in the language.

Meredith also uses exercises, such as the translation one pictured above, in order for students to reflect on different focuses within a sentence. By swapping out what the students have to replace after reading the short exemplar text, they have to reflect on the various parts of each sentence. This can either be done by folding over the paper and completing as a continuous activity or by cutting up the paper and supplying it to the student over a week as an ongoing activity.

The innovation stage

In modern languages, the innovation stage often focuses on getting the students to apply the language they are learning to different circumstances. Meredith's translation activity early on in Year 7 allows the students to examine different aspects of a text. At the beginning of each class, they have a low-stakes-quizzing activity to review learning. As the unit progresses, the quizzing develops in complexity. One of the most useful tasks can be to provide incorrect sentences and have the students identify mistakes. The students complete the activities on mini whiteboards which makes it easy for the teacher to confirm whether the answers are correct or not. (Mini whiteboards are a great resource for providing instant feedback, as this picture of a Spanish lesson shows.)

The next step is for a student to write up their response on the board and for the class to review and confirm it is correct or correct it. At some point, the activity will also be done in pairs and the students test each other. Self and peer testing often encourages deeper reflection as students try to make the mistakes harder and harder to spot. The picture here shows peer group marking in one

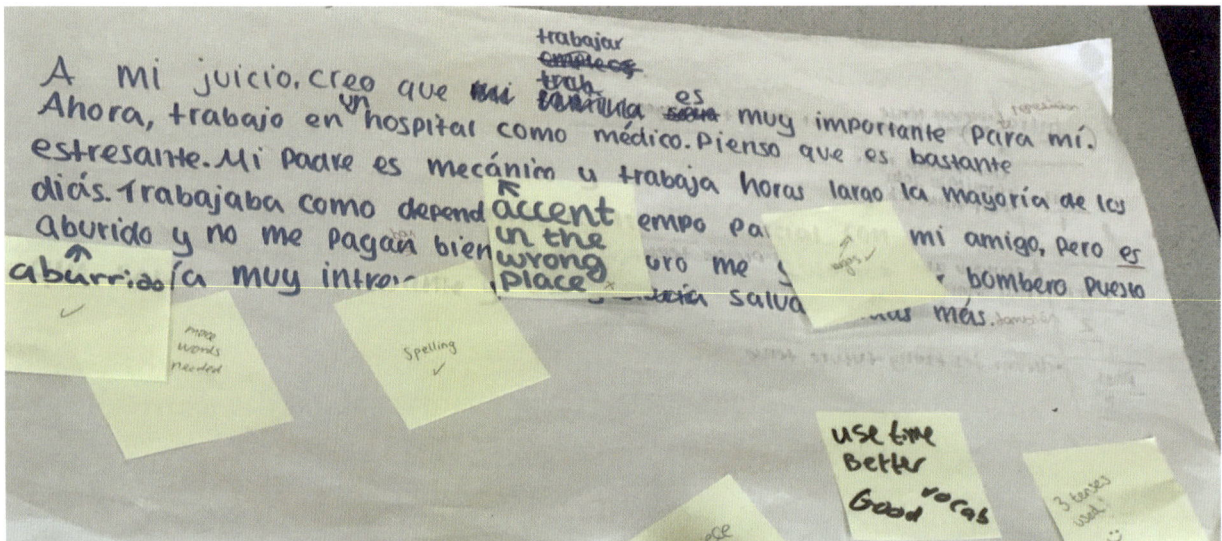

of Meredith's other classes where students are sharing their work and editing it together using Post-it notes to add corrections/suggestions to the text.

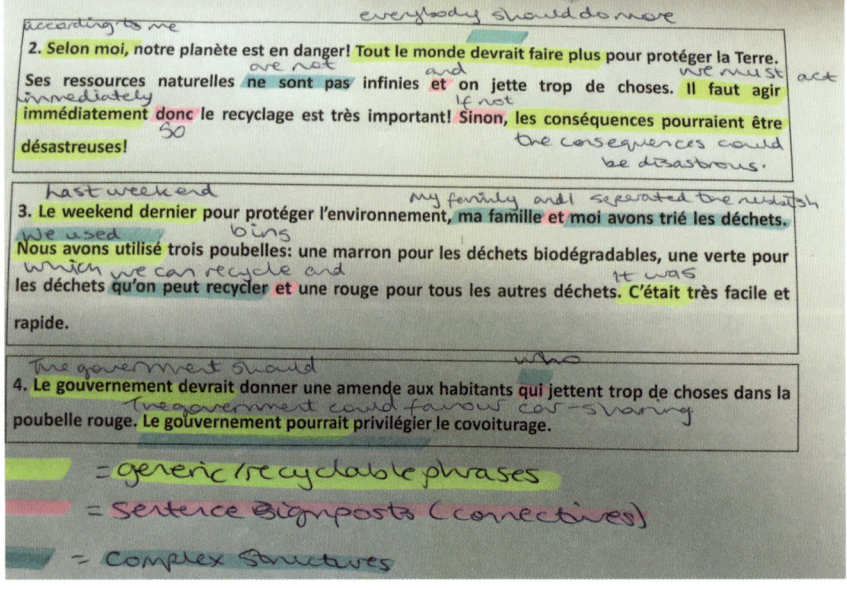

Shared writing is an essential teaching technique for teachers of any language so the students can see how to construct the sentences that are needed. This is excellently illustrated by French teacher Francoise Cusimano at Slough & Eton – **see video clip 57** – who uses shared writing to consolidate all the work she has done on linking phrases, alongside colour coding generic expressions, to help the students build up their linguistic skills in French and speak and write accurately, interestingly and coherently.

Attention to these essential linking phrases pays off – and it was an important point being made by Jade McGowan, the head of modern languages at Wexham School, when she shared what works with a cross-curricular CPD group (**see page 322**). The picture here shows the colour coding for generic/recyclable phrases (yellow) and sentence signposts (shocking pink) that is used throughout the school.

Turning a KFL grid into the structure of the whole unit

French KFL grid for formal letter writing

Appropriate for a formal letter	What I know to begin with (jot the appropriate phrases here in French)	What I now know (jot any additional appropriate phrases here in French)	What more do I need to know? (formal phrases in English you need but don't know in French)
Starting			
Thanking			
Ordering			
Sending			
Asking information			
Complaining			

Here is a useful adaptation of the KWL (What do I Know/What do I Want to know/What have I Learnt) approach mentioned at the beginning of this chapter, based on material developed by the MFL department at Ipswich High School. This shows how the grid formed the basis of the whole unit from cold to hot, with the students co-constructing their learning.

First, they adapted the approach to help develop the range of phrases students had at their command when writing a formal letter in French (a task suited for more advanced learners of French but the idea could be adapted and simplified to suit students at a much earlier stage). The first blank column is filled in at the beginning of the unit

Sorting activity to construct model text

Je vous remercie	de votre brochure que nous avons reçue la semaine dernière et que vous avez élaborée pour différents clients.
Mon patron m'a demandé	de vous écrire pour vous dire qu'il apprécie la qualité de vos produits.
Pourriez-vous	nous envoyer des échantillons et des prix pour les articles ménagers dans votre dépliant.
Nous aimerions aussi	savoir quel est le délai de livraison de vos marchandises.
Y-aura-t-il	une remise si nous achetons plus de cinquante articles.

as the cold task, the middle and final columns are filled in at the end of the unit as the hot task to indicate both the additional phrases they now know in French, and then the additional phrases they still need (but these have to be written in English since they don't yet know how to construct these expressions in French). This is a good way to build reflection on learning into the unit.

The next task introduces the model text that has been written to contain many key generic formal letter phrases. This is presented as a sorting activity. The students, in pairs, have to reconstruct the letter and check that it reads coherently by reading it aloud together. When sorted, the text will look like the slide above. In effect, they will have boxed it up.

This is followed by a task that focuses on the students internalising the key phrases they have just sorted. Here, they try to complete the phrases orally, when they no longer have access to the full text.

Completez les phrases:
a) Je vous remercie de ...
b) Mon patron m'a demandé de ...
c) Pourriez-vous
d) Nous aimerions aussi savoir ...
e) Y-aura-t-il

Text loop dominoes

	Madame	vous remercie	de votre brochure que
nous avons reçue	la semaine dernière	et que vous avez élaborée	pour différents clients.
Mon patron	m'a demandé	de vous écrire	pour vous dire qu'il apprécie
la qualité de vos produits.	Pourriez-vous	nous envoyer des échantillons	et des prix
pour	les articles ménagers	dans votre dépliant.	Nous aimerions aussi
savoir quel est le délai	de livraison	de vos marchandises.	Y-aura-t-il
une remise	si nous achetons	plus de	cinquante articles?
Dans l'attente	de votre lettre	Salutations distinguées.	

Then, to further help them internalise the correct language, they construct the letter again, in pairs, but this time using text loop dominoes that break the text down into smaller chunks of meaning, thus making the sorting task more challenging.

Once complete, they read the text together and then place all the dominoes in a pile in the correct order and see if, starting with the first domino *Madame,* they can then recall the phrase that would follow in a formal letter. They can check if they are correct by turning to the next domino. This would then lead them to the domino that ends with the phrase *de votre brochure que, etc.*

Suitable text sorting game

Appropriate for formal letter	Not appropriate for formal letter
Je vous remercie de	Mercie de ta lettre
Monsieur	Cher monsieur
Nous voudrions commander	Je veux avoir
Je vous prie d'agréer monsieur l'assurance de mes	Grosses bises
Nous vous prions de trouver ci-joint	Un grand merci pour
Suite à votre demande	Je t'envoie
Ne hésitez pas à	
Veuillez trouver ci-joint	
Nous vous serions reconnaissants de	Je veux recevoir

All languages have formal and informal expressions and many languages, like French, have a formal and an informal version of *you*. To reinforce their understanding of formal and informal phrases, the students, in pairs, are then asked to sort the following phrases into those suitable for a formal letter and those that would be inappropriate. This also has the advantage of introducing some new formal phrases to help extend the students' use of language.

The students are then asked on their own, as their hot task, to write a formal letter using the phrases they have been focusing on. They then share their letters with their partner and, together, check if they are appropriate and correct.

The initial model text could then be displayed to help with checking:

> *Madame,*
>
> *Je vous remercie de votre brochure que nous avons reçue la semaine dernière et que vous avez élaborée pour différents clients.*
>
> *Mon patron m'a demandé de vous écrire pour vous dire qu'il apprécie la qualité de vos produits. Pourriez-vous nous envoyer des échantillons et des prix pour les articles ménagers dans votre dépliant.*
>
> *Nous aimerions aussi savoir quel est le délai de livraison de vos marchandises. Y-aura-t-il une remise si nous achetons plus de cinquante articles?*
>
> *Dans l'attente de votre lettre,*
>
> *Salutations distinguées.*

Now the students can return to their KWL grid and reflect on what they have learnt, adding the formal letter phrases they are now familiar with as well as thinking of some formal phrases that they only know in English, but which it would be useful to know in French.

This unit very much relies on a series of sorting games for the students to engage in which are perfect for encouraging students to discuss and use the target language. The more learning is presented as a challenging game, through which the students co-construct their learning, the more engaging it is and, as long as the games focus on internalising things that are important for the subject, they are an excellent resource to build up.

www.ilanguages.co.uk is a useful website for languages teachers in primary and secondary schools. It has permission to use the TfW approach. These two articles from the TfW website tell you a little more including support for primary schools with no foreign language expertise:

www.talk4writing.co.uk/wp-content/uploads/2019/03/Flying-Start-iLanguages.pdf

www.talk4writing.co.uk/wp-content/uploads/2019/03/Teaching-languages-through-ilanguages-TfW.pdf

Chapter 15: Talk for Writing in computer science

John Roberts, computer science teacher at The John of Gaunt School, explains how the Talk for Writing approach is helping students in KS3 and 4 make significant progress, alongside making them good digital citizens.

In 2014, the national curriculum was reformed by the government moving from ICT (information, communication, technology) to a greater emphasis on computer science. A question asked every year by parents and students alike is, "What is the difference?" Just in case you were asking yourself the same question, the answer is that ICT is the skills and knowledge of how to use computer systems and software to communicate with an audience by using software that already exists. Computer science, on the other hand, is the use of computational thinking (problem solving) to create new software that meets the needs of an ever-changing landscape of technological advances, as well as understanding how aspects of computer systems work and how to use them safely.

To develop a clear understanding of how the new *Computer Science National Curriculum* would be implemented, the *Computing At Schools Community* developed specific progression pathways which would help with the planning of topics to help ensure that teachers knew what skills and knowledge students should be able to develop at different stages of their school lives. The pathways were identified as Algorithms, Programming and Development, Data and Data Representation, Hardware and Processing, Communication and Networks, and Information Technology. Units of work often cover aspects of more than one pathway.

One of the key issues facing secondary computer science teachers is the differences that primary feeder schools have in their own deployment of the national curriculum, due to factors like staff knowledge and confidence in delivering the different pathways, the IT systems and software available to be used and, finally, the amount of time they are willing to dedicate to the subject. The Year 7 *E-Safety Unit* focused on here is one that students are introduced to and was developed to aid in identifying the different experiences that students would have been exposed to. It also illustrates clearly how the TFW process helps to improve pupil performance. In this unit, lessons help the students understand what cyberbullying is and know the different ways to report it, as well as looking at the cultural aspect of computer use in everyday life and how, by using the SMART acronym (Safe, Meeting, Accepting, Reliable and Tell), we can all be encouraged to be good digizens (digital citizens).

In Year 7, students only have one 60-minute lesson of computer science a week which adds up to 40 hours of lessons per academic year. In each of those lessons, students work simultaneously on an assessment book which contains their TfW tasks and a Word document to expand their understanding of different scenarios.

Laying the foundations

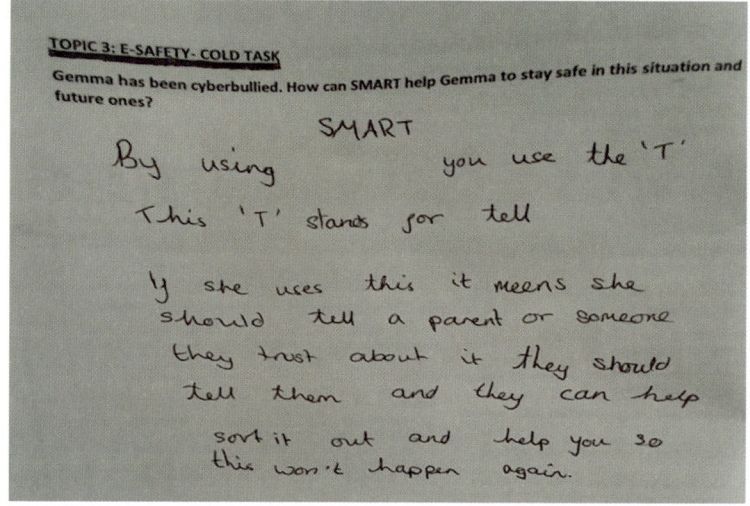

To begin to understand what the students already know on a topic, we include a cold task in the first lesson, as pictured here. This is a direct copy of what will be their assessed hot task at the end of the 7-week unit. This allows both staff and students to see how much progress a student can make within 6 taught lessons on a specific topic. This works especially well with the students as each lesson we can refer back to their original cold task and what we hope to achieve by the end-of-unit hot task. In each lesson, we also refer back to the specific aspects that they could use to demonstrate their understanding. This helps with students who may be anxious about assessments because staff, when delivering the cold task, explain to the students that they are not being assessed on that piece of work, but rather they are only required to put down anything that they might know about a topic or an exercise. In this unit, both the cold and the hot task is to create a letter to a student who has been cyberbullied at school.

During this unit, the students have to be able to understand all of these aspects: the difference between bullying and cyberbullying; what the advice is for each of the acronym letters of SMART; what a *digizen* is; what rules to follow when setting out a letter, including words like *recipient* and *text alignment*, and how to spell the associated words like *sincerely*. For the students to have made progress and have a feeling of success, they need not just to verbalise the definitions of the SMART acronym and layout the foundations of what a letter should look like but also be able to apply them effectively to an external setting/scenario.

The imitation stage – helping students recall it

Once the cold task has enabled students to demonstrate their previous knowledge, they are guided through 6 lessons. The first 5 introduce students to each one of the letters of the SMART acronym in turn, including the definition for each word represented, followed by tasks to help warm up the words and attach them to a real-world example.

To help introduce the words focused on, students are asked to fill in their never-heard-the-word grid. This is a really good way to help them identify that, although they may know words from other subjects, sometimes their meanings are not the same as they are in computer science. Once students have been given the opportunity to attempt their own version of the new key term, we give them the technical vocabulary that they are expected to use and ask them to fill in the actual meaning on the grid. Next, we warm up the words for each lesson via a few different strategies. We are not really wanting the students to be able to regurgitate the term, but rather to gain an understanding of how it is an important fact to remember, and that it needs to be considered for different scenarios. Therefore, students are either shown videos of those key terms being used or they are shown how it can be linked to specific situations. For example, when we deliver the lesson on *Meeting,* we use the BBC video *Caught in the Web,* which tells the story of an 11-year old girl called Lost Princess who started an online friendship and agreed to meet a *boy* at a concert. But when she arrived, the girl was approached by an old man who had been lying about who he was. To help internalise this, students are asked to answer some questions on what they had seen and how the definition of *Meeting* from the SMART acronym would be helpful. They can write their answers in full sentences or via the use of text mapping by collecting pictures from the internet to put together in their Word document. Before students attempt to answer these questions, a class discussion takes place identifying how the definition they wrote in their NHTW grid applies to the story of *Lost Princess*.

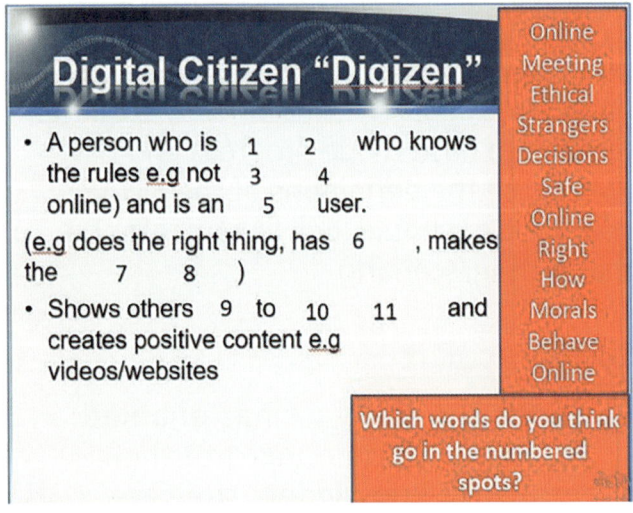

Another tactic used to help warm up the words is to use the definition as part of a missing words task. We begin by showing students a paragraph with some of the key components of the paragraph missing (as pictured on the left). We ask students to explain what each of the words means in the list of missing words before allowing them to attempt to put them into the correct location. This is a really useful task which allows you to drill down into sentence structure and how the words sound, because you are constantly reading them out aloud.

Another way in which we warm up the words is to use multiple-choice, low-stakes quizzes at the beginning of every lesson. As part of their homework, all students are given a Knowledge Organiser which has the definitions of all the key terms for that unit. Each question in the quiz references the student to a definition and asks them to identify which key term that belongs to. As the tests are completed on the computer using Microsoft Forms, the student can gain instant feedback on which ones they got right and which ones they got wrong, helping them to solidify in their heads the pattern of the definition against the key word.

> **TOPIC 3 E-SAFETY: BOXING UP. THE PLAN FOR HELPING GEMMA MANDELSON:**
> After reading the "Fakebook" conversations please complete this:
>
> **What is the JOG school address?**
> The John of Gaunt school   Wingfield road
> Trowbridge BA14 9EH
> *each item on a single line*   *Date under address*
>
> **Who started it all? How do it start?**
> Sandy Newman — posted online saying cheated on a test.
> Dear Gemma...... I am writing to you...
>
> **Who made it worse? How?**
> Gemma — for retaliating   Keiran — spreading rumors
> Ryan — for giving out number   Bailey — wanting to fight
>
> **Do you think Gemma did the right thing online?**
> No — retaliating
>
> **How is Gemma being bullied?** She is being cyberbullied by social media and text message
>
> **How can SMART help Gemma? What letters are the most important and give detail.**
> S afe — set account to private
> M eet — don't go and meet to fight
> A ccept — accepting friends you don't know
> R eliable — don't believe everything you read
> T ell — she should tell her parents
>
> **Letter ending** conclusion of what you said
> Yours sincerely Kaitlin

The lesson before students complete the hot task is where TFW really helps teachers to build the students' confidence as well as to recap any missing knowledge or misconceptions of the key vocabulary. The lesson is dedicated to boxing up how they can answer the original question and lay it out in a more formal style through the use of a letter. This lesson is a great way of having a two-way discussion by prompting with questions the key aspects of the type of answer you want them to construct. In this example, we have prompted the students with key questions on what information will be needed for the assessment at the end of the unit. This enables the teacher to cold-call questions to the students to help fill in each section. The teacher can then see if students have retained previous knowledge by asking them to explain what they would put against the prompt questions for each section of the letter. Alongside this, students are supported by a template on the rules of how to set a letter out.

The independent-application stage

In this final lesson of the unit, students apply their learning from the previous six lessons. Students are given the opportunity to verbalise all of the language covered over the previous lessons. They are asked to discuss with their partner what the layout of their letter should look like and what aspects of all the previous content they think is appropriate to mention within their letter. This is followed by a class recap of the original issues that Gemma, the recipient of the letter, has been facing. Once students have been given the chance to discuss any further ideas, they are given access to the mark scheme that they will be assessed from and they then complete the assessment.

As you can see from the example below, the difference in progress from the cold task to the hot task from the same student, tackling the same question following only 6 hours of teaching, is exceptional. The student has not only been able to format their letter correctly, but they have also managed to gain marks by talking about the main aspects of the SMART acronym that apply

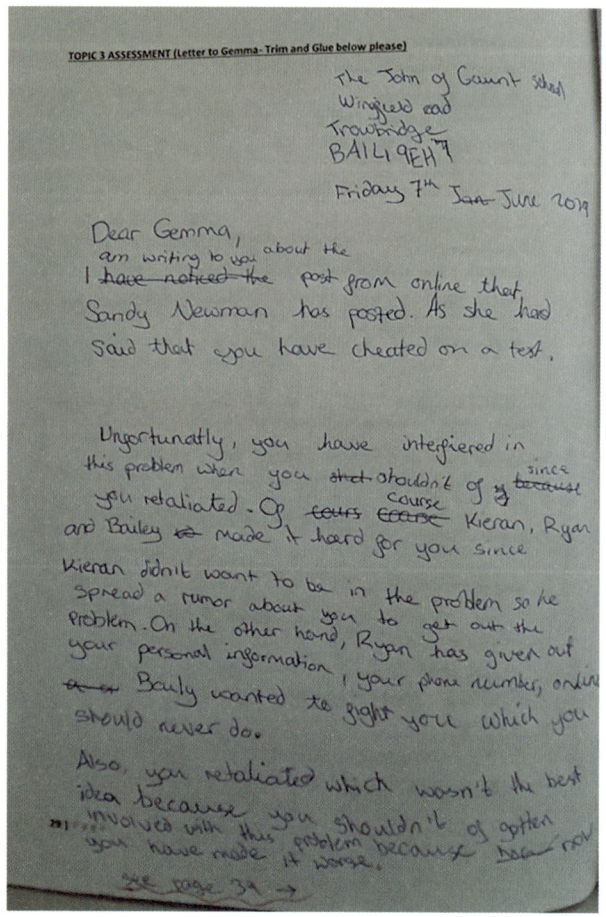
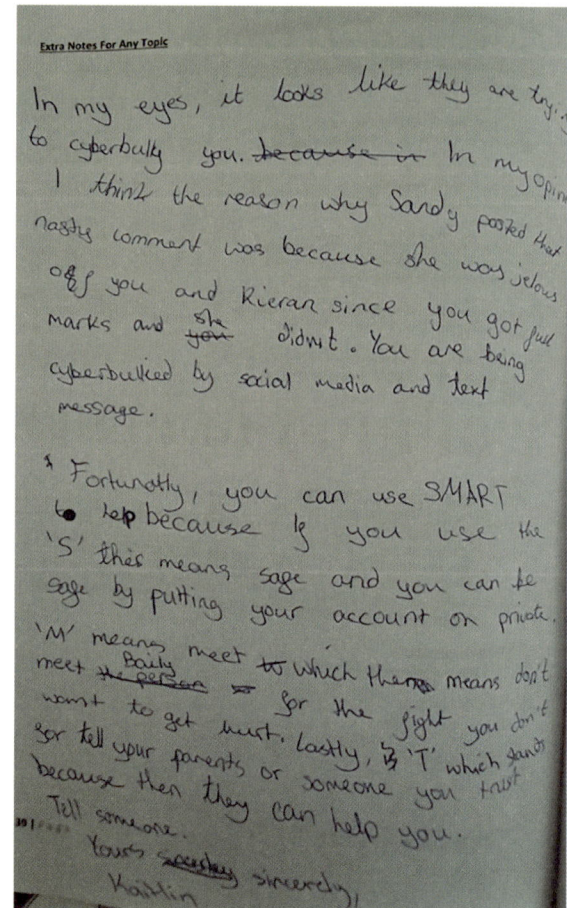

to the scenario. Moreover, they have spoken about their knowledge with confidence and have, therefore, been able to write it down coherently.

If there was more time in the curriculum, one way that we would be looking to help the students embed their learning and to show true independence, would be to use a mastery task. For example, we could introduce the students to another scenario like *gaming addiction* and ask them to write a letter to parents discussing the use of the SMART acronym to help their children ensure that they do not become victims of it.

The use of the TfW process has enabled Year 7 students, who have all arrived with varying levels of literacy and computer science knowledge, to tackle an assessment confidently and make rapid progress.

How Talk for Writing helps Year 10 students understand creative iMedia

With the National Curriculum reforms in 2014, there have been many different courses on offer at Key Stage 4 covering both ICT and computer science strands. Both strands are different with very specific skills required to complete them. Creative iMedia is currently one of the more popular courses. It is a Level 1/2 qualification that has 3 controlled assessment units and 1 exam unit. Due to the JCQ (Joint Council for Qualifications) rules on controlled assessments and the requirements of the course on plagiarism, students are not allowed to be given templates to follow and are required to develop their own style of evidence.

One area that TfW really does help with, though, is in developing understanding of how to answer exam-style questions. The exam is made up of questions based on pre-production documents meaning that the student will be expected to face questions like, "Define what a script is", or "Draw a visualisation diagram", or "Evaluate the good and not so good features of a mood board" (mood boards communicate a designer's vision at the start of a project). Here, TfW strategies are a great way of ensuring students remember key definitions and build up techniques through analysing model answers.

Many of the topics within the exam require the students to be able to explain the definitions of key planning documents and their benefits and limitations as well as creating example documents from scenarios. These include documents like mood boards, mind maps, scripts and storyboards.

When teaching each of the pre-production documents, TfW strategies work really well to introduce each of the different documents and to allow staff the time to understand what the students already know, introduce the new terminology and warm up the words, while modelling and using the language throughout practice tasks over and over again.

	Heard Before	(What I think it is)	The definition	Draw the definition
Target Audience	✓		Target audience is the person or group of people that the final product will be aimed towards	target people
Mood board		✓ I heard of it A mood map	A mood board is a visual tool that is used to help generate ideas for a product.	
Asset		Something you need to complete	Things that are necessary for product completion	
Visualise	✓		a plan for the product designer	

We start with a NHTW grid like the one pictured here to see what the students understand and to allow them to gain their first experience of the key terms they will need for the type of exam question we are looking at. The students working on Creative iMedia tend to have a lower reading age than their chronological age and are given a scribe during exams. Text mapping the definitions is a really good way of helping the students remember the definitions without worrying about the spelling. The example above shows how one lower-attaining student has used the grid and text mapping as a tool to help remember key words.

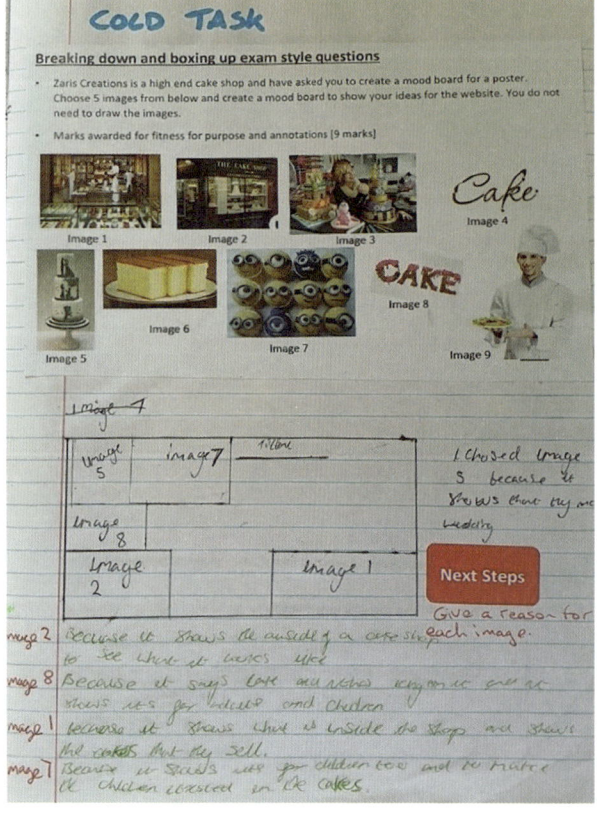

Once students have been introduced to the key terminology, they are issued a cold task to see what they can glean from the exam language and the definitions that they have begun to understand. The cold task below demonstrates students being asked to identify the correct images to use to represent a mood board. One really good aspect of this cold task is that the students are able to highlight aspects of the exam language, as part of the task. This allows the teacher to see what issues each individual student would have with similar questions. As can be seen by the next-steps feedback given by the teacher, the student has been asked to identify a reason for selecting the images they chose.

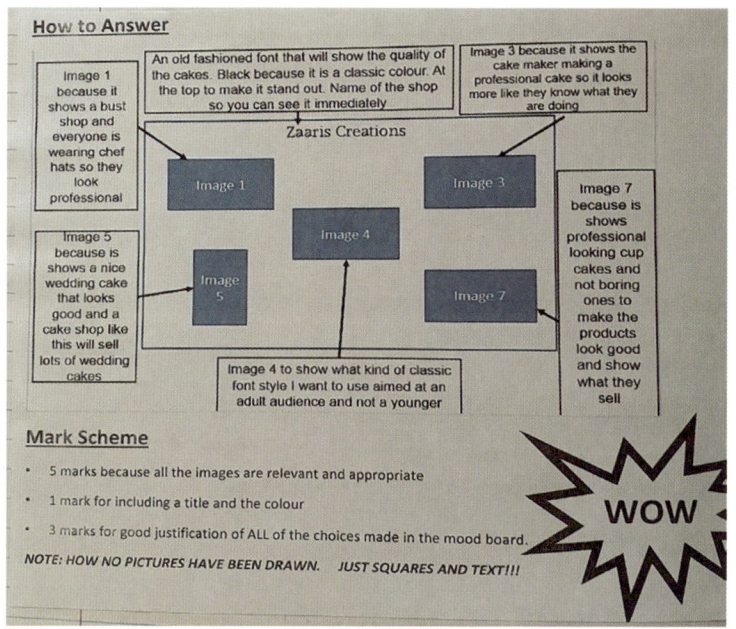

Once the teacher has had a chance to see the strengths and weaknesses of each student, we can move on to the imitation stage. Here, a model answer is shared with the students and they are helped to break down the model answer. Using the cold task as a recap, students are shown how they can get higher marks. This allows the students to understand the content of the exam language and develop a clear understanding of the structure that they can use by boxing up an answer on developing a mood board.

The innovation stage

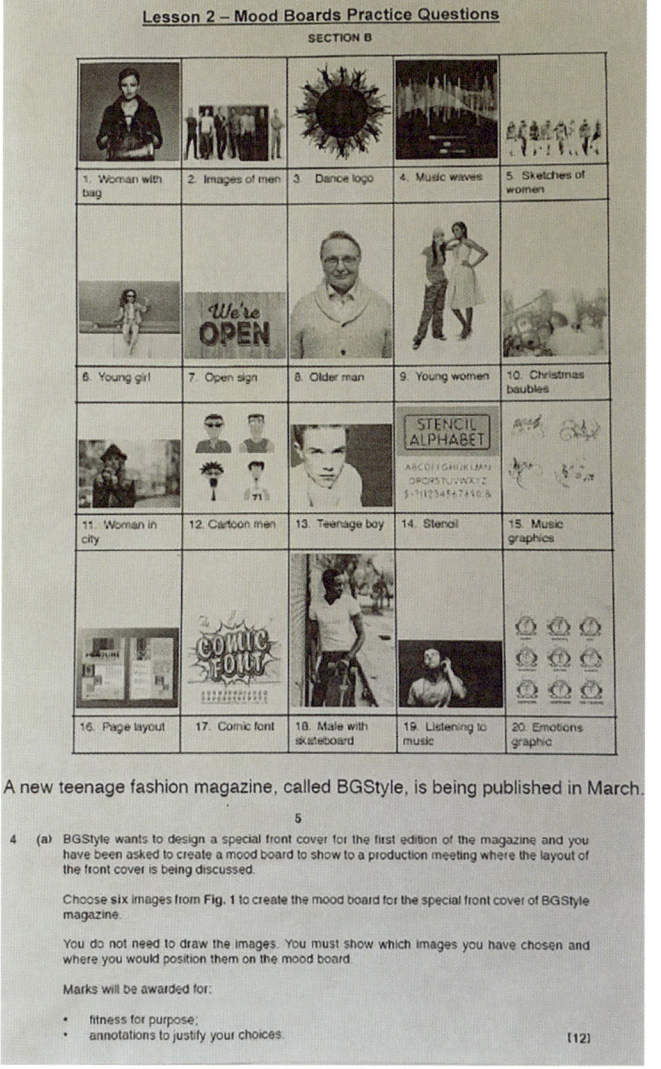

The innovation stage gives students the opportunity to do shared planning, with the teacher randomly selecting students to contribute ideas about how to answer a practice question that requires similar skills. The teacher introduces the question and asks the students to identify on a mini whiteboard what are the key points the question is asking, like, *Who is the target audience of the product? What theme should the images have?* A reminder of the model answer from the previous lesson is displayed to support discussion of what layout will best answer the question. This is followed by discussion on what language to use to best explain the decisions they have made. Students are then given time to apply their understanding by completing the question as an independent task. Here, you can see the sort of question asked and how a student answered it.

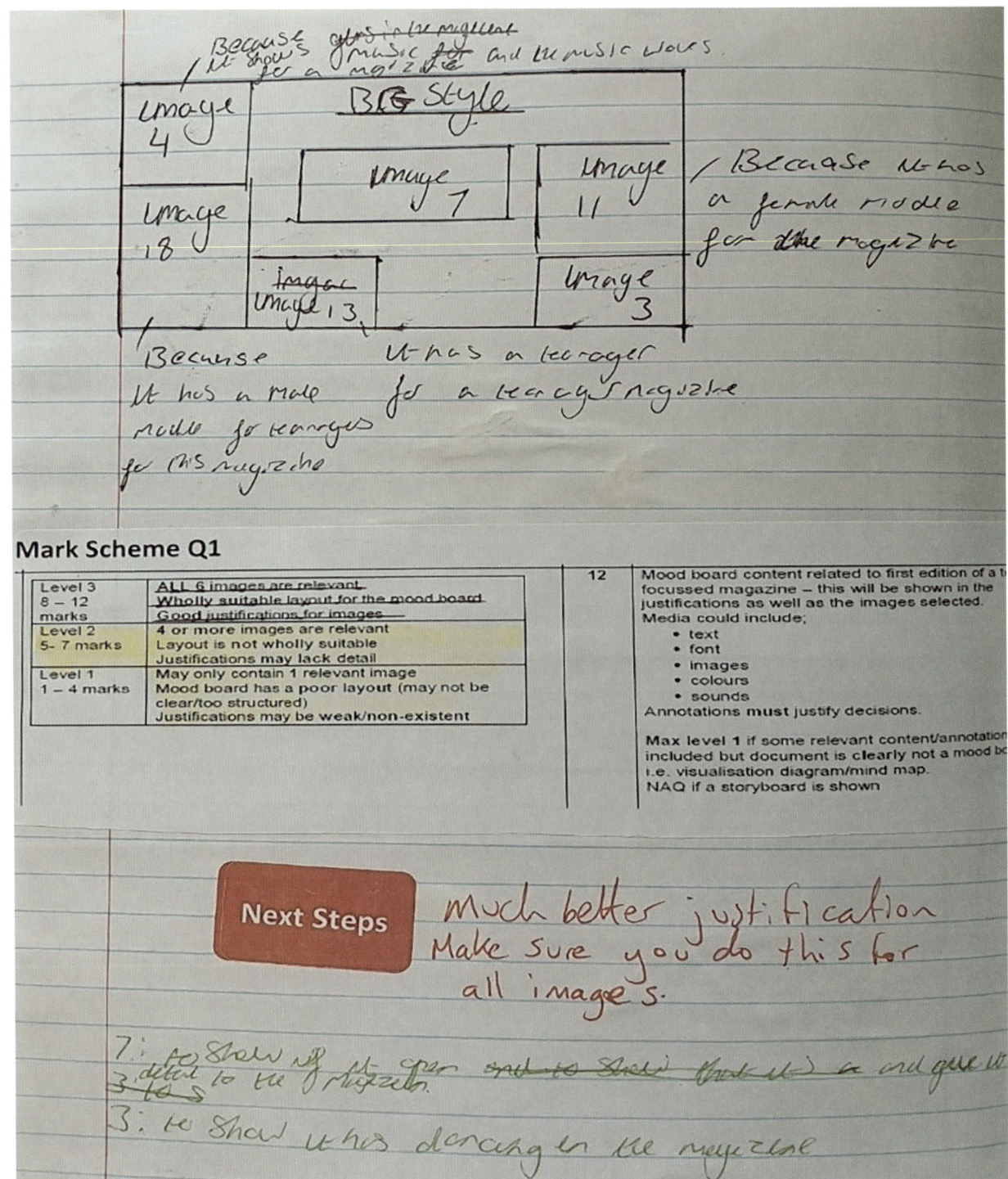

The independent application stage

This leads nicely into the independent application stage as students are again given feedback related to the mark scheme plus comments from the teacher that highlight where they missed out on marks. Here, you can see the student has attempted to make improvements (underneath the teacher's comment) to get into the habit of completing a full answer. During the response-to-marking lesson, students will be shown an example of the question from the mark scheme highlighting where all the marks could be found. During this stage, the teacher will constantly be warming up the words by discussing different key terms and asking students to identify where they are found within the practice question.

Finally, the students are introduced to their hot task, a final exam question that pulls all of the previous practice together to help demonstrate their progress. As you can see from the hot task below, the student has taken on all the elements of how to create a mood board and applied them appropriately which has enabled them to be awarded top marks, gaining a Level 3 mark-band criterion. The degree of progress shown from the cold task to hot is incredible as the student has demonstrated independently how to lay out their answer, what language to use to justify the images they have chosen and has, therefore, met all the requirements for the top mark band. This, of course, greatly increases confidence for students and teachers alike.

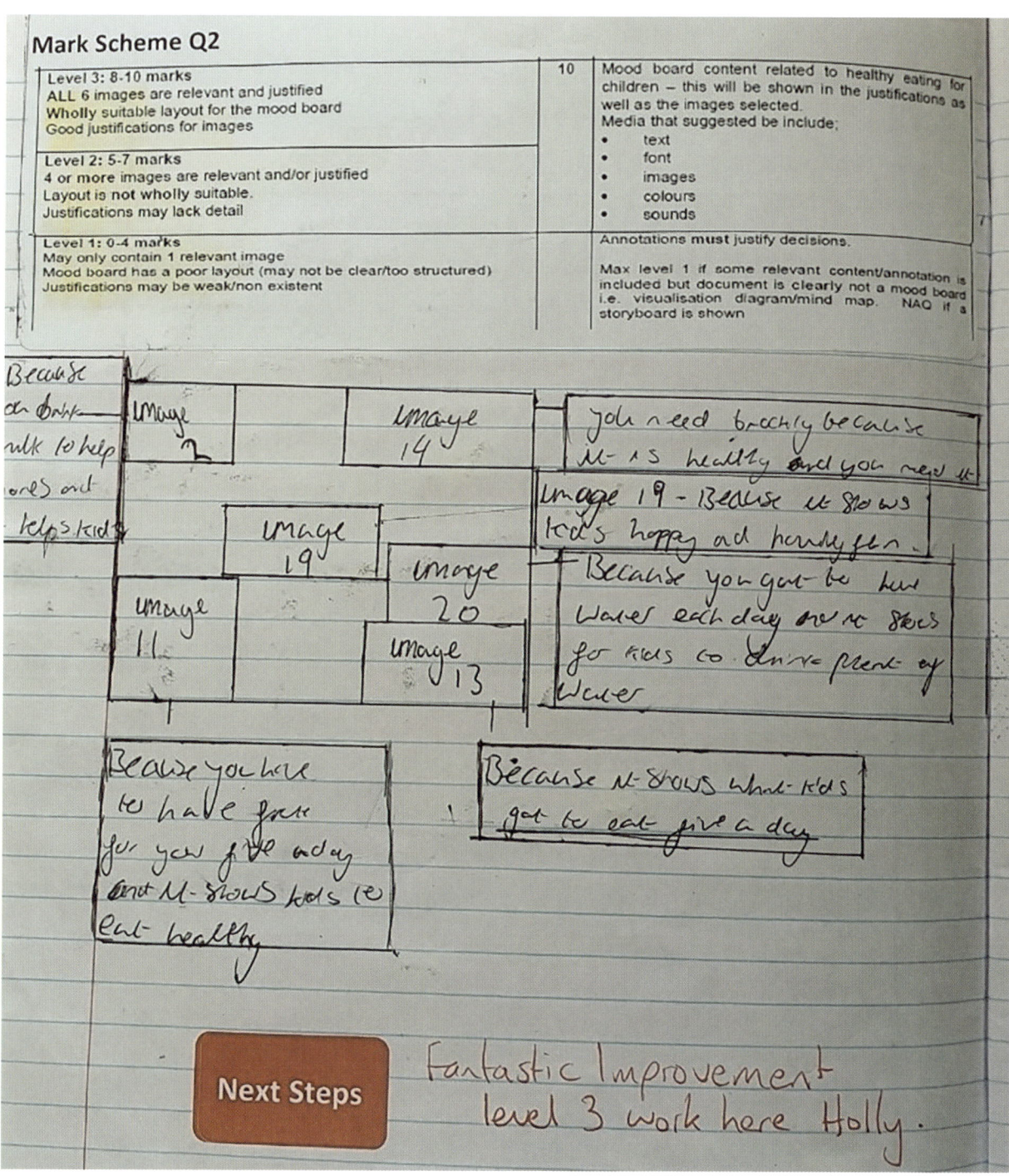

Chapter 16a: Talk for Writing in art is revolutionary

The Talk for Writing team at Briar Hill Primary School in Northampton explain how the Talk for Writing approach has revolutionised the way art is taught, alongside the quality of the art the children produce.

Since our initial training on Talk for Writing in 2016, we knew it was something that would transform our teaching forever. Staff valued and enjoyed teaching using the approach and, as a result, it became integral to the culture and core teaching methodology at Briar Hill. The simplicity and the power of its strategies have contributed to the upward trend of our end-of-key-stage outcomes. We naturally experimented with Talk for Writing across the curriculum, focusing on science, maths, RE, humanities and art.

This chapter focuses on how the Talk for Writing approach can be mirrored in art, using the '3 Is' – imitation, innovation and independent application, to structure planning. The impact of teaching art this way, for pupil outcomes and staff development alike, has been nothing short of exceptional.

Laying the foundations: curriculum planning and preparation

	Term 1	Term 2	Term 3	Term 4	Term 5	Term 6
N	Pattern	Colour and Texture	Lines	Junk Modelling	Collage	Sculpture
R	Jackson Pollack		Andy Goldsworthy		Wassily Kandinsky	
1			Line, colour, shape, collage, Modernist, Paul Klee		Line, colour, shape, watercolours, sewing surrealism, Joan Miro	
2			Self-portrait, line, cubism, oil pastels, Pablo Picasso		Life drawing, portrait, scale, pop art, Keith Haring	
3			Sculpture, public art, life drawing, clay, Antony Gormley		Line, shading, landscape, architecture, Stephen Wiltshire	
4			Oil pastel, blending, landscape, perspective, Van Gogh		Modernism, fauvism, collage, stitches. Henri Matisse	
5			William Morris, Arts and crafts, print making, watercolours, tracing		Modernism, colour theory, oil pastels, Theo van Doesburg	
6			Islamic art, calligraphy, tessellation, clay		Renaissance, life drawing, sketching, Leonardo Di Vinci	

The planning of our art curriculum took time to refine. We wanted to ensure that there was clear year-on-year progression, including a sharp focus on developing pupils' proficiency in drawing, painting, colour theory, shade and sculpture. This would equip pupils with the knowledge and skills to experiment, invent and create their own works of art, craft and design. Alongside these skills, we knew that we had to develop pupils' knowledge of a range of artists and designs, their critical awareness and their ability to critique their own work as well as the work of others. Ultimately, the artists chosen were selected to provide pupils with positive role models that they could aspire to emulate, as well as developing their understanding of their own and others' cultural heritages. Therefore, our long-term overview (a section of which is pictured above) focuses on the skills and the artists studied across the year for all year groups from nursery to Year 6. This curriculum is delivered through two art units per class each year.

Warming up the skills

The skills have become our starting point. Here we provide direct modelling, often in small steps, to ensure that all children are clear on how to improve. This stage enables ongoing assessment for learning and reviewing practice to ensure all children secure the desired artistic skill. At this stage, teachers need to identify pupils who may require additional guidance before the imitation stage. This picture shows one of our Year 5 skills lessons, where the children used watercolour to mix colour and create shade and tone. This was used to refer to when they needed to create colours in order to imitate the work of William Morris.

Warming up the history of art

As part of the preparation stage, pupils also develop their critical awareness through art history lessons. These are taught alongside the practical lessons and focus on the same artist or art movement that is being studied. The art history lessons also follow the Talk for Writing methodology, which often includes:

- teaching vocabulary explicitly, linked to the artist and the techniques focused on
- facilitating booktalk-style discussions to gather the children's initial responses to a piece of art
- text mapping to internalise procedures or key information about the style of the art/artist
- providing model texts, about the artist's life, or model texts for the analysis of pieces of art
- boxing up to help structure analysis of art or critical responses to their own and others' art
- co-constructing toolkits for analysing art/how to be a good artist.

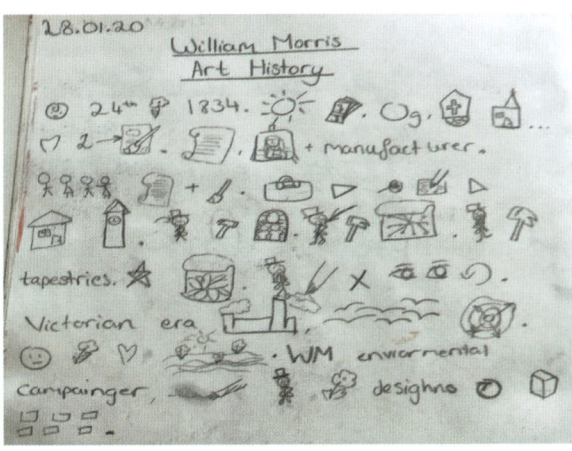

When we started teaching in this way, it became increasingly apparent that the context of the style of art and the artist's life was something that added a richness to the teaching. Pupils had a deeper understanding of why pieces of art were created in a particular style and not in another. It also put the previous 'skills lesson' into context as pupils were able to identify techniques in artwork. Text mapping helped them recall the key information. **Video clip 58** shows Year 5 teacher Katie Cross discussing William Morris's use of colour in his designs.

What a Talk for Writing unit looks like in art

In the picture below of a year 5 classroom art display, you can see how the whole process develops over a unit. It begins with the practising of skills through to the application of skills in the imitation stage, where pupils imitate artists' work (in this example, the work of Theo Van Doesburg – The Dance, 1917 – and his use of primary, secondary and tertiary colours). Then, we move on to the innovation stage, where other artwork is observed and used to influence their innovations. The final stage is where the children independently create their own art using the skills and knowledge they have obtained. This process is explained in more detail below.

The imitation stage – recreating a piece of art

Throughout the imitation stage, in the practical lessons, pupils are tasked with recreating a piece of art from the artist studied, focusing on the central skill or technique for that unit. Again, small steps, guided groups and modelling are used as the key teaching strategies to ensure that the model is imitated accurately. This enables the teacher to address any areas of difficulty and suggest how pupils might overcome them. This stage is another opportunity to identify and work with pupils who need further guidance and support. When selecting the piece of art, it is important that both the imitation and innovation stage are considered. This is because the imitation stage needs to support the children in applying the skills that they have learnt but must also work well with the innovation stimulus, so that there are enough similarities for the children to manipulate and innovate in their own way. Pupils really enjoy this phase: they have a clear goal (they know what their piece of art needs to look like) and they use the skills they have been introduced to. The scaffolds mean that all pupils are successful and, as a result, there's a great sense of achievement.

The innovation stage – changing an aspect of a piece of art

In the innovation stage, pupils are introduced to other artwork created by the artist, and asked to change a particular aspect of the key piece – this may be the style, subject or material used. During this stage, teacher modelling of their own 'shared art' is essential. This enables the teacher to think outloud as an artist demonstrating different ideas and addressing possible difficulties. For the pupils, drafting and planning of initial ideas is vital before committing themselves to whatever they are trying to create. This preparation is often completed via annotated sketches in their sketchbooks. Sometimes getting started is the most difficult part. At these times, referring back to the imitation stage helps pupils to find a starting point. Throughout the process, pupils require on going, timely feedback to help direct and improve their outcomes: use of mini plenaries is vital here to help refocus learning back onto the application of the skill they have been taught, thereby ensuring this is within their innovated piece.

Achieving independence

The independent application stage is the final stage of the process. This is where pupils take ownership of their learning from the unit and apply it to create a piece of artwork in the style of the given artist. It is where the fruits of the labour lie as pupils utilise the skills they have acquired. The pictures below illustrate the journey from imitation of Theo Van Doesberg's work, to innovation to independent application.

The Impact

Pupils at Briar Hill now demonstrate a love of art: they are confident, inspired and eager to learn both about art and from art through a challenging curriculum. From the early skills sessions to the final outcome, each pupil's progress is clear in their sketchbooks. The skills acquired from the skills sessions and the imitation stage are refined throughout the process, resulting in an independent piece of work that demonstrates improvement over time.

Talk for Writing in art is firmly embedded within the school and art now has a high profile. There are two 10-hour blocks of art a year plus a special art focus during the final weeks of the summer term. Last year, we focused on murals with every child contributing to the murals that now adorn our 'art street',

a small section of which is pictured here. Briar Hill has been awarded the nationally recognised Artsmark, Gold Status, for our work in art.

This approach to the teaching of art has developed the leadership of art in the school, and equipped novice teachers of art with the knowledge, understanding and skills they need. It has also enriched and improved the teaching of art as a whole, raising its profile so that it is taught to the same high standards as the core subjects. The enthusiasm it has instilled in the teachers can be seen from the comments here:

> *"It has helped me really understand how to teach progression in art and teach in a way that supports all children to reach their full potential."* – Hollie Tranter, Year 2 teacher
>
> *"This way of teaching art is so powerful. Children as young as 8 years old are given the scaffolds to be able to analyse famous pieces of art like Salvador Dali's* Galatea of the Spheres *– it's astonishing!"*
> – Laura Allen, Arts Lead and Year 3 teacher
>
> *"Talk for Writing in art is a clear process that allows our children to consider techniques (alongside looking at how local and international artists have used the techniques) to develop their own style and use them to create their own piece – it's great to see in action!"*
> – Ian Hickman, Year 4 teacher
>
> *"Talk for Writing in art has revolutionalised the way I teach art as a subject! It gives the children a richer and more meaningful experience of art. From the '3 Is', to the children's outcomes, to the models and boxing up of art analysis, art Talk for Writing style covers it all when planning deep, rich and meaningful art lessons."*
> – Katie Cross, Year 5 teacher & Assistant Headteacher

To find out when you can see Talk for Writing in action across the curriculum at Briar Hill Primary and related training, visit www.talk4writing.co.uk/train-with-us/briar-hill.

Chapter 16b: Talk for Writing in art (secondary)

Talk for Writing in art is still in the early stages of development in the secondary sector, but art teachers in secondary schools, like teachers in primary schools, are finding the Talk for Writing process supports students both in the theory and practice of art.

Most secondary schools allocate just one hour a week to art in KS3 which clearly limits what can be achieved. Art teachers have found that TfW not only helps students of all ages understand the technical terminology of art, aids factual recall and supports quality annotation of work but, significantly, it also develops creativity because it helps students put into practice the theoretical techniques they learn about.

Hannah Snowden, who teaches art at The John of Gaunt School, explained that when the art department first started to implement T4W strategies, they focused on KS4 in order to improve extended writing skills. They adapted their resources and created a 2-tier framework for boxing up, to help students structure their written analysis of artists' work. This worked very well: all students who engaged in the full use of these resources showed a marked improvement in this area, so this is now firmly embedded within the department.

They found implementing T4W with KS3 more challenging, so Hannah decided to really tackle this area head on and created resources for warming up the words and text mapping, which she shared among the department to trial. Ironically, they particularly found text mapping hard – it may seem strange for art teachers to find representing writing with pictures difficult but, apparently, they did, perhaps because they were all trying to make the images too artistic. Hannah persevered with text mapping and found that with a gradual build-up of text-mapped sentences, the students were generally able to recall much more information about artists than they had in previous years and were then

able to write short paragraphs about an artist or a movement. Only having one hour per week at KS3 inevitably means factual recall will be a struggle. With so much information being fed to students every day, it is not surprising that they couldn't remember much from one art lesson to the next. Previously, because time was being spent going over things again and again, sometimes students ended up just copying text into sketchbooks and no real judgement could be made as to how much

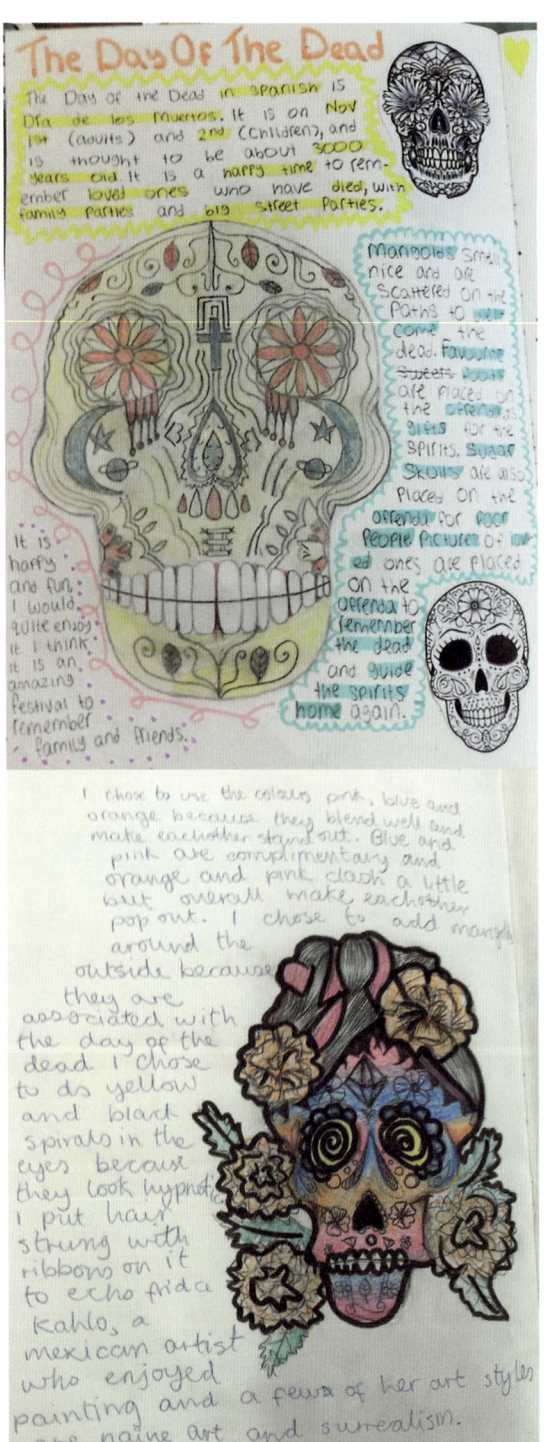

they were learning. Text mapping the information for them to keep in their books and revise from has, Hannah believes, made a significant difference in this area.

For example, for a unit on the Day of the Dead, she introduced the festival and the key concepts in the first lesson, alongside the idea of text mapping. She went through the text and pointed out how each symbol or picture could represent a word/group of words or an idea. Initially, most copied her examples but, with encouragement, they started to use their own.

As the class did practical tasks over the next few lessons, they would recap part of the text map to help embed facts and ideas and add more key concepts as necessary. For their assessment study page, they had the text maps in front of them and used them to help remember all that they had learnt about the festival so that they could write it up coherently as part of the 'factual recall' element of the assessment. This produced far better-quality written work overall than in past years, with weaker students being able to recall at least some of the facts. If you look at the example here, you can see that the student has clearly introduced the origin of the Day of the Dead and related symbolism, as well as the thinking behind it: people's desire to honour their dead.

Every lesson now, Hannah warms up the words that are new, holding up large printed versions and explaining each word and using it in context, before asking the students to add the words to their never-heard-the-word sheet if they are unfamiliar with them. She then displays the word on the wall behind her so that it is constantly on show as a reminder of the term and the correct spelling. She also helps the students use generic art phrases, as illustrated above, for example, "I chose to use …", "because they are associated with …", "because they look …" and "to echo …" to support them in making significant points coherently. All this has helped make their writing more effective and increased their understanding alongside improving the spelling.

Hannah commented: "After my 14 years of teaching experience, I found that it was definitely a smoother, more fluid way to help students complete written work based on factual recall. As a department, we aim for these skills to be continually built on in KS3, so we'll see the improvement in KS4."

Mandy Christmas teaches art and photography at Ormiston Endeavour Academy, Ipswich. When the school's TfW project team reported back enthusiastically on the impact TfW was having in the school, they were particularly singing the praises of the feedback that Mandy had recently presented to staff. Mandy had told them that previously she'd tried to improve the students' art vocabulary by getting them to write key words down as a starter, but all on one page called a *literacy mat*. The idea was that the students would have the correct spellings and could go to the page for reference when they were annotating. In reality, they didn't do that, especially if they were writing words they didn't really know or understand.

So, she decided to try out never-heard-the-word grids to see if that made a difference, presenting one like the example here on the white board at the beginning of lessons for students to quickly copy and think about, as a starter, while she took the register. For this example, she then showed some short film clips starting with an animation that told the story of Rama and Sita both visually and through commentary, followed by a presentation that had 10 facts about Diwali, written one per slide. After that, she showed two quick clips illustrating life during the festivities with film, commentary, lots of visuals and sound, and then, finally, showed a time-lapsed clip of rangoli patterns being created. In between the clips, she added extra information as necessary. During all this time, the students made notes on their NHTW grids. Most of them were then able to answer questions at the end about the key words and their meanings, and jot down some of the meanings, as illustrated below. They could explain them to others and started using them in subsequent lessons.

Students were also encouraged to draw and write the meanings if that helped, as shown here. Mandy now often asks the students to write a paragraph, using the key words and meanings, so that they can explain what they have done in the lesson and why. As there are sometimes students who will probably never be able to understand the meaning of so many words so quickly, she supports them by getting the students to swap books and, if there are any blank spaces in the book they are looking at, and they are able to write the meanings, then they do so in a different-coloured pen. This makes students try to recall information and not only supports the lower attainers, but also helps the higher attainers who feel good that they can add information that they know into someone else's book; it gives a value to their knowledge and is good for their self-esteem. It also helps the self-esteem of the lower attainers, as they no longer have as many empty spaces on their grids, and they have something to refer to.

Mandy uses a similar approach for GCSE classes but adapts it to suit what they are studying. For example, in photography, they have digital access, so they create their own document, and add words each lesson. They use the same process: ticks first and fill in any meanings they know. As Mandy explains the lesson, they add the meanings. In some lessons, she asks them to research the meanings. In art lessons, they have a printed version which they keep in their folder rather than sticking it into their sketchbook so they can use it for reference. They know that by the end of Year 11 they are expected to have used the words and explained their meaning in their sketchbooks and they add them as and when it is appropriate. They discover the meanings during the introductions to the lessons, through process, through note taking during video clips and through discussion. They know these words matter.

The art of annotation

One of the key writing challenges in art is to annotate your own work effectively and the work of other artists. Left to their own devices, students often find annotating their work very challenging as this example from a KS4 student illustrates: a few minimalist headings have been added leaving the viewer to try and piece together what is meant; several others just did the drawings and ignored the request to annotate them.

So Mandy paid great attention to how she could support the students by modelling for them what good annotations look like. For a

TALK FOR WRITING IN ART (SECONDARY) 299

I had two attempts of using biro to try to create a realistic drawing of an animal skull. The aim was to make it look Three Dimensional.

I simplified the outline too much in this drawing, which means it looks flattened and you can't see the raised eye socket on the other side. It also means that the nose looks like it is on this side rather than in the middle. The skull this side looks flat too as I didn't make it clear that the cheek bone (bone under the eye) came towards the viewer, and the jaw was underneath.

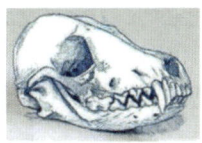
My second attempt was more successful. The shape of the eye socket was more accurate where I looked at the angles, the cheek bone is clearly closer to the viewer than the jaw bone that tucks in closer to the skull, and the teeth are textured and stick out and over the chin. I managed to create this impression of depth and solidity by more accurate outline drawing, and drawing of the features and using a wider range of tones. Even the closr cross hatching in the nose, makes it look more like a hole than in the first drawing where it still looks flat.

unit on the *Natural world and decay*, the students were first shown various artistic techniques that would enable them to use tone effectively and these were very clearly illustrated, as pictured here.

She then modelled for them how to annotate a series of drawings they had made by referring to what they were trying to achieve, the techniques used to do this and their resulting effects, as shown here. It is an excellent model because it is full of useful generic phrases that explain the causes of errors made or successes achieved that the students can magpie for art evaluation, for example, "I simplified the outline too much, which means it looks flattened …", "I didn't make it clear that …", "My second attempt was more successful …", "I managed to create this impression of depth and solidity by more accurate outline drawing ... and using a wider range of tones". The students could see the difference in the quality of the drawings as well as read clearly what approaches had been used that had led to success. Such model annotation has a clear dual benefit because, not only will it lead to better quality annotations but, because of the nature of the annotations, they help the students understand the practical steps necessary to achieve more effective drawings. This, in turn, will help students explain coherently what they are doing, thereby internalising good practice.

In addition, she provided the guide below to help the students understand what aspects to focus on when annotating, plus examples of useful sentence stems relating to each aspect:

What: This is a copy that I made of a painting by …
Why: To analyse the style of …
How: I constructed it from …
Quality: I wish that I had …
Learning: To follow this up, I will …

All this is supported by the fact that, for GCSE, the students work on paper and keep their work in a folder until they have enough work to be able to compose the page and present the work. The students then plan and compose the work and blue tack it onto the double page. They annotate on Post-it Notes and plan where the annotation will go. Mandy checks the pages before anything is stuck in and reviews the annotations. They then have the opportunity to improve the annotations. In effect, this is the innovation stage for the annotations. Then they can then stick them in. As they become more confident, they become more independent and start to work straight into the book, sometimes with

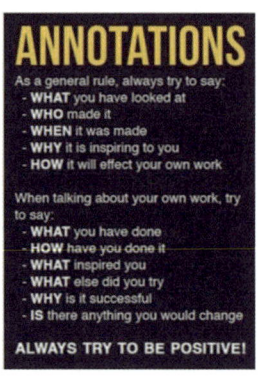

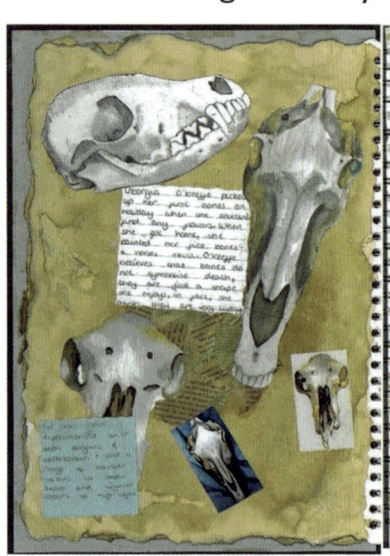
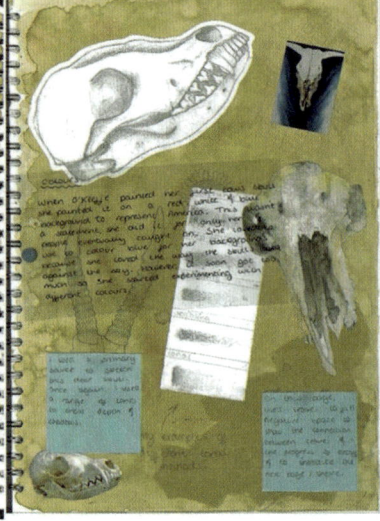

their drawings and eventually, too, with their annotations. It also gives them more confidence, as nothing is stuck in until it looks good, and then they feel proud when it is ready to be stuck in. It also means she can assist in composing the page with images and writing and, with their input, ensure it both looks good and is well expressed. She chats with students who are having difficulty with the task about what they have done and then, when she repeats their conversation, they feel confident about taking notes as she talks, which can form the basis of the Post-it Notes.

As a result, the quality of the students' work has been transformed. As pictured below, quality drawings are enhanced by excellent annotations including phrases like, "This allowed me to focus on …", " … gives the illusion that the skull is 3-dimensional …", "I looked at the negative space when drawing to make sure I was using the correct angles and proportions." You can see how the student has reflected on what they had done and taken the reader clearly through the techniques they used to increase the quality of the drawing, using technical language effectively to help the reader understand both

the processes used and the artist's intentions. The quality of the annotations enhances the quality of the drawings.

All this is strengthened by using the classroom display areas to support understanding. The left-hand part of the display pictured below is permanent; the other side is made up of laminated support sheets on hooks that students can use in the lesson or borrow overnight.

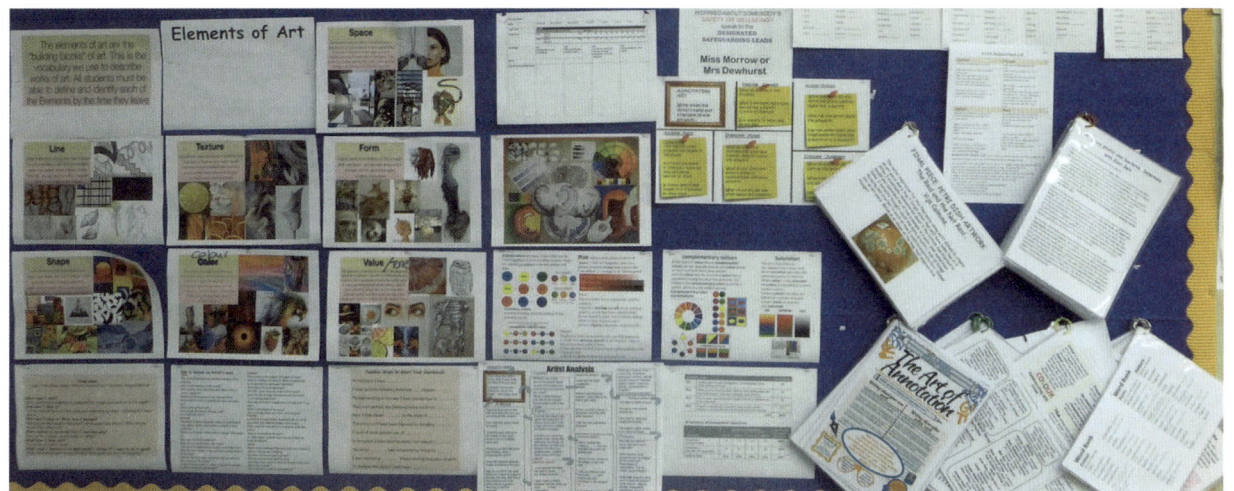

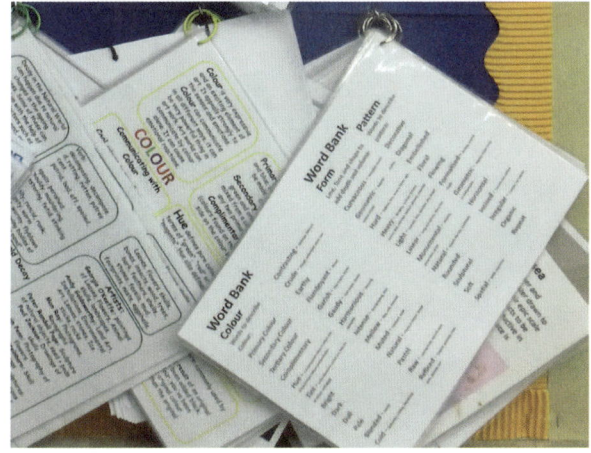

Here, you can see the quality of those resources, including word banks of key vocabulary sheets about colour and examples of effective annotating. There is also an annotation checklist to help those who may find all the visual support overwhelming so they can just use the checklist. Mandy produces model answers by writing about students' work as if it is her own and displays these for student access. Providing a good model of what quality annotations look like, alongside paying attention to the sentence stems/generic phrasing and related vocabulary that help the students annotate their work, and the work of others effectively, has really paid off.

Mandy commented, "Although, as a creative teacher, I would like students to be able to work independently and research their own artists and ideas as soon as they start the GCSE course, in reality this won't happen. Of course, it depends on what the catchment area is and the type of students you are teaching, and what previous knowledge and learning they have. I now find that it is essential to start with teaching and continually reinforcing the basics about the formal elements of art, and what is important to write about and how to write it. This means, initially, limiting the artists that are studied until the students are more confident in annotating and artist analysis. I am already seeing a difference with the GCSE students in Year 9 because of the changes I made in teaching

when they were in Year 8. I therefore leave it until the Spring Term in Year 10 before students start to research artists that I have not suggested to them in class." Mandy added, "What has also made a huge difference is having regular meetings with art teachers from the other Ormiston Trust schools, where we can share ideas and ways of working." The more opportunities teachers get to share good ideas, the more creative and effective teaching will become.

Video clip 59: Jo, Head of Art, Design & Technology at Rainham Girls, explains how Talk for Writing has helped all aspects of these practical subjects and has helped the different sections within this curriculum group work together effectively.

Chapter 17a: Becoming a Talk for Writing school

Louise Hamilton, Deputy Headteacher with responsibility for Teaching & Learning at The John of Gaunt School (JOG), describes how the school adopted the Talk for Writing approach. The school has recently become a Talk for Writing secondary training school.

Why Talk for Writing?

Louise Hamilton (right), Headteacher Paul Skipp & Julia Strong

The first time I came across Talk for Writing was when I saw our school's primary-trained nurture group teacher in action. Her use of TfW strategies led Year 7 and 8 students with low starting points to make excellent progress, and visibly enhanced their enjoyment of, and confidence in, their English lessons. Although I was amazed by the complexity of the sentence structures and vocabulary used by these students, what excited me even more was their ability to articulate the writing process they had used, from first draft to final piece. Intrigued by the principles behind the approach, I started to carry out some research online, and discovered that a few trail-blazing secondary schools were starting to use the TfW toolkit across the curriculum to great effect, having been trained by Julia Strong, the co-creator of the approach and author of *Talk for Writing in Secondary Schools* (2013). Having convinced the then Headteacher about the need to investigate the approach further, I booked a place at an information morning run by our nearest TfW secondary, Slough and Eton C of E Business and Enterprise College.

To say I was blown away by what I experienced at Slough and Eton would be an understatement. Visiting classrooms on a learning walk, I saw students working with the independence, skill and confidence of the nurture group students at my own school; it was clear that the TfW methodology was the embedded way of learning for students of all abilities and ages in every subject area within the school. In many ways, this was a shock to me. Having spoken to primary colleagues trained in the approach, I had expected to find the strategies being used in literacy-based subjects like English, history and modern foreign languages, but not so much in science, technology and maths. At Slough and Eton, all subject areas were using the approach to aid students' thinking and planning, as well as their writing, and this was having a great impact in terms of students' learning skills.

Seeing the clear metacognitive benefits of TfW was in fact one of the reasons why I was so drawn to the approach during my visit to Slough and Eton. As a senior leader in a secondary school, I was conscious of how many students struggle with knowing how to start a piece of writing and who, consequently, spend precious time in exams and assessments staring at a blank page. The traditional approach of planning using spider-diagrams didn't help our students understand how to sequence their ideas, or how to prioritise them when structuring an argument. Students clearly felt mystified by the vast array of command words and question types being covered in different subjects, and by the potential confusion caused by the same term being used in different ways in different disciplines (e.g. 'describe' in both English and maths). At Slough and Eton, TfW was providing students with a metacognitive toolkit that enabled them to think, plan and then write in a logical way, and that was equally applicable to any subject and age range.

Following the learning walk at Slough and Eton, a number of subject specialists from the school gave short presentations about how the approach could work in their areas. One presenter, who described herself as a "typical blocker", described her own initial scepticism regarding TfW, and her conviction that it would not be effective at A-level. Having tried it with A-level sociology and psychology students for a short time, however, she had been amazed by its efficacy with post-16 students, and now regarded herself as a great fan of TfW. Another presenter showed how the language of maths could be clarified for students through the 'warming up the words' stage of the approach, and how complex, multi-stage maths problems could be boxed up to simplify the calculation process for students. A PE specialist demonstrated how iPads were being used in his subject to help with modelling and co-construction of physical skills.

While listening to these presentations, I was growing more and more excited as I considered how the TfW methodology could be used at my own school. Having taught and observed hundreds of lessons, I was aware that teachers often make assumptions that students understand how to vary their writing style across subject areas. While it is true that primary school students spend a lot of time learning how to construct different non-fiction text types (e.g. instruction, recount, information, explanation, persuasion, biography, journalistic writing and discussion), this learning is seldom revisited by secondary teachers (English teachers aside) who may only know how specialist subject texts work at an experiential, somewhat innate level themselves. How often does a history teacher assume, for example, that students will understand the language of cause and effect needed to explain the factors that led to a key historical event? How many science teachers take it for granted that their students will know how to write up an experiment, without explicitly teaching, modelling and co-constructing the process? Considering these questions, I began to understand what was missing in my own teaching and in that of many of my colleagues, and why so many students struggled with a blank page.

Following my visit to Slough, I started to think about how I could share my enthusiasm for TfW with my school's Headteacher, Senior Leadership Team and governors, whose support would be essential if I was to succeed in

Dr John Kotter's 8-step process for leading change	
Stage A: Creating the climate for change	Step 1. Create urgency Step 2. Form a powerful coalition Step 3. Create a vision for change
Stage B: Engaging and enabling the organisation	Step 4. Communicate the vision Step 5. Empower action Step 6. Create quick wins
Stage C: Implementing & sustaining change	Step 7. Build on the change Step 8. Make it stick

bringing the TfW methodology to my own school. In doing so, I drew on some recent learning from my National Professional Qualification of Senior Leadership (NPQSL) regarding the leadership of change at a whole-school level. Among other models, I had studied Dr John Kotter's 8-Step Process for Leading Change, and the clarity of this process made it an obvious starting point for planning my next steps. As can be seen from the diagram above, Kotter divides any effective change process into three distinct phases: creating the climate for change; engaging and enabling the organisation; and implementing and sustaining change. In the next section, I will outline how I used Kotter's steps to bring TfW to my school.

Stage A: Creating the climate for change

Step 1. Create urgency

My first challenge was to create a sense of urgency around the need to bring TfW to JOG, so that key stakeholders within the school would agree to sign up to what would be an enormous change within the pedagogical culture of the school. To do this, I created a presentation about TfW out of my research, insights gleaned at Slough and Eton, and my observations around barriers to student progress at JOG. Seeing how closely the TfW methodology linked to research from the Education Endowment Foundation (EEF) toolkit, regarding the impact of metacognitive approaches to learning and regularity of feedback, and to Barack Rosenshine's *Principles of Instruction* (2012), I was able to create a rationale around adopting the TfW framework that was linked to a strong evidence base. At this stage, I also contacted Julia Strong to ask her for further case studies and evidence of impact, and to find out how much a training programme would cost. Even at this early point in the project, Julia was clear about what would and would not work: without absolute buy-in from the Headteacher and governors, and a strong dedication to whole school involvement, any attempt to embed TfW would be unlikely to succeed. In retrospect, it is clear to me that she was absolutely right: without this level of commitment, TfW could simply have been regarded as 'yet another initiative' to be adopted half-heartedly by some, and then dropped in lieu of something else. Such was the potential of TfW that I did not want this to happen; neither did I want to impose additional change on colleagues that would not be seen as both lasting and valuable. Due to the extensive background research and reflection that went into my presentation, I was indeed able to convince the Headteacher and governors about the value of TfW and the need to invest in it for the benefit of our students.

Step 2: Form a powerful coalition

Having secured the support of the Headteacher and governors, the training programme was agreed with Julia and the TfW team. Both Julia and I felt it was important to have her involvement over a full academic year until the implementation process was complete, both for support and guidance, and as a sign of the school's long-term commitment to the approach. Having led similar training programmes in other secondary schools, including Slough and Eton, Julia recommended that we start the training programme by creating a project team, which would be made up of 8-10 teachers from a variety of subject areas across the school, as well as myself as project leader. These teachers would be strong practitioners, known for their positivity and openness to new ideas, and respected by their colleagues. By training these teachers first, and giving them a term to experiment with the TfW approach, we hoped to do what Kotter also suggests in the second step of his model: build a powerful coalition that would help to drive wider change.

Members of the project team focusing on a vocabulary sorting activity

On the first teacher training day of the next academic year, therefore, the members of the newly formed project team were trained in every stage of the TfW process by Julia. It had been explained to team members that they would be ambassadors for the approach when it was launched across the whole school in the following term, so they were encouraged to discuss any confusion and voice questions about the approach during this initial training session. All members of the project team – representing English, maths, science, MFL, history, geography, art and PE – responded positively to the training, and began to experiment with TfW during Term 1.

At the same time as the project team were trained, Julia also delivered training to the English department. The rationale behind this is because the English department builds the foundations that other subject areas can adapt to suit the needs of their subject area. They introduce concepts like boxing up and developing toolkits and will underpin students' understanding of the roots and affixes that are the building blocks of developing vocabulary. In this way, students will be able to see how to transfer skills from one subject to another

English department training day – learning how to imitate text

and a coordinated approach to literacy across the curriculum can be achieved. During Term 1, the English faculty joined the project team in experimenting with TfW, and were therefore able to prepare the ground for introducing the approach to the whole school at the start of Term 2.

By giving the project team and the English department an additional term to become familiar with TfW, and to see for themselves how powerful its impact could be, we were essentially creating the coalition that Kotter would regard as an essential precursor to introducing wider change.

Step 3: Create a vision for change

By the start of Term 2, the project team and English department had gained confidence in using the TfW approach and were enthusiastic about its impact on students' learning. As a means of piquing their colleagues' interest, they had already presented several TfW 'taster' sessions in morning briefings and had started to post details of their practice on the school's new TfW blog. The rest of the staff were therefore intrigued by the approach and were enthusiastic about its launch on the training day at the start of Term 2.

In preparation for this training day, the project team and English department put together a showcase of their TfW practice in each subject area that could be shown as evidence of the approach working in our own specific school context. For example, while the maths lead had created a JOG-specific version of the boxing up grid I'd seen used at Slough and Eton, the History lead had found text mapping to be a powerful mechanism for presenting sequences of events and for planning essay content. Each subject lead on the project team had also collected examples of how they were using TfW in lessons, with many including short videos of students deconstructing models, miming, and so on. Importantly, they had all found ways of capturing the impact of the strategies they were using, whether through student interviews, surveys, cold-to-hot task photographs, or test data.

Although the presentation of the showcase was a crucial aspect of the initial whole-school training day, it was only a small section of six hours of lively, interactive training led by Julia. Importantly, the day started off with a seal of approval from the Headteacher, who made it clear to staff that TfW would become the default approach to teaching and learning within our school because he was impressed by the progress he had seen so far; as already stated, this endorsement from the Head is a crucial part of ensuring the ongoing success of the approach. Keen to further emphasise the importance of this event, I ensured that colleagues from neighbouring primary schools were invited, as well as all members of the JOG governing body. The power of 150 colleagues participating in Julia's 'Foxes are not pets' internalisation of text in our school hall cannot be over-emphasised: it was a clear sign that the majority of the community was committing to the TfW approach and to the journey ahead.

Stage 2 – Engaging and enabling the organisation

Step 4: Communicate the vision

Communicating the vision for how TfW would transform teaching and learning at JOG was one of the main aims of the first whole-school training day at the start of Term 2, but this aspect of Kotter's model is one that is – in my experience – continually enacted. We first shared this vision with the governors and senior leaders, then with the project team and English department, then with the whole staff, but throughout the process 'over-communication' through frequent revisiting of our TfW goals was essential to help embed this new approach to pedagogy. From the outset, I was clear with all stakeholders that fully embedding the approach would be a three-year project and shared the action plan that led the school from initial training to my ambitious goal of becoming a TfW training school by the end of the third year. In sharing this vision, I was careful to start with the 'why' of the 'Golden Circle' (Sinek, 2009): embedding TfW at JOG would directly improve the life chances of our students by improving their examination outcomes but also by providing them with an internalised metacognitive toolkit that would serve them throughout their future lives. As teachers began to experiment with TfW in their own classrooms, they could see the impact of the approach for themselves, and this strengthened their own moral imperative and belief in the vision.

Step 5: Empower action

In order to empower teachers, many of whom were understandably tentative about the practicalities of implementing TfW, I had planned for terms 2-6 of that first year to be focused on building teacher confidence in the approach through experimentation. By removing the expectation that all lessons and schemes of work would be aligned to the complete TfW process from the start, I was able to reassure those who were concerned about the impact on workload or their own ability to deliver TfW, as well as those who were still sceptical about the approach working in their specific subject area.

Starting off with an experimentation phase could quite easily have led to some teachers opting out, or to a haphazard application of the TfW principles, so it was important, in this stage, to set goals for faculties. One such goal was around teacher appraisal: the focus of everyone's teaching practice target that year was the development of TfW strategies within lessons, and this had to be evidenced through lesson observations and work sampling. A second goal was that subject teams should start collaborating on best TfW practice within their area, with a view to writing the approach into schemes of work by the end of that first year. A training day was disaggregated into six hour-long twilight sessions that were given over to subject teams to share and develop ideas; these were then presented in whole-staff briefings or captured in the school's evolving TfW blog. Throughout this experimentation phase, Julia Strong continued to visit the school to support the project team and English department, who were now supporting colleagues across the school with implementation, and to advise about the practice she saw on learning walks and in students' books. It was very important to have Julia's expert eyes during this phase, as she was able to point out examples of emerging ineffective practice, such as providing students with ready-made toolkits or boxing up, rather than co-constructing them, and to highlight where practice was most effective.

On a practical level, empowering teachers to experiment with TfW meant providing them with the necessary tools. Flipcharts and washing lines were provided to all members of the project team and the English department, who experimented with them during Term 1, before the rest of the teachers had been trained. Many of our older classrooms struggled to accommodate full washing lines due to small rooms and one whole wall being taken up by windows, so we decided to use smaller versions that could still accommodate three or four flip chart sheets at one time. Flip charts proved very useful, but we decided to limit these to the subjects that would use them most due to the ongoing cost of the flipchart paper, choosing instead to invest in miniature document cameras (visualisers) for every classroom in the school. These nifty little cameras are easy to use and to store, and enable teachers to co-construct and de-construct models, display students' work, live mark and text map for their classes. An added feature of our cameras is that anything they display can be captured in a screen shot, to be brought out in future lessons in much the same way as flip-chart paper on a washing line. Further support was offered to subject teams in the form of Talk for Writing books, as well as having a member of the Project Team assigned as a mentor and coach.

Step 6: Create quick wins

In the first experimentation-based phase of TfW implementation, it was important to create quick wins in order to maintain the appetite for change within the school, and to indicate to all key stakeholders that initial efforts were paying off. In his blog *Management is a Journey*, Robert Tanner defines these short-term wins as being unambiguously successful, visible throughout the organisation, and clearly related to the change effort. Our first quick wins had already been achieved by the time of the whole school launch, as previously discussed: a TfW-specific target had been incorporated into the appraisal system and the CPD calendar had been altered to accommodate termly twilight sessions. A further short-term win was directing teachers to create a TfW showcase board in their classrooms, so that the approach was celebrated throughout the school, and becoming – in literal terms – part of the wallpaper. Linked to this, all students within the school received assemblies on the TfW approach, so that they knew to expect the strategies in every subject area, and to reinforce the message to colleagues that TfW would indeed be a non-negotiable change to our methodology.

In term 4 of that first year, after teachers across the school had been experimenting with TfW for two terms, I worked with another member of the project team to create a new JOG-specific framework for teaching and learning known as 'The JOG Essentials'. This comprised six strands of best practice, based on the TfW principles and the closely-aligned Rosenshine *Principles of*

Instruction. Lesson planning and observation records were altered to reflect these strands of *Behaviour and Engagement, Quality of Instruction, Support and Challenge, Modelling, Questioning* and *Feedback*, and the TfW strategies were included as essential 'tools' that everyone should be using. By creating this new framework for pedagogy within the school, we were reassuring stakeholders that the changes we were making were long-term rather than a fad, and that the efforts they were putting into developing their TfW practice were worthwhile.

By the end of the academic year, TfW had become central to teaching and learning at JOG, a fact that was reinforced by a visit from Ofsted. It's report stated: "the recent introduction of TfW has been well-received and its impact was evident in lessons visited by inspectors." Other external visitors were impressed by how far we had come in just a year, with a National Leader of Education reporting that, "TfW benefits all pupils and is clearly targeted to address barriers to learning faced by disadvantaged pupils. The learning walk flagged up the programme in practice. Full buy-in from leaders ... possibly transformational." All of this evidence was communicated to staff and governors so that the whole community could take stock of our successes and see that all of our efforts were worthwhile.

Stage 3 – Implementing and sustaining change

Step 7: Build on the change

Members of staff co-constructing understanding through sorting

Having spent a year experimenting with TfW and making underlying strategic changes that would help grow and sustain it (e.g. developing the JOG Essentials), it was now time to begin the 'Embedding' phase of our project. The new academic year started with a second whole-staff training day on TfW, delivered again by Julia. And again, the Headteacher spoke to staff at the beginning of the day, to make his absolute commitment to TfW clear: but what was unusual about this was that the Headteacher – Mr Paul Skipp – was new to the school himself, having just taken up the post at JOG that very day. Although it could have been problematic to have a change of Headteacher mid-way through the TfW training process, Paul immediately recognised the power of the approach to transform students' lives through improved literacy and metacognitive skills. His unswerving support of TfW has been key to the progress we have made over the past eighteen months.

This second whole-staff training day with Julia featured a second showcase of best practice, this time delivered by colleagues who were not part of the project team, but who had embraced the approach in their lessons. Colleagues were reminded that TfW is a process rather than a toolkit of pick 'n' mix strategies, and that this second year would be focused on writing this process into schemes of work and the assessment cycles used at our school. At this point, it was very helpful to have some strong evidence of impact to share with staff: one member of our project team, our SENCO, had used the complete TfW process with her GCSE English lower-attaining class, and had achieved stunning outcomes with the majority of the class beating their targets by at least one grade (and in one case, by four grades). The fact that this teacher was able to share her class data with staff on the training day, and that she credited her students' excellent grades to following the whole TfW process from cold to hot, was more powerful for staff than anything else they heard that day. The message was clear: this approach works for our students, so we need to embed it in every subject and year group across the school as soon as possible. In this way, our collective 'sense of urgency' was renewed and strengthened.

Throughout the rest of this second year of TfW, the embedding phase was supported by once again providing subject teams with termly twilight sessions, during which departments could collaborate on writing the approach into medium-term plans and assessments. Further to this, TfW was added as a standing agenda item to all middle leaders' meetings, and to the proformas used in work sampling and for learning walks, so that progress and barriers to embedding could be explored at every opportunity. In addition to this, subject teams were asked to dedicate one of their morning briefings per term to running mini TfW showcases based on the good practice that middle leaders had seen on their learning walks. Aspects of this practice, such as the science department's subject-specific guide to using TfW, were then shared with the whole school to enable colleagues to magpie from each other, as well as being celebrated in the blog. For the second year running, all teaching staff had the embedding of TfW set as one of their appraisal targets.

During this second year, a colleague who was completing his NPQSL qualification ran an incremental coaching programme based on developing teachers' skills and confidence in the TfW process. All members of the project team were given coaching training and were then able to 'drop-in' to colleagues' lessons to support them with TfW through live coaching and follow-up conversations. Teachers who wanted more in-depth input could then sign up for more regular incremental coaching, where they could request to work on developing a specific area in their teaching e.g. text mapping, shared writing, etc. This system proved popular with staff and has now been extended to incorporate live coaching on all the JOG Essentials.

Step 8: Make it stick

At the end of our second year of TfW, I decided to approach Julia to see if JOG was ready to begin training other schools, as word about our success was spreading, and we were now receiving a lot of requests to visit the school and see the approach in action. Following an in-depth visit to look at our systems, lessons, books and data, Julia agreed that we could start organising training events for other secondaries interested in TfW. Although it had always been part of my long-term plan to achieve training school status eventually, I was delighted that we were able to achieve this so soon, and felt that it would be a real boost to our staff who had worked so hard on embedding it over the previous two years. Becoming a training school would, of course, enable us to further fulfil our sense of moral purpose around TfW by sharing our insights with other professionals in much the same way that Slough and Eton had done for me. But another reason why I was so keen for JOG to fulfil this role was to help us with the final stage of Kotter's change model: making it stick. Being a training school would, I believe, enable us to further develop and refine TfW within JOG; it would also ensure that our practice stays fresh, and our teachers remain enthusiastic.

Aside from creating 'stickability' through our role as a training school, it is the ongoing responsibility of all leaders within our school to ensure that the changes brought about through TfW are firmly anchored, and that the methodology is woven through every aspect of teaching and learning at our school. TfW is therefore central to every training session we have on the JOG Essentials, as well as remaining as a standing item in meetings; it is, furthermore, a central aspect of our quality assurance process as well as a key aspect of work sampling and lesson drop-ins. All new staff, including our ITT students, are trained in the TfW approach, and a number of our more experienced teachers are carrying out action research projects linked to developing our TfW skills in, for example, tier 2 vocabulary and A-level humanity subjects.

A final aspect of making the TfW approach stick is refusing to believe that we have reached mastery and can therefore rest on our laurels, as there is still much to work on. Having said this, JOG teaching staff are now starting to reap the benefits of the approach, with our Key Stage 4 results now showing a morale-boosting three-year improvement trend. Our students are increasingly confident with TfW, particularly the older year groups who have now had two and a half years' exposure; indeed, when students were surveyed recently about TfW, their only criticism was that they wanted more of it! As our students have become more accustomed to the TfW methodology, their metacognitive skills have noticeably developed, and this had led to more automaticity around thinking and writing skills. From a moral point of view, I remain convinced of the potential of TfW to transform lives and am therefore delighted that my colleagues and I have been asked to contribute to a book that will share our insights with other secondary school professionals.

To find out when you can see Talk for Writing in action across the curriculum at The John of Gaunt School and related training, visit https://www.talk4writing.co.uk/train-with-us/john-of-gaunt/.

Chapter 17b: Getting Talk for Writing going in your school

This chapter mainly focuses on how to get the approach going in secondary schools, but many of the key points are equally valid for both settings. It ends with invaluable advice devised by primary Talk for Writing training schools on how to sustain the process and raise achievement year on year.

Professor Robert Coe researched the conditions needed to support transforming practice in schools. It's worth reflecting on his key findings listed here. All of his conclusions have been borne out by the experiences of the Talk for Writing training team. This is why we now rarely offer one-day training for schools as it may not be a good use of time. It's important to research what approach is going to make a difference and then focus on that approach, embedding and developing it over the years.

> **Research tells us that if you want to transform practice you need:**
>
> - at least 15 hours intense input/trialling – preferably 50 hours
> - spread over at least 2 terms
> - focused on teacher's knowledge and how children learn
> - time to try ideas out and discuss
> - **with support networks to help sustain and improve**
> - that leads to feedback and evaluation
> - focused on evidence-based strategies (see EEF toolkit)
>
> *Thanks to Robert Coe – Durham University*

One of the great curses for practicing teachers, fanned by a climate that fosters a desperate need to improve results, is having managers that flit from initiative to initiative, never allowing anything to be properly developed and embedded, in their search for the magic wand that instantly rectifies all learning barriers. This is gloriously summed up by an ancient quote, courtesy of education reformer and researcher Michel Fullan:

> "Gaius Petronious nailed this problem almost two thousand years ago: 'We trained hard ... but it seemed every time we were beginning to form up into teams we were reorganised. I was to learn later in life that we tend to meet any situation by reorganising, and what a wonderful method it can be for creating the illusion of progress while producing confusion, inefficiency, and demoralisation'."

This inevitably leads to teacher cynicism about change. This problem is exacerbated by the fact that human beings are creatures of habit: research tells us that teachers tend to teach in the way that they were taught. It is not surprising, then, that changing practice is hard: we all have a tendency to return to old routines and many of us have got buckets of evidence showing how calls to change things didn't actually lead to progress. But a second quotation from Michael Fullan hits the nail on the head again, this time in a positive way:

> *"What we need is consistency of purpose, policy, and practice. Structure and strategy are not enough. The solution requires the individual and collective ability to build shared meaning, capacity, and commitment to action. When large numbers of people have a deeply understood sense of what needs to be done – and see their part in achieving that purpose – coherence emerges and powerful things happen."*

This quotation sums up what we have been trying to achieve over the years through co-constructing with schools how to develop the Talk for Writing process. The system we use is illustrated here. It needs to be co-constructed with staff through achieving staff buy-in, so that you build a critical mass of support. Once people can see the benefit of something, they will want to join in. Hopefully, the chapters written by teachers for this book reflect this enthusiasm for the Talk for Writing approach which leads to unity of purpose.

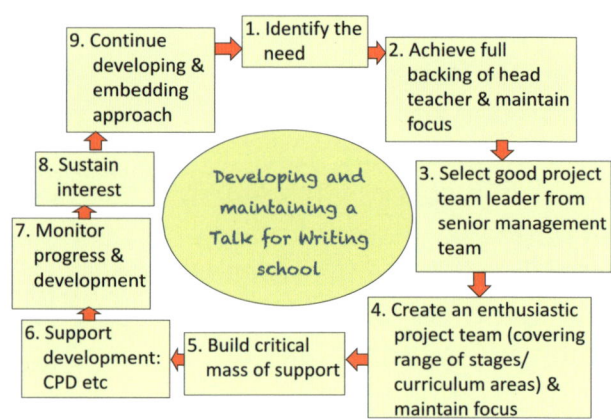

As you can also see, this is one of those dreaded, circular-development diagrams that suggests the job is never finished. Creating the best quality literacy outcomes for all our students is never 'job done'. But, whereas painting the Forth Bridge used to literally mean starting at the beginning again, once you reach stage 9, much progress should have been made and every stage will need adapting in the light of that. *Need* should be significantly different and developing and improving can become the key focus. Point 5 (*build critical mass of support*) should be redundant, but it will probably be replaced by the question of how you train all new members of staff in the approach and win their enthusiasm; point 8 (*sustain interest*) will always be relevant.

I wasn't aware of Professor Kotter's 8-step process for leading change until I read Louise's chapter (17a), but it interests me how close his steps are to the model here. Louise has made the stages and related challenges very clear, so I just want to focus on the centrality of these 7 key points:

- establishing headteacher and management team support
- establishing a quality project team
- training the English department before you train the other curriculum areas
- encouraging interactivity
- ensuring the quality of the models used
- getting going
- sustaining interest.

Establishing headteacher and management team support

Over the years, I've come across a depressingly large number of beleaguered souls (usually English teachers) who have been handed the job of sorting out literacy across the curriculum on top of a full teaching workload, when they have no clout within the school, and no one in management actually wants to listen to the impossibility of the task they have been allocated. My advice in these circumstances is simple: "Move schools." Changing how teachers teach cannot be achieved from such a position. "Can you send me a literacy policy?" is another well-known request, as if a piece of paper with a few *must dos* on it ever changed anything.

If you want to convince your management team, it's useful to trial the approach yourself and get a few enthusiasts onboard and then brainstorm why it works and present this to the management team. The approach has to be co-constructed and the need for it has to be recognised by the headteacher so that there is focus and that focus is sustained. This is all about improving teaching and learning so it needs to be a central part of the school plan with the full backing of the governors. Time needs to be found to do the work and it needs to be funded. In primary schools, sometimes headteachers lead the project team; this is unlikely to be the case in secondary schools, but the project team leader needs to be a respected member of the senior management team (SMT) who works closely with the head on developing the project.

You may find it useful to use **video clips 1, 2, 3 & 6** with your senior management team to help develop that essential ingredient SMT and headteacher support and understanding of the approach. You can't lead what you don't understand. When you monitor lessons, you have to know what

you are looking for. There are, inevitably, demands on headteachers that mean that sometimes, with the best will in the world, they cannot attend whole-school training days that focus on teaching and learning. But we've probably all had experience of headteachers who seem to have mastered the art of always saying something is very important and everyone must do it and then, somehow, never quite finding the time to ever be there themselves. Leading by example counts. In the picture above, you can see the massed ranks of the Slough and Eton staff imitating a text in the hall, framed by the flags of all the nationalities represented in the school. The small picture underneath shows the Headteacher, alongside Senior Deputy Aruna, with the Chair of Governors behind her, all joining in with gusto. School management team commitment matters.

The centrality of a quality project team

Experience has taught us that effective project teams are crucial if you want to implement Talk for Writing successfully. It is hard to over-emphasise the importance of a good project team; in the previous chapter, Louise makes this very clear. A secondary school project team should include at least one leading member of the senior management team who is the project team leader, and one key enthusiastic and respected practitioner from each of the main curriculum areas and, if that happens to be the head of the area, so much the better. The more curriculum areas covered, the more effective the project team tends to be. If possible, the literacy leads from any key primary feeder schools that use the TfW approach should be invited to some meetings to maximise the potential of making primary-secondary transfer coherent alongside learning from each other.

Do not include anyone on the team who is not enthusiastic about the potential of everyone (teachers and students alike) to learn. Negative forces within the team will hold it back; obviously, you want people who will question ideas but from the perspective of finding the best way forward rather than blocking all change. A senior manager at one school ignored my advice and deliberately placed a number of failing teachers on the project team (without telling me) with the idea that it would buck them up – not exactly guaranteed to move the whole school forward.

In grand contrast, it is worth looking at how Slough and Eton C of E Business and Enterprise College (much more Slough than Eton, as the Head pointed out) developed the approach. The management team first sent two key teachers to a secondary Talk for Writing conference to see if it seemed to meet the school's needs. They then applied to be trained. A very high-quality project team of enthusiastic teachers from a wide range of curriculum areas was selected, all led by the school's Senior Deputy and former maths teacher Aruna Sharma. The project was planned so the project team had several months to trial the approach before a whole-school training day. This trialling is absolutely key. It enabled them to build up lots of great feedback to present on that day showing that the approach worked with the type of students that were often seen as challenging. This also provided the school with internal expertise so that the whole staff could be both inspired and supported in implementing the process. Moreover, if the project team is given time to trial the approach, then, by the time the first whole-school training day arrives, there will already be significant buy-in from colleagues who will have seen the approach in action. Meanwhile, the Headteacher, Paul McAteer, had kept a close eye on how the project was progressing, visiting lessons and talking to students and teachers alike. He was thus in a position to say, at the start of the first whole-school training day, that all teachers at Slough and Eton should teach using the Talk for Writing approach. As he explained:

> *"If I'm saying to all of the staff, 'This is what we want to happen,' hopefully, it's got more of a chance of being successful. I'm delighted with the progress that the staff have made, and the pupils have made, and some of the stories that have come back to me about the development and the learning going on in classrooms plus what I see. I walk around the school every day and, when I see Talk for Writing in place, they are exciting lessons."*

Train the English team before you try to train all the curriculum areas

In secondary schools, the English department will be key to getting students to understand some of the underpinning elements of the TfW process, for example talking the text and text mapping followed by boxing up, co-constructing the generic writing toolkit, identifying key generic phrases and magpieing them. So, once the lead English teacher on the project team has started to build up sufficient expertise and confidence in the approach, it's a good idea if they train the school's English team in the approach in order to lay effective foundations for the project. The more the English department can introduce students to the approach, the easier it will be for the other departments to build on the foundations laid. This, in turn, will support the transfer of learning so that students become confident, effective communicators who can reflect on their learning and see how a skill developed in one area can be adapted and be very relevant in another.

If the English team project member is armed with all of the TfW books on English pictured here, as well as this book, plus examples from units they've trialled, then it should be easy to get the English team on board. If possible, include a visit to a Talk for Writing Primary Training School (see talk4writing.co.uk/training-centres/) so that English teachers can be inspired by the quality of the writing that the children can produce and the fluency, coherence and enthusiasm of their ability to talk about their work. Secondary English teachers typically come away amazed by the high standards that are achieved if Talk for Writing has been developed systematically throughout a primary school (**see page 141**).

Encouraging interactivity

The TfW process is all about getting teachers to focus on the ingredients that underpin effective practice. A useful way of underlining this with the project team and with the whole staff is to use the slide below and ask them to discuss which are the two most effective and the two least effective ingredients to include in our teaching repertoire if we want students to retain what they have

> **Retention:**
> which are the 2 most/least effective approaches for helping students retain information?
>
> - audio-visual
> - reading
> - discussion
> - explaining to others
> - demonstration
> - listening
> - practise by doing

been taught. Teachers tend to know the answer to this and so discussions will quickly result in people suggesting that the winners are *explaining to others* and *practice by doing*; the losers being *reading* and *listening*.

To emphasise this, show them the 'answer slide' below and ask everyone to reflect on what the top 3 have in common. Very quickly, someone will say something like "Doing it yourself" or "Interactivity". Now ask them to pretend that they are an invisible member of the secondary school Ofsted team who can drop in on lessons at any time and actually see what goes on. Ask them if they think that the practice that will be seen will be from the top or the bottom of the list. The answer, invariably, from many thousands of secondary teachers is that it will be from the bottom. So, here we have the interesting conundrum that teachers seem to know in theory what works but, in practice, they do

> **Hook your audience:**
> Retention rates in order of effectiveness
>
> - explaining to others: 90%
> - practise by doing: 75%
> - discussion: 50%
> - demonstration: 30%
> - audio-visual: 20%
> - reading: 10%
> - listening: 5%
>
> Research: National Training Laboratories, Bethel, Main USA

something else (or at least they suspect their lesser colleagues do something else). The reasons given for this range from confidence, to control, to lack of time. This is probably the key to helping change practice. We have to show them how the TfW process works so that the teachers have the confidence to try it and find out that it works themselves. In engaging the students through interactivity and the motivation that success brings, they discover that the control issue usually solves itself.

> **Does the layout of classrooms aid interactivity?**
>
> - Can everyone see the screen/whiteboard clearly?
> - Do classrooms have a flip chart/visualiser to display work in progress?
> - Does the way tables are arranged aid a range of activities or would it just best suit an exam?
> - Are mini-whiteboards provided for all classrooms?
> - Are there working walls/washing lines to display work-in-progress?
> - Is there an easy way of displaying students' work on screen? (visualiser/iPad)

One thing that really helps here is ensuring, as far is physically possible, that the layout of teaching rooms (the classroom set up) aids interactivity, as the points on this slide emphasise. The rise and rise of the ironically named interactive whiteboard has led to a great decrease in interactivity – it's worth noting the low retention score for audio visual. Yes, they are very useful for demonstration but that only wins a 30% score. It's important to help teachers recognise the importance of sorting activities (using packs of cards, not on screen) so that the students can physically move the text/words/images around and discuss what works. Changing the seating pattern so that the tables are arranged in an L shape, as illustrated below, maximises the potential of the room to be used for

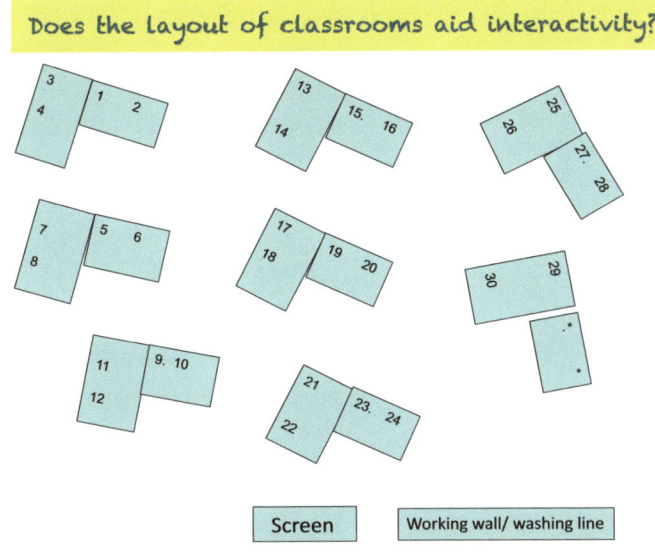

Does the layout of classrooms aid interactivity?

Screen | Working wall/ washing line

a wide range of activities without having to rearrange the room. 4 students seated in this way facilitates group discussion, paired work and individual working, while potentially maintaining focus on the teacher and screen if the tables are angled likes spokes of a wheel to face the screen. This layout also facilitates teacher support of any group while minimising the invitation to chat that 2 tables facing each other provide.

Ensuring the quality of the models used

Model text is a whole-school issue
What sort of support group would work best?

The support group needs to be able to help teachers establish appropriate quality model text that
- builds in progression throughout each year & year to year
- applies & extends pupils' literacy skills across curriculum as well as dealing with any arising issues from project

Suggestion: Have a trial run with a few people from project team supporting, and learning from, the rest.

Anyone who has ever read through all the reports written by teachers in a school will know that some teachers write better than others, and probably all of us need a bit of help ensuring that any text we have written that we present to classes is of high quality and suits its audience and purpose.

Moreover, we have to ensure that there is progression from year to year and from primary to secondary and that Year 7 doesn't become a year of repeating what you did in Year 6. Someone has to have an eye on these things across subjects and across the school. And our expectations of "what = good" will change as the progress students make increases. A frequent comment from TfW primary schools is that work that once suited a particular year is now done a year if not two years earlier. If you look at the standard of writing being achieved by pupils in Year 5 & 6 in this book, it is often higher than that being achieved in secondary schools by pupils several years older. All but one of the primary schools whose work is presented here have very challenging intakes, but what has made the big difference is that all of these schools have been doing TfW for many years and it shows.

When you ask a project team what sort of qualities the support group should have, apart from the obvious, *someone who has high literacy standards themselves*, they very quickly include qualities like being approachable, and being a good listener. The support group would have to understand what the language requirements of whatever subject being considered are – we're not trying to turn everyone into teachers of English; and they need to be the sort of people you willingly turn to for support and who will listen to the perspectives of others, so they start to understand the linguistic demands of the different subject areas. It

320 TRANSFORMING LEARNING ACROSS THE CURRICULUM

makes good sense to set up some sort of TfW support group to whom teachers can turn for help.

Getting going

With the help of this book (plus the original *Talk for Writing Across the Secondary School* which is full of useful examples and dozens of handouts that haven't been included in this book) and a good project team, a school should be able to develop the approach themselves. As emphasised here, this is best done by building up the skills of the project team before diving into providing whole-school training. If you are the most likely candidate to be the project team leader outlined above, then begin by reading this book and watching the videos. Visit a local TfW primary training school, preferably with another member of the management team and, if you are within distance of John of Gaunt, join a training day at the school. We hope to have more TfW secondary training schools soon so keep an eye on our email newsletter and the training pages of our website (talk4writing.com) to stay up to date with where you can see TfW in action.

If you want to set up a project, trial the approach yourself first in your own lessons and get a bit of evidence about the difference it can make so that you have material that will convince colleagues that this works in your school with your intake. Watch **video clip 61** to learn how Gemma Wade, Assistant Principal and Director of Teaching and Learning at Thomas Becket Catholic School in Northampton, got the approach going and made a really significant difference to the quality of teaching at her school, taking it out of special measures and into *80% good or better teaching* within a year. She had had the benefit of receiving training along with three other members of staff, but the essence of that training is now in this book, and much more besides, because it has worked examples from across the primary and secondary curriculum. Once you have your own evidence that it works, get the necessary headteacher and management buy-in and set up your hand-picked project team. Train them so they can then go away and trial the approach in their lessons and then you will have home-grown evidence to show to staff when you venture into your first whole-school training day. **Video 61** explains how showing the difference between the cold and hot work in a range of subjects was what won over that essential ingredient staff buy-in. **Video clip 6** is powerful for this but not as effective as a video of the cold to hot process in your school could be. To return to the Michael Fullan quote near the start of this chapter: "The solution requires the individual and collective ability to build shared meaning, capacity, and commitment to action …".

GETTING TALK FOR WRITING GOING IN YOUR SCHOOL

Such videos help you see the potential power of what he is describing. You might also want to show **video clips 60 & 3**, in that order. The first shows what Marissa Bow, Head of Business and Accounting at Slough and Eton thought she was going to do following her first project team training day. The second explains just how much they achieved and how good it made both the teachers and the students feel. If you look at the feedback above on the potential of Talk for Writing to transform learning, flipcharted at the first whole staff training day at Dyson Perrins in Malvern, you can see that significant staff buy in can be achieved, but this can only be achieved if you have laid the foundations.

The centrality of sustaining interest

Finally, keeping the momentum going is always going to be a challenge. Successful project teams have devised ingenious and effective ways of maintaining momentum and embedding good ideas through finding innovative ways of sharing good practices, as Louise has outlined in the previous chapter. One of her excellent ideas was to create a coaching system involving a **C**hallenge, some **S**upport and some ideas to **I**nspire – hence the initials CSI on the image pictured here. On this coaching card, you can see how the *support* comes in the form of praise for something that was liked. The *challenge* is a suggestion for something to try and the *inspire* builds on this.

Royds Hall used a non-threatening twinning approach involving teachers linking up with another teacher of their choice and dropping in on lessons so they could learn from each other. The momentum of this was increased by staff being invited to flag up key learning points from their visits in a big staffroom display which served the double purpose of keeping the initiative in the limelight, to help maintain impetus and interest, alongside the exchange of good ideas about what works.

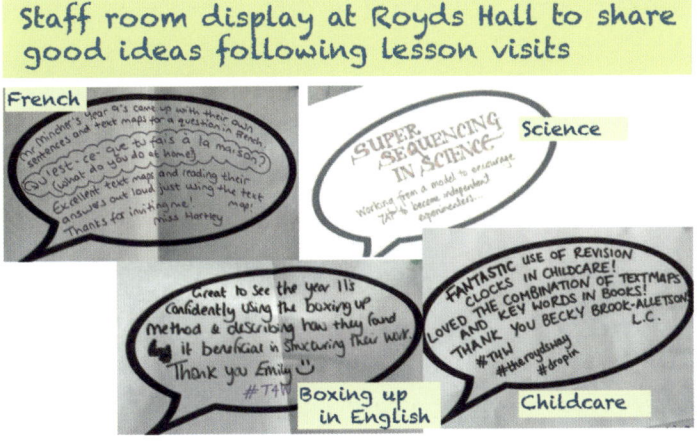

Wexham School has devised an excellent approach – all staff have 50 minutes per week continuing professional development (CPD) time on their timetables. This is in addition to planning, preparation and assessment time. They are divided into collaboration groups. To support TfW implementation, these groups are led by members of the project team. The

focus for the groups changes every half-term and always includes a TfW element within a broader pedagogical approach. For example, when I visited, the focus was on model text. The picture here shows one of the groups, led by the head of MFL, Jade McGowan. Key vocabulary in French is in the pocket chart and model text is displayed on the washing line. For the following half term, the focus was to be on teacher exposition with an emphasis on text mapping and oral rehearsal.

In conclusion, the handout below is probably the most helpful way of supporting schools in sustaining the approach as it is distilled from the expertise of schools which have helped develop this approach over many years. It is written from a primary perspective but many of the points are equally valid for either sector. This handout can be downloaded from the website to help schools develop their own approach.

Together we can co-construct a way of transforming the quality of teaching and learning in our schools and build the potential of every learner.

If you are interested in developing Talk for Writing across the curriculum in your school, please email me at Julia.Strong@Talk4Writing.com. Project team online training, as well as more traditional training, is now available.

Leadership rules for developing, maintaining and embedding a Talk for Writing School

The rules	Why they are mainly rules not just tools	Practical examples
1. Recognition that the pedagogy of Talk for Writing underpins effective teaching and learning	• It is based on what research has shown to be effective practice • It recognises poverty is no excuse: all children can make progress • Talk for Writing can unlock teachers' and children's potential – gives children the opportunity to develop their language • The rules have been developed by schools that have spent many years developing the approach	Sustainable because process is underpinned by what makes effective teaching and learning
2. Headteacher engagement with the development and embedding of the approach is central	• Head has to understand how it works so they can support the teacher who is leading the process and contribute to the development of the approach through CPD etc. • This creates headteacher credibility	1. You need to know what you are looking for on learning walks 2. Helps headteacher know what leadership looks like
3. TfW must be at heart of School Development Plan	• Talk for Writing underpins teaching and learning in a school and therefore has to be the key element in planning	
4. Establish a structure to support the development	• Unless there is a leader with the time and resources to develop the approach, it will not flourish	• Appoint someone to lead the process who has time out of the class to support colleagues • Plus a small team to support them and provide succession – include a leading teaching assistant
5. The Talk for Writing teacher non-negotiables are followed in every classroom	All teaching staff (supported by teaching assistants) must: **establish the three-stage Talk for Writing approach** (moving from **Imitation** to **Innovation** to **Independent application**) to plan and deliver units of work underpinned by formative assessment: – use the cold-hot text approach to establish what features to focus on and progress made – adapt model text to meet needs of class – create related sentence games underpinned by regular phonics and spelling work – provide shared/guided writing virtually daily. – co-construct learning — help students talk their way to understanding – use self-assessment and peer-assessment techniques including response partners **build in progression:** – teach language features established for year group – establish which stories/texts for their year group – increase and deepen reading – literature spine **make the learning visible:** washing lines or working walls to display model text, boxing up, toolkits, word banks etc, writing journals/magpie books **provide an audience and purpose**, e.g. assemblies	• Focus on quality story not on shoe-horning a story into a topic • Non-fiction is basically the same process. Start with fiction and move to non-fiction, initially doing made up non-fiction instructions for capturing a dragon etc, then transfer skills to factual non-fiction and embed across curriculum • Aim for children to be able to apply skills independently

6. Approach is underpinned by clear policy of progression, and a practical way of implementing it, within years and from year to year	• Progression is key to progress. A system needs to be established to support teachers in building progression within their teaching and from year to year, e.g., a Talk for Writing support group that helps develop:
	    ○ model text that builds in progress from year to year and across the curriculum
	    ○ the language features that each year introduces/consolidates
	    ○ the school literature spine
	    ○ staff meetings that focus on building progress into planning
		• Talk for Writing is a process that can transform a school – implementing it takes time – there are no quick fixes
		• Talk for Writing team needs to set up a system to ensure quality of model text that builds in progression. Toolkits and lists of connectives should be built up across year and go up with the children from class to class
		• If new to TfW process, it may take 3 years to turn the school into a TfW school
		Where to start? – see 15 below

7. Approach underpinned by building a school community that reads	• Reading underpins broadening and developing children's vocabulary and familiarity with phrasing, as well as opening up endless opportunities.	• Have a literature spine of quality books • Consider the visual image of reading in your school and make it as powerful as possible – especially promote peer recommendations • Model how to choose books • Make a good choice of books easily available
8. Underpinned by systematic approach to teaching phonics & spelling	• Research shows that a systematic approach to teaching phonics supports children's early reading and spelling.	• TfW recommends Sounds Write: www.sounds-write.co.uk

9. Invest in training and ongoing professional development as a continuing priority	• To refine and develop the approach:
	    ○ include regularly within INSET training programme
	    ○ plan related follow-up so teachers put what they heard into practice
	    ○ send staff to Talk for Writing conferences
	    ○ include TAs in training and provide training aimed at TAs
	• Encourage staff (in pairs or more) to visit TfW schools to develop awareness. Ensure clear focus for visit
	• Self-improvement and reflection is key
		• Key focus of staff meetings is developing T4W process

10. Monitoring is essential	- Unless something is monitored, leadership can have no idea if it is happening or not. A key way of monitoring Talk for Writing is to look at the books.
	  o Is the cold task-hot task framing learning?
	  o Can you see progress between the two?
	  o Can you see how the teaching was planned to underpin this progress?
	It is also essential to monitor that progression is planned for; that the model text for each unit builds progression with the year and from year to year

When observing lessons, what are you looking for? Use the key points below to raise staff skills:
- Are the grammar features integrated into the mode text, so grammar becomes meaningful?
- Are the features identified by the cold task integrated into the shared writing, so the way forward is modelled?

What are you looking for when you see toolkits?
- Have they been co-constructed?
- For fiction, do they allow writer to make choices? – toolkits not rules. Non-fiction may have rules.
- Are they written in language children can understand?
- Are there examples of features to help children understand?

What are you looking for with teacher feedback?
Has the teacher:
- responded as a reader to their writing?
- provided useful practical advice with examples if needed?
- made the ingredients that make it good or not so good clear?
- asked the child what would help them?
- encouraged child to reflect on learning and seek help?

Does the room physically and visually support learning?
- Look at the layout of the room: is it laid out to facilitate good shared and guided work?
- Are the noticeboards used effectively? e.g. big and bold so can be read; relevant to what is being taught; displaying children's work; used to support co-constructing learning
- When you walk into the room, can you tell from the visual environment what is being taught?
  o Is there a cumulative bank of core vocab & actions?
  o Are the three stages displayed?
  o Can the children read the display? – ask the children

Book scrutiny: Look at the books to see if there is progress
Can the children articulate their learning? Ask the children
Are success criteria appropriate and are they making a positive difference or causing confusion?
Are teachers sticking in disembodied grammatical tick lists?
Is formative and summative assessment muddled?
Are the children bunging in grammar or overwriting?
Is the feedback constructive?
Is teacher providing read-as-a-writer advice with useful examples?
Has advice been co-constructed in language the class understands?

11. In-school support for new staff/ struggling staff/ unconvinced staff	- This is a central part of developing and embedding of the approach:
	- Provide your lead Talk for Writing teacher with the time to support staff
	- Buddy up staff so that new staff/struggling staff have mentor
	- Position leading teachers strategically so they can support other teachers
	To do this:
	- provide structure that enables you to quickly assimilate NQTs
	- use 'Flipchart' (online resource storage system) to store all planning so that new teachers have immediate access to tried and tested units and all the related images, examples etc related to the unit, plus material to support shared writing; this cuts out the need for paper planning and allows teachers to focus on how to teach unit most effectively. All embedded in planning. This is transformational. Can be tweaked and refined. Can include hints for the teacher; cuts out time spent on endless planning.
	- Tell teaching candidates to demonstrate that they can teach in TfW style
	This means that:
	  o recruitment no longer an issue
	  o quality teaching is easier to assure
	  o all teachers can articulate the process

12. Measure the impact	• It is essential that impact is measured. The progress between cold and hot tasks will be key to this
13. All teaching staff support the approach and can articulate it	• If there is an effective whole-school approach to developing Talk for Writing, all staff will be applying it because they understand why it matters and should therefore be able to articulate it effectively
14. Key principles are not negotiable	Aim to change teacher behaviour; in some schools with some teachers means have to be prescriptive. Where possible, co-construct the approach: identify problems and solutions
15. Getting going • Remember: The head understanding the process is key	• Stage 1: get the process going • Stage 2: embed the practice • Stage 3: refine the process Where to start: 1. **Engage the children:** selecting effective stories to hook the children is key. Link to real experience e.g. going to a wood & practical experiments. Make it meaningful and memorable 2. **Train the teachers:** Ensure the imitation stage is effective – so focus on the art of learning stories – the storyteller must be confident and bring the story alive so train staff 3. Must know the story really well; work on this collectively. This is a key non-negotiable for teachers and TAs and the senior leadership team has to be able to do it too
16. Embed the approach	• Once the leadership team has understood the process, you can apply the approach more quickly **CPD is key to progress** • A lead practitioner is key to support all teachers and train NQTs • Provide opportunities to share teaching skills • Identify and nurture strong practice to develop strong teaching • Have an open-door policy so can see other's teaching • Develop wider literacy curriculum using the story as a vehicle • Ensure learning process is visually obvious throughout school • Use focused work scrutiny to identify training needs • Talk to the children – can they articulate the process and see how it helps them learn? • Spread to all subjects – based on teacher confidence. This makes the approach sustainable.